The Principle of Permar
over Natural Resources
in Times of Sealevel Rise

Mara Alin Brinker

The Principle of Permanent Sovereignty over Natural Resources as an Anchor in Times of Sealevel Rise

Maintaining Rights over the Maritime Zone for the „Disappearing Islands“

Springer VS

Mara Alin Brinker
Walter-Schücking Institut für
Internationales Recht
Christian-Albrechts-Universität zu Kiel
Kiel, Germany

ISBN 978-3-658-50526-4 ISBN 978-3-658-50527-1 (eBook)
https://doi.org/10.1007/978-3-658-50527-1

This Springer VS imprint is published by the registered company Springer Fachmedien Wiesbaden GmbH, part of Springer Nature.
The registered company address is: Abraham-Lincoln-Str. 46, 65189 Wiesbaden, Germany

Foreword

This thesis was accepted as a dissertation by the Faculty of Law at Christian-Albrechts-University of Kiel in the winter semester of 2023/2024. Literature and case law up to September 2022 have been considered. The case law of the International Tribunal for the Law of the Sea, as of May 2024, was subsequently added. The political and legal classification of the sovereign rights of the island states in the South Pacific is constantly evolving. It remains one of the most significant challenges for the international community in the upcoming decades.

I want to extend my special thanks to my supervisor, Professor Dr. Nele Matz-Lück, who consistently supported and advised me throughout my research project. Moreover, she enabled me to have a research stay at the Arctic University of Norway in Tromsø. This provided me with access to an immense treasure trove of current literature on the subject, enabling me to complete the first draft of my thesis.

Furthermore, I thank my second supervisor, Professor Dr. Andreas von Arnauld, for the prompt and critical correction of my draft.

Closing, I would like to thank the Honored Judge of the International Tribunal for the Law of the Sea, Professor Dr. María Teresa Infante Caffí, who opened doors for me, which I never expected to walk through. I was able to intern at the International Tribunal for the Law of the Sea in Winter 2022 and attend the Rhodes Academy of Ocean Law and Policy in 2024.

My special thanks go to my family, to my father, PD Dr. Rüdiger Kreusch-Brinker, to my sister, Dr. Dana Kristin-Brinker, and particularly to my mother, Anje Maria Brinker, who have always supported me in all my projects and accompanied me on my new adventures. I would also like to thank Antonia Heitmann-Gordon for her quick correction of my English draft. Last but not least, I would like to thank all my friends, who supported me on this long journey and always believed in my success. I am grateful for this journey and for all the friends and allies I have met and made, united in our interest and commitment to protecting the oceans.

Osnabrück
October 2025

Mara Alin Brinker

Competing Interests The author has no competing interests to declare that are relevant to the content of this manuscript.

Contents

Abbreviations

ACHR	American Convention on Human Rights
African Charter	African Charter on Human and Peoples' Rights 1986
AOSIS	Alliance of Small Island States
Arbitral Tribunal	Arbitral Tribunal constituted under Article 10 of Annex VII to UNCLOS
Atlantic Charter 1941	Declaration of Principles of 14 August 1941
BBNJ	Biodiversity Beyond National Jurisdiction Agreement
Bern Convention	Convention on the Conservation of European Wildlife and Natural Habitats 1979
CBD	Convention on Biological Diversity
CBM	Community-Based Management
CERDS	Charter of Economic Rights and Duties of States
CHM	Common Heritage of Humankind
CITES	Convention on International Trade in Endangered Species of Wild Fauna and Flora
CRAMRA	Regulation of Antarctic Mineral Resources Activities
ECOSOC	Economic and Social Council
EEZ	Exclusive Economic Zone
EU	European Union
IACHR	Inter-American Court of Human Rights
ICC	Inuit Circumpolar Council
ICCPR	International Covenant on Civil and Political Rights
ICESCR	International Covenant on Economic, Social, and Cultural Rights
ICJ	International Court of Justice
ILO	International Labour Organization
IPCC	Intergovernmental Panel on Climate Change

ISA	International Seabed Authority
ITLOS	International Tribunal for the Law of the Sea
NGO	Non-Governmental organization
NIEO	New International Economic Order
NORI	Nauru Ocean Resources
OAU	Organization of African Unity
PACER	Pacific Agreement on Closer Economic Relations
PCA	Permanent Court of Arbitration
PFII	United Nations Permanent Forum on Indigenous Issues
PIASA	Treaty on Fisheries between the Governments of certain Pacific Island States, and the Government of the United States, and the Pacific Island Air Services Agreement
PICTA	Pacific Islands Countries Trade Agreement
PNA	Nauru Agreement
PSNR	Permanent Sovereignty over Natural Resources
Rio Declaration	Declaration of the United Nations Conference on Environment and Development 1992
SIDS	Small Islands Developing States
Stockholm Declaration	Declaration of the United Nations Conference on the Human Environment 1972
TOML	Tonga Offshore Mining Ltd.
TTPI	Trust Territory of the Pacific Islands
UNCED	United Nations Conference on Environment and Development
UN-Charter	United Nations Charter
UNCHE	United Nations Conference on the Human Environment in Stockholm in 1972
UNCLOS	United Nations Convention on the Law of the Sea
UNCLOS III	United Nations Conference on the Law of the Sea
UNCTAD	United Nations Conference on Trade and Development
UNDRIP	United Nations Declaration on the Rights of Indigenous Peoples
UNEP	United Nations Environment Program
UNFCCC	United Nations Framework Convention on Climate Change
UNGA	United Nations General Assembly
UNGA Res.	Resolution of the General Assembly of the United Nations
VCLT	Vienna Convention on the Law of Treaties

WCIP	World Council of Indigenous Peoples
WHC	World Heritage Convention
WSSD	World Summit on Sustainable Development

Introduction

1

In a single day and night of misfortune, all your warlike men in a body sank into the earth, and the island of Atlantis in like manner disappeared in the depth of the sea. (Plato, Timaeus, 360 BC)

What we consider a fairytale of a time long past—the catastrophe of Atlantis, the sunken city—could be a reality in the very near future. In the South Pacific, some small—in the present globalized world, insignificant—island States are threatened by the acute menace of submergence. Some of these low-lying coral Atoll Island States—namely Kiribati, Tuvalu, and the Marshall Islands—deal with the constant loss of territory. Every upcoming storm threatens to lead to the State's complete disappearance.

The phenomenon of disappearing islands is of course a consequence of climate change "one of the greatest challenges of our time, [so that] climate—effected hazards have direct and irreversible consequences on people, property, business, financial systems, and state institutions worldwide".[1] Particularly due to this, climate change has caused so much controversy and discussion in the recent times, because it affects everyone across the planet so it cannot treat differently as "a public good", on the one hand.[2] On the other hand, no other phenomenon—in an era of Anthropocene and human dominance—provokes so much "radical inequality" not only between different peoples, but also between the different

[1] Resolution 66/288. The future we want, 27.07.2012b; A/RES/66/288; *M. E. Vaha*, "We as Peoples Have the Right to Exist": Threatened Nations and Climate Justice, Climate Justice and Human Rights (2017), 771.

[2] *T. Pfeiffer/M. A. Nowak*, All in the game, Nature (2006), 583.

M. A. Brinker, *The Principle of Permanent Sovereignty over Natural Resources as an Anchor in Times of Sealevel Rise*, https://doi.org/10.1007/978-3-658-50527-1_1

generations.[3] As the Intergovernmental Panel on Climate Change (IPCC) noted, also adapted by ITLOS, "the impact of climate change is likely to fall disproportionately upon the poorest countries and the poorest persons within countries":[4] Therefore, the expression of "climate justice" is appropriate and meaningful at the same time.

Let us take a closer look at the small Pacific island States, standing at one end of the balance of "climate inequality" and claiming, therefore, to be among the loudest advocates of "climate justice". The region is particularly vulnerable to the effects of climate change. Sea-level rise and extreme weather events, such as surging and swelling storms, including tropical cyclones, along with coastal flooding, erosion, droughts, and inundations, are the main factors contributing to the region's high vulnerability to environmental disasters and climate change.[5] Compared with the median values from 1995 to 2014, the prognosticated sea-level rise of 0.7 to 1.6 meters for 2081 to 2100 significantly increases the likelihood of the complete loss of the majority of the islands, including those in the territories of the island States, to a very high level.[6] Kaateti Toto, Kiribati's Minister of Environment, Lands and Agriculture Development, expressed the situation with the worlds "there is no place to run. Maybe our adaptation strategy should be to build an ark."[7] The following array shall help to form a better impression of the multiple impacts on the islands, which affect the population in all aspects of their life, in either geographical, environmental or socio-economic manner, and what accumulate in the high vulnerability at the end.

---

[3] *M. E. Vaha,* "We as Peoples Have the Right to Exist": Threatened Nations and Climate Justice, Climate Justice and Human Rights (2017), 769.

[4] *R. Watson,* IPCC—AR3 Synthesis Report—Climate Change 2001, 32; *C. Hamilton,* The Commonwealth and Sea-Level Rise, The Round Table (2003), 519; *Request For an Advisory Opinion submitted by the Commission of Small Island States on Climate Change and International Law,* No. 31, 21.05.2024, para. 374.

[5] *D. Chen/M. Rojas/B. Samset,* IPCC—AR6 Synthesis Report—Climate Change 2021, 1839; *R. Pachauri/A. Reisinger,* IPCC—AR4 Synthesis Report—Climate Change 2007, 15; *J. Bryant-Tokalau,* Indigenous Pacific Approaches to Climate Change: Pacific Island Countries, 2018, 20.

[6] *D. Chen/M. Rojas/B. Samset,* IPCC—AR6 Synthesis Report—Climate Change 2021, 1839.

[7] *S. Willcox,* Climate Change Inundation and Atoll Island States: Implications for Human Rights, Self-Determination and Statehood, 2015, 18.

Water

One of the greatest threats, and an accelerator of the total uninhabitability of the islands, is the limited freshwater resources. Some islands are already suffering from a reduced natural freshwater supply due to the absence of primary water sources, such as lakes or permanent watercourses.[8] Consequently, the supply of the whole population depends on "lenses of fresh water floating on salt water in the porous sand under the islands".[9] However, because of the extreme weather events, increasingly haunting the islands during year in, year out, "freshwater lenses are overwashed, which increases the salinity of the water and thus reduces its viability for drinking and agriculture." [10] Moreover, sea-level rise results in the salinization of freshwater lenses, so that the volume of the lenses could be reduced by 50 to 65 percent.[11] Additionally, climate change is expected to decrease rainfall in the South Pacific by 10 to 20 percent.[12] This led to an extreme increase in dependence on external water supplies, because "most low-lying atoll countries rely almost entirely on rainwater."[13] The extreme remoteness of the islands, in combination with the lack of storage during the stormy wintertime, makes a permanent supply of water difficult to maintain.[14] Consequently, the likelihood of inhabitable conditions increases with each new contamination of a freshwater lens.

Infrastructure and socio-economic conditions

The loss of significant parts of the islands would inevitably trigger migration, as most of the population and infrastructure are located at elevations of 2 meters or more above sea level. [15] In the case of Tuvalu, for instance, over 90 percent of the housing and most of the infrastructure are located near the coast, where coastal erosion is particularly severe and sea-level rise is three times the global

[8] *W. C. Burns*, in: A. Gillespie/W. C. Burns, Climate Change in the South Pacific: Impacts and Responses in Australia, New Zealands, and Small Islands States, 2003, 241.

[9] Ibid.

[10] D. Chen et al. (note 6), 1839; *J. McAdam*, Climate change, forced migration, and international law, 1st ed., 2013, 131.

[11] W. C. Burns (note 8), 242; S. Willcox (note 7), 14; *R. Pachauri/A. Reisinger,* IPCC—AR4 Synthesis Report—Climate Change 2007.

[12] W. C. Burns (note 8), 242; S. Willcox (note 7), 14; R. Pachauri and A. Reisinger (note 11).

[13] R. Pachauri and A. Reisinger (note 11), 343; W. C. Burns (note 8), 242.

[14] R. Pachauri and A. Reisinger (note 11), 689.

[15] Republic of Kiribati, National Adaptation Program of Action (NAPA), 2007, iii; *I. Kelman,* Islandness within climate change narratives of small island developing states (SIDS), Island Studies Journal (2018), 157.

average.[16] In the case of the Marshall Islands' capital, the urban atoll of Majuro, which has a population of 20,000 people, approximately 37% of the building stock is at risk of permanent inundation due to a one-meter sea-level rise by the end of this century.[17]

A side effect of sea-level rise is the extreme population distribution on the remaining landmass. For instance, Kiribati's main island and capital, the Atoll Tarawa, suffers from high overpopulation, as more than half of the population—approximately 56.000 out of around 95.000—live here, on an atoll of 32 square kilometers and 39 kilometers in length.[18] The collateral consequences include not only a lack of employment, food, water, security, and environmental sustainability, but also lead to a degradation of underdevelopment, so that, *e.g.*, only 20 percent of households have access to a sewerage system, and 64 percent do not use toilets.[19] Less than 25 percent of the population has a job, and the majority is in governmental administration.[20] The same can be said about Funafuti—the capital and only urban center of Tuvalu, with an extremely high population density of 1,610 people per square kilometer.[21] The highly dense population in close proximity to the coastal areas promotes "additional stress to an already vulnerable marine ecosystem".[22] The population is suffering under relative poverty, which means, in particular, a "poverty of opportunity", due to the remoteness of the island States themselves and the islands among each other.[23] However, sea-level rise does not only cause direct geographical damage. Still, it is "likely to be of a magnitude that would disrupt virtually all economic and social sectors in these countries".[24] Tourism, a primary source of economic growth in these countries, is experiencing a downturn or even complete disruption due to the

[16] S. Willcox (note 7), 16 et seq.

[17] The World Bank, Adapting to rising sea levels in Marshall Islands: Understanding the Pacific atoll nation's adaptation pathways to build resilience to sea level rise and climate change, 2021.

[18] J. McAdam (note 10), 124; Republic of Kiribati, National Adaptation Program of Action (NAPA), 2007, 13.

[19] Republic of Kiribati (note 18), 16, 165; J. McAdam (note 10), 125.

[20] Republic of Kiribati (note 18), 7; J. McAdam (note 10), 125.

[21] *U. Government of Tuvalu,* Tuvalu's National Adaptation Programme of Action, 2007, 15 et seq.

[22] Ibid., 16.

[23] Ibid.

[24] *R. Watson,* IPCC—AR3 Synthesis Report—Climate Change 2001, 236.

multifaceted effects of climate change, including beach erosion, coral bleaching, coastal inundation, and the destruction of cultural heritage sites.[25]

Agriculture, fishing, and natural resources

Considering the extreme remoteness of the islands, it is not surprising that the Atoll Island States depend heavily on the agricultural and fishing industries, as they are their primary sources of income and nutrition.[26] However, this income is also threatened by climate change, *e.g.*, in Tuvalu, where increasing saltwater intrusion has destroyed more than 60 percent of the pulaka plantations. In comparison, the remaining 40 percent are at immense risk of saltwater intrusion.[27] Additionally, the increasing frequency of extreme weather events, such as cyclones and droughts, will likely result in average crop losses of 50 to 60 percent of agricultural products like pulaka, coconut, banana, root crops, and breadfruit.[28] Consequently, it is not surprising that the island States are already highly dependent on food imports, with this tendency increasing, while employment in the primary sector has fallen to three percent.[29]

Moreover, rising sea temperatures have a significant impact on fisheries. For instance, sea turtles and clams are susceptible to temperature changes, while the growth of toxic algae and jellyfish is favored by warmer water.[30] In the case of Kiribati, once a leading tuna-fishing nation, production has decreased significantly because the fish migrate further north.[31] Meanwhile, in inland areas, hypersaline conditions in some shallow lagoons led to the complete extinction of small island fisheries, adversely affecting productivity in certain regions.[32]

Considering all these facts, the question arises, how can we deal with the impending disappearance of the island States? Is there any solution in international law? Of course, we can rely on the broad mitigation and adaptation strategies that international law has already established, starting with the first obligations in the Kyoto Protocol of 1997, which addressed carbon emissions

[25] S. Willcox (note 7), 15.

[26] Ibid., 14.

[27] U. Government of Tuvalu (note 21), 28.

[28] Ibid; W. C. Burns (note 8), 243.

[29] *U. Government of Tuvalu,* Tuvalu's National Adaptation Programme of Action, 2007; Republic of Kiribati (note 18), 7.

[30] W. C. Burns (note 8), 241.

[31] Republic of Kiribati (note 18), 5, 13.

[32] W. C. Burns (note 8).

and created a market-based regulation system.[33] This was followed by the Paris Agreement under the United Nations Framework Convention on Climate Change (Paris Agreement) in 2015, which obligated the 174 ratifying parties to limit the temperature increase to 1.5 to 2 degrees.[34]

> *"Holding the increase in the global average temperature to well below 2°C above pre-industrial levels and pursuing efforts to limit the temperature increase to 1.5°C above pre-industrial levels, recognizing that this would significantly reduce the risks and impacts of climate change."*

So, even if the ambitions are high, in the light of the immense impact of climate change, it seems unsurprising that disillusionment has set in among the Atoll islanders in the sense "that traditional ways of coping with the extreme weather events are no longer adequate because the nature of the events has changed from being manageable to being unmanageable."[35] In the words of a former Tuvaluan cabinet member:

> *"On the island where I live, Funafuti, it is possible to throw a stone from one side of the island to the other. Our islands are very low-lying. When a cyclone hits us, there is no place to escape. We cannot climb any mountains or move away to take refuge. It is hard to describe the effects of a cyclonic storm surge when it washes right across our islands. (...) The devastation is beyond description."*[36]

Consequently, the time of adaptation and mitigation seems to have already passed for the Pacific island States. The focus must lie on other solutions, far removed from the idea of maintaining territory. The core question is how we can deal with the fact that these island States will most likely be entirely inundated in the near future. How can we claim a submerged area of the sea if there is no territory left? Will they have any claims at all when the landmass disappears? Does international law offer any possibility for the population of a sunken landmass to claim a vast part of the ocean and still be considered an existing State? Figuratively speaking: Do Plato's long-lost people have any rights and claims to the area into the sea, which used to be their territory?

---

[33] *P. Minnerop,* Climate Protection Agreements, Max Planck Encyclopedias of International Law (2018), para. 2.

[34] *P. Minnerop,* Climate Protection Agreements, Max Planck Encyclopedias of International Law (2018), para. 18.

[35] Republic of Kiribati (note 18), 35.

[36] S. Willcox (note 7), 12.

One principle in international law will serve as the crucial foundation and starting point for this research project in finding a solution to the issue of disappearing islands: the principle of permanent sovereignty over natural resources. This principle, which has received ever-growing attention and influence in the international political economy, can also make a difference for the inhabitants of the disappearing islands.[37] Moreover, this principle has become of high importance, because "rights over resources are at the center of contemporary political and philosophical thought—we talk about indigenous rights to resources, the equal distribution of natural resources, the resource curse, responsibility for climate change affecting our natural resources, and so on".[38] Consequently, can we make this principle feasible in the context of the threatening situation of the disappearing islands? Can it serve us to comply with the desire and probable future claim of the inhabitants of the island States to maintain their rights over their maritime resources in the ocean? This principle is fascinating to address because the ocean's natural resources are the islanders' most valuable goods. Therefore, the question of maintaining rights in this area is a matter of power over natural resources—or, in juridical terms, sovereignty over them.

Consequently, this research project aims to explore the connection between the principle of permanent sovereignty over natural resources and the urgent threat of climate change to the disappearing islands in the South Pacific. First of all, the principle of permanent sovereignty over natural resources is set in the historical context (1), then, the main pillars of the principle are developed—State sovereignty and right of self-determination (2), followed by the question of the right—or rather principle—holder of the permanent sovereignty over natural resources (3). Afterwards, the project addresses the question of the changing pillars of the principle of permanent sovereignty over natural resources in the context of climate change, State sovereignty, and the right of self-determination, followed by the remaining question of whether the principle of permanent sovereignty over natural resources must also undergo a change (4). The last two chapters focus on the possibilities that international law offers for the disappearing island States (5) and on whether this new concept would fit with the most relevant international treaty for the oceans: the United Nations Convention on the Law of the Sea (6).

---

[37] *Y. Tyagi,* Permanent Sovereignty over Natural Resources, Cambridge Journal of International and comparative Law (2015), 589.

[38] *C. Nine,* Global justice and territory, 1st ed., 2012, 116.

The Principle of Permanent Sovereignty over Natural Resources: History and Development

2

All rights and laws are still transmitted, like an eternal sickness of the race,

From generation unto generation fitted And shifted round from place to place. (*J. W.* von *Goethe*, Faust I, 1808, 1:IV)

This chapter will focus on the history and development of the most relevant principle of permanent sovereignty over natural resources. Starting with the creation of this principle in the aftermath of World War II, we will follow its development over the previous seventy years, as shaped and guided by resolutions of the United Nations General Assembly (UNGA). It evolved into a fundamental principle of international law and was adopted in various jurisdictions and global declarations. Nowadays, it has taken its rightful place in the doctrine of international law, although the legal status remains unresolved among scholars.[1] Let us look closer at the principle of permanent sovereignty over natural resources, also known as PSNR.

[1] *N. Schrijver*, Sovereignty over Natural Resources: Balancing Rights and Duties, 1997, 221; *S. van Wyk*, The Impact of Climate Change Law on the Principle of State Sovereignty over Natural Resources, 2017, 44.

M. A. Brinker, *The Principle of Permanent Sovereignty over Natural Resources as an Anchor in Times of Sealevel Rise*, https://doi.org/10.1007/978-3-658-50527-1_2

2.1 Development of the Principle of Permanent Sovereignty over Natural Resources

2.1.1 Preliminary Words

Initiated by the freedom movements of the colonial States, PSNR was developed primarily through UNGA resolutions in the 1950s and 1960s.[2] Introduced by the Latin American States and supported by Eastern European socialist countries, the policy first focused on the dispute between the Cold War parties.[3] Later, after decolonization, the issue became much more prominent in the North-South conflict.[4] The North-South conflict is a term used to describe the disparity between developed and developing countries, referring to the divide between the wealthy North and the impoverished South. To this day, this principle remains primarily applicable in the conflict between developed and developing States, or, in other words, between capital-exporting and capital-importing countries.[5]

With the groundbreaking Resolution 1803 (XVII) in 1962, the principle of permanent sovereignty over natural resources was officially established in the international regime by the United Nations General Assembly (UNGA). For the last time, this Resolution represented the complete consensus of developed and developing countries. Hence, the two Human Rights Covenants of 1966[6] incorporated the principle as well, reflecting a configuration of the right of people to self-determination and strengthening the people of developing States.[7] Consequently, the principle of permanent sovereignty over natural resources symbolized liberation and governance for the developing States.

---

[2] Resolution A/RES/523 (VI): Integrated economic development and commercial agreements, 12.01.1952; A/RES/523 (VI); Resolution A/RES/545 (VI): Inclusion in the International Covenant or Covenants on Human Rights of an article relating to the right of peoples to self-determination vol. 1952, 05.02.1952; A/RES/545 (VI); Resolution A/RES/626 (VII): Right to Exploit Freely Natural Wealth and Resources, 21.12.1952; A/RES/626(VII); Resolution A/RES/15/1514: Declaration on the Granting of Independence to Colonial Countries and Peoples, 14.12.1960; A/RES/15/1514; Resolution A/RES/1515: Concerted Action for Economic Development of Less Developed Countries, 15.12.1960; A/RES/1515; Resolution A/RES/1803 (XVII): Permanent sovereignty over natural resources, 14.12.1962; A/RES/1803 (XVII).

[3] N. Schrijver (note 1), 6, 33.

[4] Ibid., 33.

[5] Ibid.

[6] International Covenant on Civil and Political Rights, 16.12.1966; ICCPR; International Covenant on Economic, Social and Cultural Rights, 16.12.1966; ICESCR.

[7] N. Schrijver (note 1), 36 et seq.

Even though the formerly developing countries could increase their influence in institutions like the United Nations Conference on Trade and Development (UNCTAD), the discussion became more controversial, and the fronts hardened between the formerly subdued States and the Northern countries.[8] Symptomatic of this controversy were the nationalization awards in the 1970s, which involved the nationalization of oil platforms in Libya and Kuwait, mainly owned by British companies.[9]

In this decade, the discussion about sustainable development policies has also received much more attention. Consequently, the principle of permanent sovereignty over natural resources shifted to a context of environmental preservation and sustainable use.[10] As a result, the principle of PSNR was integrated into Principle 21 of the Declaration of the United Nations Conference on the Human Environment 1972 (Stockholm Declaration)[11], and later on, with a slight deviation, the formulation of this principle found its way into the Declaration of the United Nations Conference on Environment and Development 1992 (Rio Declaration)[12]:[13]

> *"States have, in accordance with the Charter of the United Nations and the principles of international law, the sovereign right to exploit their own resources pursuant to their own environmental and developmental policies, and the responsibility to ensure that activities within their jurisdiction or control do not cause damage to the environment of other States or areas beyond the limits of national jurisdiction."*[14]

Nowadays, the PSNR constitutes customary international law because various international jurisdictions recognize the principle, which dates back to the

---

[8] *S. Hobe*, in: M. Bungenberg/S. Hobe, Permanent Sovereignty over Natural Resources, 2015, 7; *N. Schrijver*, in: M. Bungenberg/S. Hobe, Permanent Sovereignty over Natural Resources, 2015, 19.

[9] *BP Exploration Company (Libya) Limited vs. Libya,* 10.10.1973; *LIAMCO vs. Libya (Libyan American Oil Company vs. The Government of the Libyan Arab Republic),* 12.04.1977, 24.03.1982.

[10] N. Schrijver (note 1), 34.

[11] Declaration of the United Nations Conference on the Human Environment, 16.06.1972; Stockholm Declaration.

[12] Declaration on Environment and Development, 12.08.1992; Rio Declaration.

[13] S. van Wyk (note 1), 40.

[14] Declaration on Environment and Development (note 12): Principle 2.

1920s.[15] In particular, in international environmental law, it plays an essential role in interpreting the limits a State faces regarding natural resources.

2.1.2 The Creation of PSNR in the Resolutions of the General Assembly

This first part will focus on the development of the principle in the 1950s and 1960s, marked by a series of United Nations General Assembly resolutions culminating in Resolution 1803 (XVII) in 1962.

2.1.2.1 The General Assembly as a Lawmaker?

One of the primary sources of the here-discussed principle was the resolutions of the United Nations General Assembly (UNGA Res.). Although the General Assembly is a political organ of the United Nations, many of its resolutions have found wide acceptance in international law. A large majority views them as the modern source of international law because of "their flexibility, rapid formulation, and democratic nature" to confront the challenging questions of the international community, which arise periodically.[16] Even though the principles evolved by the General Assembly are often described as a "para-legal ideology of power economics" and therefore as "meaningless"[17], this institution is recognized as a "quasi-law-maker"[18] or as a "midwife for the delivery of nascent rules."[19]

In particular, in environmental protection, we notice the steady importance of the UNGA as the leading voice and „principal policy-making and appraisal organ for the protection of the global environment“.[20] The decisions of the UNGA do not have a self-executing character. They can therefore only be titled "soft law"; its decisions work as a "catalyst for law-making".[21] The UNGA was consequently

---

[15] *Y. Tyagi,* Permanent Sovereignty over Natural Resources, Cambridge Journal of International and comparative Law (2015), 596.

[16] *M. Bedjaoui*, Towards a new international economic order, 1979, 140; N. Schrijver (note 1), 33.

[17] N. Schrijver (note 1), 33; *G. Schwarzenberger*, Economic world order?: A basic problem of international economic law, 1970, 49.

[18] *R. Falk*, in: N. G. Onuf, International legal theory, 2008, p. 782, 18, 20; N. Schrijver (note 1), 34.

[19] N. Schrijver (note 1), 34.

[20] *N. Matz-Lück/L. Christiansen,* UNGA as the Anchor: Global Environmental Conferencing, Environmental Policy and Law (2020), 521.

[21] Ibid.

host of several global UN environmental conferences, from the United Nations Conference on the Human Environment in Stockholm in 1972 (UNCHE), up to the United Nations Conference on Environment and Development (UNCED) in Rio de Janeiro in 1992, and the World Summit on Sustainable Development (WSSD) in Johannesburg in 2002.[22] The primary purpose of these conferences is to raise participants' awareness of the growing environmental challenges and to demonstrate practical ways to address them in a more coordinated manner.[23]

Consequently, soft law often finds its application where treaty-making seems too delicate, or the already adopted treaties, with "their universal consent by compromise and their weak 'soft law' language," require specific anchors for interpretation to bridge the gap to concrete application.[24] From this point, the way is not far to turn from these political declarations—and nothing else is a UNGA resolution—to customary international law.[25] In the development of the principle of permanent sovereignty over natural resources, the resolutions of the UNGA played a key role, which we will examine now.

2.1.2.2 The First Steps to the Principle of Permanent Sovereignty over Natural Resources

For the first time after World War II, the discussion of a kind of predecessor of the principle of permanent sovereignty over natural resources came up in the sixth session of the General Assembly, where "long-term trade agreements" between the –at that time so-called– underdeveloped countries and the developed countries concerning "economic development of the underdeveloped countries" were discussed.[26] At this time, the controversy surrounding these agreements, which aimed to deliver machinery and equipment to underdeveloped countries in exchange for raw materials, centered on whether to include economic or political statements about the violation of sovereign rights.[27] Underdeveloped countries wanted to minimize the influence of the United States on their land. The United States, however, wished to secure strategic raw materials under the guise of the paragraph to maintain "the interests of an expanding world economy."[28]

---

[22] Ibid, 522.

[23] Ibid.

[24] Ibid., 523, 527.

[25] Ibid., 523.

[26] Doc. A/C2/L81, 26.11.1951; N. Schrijver (note 1), 39.

[27] N. Schrijver (note 1), 39; Doc. A/C2/L81 (note 26), para. 5.

[28] N. Schrijver (note 1), 40; Doc. A/C2/L120, 20.12.1951, sub.1; UN Doc. A/C2/L120, 20.12.1951, sub.1.

In conclusion, Resolution 523 (VI) enshrined "for the first time, the sovereign right of 'under-developed countries', determining freely the use of their natural resources", however, with the obligation—for the last time—"to utilize such resources not only in their own national interests but also to further the expansion of the world economy."[29]

This resolution was followed by one of the General Assembly's landmark resolutions on the principle of permanent sovereignty over natural resources, resolution 626 (VII) of 21 December 1952. The first resolution of the United Nations General Assembly addressed the permanent sovereignty over natural resources, also known as "the genesis of the principle of permanent sovereignty."[30] Introduced by Chile, one of the strongest representatives of the developing countries and counterpart of the United States in the United Nations, this resolution is considered the expression of the balance between the interests of the developing and developed countries, in particular, by strengthening the right of the economically weak countries to utilize and exploit their natural resources on their own.[31]

For the first time, the reference to the "right of people" was introduced, referring to their right to exploit their natural resources and reflecting the right of self-determination adopted from Article 1.2 of the UN Charter.[32] However, even though the United States recognized the Member States' intention to "further their peoples' welfare by exploiting their resources through nationalization," it criticized the fact that the "reciprocal responsibility towards private investors concerning their expropriated property" was overlooked.[33] In the following discussion, the main problem of the so-called "nationalization-resolution" for developed countries is the lack of security for capital-investing States, particularly the absence of "fair and equitable compensation."[34] India described this phenomenon with the example of water: "Capital, like water, will find its own

[29] Resolution A/RES/523 (VI): Integrated economic development and commercial agreements (note 2).

[30] *I. Brownlie/J. Crawford*, Brownlie's principles of public international law, 2019, 539; N. Schrijver (note 1), 36.

[31] *Y. T. Chekera/V. O. Nmehielle,* The International Law Principle of Permanent Sovereignty over Natural Resources as an Instrument for Development: The Case of Zimbabwean Diamonds, African Journal of Legal Studies 6 (2013), 36; N. Schrijver (note 1), 34, 42–43; Doc. A/C2/L.165, 05.11.1962, and Corr. 1–3.

[32] Doc. A/C2/L.165 (note 31), and Corr. 1–3; N. Schrijver (note 1), 42 et seq.

[33] Ibid., 45.; Doc. A/C2/SR237, 11.12.1952, 280, para. 41.

[34] N. Schrijver (note 1), 47 et seq; Doc. A/PV.411 (VII), 21.12.1952, 488, para. 74.

level. It will not flow into countries that do not provide conditions of security and stability."[35]

In conclusion, the adoption of Resolution 626 (VII) did not clarify the principle of permanent sovereignty nor establish a precise legal instrument. However, the General Assembly took root for the first time "as a platform for political debate and as a stock-taker of the views of the various groups of member States."[36]

2.1.2.3 The Inclusion of the Right of Self-Determination

With the inclusion of the right of people to self-determination in the two Covenants on Human Rights, referring to Article 1.2 of the UN Charter, by the Resolution 545 (VI) of 5 February 1952, a new debate about the importance of the right of self-determination, referring to the permanent sovereignty over natural resources, was sparked.[37] This time, the discussion specifically addressed integrating the right to self-determination into the draft covenants.

Chile started its appeal with the proposal that "the right of the peoples to self-determination shall also include permanent sovereignty over their natural wealth and resources. On no account may a people be deprived of their means of subsistence on the grounds of any rights that other States may claim."[38] Chile wanted to strengthen the position of the people in contrast to the States, so that "the people would be enabled to remain master of their natural wealth and resources."[39] This led to the question of the definition of sovereignty and its right-holder: could the strengthening of peoples' rights create a weighty counterbalance to the concept of State sovereignty?[40] The question of the concept of international law as a whole was at stake, which was based on the validity of treaties and agreements, and so on, and the absolute sovereignty of States.

This core question reinforced the fear of the capital-exporting and developed States, leading them to downplay this proposal on a technicality: the Commission on Human Rights was not competent to deal with the rights and duties of States.[41]

---

[35] N. Schrijver (note 1), 48; Doc. A/PV.411 (VII) (note 34), 488, para. 78.

[36] N. Schrijver (note 1), 48.

[37] Ibid., 49; Resolution A/RES/545 (VI): Inclusion in the International Covenant or Covenants on Human Rights of an article relating to the right of peoples to self-determination (note 2).

[38] N. Schrijver (note 1), 49; Doc. E/CN4/L24 vol. 1952, 16.04.1952.

[39] N. Schrijver (note 1), 49; Doc E/CN4/SR260, 06.05.1952.

[40] N. Schrijver (note 1), 49.

[41] Ibid., 50; Doc E/CN4/SR260 (note 39), 7.

Consequently, the USA rejected the right of people to permanent sovereignty over natural resources, while developing countries saw it as an opportunity to enjoy human rights in their entirety.[42] Chile only saw a possibility to

> *"exercise the right of self-determination unless [the country] were master of its own resources (...). Self-determination had to be based on economic independence. [It] would be an illusion in a country whose natural resources were controlled by another State."*[43]

In the end, most developing States adopted paragraph 2 of Article 1 of the Covenants, which was widely discussed.[44] Hence, for the first time, the link between the right to self-determination and the permanent sovereignty of natural resources was tied.

2.1.2.4 The Creation of the "Principle of Permanent Sovereignty over Natural Resources"

In the following years, this debate was conducted in a much more heated and intensive manner and culminated in the adoption of Resolution 1803 (XVII) of 14 December 1962, which established the doctrine of permanent sovereignty over natural resources for the first time.[45] The controversial issue leading up to this Resolution was once again the question of the link between the right of self-determination and permanent sovereignty over natural resources. While the developing States persevered on the connection, the Western countries retained the opinion that it would be "illogical to use the term 'sovereignty' about peoples which were not yet sovereign States."[46]

A divisive point lay in the commission's remit itself. Thus, the Director of the UN Office of Legal Affairs argued that it would be "defining or restricting the rights of foreign nationals, companies or governments to own or exploit the natural resources of a country".[47] Chile, meanwhile, representing the position of the developing countries, strengthened the opinion that political independence had

[42] N. Schrijver (note 1), 51 et seq; Doc. A/C3/SR 646, 27.10.1955, 108, 110, para. 15, 34.

[43] N. Schrijver (note 1), 52; Doc. A/C3/SR 646 (note 42), 104, para. 11.

[44] N. Schrijver (note 1), 55; Doc. A/C3/SR676, 29.11.1955, 261 et seq.

[45] S. Hobe (note 8), 1; *D. Cambou/S. Smis,* Permanent Sovereignty over Natural Resources from a Human Rights Perspective: Natural Resources Exploitation and Indigenous Peoples' Rights in the Arctic, Michigan State International Law Review (2013), 352.

[46] N. Schrijver (note 1), 58; *C. Armstrong,* Justice and natural resources: An egalitarian theory, 2017, 162.

[47] N. Schrijver (note 1), 59; Doc. A/AC97/SR.1., 18.05.1959, 4.

to go hand in hand with economic freedom, so that "national sovereignty must be exercised over the entire territory and wealth of a nation".[48] Another point of controversy centers on how developing countries and their people can exercise their self-determination over their natural resources, particularly when they lack sufficient capital.[49] Therefore, the discussion centered on compensation, and the term "appropriate compensation" emerged for the first time.[50]

Due to the lack of consensus, the General Assembly adopted two additional resolutions in 1960. Later recognized as the "political decolonization declaration"[51], the first affirmed the right of self-determination for peoples, primarily in colonial countries, by underlining the right of free determination of their political status and the promotion of their economic, social, and cultural development. In the second one, they separately emphasized the exercise of sovereignty by every State, particularly regarding the disposition of its natural resources, while also considering States' duties under international law.[52]

After three years of discussion, based on the most balanced Chilean draft, which required that the principle "must be exercised for the benefit of the people of the State concerned" and on the other hand, the needs of the capital-owning States in "protecting [the capital] on the same conditions as domestic capital similarly invested", stood a resolution with eight paragraphs.[53] The UNGA Res. 1803 (XVII) included the right to permanent sovereignty over their natural wealth and resources as well as its free exercise for nations as well as for people, and the right to "nationalization for the State by reasons of public utility, security, and national interest".[54]

2.1.2.5 The Significance of Resolution 1803 (XVII)

First, it embodies the most critical resolution on permanent sovereignty over natural resources, as it guided the development of these resources in the years that

---

[48] N. Schrijver (note 1), 60.

[49] Ibid.

[50] Ibid.

[51] N. Schrijver (note 8), 18.

[52] S. van Wyk (note 1), 63; Resolution A/RES/15/1514: Declaration on the Granting of Independence to Colonial Countries and Peoples (note 2); Resolution A/RES/1515: Concerted Action for Economic Development of Less Developed Countries (note 2).

[53] N. Schrijver (note 1), 65.

[54] Ibid., 74; Resolution A/RES/1803 (XVII): Permanent sovereignty over natural resources (note 2).

followed.[55] It symbolized the long-expected and controversially discussed link between economic independence and the right to self-determination, which also features a "general limitation of the principle of State sovereignty under international law".[56] Moreover, it represents the last resolution dealing with the concept backed by a broad majority of all ethnic groups represented by various States, "as it embodied a balance between the interests of capital-importing and capital-exporting countries".[57] In summary, this resolution outlined one of the "most profound and consequential international reforms concerning ownership, control, and use of land and natural resources"[58] and is therefore considered an "economic decolonization declaration," the equivalent of the Resolution 1514 (XV), mentioned above, the "political decolonization declaration".[59] Not without reason, this resolution stands for "the cradle of a well-developed system of nationalization", including the right of the host State to nationalize and expropriate, as well as appropriate compensation for the foreign investor.[60]

As a "somewhat hybrid resolution" because of the "widely-accepted oration least widely-held views",[61] this resolution represents the "kickoff for the development of an international law on natural resources consisting of principles of customary international law as well as treaty law."[62] Some scholars even consider the Resolution to be *ius cogens* under Article 53 of the Vienna Convention on the Law of Treaties; others have spoken of a declaratory, quasi-law-making, and programmatic function in international law.[63]

---

[55] D. Cambou and S. Smis (note 45), 352; *F. Nawrot,* Principle of permanent sovereignty over natural resources in rulings of international courts, Prawne Problemy Gronictwa i Ochrony Srodowiska (2020), 100.

[56] Y. T. Chekera and V. O. Nmehielle (note 31), 75; *R. Pereira/O. Gough,* Permanent Sovereignty over Natural Resources in the 21st Century: Natural Resource governance and the Right of Self-Determination of Indigenous Peoples under International Law, Melbourne Journal of International Law 14 (2013), 458.

[57] *N. Kofele-Kale,* The international law of responsibility for economic crimes: Holding state officials individually liable for acts of fraudulent enrichment, 2nd ed., 2006, 84–85, 94–95; Y. T. Chekera and V. O. Nmehielle (note 31), 74.

[58] *P. Gümplová,* Sovereignty over natural resources—A normative reinterpretation, Global Constitutionalism (2019), 11.

[59] N. Schrijver (note 8), 18.

[60] R. Pereira and O. Gough (note 56), 456.

[61] N. Schrijver (note 8), 17.

[62] *M. Bungenberg and S. Hobe (eds),* Permanent Sovereignty over Natural Resources, 2015, V.

[63] N. Schrijver (note 8), 17.

The resolution exhibits certain aspects of a declaratory resolution, characterized by reiterating and emphasizing the content of other doctrines already established in different resolutions, as seen, *e.g.*, in paragraphs one and two. Here, the basic principles are laid down: all States have the right to PSNR, and the exploration, development, and disposition of natural resources comply with domestic law. Furthermore, in the other paragraphs, general principles are reiterated and formalized, such as the treatment of foreign investors in paragraphs three and four, the importance of sovereign equality in paragraph five, and the observation of the exercise of the principle in good faith in paragraph eight.[64]

However, this ruling also contains quasi-legal creating effects, as seen in paragraph one, where the principle is attributed to both the States and the people, along with duties that refer to the interests of national development and the well-being of the people. Notably, paragraph four marked a milestone and a shift away from the formerly predominant traditional international law, permitting previously prohibited policies, such as the above-discussed nationalization and the provision of adequate compensation to expropriated foreign investors.[65] The same paragraph formalizes the reference to international adjudication and arbitration, allowing both developing and developed States to invoke their national standards under the Calvo doctrine or the minimum standard.[66]

The Calvo doctrine, developed by the Argentine jurist Carlos Calvo, requires that the same treatment given to nationals—citizens or investors—be equally applied to foreign investors by the national jurisdiction. The so-called Calvo doctrine has been incorporated into the legislation of many developing States, particularly in Latin America. [67] In contrast, the international minimum standard, favored by developed States and now recognized as customary international law, is based on the general principle of the fair and equal treatment of all foreign investors.[68]

In conclusion, the principle of permanent sovereignty over natural resources originated in soft law before being incorporated into treaty law.[69] Already recognized in judicial decisions of international courts and tribunals, such as the human rights courts, the principle was finally recognized as customary international law

[64] Ibid.

[65] Ibid.

[66] S. Hobe (note 8), 6.

[67] *A. K. Bjorklund*, in: A. Reinisch, Standards of investment protection, 2008, 31.

[68] Ibid., 32.

[69] N. Schrijver (note 8), 18.

by the International Court of Justice (ICJ) in 2005.[70] Nowadays, it constitutes one of the "bedrock principles of international law", applied *inter alia* in international environmental law, international economic law, and the law of the sea.[71]

Born from the idea of protecting the economic independence and development of resource-rich countries, and against the backdrop of the colonized countries' liberalization, the crux lies in a fair and equitable allocation of resources.[72] Thus, Resolution 1831 (XVII), which was adopted a few days after the above-developed Resolution in 1962, "was the last attempt to spring from the vestiges of colonialism".[73] This Resolution focused on the connection between economic development and the conservation of nature, aiming to find a way to give developing countries greater control over their natural resources.[74] In the following, the General Assembly sought to establish a link between resources and development, particularly to strengthen foreign investment. Thus, the Resolution 2158 (XXI) of 25 November 1966 expressed that "it is essential that the exploitation and marketing [of the natural resources] should be aimed at securing the highest possible rate of growth of the developing countries."[75]

2.1.3 The Development of the PSNR in Soft Law

In the following years, a growing interest in implementing the principle of permanent sovereignty over natural resources was observed, allowing developing host countries to promote and demonstrate their development.[76] Thus, the new resolution shifted the focus to the link between resource sovereignty and development, particularly concerning foreign investment.[77]

These tendencies were also highlighted in the jurisdiction, *i.a.*, in the *Texaco*, *Liamco*, and *Aminoil* awards of the 1970s.[78] These awards were exemplary for the conflict between the growing entitlement of the developing countries to become

---

[70] *Case Concerning Armed Activities on The Territory of the Congo (Congo vs. Uganda)*, 19.12.2005, 18, 19, 81, para. 222; M. Bungenberg and S. Hobe (note 62), V.

[71] P. Gümplová (note 58), 11.

[72] M. Bungenberg and S. Hobe (note 62), V.

[73] S. van Wyk (note 1), 269.

[74] Ibid.

[75] S. Hobe (note 8), 7.

[76] S. van Wyk (note 1), 228.

[77] S. Hobe (note 8), 7.

[78] *Texaco Overseas Petroleum Co. vs. Libya,* 19.01.1977; *LIAMCO vs. Libya (Libyan American Oil Company vs. The Government of the Libyan Arab Republic),* 12.04.1977; *The*

their own master over the natural resources in their territory through the use of the recognized legal instrument of nationalization and the claim of the developed countries, represented here by powerful oil companies, to fair and equitable compensation, mainly to the detriment of the developing countries.[79] All these awards share the common feature that the States nationalized oil companies—in these cases, Libya and Kuwait—without adequate compensation, compelling the oil companies to claim this entitlement.[80]

2.1.3.1 The New International Economic Order

The New International Economic Order (NIEO) was established in the 1970s with the clear objective of strengthening and enforcing the rights of developing countries, particularly regarding permanent sovereignty over natural resources. At the same time, the PSNR over marine resources gained importance in the international fora.

2.1.3.1.1 The Development of the New International Economic Order

Resolution 3201 (S-VI) ushered in the era of the NIEO, which is based on the idea of "to make the world economy more equitable and to create domestic prosperity" and acknowledges full sovereignty for developing countries.[81] The values of self-determination and sovereign equality were emphasized, and it was proclaimed that "the right of every country to adopt the economic and social system that it deems most appropriate for its own development" and to enjoy "full permanent sovereignty...over its natural resources and all economic activities."[82] The industrial and social development of developing countries came to the fore, initiated by the General Assembly's Resolution 2692 (XXV), which invited the Economic and Social Council (ECOSOC) to prepare reports on this topic, also in reference to the principle of PSNR.[83]

The NIEO debate emerged from the challenges faced by developing countries. In the early 1970s, the world faced severe consequences, including economic

American Independent Oil Company vs. The Government of the State of Kuwait (Aminoil vs. Kuwait), 24.03.1982.

[79] C. Armstrong (note 46), 167.

[80] Ibid.

[81] S. van Wyk (note 1), 246.

[82] *A. Stilz,* Territorial sovereignty, 2019, 222; Resolution A/RES/3201(S-VI): Declaration on the Establishment of a New International Economic Order (note 82).

[83] N. Schrijver (note 1), 89.

stagnation, high inflation, and increasing monetary instability, culminating in the 1973 oil crisis.[84] These events led to a militant attitude among developing countries, supported by nationalization movements in Latin America, as seen in Chile, Peru, and Venezuela, and in the Middle East, notably in Iraq and Libya.[85]

Moreover, Resolution 3016 (XXVII) in 1972 introduced a prohibition on economic and political coercion to maintain international peace and security.[86] This concept was also incorporated in Resolution 46 (III) of the UNCTAD. It repeated the free disposition of the natural resources in the interest of the economic development and the well-being of its own people. On the one hand, it underlined the violation of the principle of self-determination of people by "external, political or economic measures or pressure to bear on the exercise of these rights".[87]

Resolution 3201 (S-VI) announced the NIEO, based on the idea of "sovereignty equality, interdependence, common interest and cooperation among all States" to "make possible to eliminate the widening gap between the developed and the developing countries and ensure steadily accelerating economic and social development and peace and justice for present and future generations".[88] This Resolution wanted to accrue the developing States to an adequate exercise of "its full and permanent sovereignty over its natural resources".[89] After a period of Western dominance particularly through the acquisition of mining and exploitation concessions for dumping prices, "the backlash came" and the developing countries began to nationalize their natural resources once again. Initially, developed countries could still count on adequate compensation, but the amount of return was considered at the discretion of the expropriating States and therefore out of reach for them.[90] Even though the international minimum standard—as part of the law of aliens—was considered too generous for the expropriated investors.

---

[84] Ibid., 93.

[85] Ibid.

[86] Resolution A/RES/3016(XXVII): Permanent sovereignty over natural resources of developing countries, 18.12.1972b; A/RES/3016(XXVII).

[87] *Compare:* Proceedings of the United Nations Conference on Trade and Development; Third Session; Santiago de Chile, 13.04.1972, Volume I—Report and Annexes, *General Principle 1*; N. Schrijver (note 1), 93.

[88] *S. P. Ng'ambi,* Permanent Sovereignty Over Natural Resources and the Sanctity of Contracts, From the Angle of Lucrum Cessans, Loyola University Chicago International Law Review (2015), 154.

[89] Resolution A/RES/3201(S-VI): Declaration on the Establishment of a New International Economic Order (note 82); N. Schrijver (note 1), 99.

[90] M. Bungenberg and S. Hobe (note 62), VI.

The Western countries, by contrast, criticized the broad scope of economic activities concerning the extent of permanent and full sovereignty, including the right to nationalization and the transfer of ownership.[91] Further, any reference to compensation for nationalization measures was missed, even though the full compensation for the exploitation of States and people under foreign occupation, alien and colonial domination, or apartheid was underlined.[92] While some scholars spoke of "the end of complete Northern hegemony and the emergence of a new interdependence of power and wealth,"[93] others foresaw total impoverishment due to a state-led, command-and-control philosophy in developing countries.[94]

In 1974, the Charter of Economic Rights and Duties of States (CERDS) was adopted by Resolution 3281 (XXIX), arising from the idea of the NIEO. Although this document acknowledged the main principles of permanent sovereignty over natural resources, as outlined in Resolution 1803 (XVII), for example, the principle of fulfilling international obligations in good faith,[95] it established fundamental discrepancies.[96] The principal difference was the return to protection and nationalization, achieved by strengthening the host State's courts' laws and jurisdiction to settle investment disputes. This was the attempt to deny the "ability of foreign investors to rely on international standards in the event of expropriation of the investment".[97]

Thus, the Charter was supported by most developing countries but not by developed countries.[98] As a result, the exacerbation of the conflict was unavoidable and aggravated in such a way that "other international fora North-South encounters became increasingly confrontational and unproductive despite the fact there were genuine concerns on the part of both developed and developing countries about operations of the global economic system".[99]

---

[91] N. Schrijver (note 1), 99 et seq.

[92] Ibid., 99.

[93] S. P. Ng'ambi (note 91), 154.

[94] T. W. Wälde (note 83), 123.

[95] N. Schrijver (note 1), 99; *G. Elian*, The principle of sovereignty over natural resources, 1979, 118 et seq.

[96] R. Pereira and O. Gough (note 56), 456.

[97] Ibid.

[98] Ibid.

[99] *K. Hossain*, in: N. Schrijver/F. Weiss, International law and sustainable development, 2004, vii.

The CERDS reflected the main ideas of the New International Order, following a "state-led and command-control based philosophy" and promoting constitutive collaboration to uphold the sovereign equality of all States.[100] A decrease in foreign investment in the natural resource project ultimately led to increased investment problems for developing States.[101] The failure of this idea was exemplified by Tanzania, which followed the NIEO as one of the most consistent and ended up as one of the "most aided countries that fell into the deepest poverty trap."[102] It is probably due to the incompatibility between the approach of the expense of equality and solidarity and the main idea of the international economy, which is based on international trade, finance, and investment, and consequently, on "the self-interest of the rich West embodied in the freedom of the market."[103]

2.1.3.1.2 Permanent Sovereignty over Marine Resources

At the same time, the discussion about protecting marine resources, particularly concerning the principle of permanent sovereignty over natural resources, intensified.[104] During the debate on the Declaration on Permanent Sovereignty over Natural Resources, Resolution 1803 (XVII) in 1960, Peru raised the law-of-the-sea issue for discussion.[105] Even though Peru wanted to call attention more to the "urgent threat of certain marine species up to their complete disappearance", the matter of greater protection and "wealth of the seas" appeared for the first time on the agenda.[106]

In the following, the UNCTAD III in 1972 also addressed the right of coastal States over their marine resources in Principle XI of Resolution 46(III).[107] Moreover, the General Assembly adopted Resolution 3016 (XXVII) in the same year, which referred to the "permanent sovereignty over natural resources of developing countries".[108] Here, the wording and context were broadened so that the

---

[100] *P. J.* de *Waart*, in: N. Schrijver/F. Weiss, International law and sustainable development, 2004, 287; N. Schrijver (note 1), 99; T. W. Wälde (note 83), 123.

[101] N. Schrijver (note 1), 113.

[102] T. W. Wälde (note 83), 123.

[103] P. J. de Waart (note 103), 287.

[104] G. Elian (note 98), 124–126.

[105] N. Schrijver (note 1), 63; Doc. A/AC.97/SR.10, 01.03.1960, 8 et seq.

[106] N. Schrijver (note 1), 63; Doc. A/AC.97/SR.10 (note 108), 8 et seq.

[107] Principle XI: "*Coastal States have the right to dispose of marine resources within the limits of their national jurisdiction, which must take duly into account the development a welfare needs of their peoples.*"

[108] N. Schrijver (note 1), 92.

resources "found in the seabed and the subsoil thereof within their national jurisdiction and in the superjacent waters" were part of the permanent sovereignty of the developing countries.[109]

2.1.3.2 The Stockholm Declaration (1972)

The NIEO heralded a new decade, focusing on protecting the Human Environment.[110] Hence, in the 1970s, the first United Nations Conference on the Protection of the Human Environment was held, culminating in the adoption of the Stockholm Declaration in 1972.[111]

Initially, the Stockholm Declaration was considered a guideline to specify goals and objectives, similar to the Resolutions of the General Assembly. This resolution should highlight the connection between the environment and development, and, in addition, bring to the forefront the interests of developing countries.[112] The Stockholm Conference, held from June 5 to 16, 1972, was attended by 113 states and was guided by the principle that "each State has inalienable sovereignty over its environment and natural resources."[113]

During the Conference, it was emphasized that improving and defending the human environment should be a fundamental objective, alongside peace and economic and social development. Thus, the attendees concluded that international cooperation was unavoidable in supporting developing countries in addressing the increasing environmental problems. In particular, the local and national governments were most burdened by large-scale environmental policy programs.[114]

Principle 21 of the Stockholm Declaration is of significant importance for developing and evolving the principle of permanent sovereignty over natural resources.[115] In the final version, it is worded as follows:

> *"States have, in accordance with the Charter of the United Nations and the principle of international law, the sovereign right to exploit their own resources pursuant to their own environmental and developmental policies, and the responsibility to ensure that*

---

[109] Resolution A/RES/3016(XXVII): Permanent sovereignty over natural resources of developing countries, 18.12.1972a; A/RES/3016(XXVII).

[110] N. Schrijver (note 8), 19.

[111] *Declaration of the United Nations Conference on the Human Environment (note 11).*

[112] N. Schrijver (note 1), 121.

[113] Ibid., 122.

[114] Ibid., 123.

[115] *F. Nawrot,* Principle of permanent sovereignty over natural resources in rulings of international courts, Prawne Problemy Gronictwa i Ochrony Srodowiska (2020), 101.

activities within their jurisdiction or control do not cause damage to the environment of other States or of areas beyond the limits of national jurisdiction."

The question arose about how the environment should be associated with the sovereign right, and whether it should represent content or limitation for the exercise of permanent sovereignty.[116] Consequently, it is apparent in the environmental context, in which the sovereignty over natural resources stands, that the restriction is difficult ("*pursuant to their own environmental policies*").[117] What initially seemed a dichotomy of rights and duties of States—on the one hand, the rights over their natural resources and on the other hand, their duty to prevent environmental damage—is perfectly balanced in this principle.[118]

This principle played a decisive role in environmental policy in the following years and, in general, in the development of permanent sovereignty over natural resources. This principle is considered customary international law, as confirmed by the ICJ in its *1996 Advisory Opinion on the Legality of the Threat or Use of Nuclear Weapons.*[119] Afterwards, it entered various international treaties, like in the preambles of the Convention on the Conservation of European Wildlife and Natural Habitats 1979 (Bern Convention) and the Convention on Long-Range Transboundary Air Pollution 1979.[120]

The primary reason for this prominent position in international law is that this principle combines various doctrines established as essential in international environmental law over the years. Hence, the obligation to exercise due care for

[116] *Doc. A/CONF 48/PC.12 Annex II,* 14.06.1971, 12 et seq.

[117] N. Schrijver (note 1), 127.

[118] *F. Weiss/B. Scherzer*, in: M. Bungenberg/S. Hobe, Permanent Sovereignty over Natural Resources, 2015, 46; S. van Wyk (note 1), 90.

[119] S. van Wyk (note 1), 40 et seq.; F. Weiss and B. Scherzer (note 121), 46; *P. Sands*, Principles of international environmental law, 2018, 192.

[120] *Compare:* Preamble of the Bern Convention: "*Bearing in mind the widespread requests for common action made by governments or by international bodies, in particular the requests expressed by the United Nations Conference on the Human Environment 1972 and the Consultative Assembly of the Council of Europe;";* Preamble of Convention on Long-range Transboundary Air Pollution: *"Considering the pertinent provisions of the Declaration of the United Nations Conference on the Human Environment, and in particular principle 21, which expresses the common conviction that States have, in accordance with the Charter of the United Nations and the principles of international law, the sovereign right to exploit their own resources pursuant to their own environmental policies, and the responsibility to ensure that activities within their jurisdiction or control do not cause damage to the environment of other States or of areas beyond the limits of national jurisdiction";* S. van Wyk (note 1), 236 et seq.

the environment and nature is known nowadays as the principle of good neighborliness or the no-harm principle.[121] This principle, initially developed through a private law analogy known as "sic utere tuo ut alienum non laedas," which means the obligation not to cause transboundary environmental damage, is a customary law principle.[122] Moreover, the principle marks the beginning of the sustainable use of natural resources, which was adopted, refined in the UN Environmental Plan of 1978 and the World Charter for Nature of 1982, and ultimately defined as the principle of sustainable development in the Brundtland Report of 1987.[123] Nowadays, it represents one of the central elements of international governance, incorporated in international treaties and applied in international dispute settlements.[124]

2.1.3.3 UN Environmental Program Guidelines (1978)

The Stockholm Declaration later served as the basis of the United Nations Environment Program (UNEP) Guidelines in 1978, which focused on transboundary resources and the principles related to them.[125] Initially, only intended to be "a coordinator and catalyst in the field of environmental policy"[126], the Program laid the foundation for an international and national management of natural resources. The UNEP still provides the impetus for a new environmental spirit in the international community, including the private sector. Thus, it set standards for multilateral environmental agreements and increased motivation and responsibility among private entities, creating space for civil society participation in political or legislative processes.[127]

The development was stimulated by the wording of Principles 21 and 22 of the Stockholm Declaration, which emphasized the no-harm rule in a different context, referring to "*significant harmful effects in zones situated outside their national jurisdiction*", also using "*their technical data with a view to avoiding significant harm that may occur in the environment of the adjacent areas*".[128]

---

[121] Ibid., 57; F. Weiss and B. Scherzer (note 121), 46; N. Schrijver (note 8), 27.

[122] F. Weiss and B. Scherzer (note 121), 47.

[123] N. Schrijver (note 8), 27; M. Bothe (note 125), 555 et seq.

[124] F. Weiss and B. Scherzer (note 121), 55.

[125] N. Schrijver (note 8), 19.

[126] *N. Schrijver*, Development without Destruction: The UN and Global Resource Management, 2009, 57.

[127] *O. Ruppel/K. Ruppel-Schlichting*, Environmental Law and Policy in Namibia, 2011, 71.

[128] N. Schrijver (note 1), 128.

Thus, over the following years, the theory was further developed, building on the basic idea that the most significant environmental damage stemmed from the irrational and wasteful exploitation of natural resources. This exploitation threatened the exercise of permanent sovereignty over natural resources by other countries, particularly developing countries.[129] The idea of different resource management was also implemented in the following General Assembly Resolution 35/7 of 1980, repeated in the Resolution 36/6 and 37/7 in 1981 and 1982, which proclaimed the World Charter of Nature[130]:

> *"Solemnly invites the Member States, in the exercise of their permanent sovereignty over their natural resources, to conduct their activities in recognition of the supreme importance of protecting natural systems, maintaining the balance and quality of nature and conserving natural resources, in the interest of present and future generations."*

Taking this into account, the idea of shared resources came to the agenda of the United Nations, reflecting the mutual obligations of neighboring States and uniting the principles of good neighborliness and due diligence.[131] Hence, in 1973, the General Assembly adopted Resolution 3129 (XXVIII), which entrusted the mission of formulating international standards in that realm to the General Assembly. In 1975, the UNEP established an intergovernmental working group.[132] Moreover, the General Assembly encouraged this initiative, including the principle of shared resources in the Charter of Economic Rights and Duties of States of 1974.[133] Hence, the Charter required that

> "*Each State must co-operate based on a system of information and prior consultation to achieve optimum use of such resources without causing damage to the legitimate interests of others.*"[134]

---

[129] Ibid.

[130] N. Schrijver (note 130), 57; N. Schrijver (note 1), 128.

[131] N. Schrijver (note 1), 130.

[132] A/RES/3129(XXVIII): Co-operation in the field of the environment concerning natural resources shared by two or more States., 13.12.1973; A/RES/3129(XXVIII); N. Schrijver (note 1), 131.

[133] N. Schrijver (note 130), 57.

[134] Ibid., 57 et seq; Charter of Economic Rights and Duties of States, 12.12.1974; A/RES/3281(XXIX), Art. 3.

Finally, in 1978, the Draft Principles of the UNEP Guidelines on Shared Resources were established. In the fifteen principles, the focus is on the conservation and harmonious use of the resources with a view to controlling, preventing, reducing, or eliminating adverse environmental effects which may result from the utilization of such resources."

This guideline created a new leadership of "worldwide academic partnership" to inspire, inform, and enable nations and people to improve their quality of life, without compromising that of future generations."[135] Furthermore, by adhering to the principle of good faith and in the spirit of good neighborliness, it also had an effect on civil society, motivating them to be more environmentally responsible and creating much-needed space for their participation.[136] In conclusion, it also enhances development, particularly in developing countries.[137] The UNEP is a cornerstone in the development of sovereignty over natural resources because, for the first time, international law principles such as diligence and due care, good neighborliness, and state responsibility for extraterritorial damage were consolidated in a single international document.[138] Until today, this document shows its effects up to the basics of civil society and how the former Executive Director of the UNEP noticed:

> "*Sustainable development cannot be achieved unless laws governing society, the economy, and our relationship with the Earth connect with our deepest values and are put into practice internationally and domestically.*"[139]

2.1.3.4 Brundtland Experts Group on Environmental Law

Sustainable development was a key point in 1983, as outlined in the World Commission on Environment and Development's report, Our Common Future, which led to the emergence of the Brundtland Report in 1987.[140] Already under discussion in 1970, Resolution 35/56 of the General Assembly brought the principle of sustainable development to the fore, and in 1985, the ASEAN Agreement on the Conservation of Nature and Natural Resources explicitly mentioned it.[141] Finally, the Brundtland Report emphasized the importance of sustainable development for

---

[135] O. Ruppel and K. Ruppel-Schlichting (note 131), 71, 357.

[136] Ibid., 71; N. Schrijver (note 1), 133.

[137] N. Schrijver (note 1), 133.

[138] N. Schrijver (note 8), 19.

[139] O. Ruppel and K. Ruppel-Schlichting (note 131), 260.

[140] N. Schrijver (note 130), 9; Resolution A/Res/38/161: Process of preparation of the Environmental Perspective to the Year 2000 and Beyond, 19.12.1983; A/RES/38/161.

[141] F. Weiss and B. Scherzer (note 121), 52.

"preserving peace, reviving growth and changing [the] quality [of environment and development policies], remedying the problems of poverty and satisfying human needs, addressing problems of population growth and of conserving and enhancing the resource base, reorienting technology and managing risk and merging environment and economics in decision-making."[142]

In this report, for the first time after a long discourse of political, economic, and legal approaches, the meaning of sustainable development was clarified:[143]

"Sustainable development is development that meets the needs of the present without compromising the ability of future generations to meet their own needs."

Thus, this report represented the starting point of a general trend in international law adopted in the following years, which defined sustainable development as a general source, including, *i.a.*, the PSNR.[144] Although the concept has changed over the years, sometimes from "sustainable development" to "sustainable growth", the crucial point of the idea includes the recognition effect in international instruments, "covering various issue-areas and is solidly embedded in treaty practice".[145] In environmental law, this definition has served as the basis. In various other legal fields, the term was and is the basis "to integrate economic, development, human rights, and environmental issues".[146]

Hence, the Brundtland Report advocated for "ecological modernization" that impacts all relevant political fields by acknowledging the structural problems concerning the environment, while recognizing that "existing political, economic, and social institutions can internalize this care for the environment."[147] The innovation of this concept was significant due to its references to future generations, with the idea of "react and cure" at the heart of the Brundtland Report and the

---

[142] *G. H. Brundtland,* Report of the World Commission on Environment and Development: Our Common Future, 1987, Res. 42/187, para. 5; *T. A. Mensah,* in: I. Buffard/J. Crawford/A. Pellet/S. Wittich, International Law Between Universalism and Fragmentation, 2008, 798.

[143] *M. Campins-Eritjia/J. Gupta,* in: N. Schrijver/F. Weiss, International law and sustainable development, 2004, 254; N. Schrijver (note 8), 19.

[144] *N. Schrijver,* Evolution of Sustainable Development in International Law, 2008, 104; *G. Loibl,* in: N. Schrijver/F. Weiss, International law and sustainable development, 2004, 97.

[145] N. Schrijver (note 148), 104; G. Loibl (note 148), 114.

[146] M. Campins-Eritjia and J. Gupta (note 147), 253.

[147] *A. Gillespie and W. C. Burns (eds),* Climate Change in the South Pacific: Impacts and Responses in Australia, New Zealands, and Small Islands States, 2003, 35.

idea of "exceeding the capacities of State authorities."[148] Hence, for the first time, this report introduced the concept of intergenerational justice, which was subsequently expanded to encompass entire economies and societies.[149]

In particular, Article 2[150] of the Legal Principles of the Expert Group—referring explicitly to the PSNR—invited the States to not only apply this idea to policies on matters within and between the States but also to include it in all considerations within the sovereign territory, the border areas, and transboundary natural resources, as well as areas beyond national jurisdiction and resources therein.[151] The report aimed to initiate a new process to harmonize the "exploitation of resources, the direction of investments, the orientation of technological development, and institutional change"[152] and to "enhance both current and future potential to meet human needs and aspirations."[153] Hence, as classical soft law, the Report summarized many well-meaning ideas. Still, some scholars called it a mere "summary of proposed Legal Principles for Environmental Protection and Sustainable Development adopted by its Legal Expert Group", which did not establish new legal principles or obligations.[154]

In particular, developing countries promoted the implementation of the Brundtland Report to address social issues and further advance human rights.[155] However, the structural problems between developing and developed countries were insufficiently discussed in the context of the same combination of international aid and the promotion of free trade.[156] Thus, the thesis of the Brundtland

---

148 *M. Fitzmaurice*, in: I. Buffard/J. Crawford/A. Pellet/S. Wittich, International Law Between Universalism and Fragmentation, 2008, 222; A. Gillespie and W. C. Burns (note 151).

149 *U. Baxi*, in: S. Alam/J. H. Bhuiyan/J. Razzaque, International Natural Resources Law, Investment and Sustainability, 2019, 46.

150 Resolution A/42/427. Report of the World Commission on Environment and Development: Our Common Future: Annexe 1, 04.08.1987; A/42/427, Art. 2: "*States shall conserve and use the environment and natural resources for the benefit of present and future generations.*"

151 N. Schrijver (note 1), 133.

152 G. H. Brundtland (note 146), 17, para. 30; M. Campins-Eritjia and J. Gupta (note 147), 253.

153 G. H. Brundtland (note 146), 44, para. 15; M. Campins-Eritjia and J. Gupta (note 147), 253.

154 N. Schrijver (note 1), 134.

155 M. Campins-Eritjia and J. Gupta (note 147), 253.

156 Ibid.

Report focused, on the one hand, on greater citizen participation in decision-making regarding political and economic matters. On the other hand, emphasis was placed on self-reliance and self-correction after acquiring the necessary knowledge across all fields, including economic, social, productive, financial, and administrative realms.[157]

Moreover, the Brundtland Report came up at a time of tension between State sovereignty and international environmental law, described by the Brundtland Commission as the following dichotomy:

> "(…) *the planet was a large world in which human activities and their effects were neatly compartmentalized within nations, within sectors (energy, agriculture, trade), and within broad areas of concern (environmental, economic, social). These compartments have begun to dissolve. This applies in particular to the various global "crises" that have captured public attention over the past decade. These are not separate crises: environmental crises, developmental crises, and energy crises. They are all one.*"[158]

The Brundtland Report described a gradual dilution of the sovereignty of States, provoked by the interaction of various substantial issues of a general economic and environmental nature, also called the "interlocking crisis."[159] Even though the report proclaimed no "encroachment upon national sovereignty" at all, for the developing countries, in particular, this compromise represented rather a curtailment of their sovereign rights for the sake of environmental protection.[160] This interplay between State sovereignty and environmental law, first mentioned in Principle 21 of the Stockholm Declaration, remained one of the most debated themes in the years that followed. The PSNR stood between these two debated fields, which were not clearly defined as principles: strengthening state sovereignty or protecting natural resources.

Also in the Rio Declaration, the debate on more effective environmental protection continued, and, *e.g.*, the principle of sustainable development was established as a substantial doctrine, which later became legally grounded in various treaties at both national and international levels.[161] In conclusion, the

[157] Ibid.

[158] S. van Wyk (note 1), 90.

[159] Ibid.

[160] N. Schrijver (note 1), 135.

[161] N. Schrijver (note 148), 104; G. Loibl (note 148), 97.

principle of sustainable development is of great importance today, particularly because it "remains almost infinitely malleable".[162]

2.1.3.5 Rio Declaration on Environment and Development 1992

Since 1989, the General Assembly had already been considering a "second Stockholm Conference" to strengthen and improve the environmental concepts developed since 1972. The developing States expressed their concerns about the declining importance of their national sovereignty over their natural resources. In their opinion, it was a future concern that developed countries would misuse environmental considerations, enshrined in particular in Principle 21 of the Stockholm Declaration, to exert influence over their domestic affairs. Moreover, developing countries faced increasing obligations regarding environmental protection in international development and trade agreements, and their concerns became a subject of political interest.[163] Hence, to address all concerns and claims, the UNCED in 1992 emphasized environmental improvement while focusing on development. Not for nothing, the Conference took place in Rio de Janeiro, Brazil, a developing State that suffered from high environmental pollution and rainforest deforestation, representing a "degradation of the global life-support systems."[164]

The Rio Declaration 1992, which emerged from the so-called "Earth Summit" on 14 June 1992 in Rio de Janeiro, Brazil, laid the foundation for a new focus on environmental problems and therefore represents one of the primary sources of environmental principles.[165]

Accompanied by the right to a healthy environment, newly developed during this Conference, the principle of sustainable development occupied the prominent position of principle 1[166].[167] While the Rio Declaration does not explicitly address sustainable development, it serves as the basis for the Declaration's overall understanding. It can therefore be recognized in various other principles, *e.g.*, in Agenda 21 and the sustainable development as defined in Principle 3:

---

[162] *A. Boyle*, in: M. Kaltenborn/M. Krajewski/H. Kuhn, Sustainable Development Goals and Human Rights, 2019, 172.

[163] *J. A. Hofbauer*, The Principle of Permanent Sovereignty over Natural Resources and Its Modern Implications, 2009, 15 et seq.

[164] N. Schrijver (note 1), 135.

[165] *N. Schrijver and F. Weiss (eds)*, International law and sustainable development, 2004, 3.

[166] *Compare: Declaration on Environment and Development (note 12), Principle 1: "Human beings are at the center of concerns for sustainable development. They are entitled to a healthy and productive life in harmony with nature."*

[167] N. Schrijver (note 1), 136.

> *"The right to development must be fulfilled so as to equitably meet developmental and environmental needs of present and future generations."*[168]

In sum, in light of these principles, the Rio Declaration represents "an evolution of the concept of the right to a healthy environment, translated into the principle of sustainable development and the rights of future generations".[169]

The idea of "common but differentiated responsibilities" became a catchword for sustainable development. It is recognized in many international "soft law" documents, such as the Declaration, the UN Framework Convention on Climate Change, and Agenda 21, which followed shortly after the Rio Declaration, reinforcing the central doctrine.[170] To this day, the principle is recognized as a legal or fundamental principle of international environmental law.[171]

However, the most formative principle of the Rio Declaration is Principle 2, which builds upon Principle 21 of the Stockholm Declaration and maintains the exact wording, however, with the small addition of two words:[172]

> *"States have, in accordance with the Charter of the United Nations and the principle of international law, the sovereign right to exploit their own resources pursuant to their own environmental* ***and developmental*** *policies, and the responsibility to ensure that activities within their jurisdiction or control do not cause damage to the environment of other States or areas beyond the limits of national jurisdiction."*

To meet the needs and claims of the developing countries, the Rio Declaration set "emphasis on the connection of the principle with the aim of development", one of the original intentions of the principle of permanent sovereignty over natural resources.[173] Hence, the Declaration aimed to bridge the gap between the demands of developing countries to exploit and utilize their natural resources and the growing interest in strengthening environmental policies.[174] Thus, the intention was to "incorporate the environmental preservation in the development process," acting at different levels, such as sustainable conduct, transnational

---

168 M. Campins-Eritjia and J. Gupta (note 147), 255.

169 *S. Giorgetta*, in: N. Schrijver/F. Weiss, International law and sustainable development, 2004, 393.

170 N. Schrijver (note 1), 139.

171 *Y. Matsui*, in: N. Schrijver/F. Weiss, International law and sustainable development, 2004, 95.

172 N. Schrijver (note 8), 21.

173 J. A. Hofbauer (note 167), 7.

174 Ibid.; N. Schrijver (note 8), 21.

cooperation, and resource management, and always being aware of environmental principles.[175]

Consequently, the Rio Declaration served as the foundation for several international environmental documents and treaties in the years that followed, exerting influence on state conduct.[176] The most famous ones are the UN Framework Convention on Climate Change and the Convention on Biological Diversity, as well as treaties like the African Charter on Human and Peoples' Rights (African Charter 1986), which integrated various ideas from the environmental doctrine of the Stockholm Declaration.[177] For instance, the Convention on Biological Diversity (CBD) provides an informative definition for sustainable use in the context of Biological Diversity in Article 2, and the African Charter addresses a "right of all peoples to freely dispose of their wealth and natural resources in Article 21.[178] As a result, the main principles of the Rio Declaration gained more importance in international law, and the principle of permanent sovereignty over natural resources was further echoed in international treaties.[179]

Moreover, the Stockholm Declaration assumed responsibility for people, or "humans," rather than just States[180], while the Rio Declaration was more focused on the "needs of developing countries" and the goal of poverty eradication.[181] In conclusion, the trend indicates a shift from a "people-oriented" international policy to a more "State-oriented" international policy. On the other hand, the principle of public participation was established in a global declaration, ensuring that the population's position towards the State was determined and strengthened within a formal procedure.[182]

In this context, the question arose whether this developed environmental regime enjoyed the same authority as the treaty law, on which it was based. Although this declaration was followed by numerous resolutions, decisions

[175] J. A. Hofbauer (note 167), 7.

[176] Ibid.; G. Loibl (note 148), 97.

[177] N. Schrijver (note 8), 21; Y. T. Chekera and V. O. Nmehielle (note 31), 76; N. Schrijver (note 1), 138.

[178] Y. T. Chekera and V. O. Nmehielle (note 31), 76; N. Schrijver (note 1), 138; *B. Lewis*, Environmental Human Rights and Climate Change: Current Status and Future Prospects, 2018, 32.

[179] Y. T. Chekera and V. O. Nmehielle (note 31), 76.

[180] *Compare:* Declaration of the United Nations Conference on the Human Environment (note 11), Principle 1: *"Man (...) bears a solemn responsibility to protect and improve the environment for present and future generations."*

[181] N. Schrijver (note 1), 140.

[182] S. Giorgetta (note 173), 304.

of various international courts and tribunals, and numerous scholarly works, the regime lacks strong assertiveness.[183] It still represents soft law, which gives an "ineffective legal response to environmental degradation".[184] While the Stockholm Declaration was even celebrated as "a triumph of unrestrained anthropocentricity", the influence of environmental law decreased from conference to conference.[185] Hence, thirty years later, in 2002, the World Summit on Sustainable Development in Johannesburg placed more emphasis on developmental goals than on promoting environmental affairs.[186]

2.1.4 The PSNR in the UN Convention on the Law of the Sea 1982

As a countermeasure to the dilution of State sovereignty, the United Nations Convention on the Law of the Sea (UNCLOS) was adopted in 1982, following nine years of negotiations at the UN Conference on the Law of the Sea. This Convention represented, *i.a.*, a restructuring of the sovereign rights over the sea off the coast, including sovereignty over natural resources.[187]

In this way, the breadth of the territorial sea was stipulated to be up to twelve nautical miles (nm) from the coastline. This stipulation included the sovereign rights over the territory's natural resources. The "absolute territorial integrity" was only limited by the right of "innocent passage" by foreign vessels through these waters.[188] Moreover, the concept of the continental shelf and the Exclusive Economic Zone (EEZ) was recognized as new zones, extending up to 200 nautical miles from the coast. Even though the full sovereignty did not expand in this zone, the State gained "a form of instrumental sovereignty",[189] which included full sovereignty over natural resources, the living and non-living, as

[183] *P. Gümplová,* Restraining permanent sovereignty over natural resources, Quarderns de Filosofia 53 (2014), 108.

[184] Ibid.

[185] N. Schrijver (note 1), 140.

[186] P. Gümplová (note 187), 97, 108.

[187] N. Schrijver (note 8), 20.

[188] Convention on the Law of the Sea 1982, 10.12.1982a; UNCLOS, Art. 2, 3, 17.

[189] *A. Østhagen*, Coast Guards and Ocean Politics in the Arctic, 2020b, 15; *R. Strating/J. Wallis,* Maritime sovereignty and territorialisation: Comparing the Pacific Islands and South China Sea, Marine Policy (2022a), 2.

well as those of the seabed[190], the subsoil,[191] and the superjacent waters.[192] On the other hand, UNCLOS established the principle of the "common heritage of humankind" (CHM) to govern the high seas, and the International Seabed Authority (ISA) is tasked with regulating deep-sea bed mining in these areas.[193]

However, the UN Convention on the Law of the Sea also imposed a range of duties and obligations on States concerning the management of marine natural wealth and resources. Article 193 postulates the general duty to protect and preserve the marine environment, hand in hand with the liberty of exploitation of natural resources, which is given by the extension of the sovereign rights:

> *"States have the sovereign right to exploit their natural resources pursuant to their environmental policies and following their duty to protect and preserve the marine environment."*

Consequently, already here, States' exercise of their sovereign right is constrained by the obligation to protect and preserve the marine environment, which shows the importance, "the Convention attaches to the protection and preservation of the marine environment", as recognized in the Advisory Opinion of ITLOS in 2024.[194] Ten years later, the Convention on Biological Diversity adopted this concept in its Article 3, referring in particular to the biodiversity of the oceans:

> *"States have, in accordance with the Charter of the United Nations and the principles of international law, the sovereign right to exploit their own resources pursuant to their own environmental policies, and the responsibility to ensure that activities within their jurisdiction or control do not cause damage to the environment of other States or areas beyond the limits of national jurisdiction."*

Furthermore, the influence of Principle 21 of the Stockholm Declaration was already noticeable, as coastal States had the duty to maintain the sustainable yield of fish stocks. In contrast, landlocked developing countries were permitted to fish in the EEZ if there was a surplus of fish.[195] Besides that, the Convention on the

---

190 Convention on the Law of the Sea 1982, 10.12.1982b; UNCLOS, Art. 1(1), 56(1)a).

191 Convention on the Law of the Sea 1982 (note 192), Art. 1(1), 49, 56(1)a).

192 Art. 56.1 (a), 78, 135 UNCLOS.

193 A. Stilz (note 85), 223.

194 *Request For an Advisory Opinion submitted by the Commission of Small Island States on Climate Change and International Law,* No. 31, 21.05.2024, paras. 187, 380.

195 *Compare:* Convention on the Law of the Sea 1982 (note 194), Art. 63; N. Schrijver (note 8), 20.

Law of the Sea established, together with the declaration of the "common heritage of humankind," a concept of management of the deep seabed beyond national jurisdiction. This detailed international cooperative system also imposes duties on the States.[196] Unlike the matter of "common heritage", the "common concern"—originally developed in the 1993 CBD for protecting resources within the territory—looks for the legal gap, the common heritage of humankind leaves, and concerns global commons within and outside of national jurisdiction, by trying to bypass the legal gap in matters like climate and biodiversity.[197] In conclusion, concepts like sustainability and biological diversity—even if not mentioned in the Convention—were already considered in the context of the law of the sea in the Stockholm Declaration before developing UNCLOS and became key factors later on in the New Declarations of the 1990s, in particular the Rio Declaration and the Convention on Biological Diversity.[198]

2.1.5 The Development of the Principle of Permanent Sovereignty over Natural Resources in Case Law

As already discussed above, the PSNR has evolved through different stages over the last half-century. These levels can also be noted in case law. At the outset of this principle, the debate over nationalization and privatization reflected the steadily growing conflict between developed and developing countries. In the 1980s, the question of State responsibility came to the fore, particularly amid the growing environmental crisis. To date, this question remains the most impactful issue in the case studies of the principle of permanent sovereignty over natural resources.

---

[196] N. Schrijver (note 8), 20; *M. Dervovic,* Sharing Arctic Science: Applying the Common Heritage and Common Concern of Humankind in the Arctic, The Yearbook of Polar Law 13 (2021).

[197] *P. H. Sand*, in: F. Biermann/R. Brohm/K. Dingwerth, "Global environmental change and the nation state", 2002, 194 et seq; *M. Dervovic,* Sharing Arctic Science: Applying the Common Heritage and Common Concern of Humankind in the Arctic, The Yearbook of Polar Law 13 (2021), 312 et seq.

[198] S. Hobe (note 8), 8.

2.1.5.1 The 50s to the 70s: the Principle of Permanent Sovereignty over Natural Resources and Nationalization

One of the first cases dealing with the new principle of permanent sovereignty over natural resources was the Anglo-Iranian Oil Company Case in 1952. The Anglo-Persian Oil Company was a British-owned petroleum producer that obtained exclusive rights to extract and process petroleum in Persia—now Iran—in 1933.[199] In 1951, the Iranian government nationalized the company. It annulled the 1933 oil concession agreement, violating the so-called Hull doctrine of international investment law, which requires prompt, adequate, and effective compensation.[200] The United Kingdom, unable to accept the situation, unsuccessfully attempted to persuade Iran to settle the dispute through arbitration and ultimately called upon the International Court of Justice in 1951.[201] Although the court refused its jurisdiction with the final judgment of 1952 justified with the lack of coincidence of the term "international convention" in Article 38 (1) of the court's Statute with the concession contract, a case concerning the nationalization of natural resources had appeared on the stage of international jurisdiction for the first time.

This dispute highlighted one of the problems at the time, so, for the first time, the spotlight was shone on sovereignty over national resources in international investment law. Similar problems had arisen previously in 1938 regarding the land reforms in Mexico, which the Hull doctrine traced back to. The same issue famously resurfaced in the 1970s concerning the foreign oil companies in Libya.[202] Like Iran 20 years prior, Libya nationalized oil production and refused the offer to resolve the dispute by arbitration.[203] Later on, the cases went down in history as the first arbitration awards concerning the principle of permanent sovereignty over natural resources.

Informed by the UN Resolutions on the PSNR, these cases marked a shift in arbitration regarding sovereignty over natural resources. While Libya sought to have the case dismissed on the grounds of a lack of jurisdiction, the President

---

[199] N. Schrijver (note 1), 41.

[200] *M. Bungenberg*, in: M. Bungenberg/S. Hobe, Permanent Sovereignty over Natural Resources, 2015, 127.

[201] N. Schrijver (note 1), 41.

[202] *Compare: United Fruit Company in Guatemala (1953), The Chilean Copper Industry (1972);* M. Bungenberg (note 205), 127; *M. Ahmed/N. Sirohi,* Permanent Sovereignty over Natural Resources and the Indigenous People: Revisited, Civil and Military Law Journal 51 (2015), 112.

[203] M. Bungenberg (note 205), 127.

of the ICJ, who had affirmed that these disputes were not subject to arbitration because the nationalization was an act of sovereignty, dissented, along with the other arbitrators. They stressed that contracts between States and private persons can be "internationalized" in the Texaco[204] and the BP case[205]. Moreover, in the Limaco[206] case, the principle of international law was affirmed in accordance with the sanctity of property and contracts, and the arbitrators recognized the rights and obligations associated with expropriation.[207] Thus, in the Texaco award, Arbitrator Dupuy affirmed that the rules of nationalization and compensation in the context of the principle are to be used as international customary law due to their everyday use among the States, referring also to the "*opinion Juris communis*" of the Resolution 1803 (XVII) and thereby overriding the non-legally binding status of UNGA resolutions.[208]

However, these awards also confirmed expressively the sovereignty over natural resources as "an expression of the territorial sovereignty of the State, which gives the State the prerogative to choose and build its economic system".[209] Similarly, the Aminoil award remarked, "all the natural wealth and resources are the property of the State."[210] Consequently, the principle of permanent sovereignty over natural resources was recognized under the limits of respecting "other contractual agreements and compensation obligations".[211]

In conclusion, the principle of permanent sovereignty over natural resources was first recognized in international jurisprudence.[212] In this context, the problem of nationalization was mentioned, along with the question of how far the permanent sovereignty of a state, particularly a developing state, can extend.

---

204 *Texaco Overseas Petroleum Co. vs. Libya, 19.01.1977.*

205 *BP Exploration Company (Libya) Limited vs. Libya,* 10.10.1973.

206 *LIAMCO vs. Libya (Libyan American Oil Company vs. The Government of the Libyan Arab Republic),* 12.04.1977.

207 M. Bungenberg (note 205), 128.

208 *Texaco Overseas Petroleum Co. vs. Libya,* 19.01.1977, p. 30, para. 87; M. Bungenberg (note 205), 128; S. Hobe (note 8), 10.

209 *Texaco Overseas Petroleum Co. vs. Libya, 19.01.1977, 21, para. 59*; S. van Wyk (note 1), 230.

210 *LIAMCO vs. Libya (Libyan American Oil Company vs. The Government of the Libyan Arab Republic),* 12.04.1977, para. 189–191, 228, 309; *The American Independent Oil Company vs. The Government of the State of Kuwait (Aminoil vs. Kuwait),* 24.03.1982, para. XXXVII., 90; S. van Wyk (note 1), 230.

211 S. van Wyk (note 1), 230.

212 Ibid.

Furthermore, the limitations of this principle were revealed, particularly the conflict between property rights and nationalization. Various UN Resolutions have affirmed the right to property as an inalienable or unconditional right; therefore, a consensus must be reached in accordance with the principle of proportionality between the right to property and the principle of PSNR.[213]

In these initial awards, the principle of permanent sovereignty was affirmed and strengthened for individual Nation-States. However, developing countries were also required to respect international principles when exploiting their national resources and to establish rules compliant with international law.[214] In the 1990s, these obligations were substantiated in the protection of the environment and human rights, as the ICJ showed in the Advisory Opinion on the Legality of the Threat or Use of Nuclear Weapons, where it stressed:

> *"The environment [...] represents the living space, the quality of life, and very health of human beings, including generations unborn. [...] The existence of the general obligation of States to ensure that activities within their jurisdiction and control respect the environment of other States or of areas beyond national control is now part of the corpus of international law relating to the environment."*[215]

2.1.5.2 National Sovereignty and State Responsibility

The principle of territorial sovereignty also imposes specific responsibilities and obligations, which are not a new concept in international law. For the first time, it came up in the *Island of Palmas* case in 1928, where the sole arbitrator and President of the Permanent Court of International Justice, Huber, stressed that

> *"...sovereignty in the relations between States signifies independence. Independence regarding a portion of the globe is the right to exercise therein, to the exclusion of any other State, the functions of a State... Territorial sovereignty involves the exclusive right to display the activities of States. This right has as a corollary a duty: the obligation to protect, within the territory, the rights of other States, in particular their right to integrity and inviolability in peace and war, together with the rights each State may claim for its nationals in foreign territory. Without manifesting its territorial sovereignty in a manner corresponding to circumstances, the State cannot fulfil this duty."*[216]

---

[213] Ibid., 249 et seq.

[214] M. Bungenberg (note 205), 129.

[215] *Legality of the Threat or Use of Nuclear Weapons,* 08.07.1996, 241, para. 29; *Request For an Advisory Opinion submitted by the Commission of Small Island States on Climate Change and International Law,* No. 31, 21.05.2024, para. 166.

[216] *Island of Palmas case (Netherland vs. United States),* 04.04.1928, 829 et seq., N. Schrijver (note 1), 236; *T. Aqorau,* in: M. Powles, Pacific futures, 2006, 217.

So, in 1928, the consciousness of the duties of a State not only towards its people but also towards other States, in particular, in its own territory, existed. Later, the no-harm principle in environmental law emerged from this general idea. Furthermore, in 1938, one of the most famous cases was decided by an international arbitral award, the *Trail Smelter* case between the United States and Canada.[217] This case concerned the Columbia River Valley on the Canadian-US border, which suffered from high air pollution due to contamination from the zinc and lead smelter plants in Canada.[218] Therefore, this case represented the first international environmental case, even though it was not publicly presented as such.[219] For the first time, a State was held liable for environmental damage to another State. The key phrase, which represents to this day the best-known paragraph of the award, is:

> *"Under the principle of international law…no State has the right to use or permit the use of its territory in such a manner as to cause injury by fumes in or to the territory of another or the properties or persons therein, when the case is of serious consequence and the injury is established by clear and convincing evidence."*[220]

Although the arbitrators found it challenging to decide on the "subject material", they were unable to define the detrimental act, which could only be relative, referring to the "acting" State.[221] They decided, based on clear and convincing evidence, that the injury occurred on the territory of the neighboring State, which invoked the region's original status and use.[222]

This jurisdiction was enhanced in the *Corfu Channel* case in 1949. In this case, the ICJ had to address whether Albania had a duty to warn British warships about the minefield off its coast, specifically while passing through the Corfu Channel.[223] Here, the ICJ consolidates the obligation of States:

---

[217] *Trail Smelter case (United States vs. Canada),* 16.04.1938, 11.03.1941, p. 236; N. Schrijver (note 1), 236.

[218] *Trail Smelter case (United States vs. Canada),* 16.04.1938, 11.03.1941, 1905–1982; N. Schrijver (note 1), 236.

[219] *Trail Smelter case (United States vs. Canada),* 16.04.1938, 11.03.1941, 1905–1982; N. Schrijver (note 1), 236.

[220] *Trail Smelter case (United States vs. Canada),* 16.04.1938, 11.03.1941, 1905–1982, 1965.

[221] *X. Fuentes,* in: N. Schrijver/F. Weiss, International law and sustainable development, 2004, 23.

[222] Ibid., 23 et seq.; *E. M. Denters,* in: N. Schrijver/F. Weiss, International law and sustainable development, 2004, 238;

[223] X. Fuentes (note 226), 23; N. Schrijver (note 1), 237.

> *"not to allow knowingly its territory to be used for acts contrary to the rights of other States."*[224]

Thus, the ICJ stressed that not only was it the duty of the State to ensure that this territory was not used for acts violating the rights of other States, but also to terminate any unlawful activity.[225] The question of allocation of rights was also addressed in this case and found its basis in "Great Britain's entitlement to a right of innocent passage through the channel and a right to receive treatment from other States according to elementary considerations of humanity."[226] In conclusion, the cornerstone for the no-harm principle was laid between the 1930s and the 1950s; the context of environmental law was later established in the Nuclear Weapon case in 1996.[227] This also marks a milestone for the PSNR, emphasizing state sovereignty over the rightful use of natural resources rather than their exploitation for unlawful purposes.

2.1.5.3 Environmental Responsibility Beyond the Borders of the Nation-State

In 1996, the ICJ affirmed its position in the Corfu Channel case and extended it to environmental damages. In the Advisory Opinion on the *Legality of the Threat or Use of Nuclear Weapons*, the court concluded that:

> *"The environment is not an abstraction but represents the living space, the quality of life, and the very health of human beings, including generations unborn. The existence of the general obligation of States, to ensure that activities within their jurisdiction and control respect the environment of other States or areas beyond national control is now part of the corpus of international law relating to the environment."*[228]

In this judgment, the influence of the principles of the Rio Declaration, such as the no-harm principle and intergenerational equity, was not only recognized but also served to unify jurisdiction for future ICJ decisions on state responsibility towards other States. This includes the currently defined no-harm principle. The case demonstrated that the principle of State responsibility is not a determinative

---

[224] *The Corfu Channel Case,* 25.03.1948, 22.

[225] J. A. Hofbauer (note 167), 31.

[226] X. Fuentes (note 226), 24.

[227] E. M. Denters (note 227), 238.

[228] *Legality of the Threat or Use of Nuclear Weapons,* 08.07.1996, 226, 241–242; S. van Wyk (note 1), 271.

doctrine, but must be interpreted flexibly. Consequently, in the context of international environmental law, the application is viewed as a particular field within which it is situated.[229]

Hence, the court stressed that the environmental issues had not to be considered as an absolute rule, but rather like another argument in the framework of practical concordance and proportionality[230]:

> *„The issue is not whether the treaties relating to the protection of the environment are or are not applicable during an armed conflict, but rather whether the obligations stemming from these treaties were intended to be obligations of total restraint during military conflict.*
>
> *The Court does not consider that the treaties in question could have been intended to deprive a State of its right to self-defense under international law due to its obligation to protect the environment. Nonetheless, States must take environmental considerations into account when assessing what is necessary and proportionate in the pursuit of legitimate military objectives. Respect for the environment is one of the elements that go into assessing whether an action is in conformity with the principles of necessity and proportionality."*[231]

This view was reiterated one year later in the Gabcikovo-Nagymaros case, concerning the Danube River basin between Hungary and Slovakia. Hence, the court illustrated in the framework of proportionality, what possibilities existed for Hungary to find a sustainable and environmentally friendly solution:

> *...even supposing, as Hungary maintained, that the construction and operation of the dam would have created serious risks, Hungary had means available to it other than the suspension and abandonment of the works, of responding to that situation. It could, for example, have regularly discharged gravel into the river downstream of the dam. It could likewise, if necessary, have supplied Budapest with drinking water by processing the river water in an appropriate manner. The two Parties expressly recognized that that possibility remained open even though...the purification of the river water, like the other measures envisaged, clearly would have been a more costly technique."*[232]

In conclusion, the decision again underlined that there is "a general obligation of States to ensure that activities within their jurisdiction and control respect the environment of other States or areas beyond national control," which is part of

---

[229] X. Fuentes (note 226), 21.

[230] Ibid., 21 et seq.

[231] *Legality of the Threat or Use of Nuclear Weapons,* 08.07.1996, para. 30.

[232] *Case Concerning The Cabcikovo-Nagymaros Project (Hungary vs. Slovakia),* 25.09.1997, 40, para. 55.

the corpus of international law.[233] Moreover, all these decisions helped strengthen and consolidate the status of Principle 21 of the Stockholm Declaration and Principle 2 of the Rio Declaration as general principles of international law.[234] So, in the *Gabcikovo-Nagymaros* Project, the court underlined:

> *"New norms and standards have been developed, set forth in a great number of instruments during the last two decades. Such new norms must be considered, and these standards should be given proper weight, not only when States contemplate new activities but also when continuing activities begun in the past. This need to reconcile development with protection of the environment is aptly expressed in the concept of sustainable development."*[235]

The fact is that Principles 21 of the Stockholm Declaration and Principle 2 of the Rio Declaration are often consulted for interpretation in decisions of international importance, *e.g.*, by the International Court of Justice. Consequently, this principle "is capable of establishing a customary rule that States should refrain from causing material damage to other States in all circumstances".[236] Moreover, it is reflected in the internationally recognized standard to "*sic utere tuo ut alienum non laedas*", which refers to the obligation of States to use their own property so as not to injure that of other States.[237]

2.1.5.4 The Importance and Perspective of the Principle of Permanent Sovereignty over Natural Resources

However, what does this mean for the principle of permanent sovereignty over natural resources? Does it mean the principle is accepted in international jurisdiction, as it was already mentioned in the 1970s? Is it merely of the same status as Principle 21 of the Stockholm Declaration or Principle 2 of the Rio Declaration, where the principle is included? Does the principle of permanent sovereignty over natural resources already reach the status of customary law because of international jurisdiction? Moreover, how does the authority, referring to Principle 21 or Principle 2 of the Rio Declaration, interact with the principle of permanent sovereignty over natural resources?

---

[233] X. Fuentes (note 226), 22.

[234] Ibid.

[235] *Case Concerning The Cabcikovo-Nagymaros Project (Hungary vs. Slovakia)*, 25.09.1997, 75, para. 140; N. Schrijver (note 148), 142.

[236] X. Fuentes (note 226), 23 et seq.

[237] F. Weiss and B. Scherzer (note 121), 46.

The rule against transboundary harm conflicts with the principle of permanent sovereignty over natural resources, as it also limits a Nation-State's absolute sovereignty. Adjusting the newly adopted Stockholm Declaration in 1972, the General Assembly bridged the principle of PSNR to environmental concerns, formulating that it is *"the State duty with specific reference to PSNR and provides that it is concerned about the environmental impact of the irrational and wasteful exploitation and consumption of natural resources"*.[238] Therefore, sustainable development was already a concern in 1974. This commitment not only referred to transboundary environmental harm to another State, but also extended beyond the established obligation to the duty to conserve and sustainably use natural resources within and beyond territorial sovereignty.[239]

It became apparent that problems concerning at least two States or more could not be resolved by a single one, as well as the benefits from which a State profited, *e.g.*, from the exploitation of natural resources. Therefore, the "common concern of humankind gained momentum" in these times, imposing obligations to the States towards the environment and the well-being of people, including present and future generations, in terms of other principles of international law, such as PSNR.[240] In considering environmental impacts, the principle of PSNR must continually redefine and understand its rights and terms, thereby undergoing endless evolution.

Therefore, the question arises of how to approach the above-mentioned allocation problem regarding shared natural resources. The simple limitation of responsibility within a Nation-State's territory does not apply to shared natural resources, such as watercourses, fisheries, and oil and gas deposits.[241] This was already apparent in the precedent-setting *Trail Smelter* case. Still, a recent example—the San Juan River case between Costa Rica and Nicaragua—reiterated the concern in 2015.[242] In this case, on the one hand, the court found that Costa Rica had to tolerate Nicaragua's efforts to improve the San Juan River; on the other hand, Costa Rica had the right to seek indemnification as appropriate. In conclusion, this case underscores the growing interdependence among States and the need for equitable management of shared natural resources, particularly

[238] Resolution A/RES/3326 (XXIX): Report of the Governing Council of the United Nations Environment Programm, 16.12.1974; A/RES/3326 (XXIX); S. van Wyk (note 1), 270.

[239] S. van Wyk (note 1), 270; Resolution A/RES/3326 (XXIX): Report of the Governing Council of the United Nations Environment Programm, 16.12.1974; A/RES/3326 (XXIX).

[240] S. van Wyk (note 1), 270.

[241] X. Fuentes (note 226), 24.

[242] *Construction of a road in Costa Rica along the San Juan River,* No. 1088, 16.12.2015.

in research and exploration projects, to address the pressing issue of climate change.[243]

In summary, Principle 21 of the Stockholm Declaration and Principle 2 of the Rio Declaration today represent a general rule applicable to the prohibition of the infliction of material damage on all kinds of natural resources, "irrespective of whether or not there are supplementary rules about allocation of rights upon those resources."[244] This simplifies handling shared resources, but environmental issues might be forgotten.

2.1.6 Concluding Remarks

In conclusion, the principle of permanent sovereignty over natural resources passed through several phases of development. In the 1950s and 1960s, it stood for the liberation of colonized countries and represented, alongside the right of self-determination, an image of full sovereignty over their territory by developing States. Defined for the first time in Resolution 1803 (XVII) in 1962 by the General Assembly, it established a fundamental principle in international law. However, as was also pointed out in the controversial debate concerning this Resolution, this principle has never been free from conflict. Moreover, the scope of this principle has repeatedly been a contentious issue between developing countries and developed countries, particularly in the realms of investment and nationalization.[245] Consequently, it "establishes a bridge between economic, social and cultural and civil and political rights".[246]

In the 1970s, after several jurisdictions addressed the recognition and scope of the principle—particularly concerning the nationalization of natural resources and the requirement for adequate compensation—the principle was set in a new context. In the following discussion of environmental protection and sustainable development, the principle found its new scope of application. In defining the due diligence between neighboring States and the responsibility of States to the environment, the "full" sovereignty over natural resources was once again limited by the newly established environmental principles of international law.

---

243 S. van Wyk (note 1), 276 et seq.V.

244 X. Fuentes (note 226), 24.

245 Y. Tyagi (note 15), 602.

246 Y. Tyagi (note 37 in Chap. 1), 599.

In particular, the Stockholm Declaration and the Rio Declaration included Principles 21 and 2, respectively, which are now widely recognized as fundamental principles of environmental law and serve as a general basis for a wide range of environmental principles.

Consequently, the principle of permanent sovereignty over natural resources also found its way into the jurisdiction of international environmental law and the accompanying obligations. Hence, in this context, it was recognized as international customary law in 1996; has it already reached the status of *ius cogens*?

2.2 Legal Status of the Principle of Natural Resources Today

Consequently, the principle of permanent sovereignty has already attained the status of international customary law, as various jurisdictions have addressed it.[247] In Resolution 1803 (XVII) of 1962, the principle was considered an international legal right, followed by the two famous principles of the Stockholm Declaration and the Rio Declaration, which are regarded as customary law by the ICJ (see above). Moreover, it symbolizes a prerequisite for economic development and has been incorporated into various international treaties.[248] Even though treaty law usually replaces custom, the principle remains recognized as customary international law today.[249]

The ICJ had the opportunity to address the legal status of the PSNR principle in the *East Timor* case of 1995.[250] The Court did not expressly address the status of the principle, although Portugal claimed it. In the end, the judges pointed out that the principle of permanent sovereignty represents "*one of the essential*

[247] Ibid., 596.

[248] *Compare: International Covenant on Civil and Political Rights (note 6); International Covenant on Economic, Social and Cultural Rights (note 6); Vienna Convention on Succession of States in respect of Treaties, 23.08.1978; Vienna Convention on Succession of States in respect of State Property, Archives and Debts, 08.04.1983; African Charter on Human and Peoples' Rights, 27.06.1981; Banjul Charter; Convention on the Law of the Sea 1982 (note 194), Convention on Biological Diversity, 22.05.1992; CBD; Paris Agreement to the United Nations Framework Convention on Climate Change, 12.12.2015; UNFCCC; African Convention On the Conservation of Nature and Natural Resources, 11.07.2003; The Energy Charter Treaty, 17.12.1994.*

[249] S. van Wyk (note 1), 40, 43.

[250] R. Pereira and O. Gough (note 56), 462.

principles of customary international law with erga omnes character".[251] In 2005, the ICJ affirmed the legal status of this principle under customary international law in the Armed Activities on the Territory of the Congo case, which involved the ICJ's consideration of illegal resource exploitation during armed conflicts.[252] Consequently, the court confirmed that

> *"while recognizing the importance of (this) principle (of permanent sovereignty over natural resources), which is a principle of customary international law, the Court notes that there is nothing in these General Assembly resolutions that suggests that they are applicable to the specific situation of looting, pillage, and exploitation of certain natural resources by members of the army of a State militarily inventing in another State (…)."*[253]

On the one hand, the court affirmed the status of the principle as customary international law; on the other hand, it did not apply in the concrete situation of *ius in bello*. The Court had already stated accordingly in the *Israeli Wall Advisory Opinion* that at least human rights conventions remain applicable in times of armed conflict, but not all the rights of the people.[254] In conclusion, the ICJ adopted the opinion of the General Assembly, which already reaffirmed a "right of peoples under occupation to restitution and full compensation for the exploitation, the loss and the depletion of and damages to the natural resources in territory under occupation".[255] This opinion is not free from criticism for failing to acknowledge the lack of binding effect of UNGA resolutions.[256]

The *erga omnes* character is still under discussion for the principle, namely, whether the principle also represents a peremptory norm and complies with the *ius cogens* characteristics. The recognition of the *erga omnes* character would provoke a procedural effect, while the status of *ius cogens* is of a substantive nature.[257] Therefore, these two principles cannot be equated. Moreover, the *erga*

---

[251] *East Timor Judgement,* 30.06.1995, 90, 102, para. 29; R. Pereira and O. Gough (note 56), 462 et seq.

[252] *Case Concerning Armed Activities on The Territory of the Congo (Congo vs. Uganda),* 19.12.2005; R. Pereira and O. Gough (note 56), 463.

[253] *Case Concerning Armed Activities on The Territory of the Congo (Congo vs. Uganda),* 19.12.2005, para. 244.

[254] *Israeli Wall,* 09.07.2004, para. 102, 136.

[255] *Compare:* Resolution A/RES/3336 (XXIX): Permanent sovereignty over national resources in the occupied Arab territories., 17.12.1974; A/RES/3336 (XXIX).

[256] *M. Weisburd,* The International Court of Justice and the Concept of State Practice (2009), 330; R. Pereira and O. Gough (note 56), 463.

[257] *M. N. Shaw,* International law, 6th ed., 2008, 124; S. van Wyk (note 1), 44.

omnes character allows deviating from it, while *ius cogens* is not dispositive. However, the barrier is considerable, "deeming to be of a different or higher status than others, whether derived from custom or treaty".[258] To achieve the status of principles like the prohibition of slavery or the general prohibition on the use of force, compliance with two requisites is required, as stipulated in Article 53 of the Vienna Convention on the Law of Treaties.[259]

This Article requires that the legal consequence of the recognition as *ius cogens* be that it would equate to an act of unlawfulness for states to derogate from that norm in future agreements.[260] However, the second and main requirement implies that the principle is accepted as the norm by "the international community of States as a whole" or at least by "a very large majority of States", thereby safeguarding its predominant and overriding interests and values.[261] This consideration follows the purpose that *ius cogens* shall ensure the "*common good of the international community*", opposing the individual interests of States.[262] However, the principle of permanent sovereignty over natural resources also includes limitations, as shown above, concerning international environmental law.[263] The applicability of this principle is even questionable in light of the PSNR, despite some scholars' attempts to equate it with the principles of sovereign equality of States and non-intervention.[264] Although several multilateral treaties have incorporated the principle, it is very unlikely that the principle has reached, or will reach, the status of general acceptance by a majority of States.[265]

Another argument for a special status of the PSNR is the part of the name "permanent", which is also tantamount to "full" and "inalienable", indicating a general acceptance in the international community or even compliance with *ius*

---

[258] S. van Wyk (note 1), 44; M. N. Shaw (note 262), 117.

[259] Vienna Convention on the Law of Treaties, 23.05.1969, Art. 53: *A peremptory norm of general international law is a norm accepted and recognized by the international community of States as a whole as a norm from which no derogation is permitted and which can be modified only by a subsequent norm of general international law having the same character.*

[260] *R. Pereira*, in: K. Makuch, Environmental and Energy Law, 2012, 203; R. Pereira and O. Gough (note 56), 463; S. van Wyk (note 1), 45.

[261] *A. Orakhelashvili*, Peremptory norms in international law, 1st ed., 2006, 46; S. van Wyk (note 1), 445; N. Schrijver (note 1), 376.

[262] S. van Wyk (note 1), 45; A. Orakhelashvili (note 266), 46 et seq.

[263] S. Hobe (note 8), 11.

[264] Y. Tyagi (note 15), 594; F. Nawrot (note 55), 100.

[265] R. Pereira and O. Gough (note 56), 463.

cogens. However, it is likely only an indicator of the relationship between rules and exceptions, generally applied in international law, according to which

> *"Sovereignty is the rule and can be exercised at any time, that limitations are the exception and cannot be permanent, but limited in scope and time."*[266]

Consequently, we can conclude that the adjective "permanent" is "misfitting in [the present-day] ever-changing world".[267] Even though the principle has found its limits in the context of the territory's border, it is not applicable in the High Seas, where the principle of the common heritage of humankind is dominant.[268] Moreover, the principle developed from the right of people to self-determination already has the status of *ius cogens*.[269] In conclusion, as Schrijver has already noted, all the core elements of this principle could carry this status.[270] In conclusion, some supporting views regard the principle of permanent sovereignty over natural resources as *ius cogens*; however, the prevailing view does not follow this line.[271] Consequently, it can be at least described as a "fundamental principle and right of international law" and classified under the UN principles as "part of the treaty law and customary international law", representing ideals or policies, which likely deserve to become written law but have no legal value, or "indicate the core idea of several single provisions".[272]

---

[266] N. Schrijver (note 1), 263.

[267] Y. Tyagi (note 15), 614.

[268] Convention on the Law of the Sea 1982 (note 194), Art. 137; S. Hobe (note 8), 11.

[269] S. van Wyk (note 1), 45; N. Schrijver (note 1), 375.

[270] N. Schrijver (note 1), 221; S. van Wyk (note 1), 46.

[271] R. Pereira and O. Gough (note 56), 463; S. van Wyk (note 1), 46.

[272] *G. Winter*, in: G. Winter, Multilevel governance of global environmental change, 2006, 589, S. van Wky (note 1), 46.

indeed. However, it is likely only an indicator of the relationship between rules and exceptions, generically applied to international law, according to which

3 The Primary Pillars of the Principle of Permanent Sovereignty over Natural Resources

The starting point of international relations is the existence of States... each of which... asserts sovereignty in relation to a particular portion of the earth's surface and a particular segment of the human population. (*T. Kuehls*, in: K. T. Litfin, The greening of sovereignty in world politics, 1998, 31)

As already seen above, the principle of permanent sovereignty over natural resources, as developed in the 1950s, is rooted in two main principles: the sovereignty of States and the right of people to self-determination.[1] This combination reflected two contradictory tendencies, now united in one principle: economic development in the so-called developing countries and the international legal principle of self-determination, which includes the obligation to cooperate to advance independence in these countries. This was the guidance for developing the principle of self-determination for people. On the contrary, the fundamental principle of territorial sovereignty served as the determining factor in orientation and as a counterbalance for the developed countries.[2] At this time, these two principles formed essential parts of general international law, so the right was considered to have a "sound basis in international law".[3] Consequently, introducing the principle of permanent sovereignty over natural resources represented a "radical break with the preceding era".[4] It does not only mean the end of the

[1] N. Schrijver (note 8 in Chap. 2), 15, 17.

[2] M. Bungenberg and S. Hobe (note 62 in Chap. 2), 10.

[3] Ibid.

[4] *T. Biersteker/C. Weber*, in: T. Biersteker, State sovereignty as social construct, 1996, 284.

M. A. Brinker, *The Principle of Permanent Sovereignty over Natural Resources as an Anchor in Times of Sealevel Rise*, https://doi.org/10.1007/978-3-658-50527-1_3

dominance of State sovereignty over their people but, in particular, for the developing countries, to be "freed from colonial domination" in granting "the right of free disposal over the natural wealth and resources".[5] Consequently, it marked the first appearance of people in international law, shifting from an ownership to a governance orientation.[6]

However, what do these two fundamental principles in international law mean, and what made them so significant and dominant in international law? The description and development of these principles will be the subject of this chapter.

3.1 The Sovereignty of States

The concept of a "state-centric world" emerged in Europe in the 19th century, as businesses and trade unions expanded rapidly and were increasingly organized within a larger state-based framework.[7] Trying to connect sovereignty, territory, and people—the Nation-State, born in the European state system—is, at the same time, based on and realizes the idea of self-determination.[8] The modern conception of a State still consists of a "supreme domination over a particular portion of the earth's surface."[9] Consequently, the connection between political civilization and its territory seems inseparable.[10] However, from today's perspective, this territorial organization also marked the beginning of international reorientation, starting with demarcations, then the first diplomatic goals, and culminating in the founding of international organizations.[11] However, what does the idea of the State and the people include? How did the idea of the State as a legal person emerge and develop? What is a nation? And, what does today's sovereignty of States mean?

[5] *A. Cristescu,* The right to self-determination: Historical and current development on the basis of United Nations instruments, 1981, 25, para. 176.

[6] M. Bungenberg and S. Hobe (note 62 in Chap. 2), vi.

[7] *T. Gullberg*, State, territory and identity: The principle of national self-determination, the question of territorial sovereignty in Carinthia and other Post-Habsburg territories after the First World War, 2000, 1; *J. Agnew*, Globalization and Sovereignty: Beyond the Territorial Trap, 2018, 31; S. van Wyk (note 1 in Chap. 2), 77.

[8] T. Gullberg (note 12), 1.

[9] *J. Crawford*, The creation of states in international law, 2nd ed., 2006, 48; J. McAdam (note 10 in Chap. 1), 130.

[10] *J. A. Simmons,* On the Territorial Rights of States, Philosophical Issues (2001), 301.

[11] T. Gullberg (note 12), 2.

For instance, the Peace of Westphalia, well known as the first international treaty and probably the precursor to a State system, determined that "where unity was established by Nation-States exercising sovereignty over certain territories."[12] This settlement occurred at a time in history when territorial control, borders, and customs regulations were newly established. This was partly due to the government claiming authority over its citizens and, in line with this, insisting that "interference in their internal affairs is unlawful."[13] These days, this "historical supremacy of the principle of State sovereignty sets the basic fundamental constitutional doctrine of the law of nations", which sometimes makes it difficult to breach.[14] However, we must remind ourselves that the creation and recognition of States are ultimately a legal fiction.[15] Moreover, international law sets a broad range of limitations on the nature and scope of action for States, *i.e.,* concerning the use of force or the principle of *sic utere tuo ut alienum non laedas.*[16]

However, the term "state" could be given a broader meaning, also including traditional indigenous decision-making procedures as an "institution (1) binding collective rule setting and (2) the ability to enforce its determinations in case of disputes." In this context, we have to observe that the modern interstate system and the configuration of States are a "product of European colonialism."[17]

3.1.1 Occupancy Rights: The Beginning of a State?

Territoriality is described by Robert Sack as "the attempt by an individual or group to affect, influence, or control people, phenomena, and relationships, by

[12] *C. Blanchard,* Evolution or revolution? Evaluating the Territorial State-Based Regime of International Law in the Context of the Physical Disappearance of Territory Due to Climate Change and Sea-Level Rise, Canadian Yearbook of International Law 53 (2015), 73.

[13] *F. Venter*, in: L. J. Kotzé, Transboundary Governance of Biodiversity: Transboundary Governance of Biodiversity, 2014, 76.

[14] *H. A. Northcott,* Realisation of the right of indigenous peoples to natural resources under international law through the emerging right to autonomy, The International Journal of Human Rights 16 (2012), 77.

[15] Ibid; *P. Ferrara*, in: M. Kotzur/N. Matz-Lück/A. Proelß/R. Verheyen/J. Sanden, Sustainable ocean resource governance: Deep sea mining, marine energy and submarine cables, 2018, 206.

[16] H. A. Northcott (note 19), 77; M. Bothe (note 125 in Chap. 2), 540.; Latin for „*Use your own property in such a manner as not to injure that of another*".

[17] Ibid., 15.

delimiting and asserting control over a geographic area".[18] Consequently, the idea of territorial sovereignty provides the initial impetus long before the 19th and 20th centuries and European Colonialism.

Hugo Grotius, also known as the inventor of the "mare liberium" theory, postulated the theory of common ownership as "moral rights over material resources for humans" as part of the idea of occupancy rights.[19] He argues "a certain form of ownership did exist" before the institution of private property, but as an "ownership in a universal and indefinite sense".[20] Supported by other scholars of this time, such as Thomas Hobbes and John Locke, he established the "ownership status of the earth". He introduced the concept of a "global common" and its conditions of privatization.[21] Various philosophers like Hannah Arendt took up this idea, considering in The Human Condition that "the earth is the very quintessence of the human condition and earthly nature, for all we know, may be unique in the universe in providing human beings with a habitat in which they can move and breathe without effort and artifice".[22]

Stilz concluded that this "right to use our commonly owned earth without interference is a *'primitive right'*".[23] These primitive rights are as extensive "as far as Nature required", while there are also things not directly tied to survival—like our right to use the sea to sail from place to place.[24] According to Grotius, there are things that "are necessary to being, while others are necessary only to well-being; or one might say that they relate respectively to safety and comfort".[25] Stilz further remarked that the primitive rights, which can lead to State's foundational title to land, consisted of "a bundle of rights, held by individual inhabitants, to occupy those areas essential to their comprehensive life projects, to enjoy security in these projects, and to access a range of options for revising

---

[18] *R. D. Sack*, Human territoriality, 1st ed., 1986, 19; A. Stilz (note 85 in Chap. 2), 25; T. Gullberg (note 12), 2.

[19] A. Stilz (note 85 in Chap. 2), 61; *M. Risse*, On global justice, 2012, 83; *J. A. Simmons*, Boundaries of authority, 2016, 193.

[20] *H. 1.-1. Grotius*, The Freedom of the seas or the right which belongs to the Dutch to take part in the East Indian trade, 1916, 22 et seq.; A. Stilz (note 85 in Chap. 2), 61.

[21] M. Risse (note 25), 80.

[22] Ibid., 80 et seq.

[23] A. Stilz (note 85 in Chap. 2).

[24] Ibid., 62.

[25] Ibid; *H. Grotius*, De jure praedae commentarius, 1604, 23.

them".[26] As distinguished to property rights, the land "remains in common ownership" in the understanding of primitive rights to geographic space "compatible with limited exclusionary practices".[27]

This principle of "res communis" is based on the same idea as the principle of "mare liberum", that this territory is unavailable for acquisition for all States. [28] In contrast to this, "res nullius" incorporates the idea of unsubjected territory, so that this area is thus available for appropriation and settlement.[29] Consequently, unlike the sea, States are legitimized to "do business" as legal persons in the world community, which also includes, i.e., the legitimate use of physical force.[30]

This "business" includes, according to the Lockean hierarchical account, the rights over subjects and the rights against aliens. The latter only reaches the extent that it is necessary to "properly exercise [the States'] authority" on the one hand and, on the other hand, respect the rights to non-interference, self-determination, and free interaction with other agents, as well as the individuals' natural rights to self-government.[31] However, is this hierarchical justification morally justified in referring to a particular territory?[32] One argument is the perpetuation of territorial integrity, which includes the effective control and protection of the territory for the subjects who work and reside within it.[33] Locke resolves the question of interior land will as an "international understanding of the common property of all members of a political society" accompanied by, in addition to the territorial control, the State as a "contract of association" given by a political society that sets up a particular form of government and moral background.[34]

3.1.1.1 Property Rights and the Theory of Occupancy Rights

Consequently, the distinction between property rights and occupancy rights must be questioned. Already in earlier times, before the territorialized State was

[26] A. Stilz (note 85 in Chap. 2), 73.

[27] Ibid; M. Risse (note 25), 83.

[28] J. A. Simmons (note 15), 304; M. Bothe (note 125 in Chap. 2), 551.

[29] J. A. Simmons (note 15), 304; M. Bothe (note 125 in Chap. 2), 551.

[30] J. A. Simmons (note 15), 303, 306.

[31] Ibid., 307.

[32] Ibid.

[33] Ibid., 312.

[34] Ibid., 314; *B. M. Barry*, Democracy, power and justice: Essays in political theory, 1989, 161.

"invented", "territoriality represented power and prosperity for individuals, manifested in land ownership".[35] Anna Stilz stressed, that the base of "State's territorial sovereignty is a prior "property-like" entitlement to the area it governs" so that the State acts as "an agent" for its members, who hold the "occupancy rights in these spaces".[36] In the same way, Simmons describes the "State's territory as the portion of earth's surface acknowledged to "belong" to the State by the "world community".[37] Already, Judge Huber stressed in the *Island of Palmas* case, referring to the law of property as "a rationalization of the factual distribution of possession" that:[38]

> *"...practice, as well as doctrine, recognizes – though under different legal formulae and with certain differences as to the conditions required – that the continuous and peaceful display of territorial sovereignty (peaceful in relationship to other States) is as good as a title.... Just as before the rise of international law, boundaries of lands were necessarily determined by the fact that the power of a State was exercised within them, so too, under the reign of international law, the fact of peaceful and continuous display is still one of the most important considerations in establishing boundaries between States."*[39]

However, what are the differences between property rights and occupancy rights? How was the State entitled to the occupancy rights over a territory?

In the same way that the classical definition of property states that property owners are allowed to use and control objects, States, in their own right, "claim rights to use and control parts of the globe."[40] These so-called Proprietarian theories are based on the property-like aspects of State systems, viewing the foundational title as a natural right to property by emphasizing the claims people derive from the land they inhabit.[41] Similarly, Locke considered the State as two-faceted, with the property "as the benefit and sole advantage of the proprietor", standing opposite the government, "preserving of every man's right and property by preserving him from the violence or injury of others".[42] According to Locke,

---

[35] T. Gullberg (note 12), 2.

[36] A. Stilz (note 85 in Chap. 2), 22.

[37] J. A. Simmons (note 15), 303.

[38] *R. Jennings*, The Acquisition of Territory in International Law, 1963, 2017, 20.

[39] *Island of Palmas case (Netherland vs. United States),* 04.04.1928, p. 839.

[40] A. Stilz (note 85 in Chap. 2), 33.

[41] Ibid.

[42] C. Nine (note 38 in Chap. 1), 74; B. M. Barry (note 40), 162 et seq.; *compare*: *Lockean consent theory.*

the state's territory is built on the union of individual natural property rights and the agreement between property owners "to submit both themselves and the land on which they live and work to the State's authority," constructing a State of individual rights.[43]

Unlike the proprietary theories, the territory does not "belong" to the State in the same intense and absolute way as property belongs to its owners, as the so-called occupancy rights have a weaker character.[44] Unlike the full range of liberal ownership, which includes property rights such as the right to bequest or exclude people from property, occupancy rights do not extend as far.[45] They only include the right to reside permanently on the territory, to participate in the social, cultural, and economic life, as well as return to it.[46] The right to occupancy "is more geographically capacious than private ownership is, though it confers a more limited control over resources".[47] In conclusion, the requisites for the State's foundational title to land "consist in a bundle of moral rights of occupancy held by the inhabitants of a place", giving the group the collective claim to its "homeland".[48] Consequently, occupancy can be called a weaker form of property.[49]

Nonetheless, nowadays, property and sovereignty are strictly separated domains within the legal system of a State.[50] The State as such is and remains "the definer and enforcer of property rights".[51] The power to define and protect property rights—within State borders as well as beyond them—stands as a symbol of wealth and as a representation of the flow of capital.[52] Consequently, control over property, whether over solid assets like real estate or mobile assets like capital, remains a key aspect of the monopoly of sovereignty, particularly in times of globalization, when State boundaries have become increasingly uncertain and cash flows faster and less transparently.[53]

---

[43] A. Stilz (note 85 in Chap. 2), 33 et seq; J. A. Simmons (note 25), 178 ff; T. Kuehls (note 5), 43; B. M. Barry (note 40), 162–163, 165.: *compare*: Lord Actor, Nationality, 1909.

[44] A. Stilz (note 85 in Chap. 2), 34.

[45] Ibid., 34 et seq.

[46] Ibid.

[47] Ibid., 35.

[48] Ibid., 35 et seq.

[49] Ibid., 35.

[50] *G. Elian/A. Bantas*, The principle of sovereignty over natural resources, 1979, 14.

[51] J. Agnew (note 12), 106.

[52] Ibid.

[53] Ibid., 106 et seq.

The question remains: how can a state emerge from the simple idea of a bundle of moral rights of occupancy? What makes the State what it is? Consulting Kant's political theory, "the status of territorial rights remains in question".[54]

3.1.1.2 Territorial Rights

As already noted, individuals' interests represent the heart of occupancy rights.[55] Consequently, we must close the gap between individual occupancy rights and State-level territorial rights, including, in particular, the right to territorial jurisdiction.[56] First of all, we have to define the territory as such, which is "the geographical domain of political or jurisdictional authority", as opposed to land, which is "the part of the earth's surface that is not covered by water".[57] As we saw above, the territory is distinct from the property, but we can identify some similarities between the two concepts.[58] Consequently, the territorial right-holder can dispose of a cluster of rights, including rights to jurisdiction, to control the flow of goods, and to natural resources.[59] This differentiation is essential for the further research project.

To legitimately acquire the full scope of jurisdiction over the territory, the State has to comply with the following conditions; (1), an effectively implemented system of law in the territory, which meets the requirement of fundamental justice; (2) the State's institutions, which have "to reflect the shared political will of a significant majority of cooperators among those rightful occupants; and, (3), "a lack of an institutional alternative".[60] Only the alliance between jurisdictional rights over persons and resources within the territory, on the one hand, and the ownership rights over the resources and authorities, which govern residence, immigration, and citizenship rights, on the other hand, can cover the conceptual, political, and legal scope of territorial rights.[61] Here, we can already recognize the input of occupancy rights, which has been expanded to authority rights. In addition, jurisdictional rights include the power to legislate, adjudicate, and enforce property rights, establish rules regarding unowned goods within the region, and

---

[54] A. Stilz (note 85 in Chap. 2), 59.

[55] Ibid., 55.

[56] Ibid., 34, 55–56.

[57] *M. Moore*, in: A. Santos Campos/S. Cadliha, Sovereignty as value, 2021, 148.

[58] Ibid.

[59] Ibid., 149.

[60] A. Stilz (note 85 in Chap. 2), 56.

[61] C. Nine (note 38 in Chap. 1), 6 et seq.

enter into treaties that alienate or transfer powers to another collective.[62] A benefit of this definition of territorial rights is the independence of property rights: "property rights could be before, follow from, or arise in conjunction with territorial jurisdiction".[63]

As a counterpoint to that, Simmons, referring to the individualistic Lockean theory of territory, regards territorial rights as a cluster of rights, while individuals are sovereigns over their personal property.[64] Territorial rights, according to Simmons include inter alia,(1) rights to exercise jurisdiction, (2) rights to complete control over land and resources within the territory in a reasonable manner, (3) rights to capitalize on and regulate uses, (4) rights to control or prohibit movements across the borders, and (5) rights to limit or restrict "dismemberment" of State's territory.[65] Consequently, according to the Lockean view, "those resources actually figure in the morally acceptable plans and projects of their members".[66]

Territorial rights are primarily "a set of jurisdictional powers to make, adjudicate, and enforce law", in contrast to the lower-level ownership rights "to access, use, manage, sell, or retain the value from a particular good".[67] In other words, all these different rights are entitlements that represent and enforce particular moral values. While individual property rights are designed to promote personal autonomy and well-being, territorial rights, understood as jurisdictional authority, also serve these values.[68] Therefore, it is not surprising that the Lockean theory of territorial rights is divided into two interpretations: the individualistic and the collectivistic accounts.[69] While the individualistic account is based on the idea that property owners "contract together to form a State with territorial jurisdiction", the collectivistic account is based on the collective labor on the land to gain territorial rights over said land".[70] If these people gain the "membership of political society" by the individualist or collectivistic account, they are "legitimately subject to its authority" and have the obligations of citizens, which submit them

62 Ibid., 8.

63 Ibid., 10.

64 Ibid., 11; J. A. Simmons (note 15), 306.

65 C. Nine (note 38 in Chap. 1), 10 et seq.

66 J. A. Simmons (note 25), 209.

67 C. Nine (note 38 in Chap. 1), 11.

68 Ibid., 12, 82–83.

69 J. A. Simmons (note 25), 209.

70 C. Nine (note 38 in Chap. 1), 72; B. M. Barry (note 40), 516.

to the State's jurisdiction.[71] In consequence, we have to conclude that the legal construct of the State as such cannot exist without a reference point.

Kant, in contrast, argued that "States' rights are primitive, that they are not derived through delegation of jurisdictional rights by individuals."[72] According to Kant, there are no "natural titles to ownership"; even the State can create and coordinate interpersonal connections among human beings. Therefore, they "have the duty to accept the authority of States."[73] However, according to this theory, "the status of territorial rights [of the State] remains in question" until the constitution of a universal political association.[74] Consequently, the State as a territorial entity remains illegitimate. It can be legitimized "only if its citizens are also politically committed to establishing a global authority realizing an all-inclusive principle of right".[75] Kant also acknowledged this aspect, introducing a third actor besides the individuals and States: the people, who hold the "meta-jurisdictional authority" over territorial jurisdiction.[76] According to Kant, the State is the amalgamation of political institutions, "claiming a monopoly in a particular territory", while people continue to exist without these State institutions, like a moral authority or "moral personhood".[77] Therefore, according to some scholars, people might continue to claim resources. They are the right-holders of resources, in contrast to the State, which establishes a rule of law for these rights.[78]

Like these ideas, Locke established the collectivistic Lockean theory, "allowing" a collective to acquire rights over territory, without prior reference to property rights or individual consent, one of the main weaknesses of his individualistic theory.[79] According to this theory, the collective can constitute territorial rights if its ties to the territory are "morally valuable" because, as already explained, "entitlements are justified from a set of moral principles" to help to

---

[71] J. A. Simmons (note 25), 209.

[72] C. Nine (note 38 in Chap. 1), 55., Kant's Gesammelte Schriften, 1900, 6:312.

[73] Ibid., 54 et seq.

[74] A. Stilz (note 85 in Chap. 2), 33.

[75] Ibid., 59; *A. Banai,* The territorial rights of legitimate states: a pluralist interpretation, International Theory (2014), 142; *L. Ypi,* A permissive theory of territorial rights, European Journal of Philosophy (2014), 293.

[76] C. Nine (note 38 in Chap. 1), 55; A. Banai (note 81), 144.

[77] C. Nine (note 38 in Chap. 1); *D. Miller*, Citizenship and national identity, 1st ed., 2000, *D. Miller*, National responsibility and global justice, 1st ed., 2007, 185 et seq; *D. Miller*, On nationality, 1995, 19.

[78] C. Nine (note 38 in Chap. 1), 55 et seq.

[79] Ibid., 82.

realize relevant liberal values.[80] Therefore, for instance, territorial rights serve to protect and promote the values concerning the territorial relationship of the people to the land, but not the property relationship of individuals.[81]

3.1.2 The Creation of the Nation-State

The best concept of Nation-States holding territorial sovereignty independently dates back to the beginning of World War I, when the European continent experienced one of the most tremendous upheavals in history.[82] Like President Wilson stated in 1918:

> *"Peoples and provinces are not to be bartered about from sovereignty to sovereignty as if they were chattels and pawns in a game."*[83]

In consequence, the Nation-States, as the general basis for the European State system, were born, endorsing the claims to self-determination and supported by the League of Nations,[84] so that "today no State possesses legitimacy which does not claim to represent the will of the nation".[85] This implied the connection between sovereign, territory, and people, so that "a State's internal sovereignty and the existence of the State itself is threatened" when the composition of a nation is uncertain and the State sovereignty itself "becomes shaky".[86] In simple words, it means "those who inhabited a territory which a State defined as its own were to identify with the State's ideology, which that State used to legitimate its territorial stipulations."[87]

---

[80] Ibid., 82 et seq.

[81] Ibid., 83.

[82] T. Gullberg (note 12), 1; J. Agnew (note 12), 81; *B. Knoll*, The legal status of territories subject to administration by international organisations, 2008, 56 et seq.

[83] B. Knoll (note 88), 57; *R. N. Chowdhuri*, International mandates and trusteeship systems, 1955, 53 et seq.

[84] B. Knoll (note 88), 58.: *"Europe is being liquidated, and the League of Nations must be the heir to this great estate."*

[85] T. Gullberg (note 12); B. Knoll (note 88); *R. L. Doty*, in: T. Biersteker, State sovereignty as social construct, 1996, 122.

[86] T. Gullberg (note 12); R. L. Doty (note 91), 122.

[87] T. Gullberg (note 12), 1; *D. Deudney*, in: K. T. Litfin, The greening of sovereignty in world politics, 1998, 314.

The notion "nation" is often used simultaneously with the notion "State",[88] determining "a function of a State's (...) ability (...) to impose fixed and stable meanings about who belongs and who does not belong to the nation."[89] However, what is a nation in contrast to the State? How is the term used today?

Anna Stilz defined the nation in contrast to the so-called "collectivist theories" and the concept of "peoplehood."[90] According to these so-called nationalists, a nation is a "group defined by cultural features its members believe themselves to share," as opposed to a peoplehood, which is a self-determining group related by some other tie.[91] The word "nation" derives from the Greek "ethnos," meaning "a people" and referring to groups bound by shared culture and folklore.[92] According to Miller, this group is "a transhistorical group of people united by shared traits", which "centrally include a common public culture, a set of understandings about how their collective life should be led", in the spirit to be or become politically self-determining.[93] United by the spirit, the nation claims rights to a specific territory. It is acquired by adding material and symbolic value, such as the cultivation of land or the creation of buildings and roads.[94] Consequently, these "places and areas within that territory acquire symbolic significance for that nation".[95] In conclusion, "nations, as of natural persons, are bound by natural law".[96]

In contrast to the State, an "artificial person" is a "legal and political concept, whereas a nation is a cultural one."[97] Advanced by this development, the cultural nations claim self-determination due to three reasons: (1) the crucial interest of

---

[88] B. M. Barry (note 40), 172.: *compare.: „United Nations" is an organization of States.*

[89] R. L. Doty (note 91), 122; T. Biersteker and C. Weber (note 9), 278.

[90] A. Stilz (note 85 in Chap. 2), 27 et seq.

[91] A. Stilz (note 85 in Chap. 2), 28; C. Nine (note 38 in Chap. 1), 58; A. Banai (note 81), 141; D. Miller (note 83), 27.

[92] J. Agnew (note 12), 96.

[93] A. Stilz (note 85 in Chap. 2), 28; *A. Banai/M. Moore/D. Miller/C. Nine/F. Dietrich,* Symposium 'Theories of Territory beyond Westphalia', International Theory 6 (2014), 102; D. Miller (note 83), 124 et seq; *D. Miller,* Territorial Rights: Concept and Justification, Political Studies (2012), 258.

[94] A. Stilz (note 85 in Chap. 2); D. Miller (note 83), 218 et seq; D. Miller (note 100), 258.

[95] A. Stilz (note 85 in Chap. 2).

[96] *P. Ferrara,* in: M. Kotzur/N. Matz-Lück/A. Proelß/R. Verheyen/J. Sanden, Sustainable ocean resource governance: Deep sea mining, marine energy and submarine cables, 2018, 222.

[97] *A. Icduygu,* in: E. Kofman, Globalization: Theory and practice, 2003, 152.

individuals to preserve their national culture, which is (2) determined by a particular territory, and (3) preserved by the group's self-governance.[98] Consequently, the cultural aspects of a group shape the nation and define it at the same time.[99] In conclusion, according to Miller, the best implementation of a Nation-State would be in a multi-national State where "the dominant group has a strong incentive to use that authority to impose its culture on the weaker groups".[100] Moreover, it allows minority or oppressed groups to define the political power they wish to challenge.[101]

These considerations suggest that the concept of a Nation-State is outdated, particularly because it implies equating political groups with cultural groups.[102] The official texts of the United Nations Conferences seem to convey a similar idea of nationhood, as the word "nation" is used only in a broad, non-political sense.[103] This stands in stark contrast to the nowadays dominant opinion of a political understanding as "demanding various forms of autonomy or self-government".[104] Buchanan also stressed that only the focus on the cultural aspects of a group does not portray the identification of a group well: "At least in the modern world, individuals have diverse sources of identity, among which nationality is only one, and not the most important one".[105] Other sources are, *e.g.*, religion, political ideologies, or professional commitments. Consequently, "the idea of the Nation-State as the sole basis of the political organization must be abandoned".[106]

Therefore, Moore considers that the cultural aspect of a nation should not be stressed too much, and he states that, "nationalist identities are primarily political identities; they are concerned with the political community with which one identifies, and are normally characterized by the aspiration for some kind of political or institutional recognition of this community."[107] The problem with this definition is that a political commitment is as challenging to articulate as

---

98 A. Stilz (note 85 in Chap. 2), 28; C. Nine (note 38 in Chap. 1), 58.

99 C. Nine (note 38 in Chap. 1), 59.

100 A. Stilz (note 85 in Chap. 2), 28; D. Miller (note 83), 33 et seq.

101 C. Nine (note 38 in Chap. 1), 58 et seq.

102 Ibid; *C. R. Beitz*, Political theory and international relations, 1999, 115.

103 A. Cristescu (note 10), 38.

104 C. Nine (note 38 in Chap. 1), 59.

105 Ibid; C. R. Beitz (note 110), 114; *A. E. Buchanan*, in: A. E. Buchanan/M. Moore, States, nations, and borders: The Ethics of Making Boundaries, 2003, 250.

106 C. R. Beitz (note 110), 114.

107 C. Nine (note 38 in Chap. 1), 60; *M. Moore*, The Ethics of Nationalism, 2001, 9, 14–15.

one based on cultural factors. Therefore, many nationalists view the solution as a combination of cultural and political factors that constitute a nation.[108] However, it must be emphasized that a nation cannot exist if it focuses solely on cultural aspects without political ambition.[109] To constitute a nation, there must be political institutions and communities, because "nationality is created and reinforced through State institutions".[110] However, basing Statehood on the concept of nationhood shows us its weaknesses, because "States cannot be neutral with respect to nationality".[111] State institutions should—ideally—represent not only the majority or elite but also consider minority groups.[112] They represent the "individuals' legitimate public preferences".[113] These preferences can originate in cultural identities to ground a claim to self-determination in a territory, but this is not necessarily the case, as seen in examples of multicultural nations such as Canada and Belgium.[114] Consequently, even though strong nationalist tendencies have been observed in Europe in recent years, the Nation-State has occasionally declined.

3.1.3 Territorial Sovereignty

Having already discussed territorial rights, how do these culminate in territorial sovereignty? When we talk about sovereignty today, we have States' territorial sovereignty in mind.[115] This is also the classical definition on which the 1933 Montevideo Convention based its definition of a State, originating from the European State system.[116] In particular, the requirements of a government and the capacity to enter into relations with other States reflect the main pillars for the concept of sovereignty. In sum, the sovereign State system is based on a "final authority over most if not all social, economic, and political matters, which

[108] C. Nine (note 38 in Chap. 1).

[109] Ibid., 60; M. Moore (note 115), 48 et seq.

[110] C. Nine (note 38 in Chap. 1), 61; M. Moore (note 115), 15 et seq.

[111] C. Nine (note 38 in Chap. 1).

[112] Ibid., 61.

[113] Ibid.

[114] Ibid., 62 et seq.

[115] S. van Wyk (note 1 in Chap. 2), 83.

[116] *L. W. Pauly/E. Grande*, in: E. Grande/L. W. Pauly, Complex Sovereignty: Reconstituting Political Authority in the Twenty-First Century, 2005, 7.

should rest with those in control of the territorial units that make up the system."[117] However, how is "the State" defined, and what does the sovereignty of States mean?

3.1.3.1 Definition of Statehood

Article 1 of the 1933 Montevideo Convention on Rights and Duties of States prescribes four requirements, which constitute a State: a permanent population, a defined territory, a government, and the capacity to enter into relations with other States.

The criterion of the required territory, the main point of discussion for this thesis, represents the bordered area, where the subject of international law can exercise its authority.[118] This criterion is the most obvious. As Crawford put it: "Evidently, States are territorial entities".[119] The role of the territory is crucial in several ways, as it not only marks "a portion of the earth's surface"[120] but also defines the scope for determining control, jurisdiction, and authority for the State itself and within the framework of international law.[121] Consequently, territorial Statehood promotes relative stability between people of different ethnicities inside the territory. This principle of stability, peace, and security is recognized by international law.[122] In this context, it was already concluded in the 1970s that "territory which was once connected to the land and then submerged by the sea can continue to be regarded as a connected part of State territory".[123] Consequently, even though the territory is defined as "the physical basis that ensures that people can live together as organized communities,"[124] it has to be seen more figuratively, as the "jigsaw puzzle of solid color pieces fitting neatly together."[125]

---

[117] *A. B. Murphy*, in: T. Biersteker, State sovereignty as social construct, 1996, 82.

[118] *R. Jennings, A. Watts and L. F. L. Oppenheim (eds)*, Oppenheim's international law, 9th ed., 1992, 564 (bei Aufl. 2008).

[119] J. McAdam (note 10 in Chap. 1), 128; J. Crawford (note 14), 46.

[120] J. McAdam (note 10 in Chap. 1), 130.

[121] Ibid; *M. A. Brinker*, The Right of Self-Determination in the context of Climate Change: How to deal with the disappearing islands in the exemplary case of the Atoll State Kiribati under the International Law, 2020, 19.

[122] *I. Brownlie*, in: M. D. Evans, Aspects of statehood and institutionalism in contemporary Europe, 1997, 6.

[123] *Case "Sealand"*, 9 K 2565/77, 03.05.1978, 686.

[124] *J. Grote Stoutenburg*, in: M. B. Gerrard/G. E. Wannier, Threatened Island Nations: Legal Implications of Rising Seas and a Changing Climate, 2013, 61.

[125] *K. Knop*, in: J. Crawford/M. Koskenniemi, The Cambridge companion to international law, 2012, 95; *M. A. Brinker*, The Right of Self-Determination in the context of Climate

Secondly, the permanent population represents a collective settlement or a stable community.[126] In the relevant context, this criterion will be challenged by the complete submergence of the territory, as uninhabitable land will trigger an exodus long before it.[127] Therefore, these criteria also marked the differentiation between an island according to Article 121 para. 1 UNCLOS and an uninhabitable rock according to Article 121 para. 3 UNCLOS.[128] However, there is neither a minimum population requirement nor is it necessary that most of the population live inside the territory.[129] For example, in some Pacific island States, 56.9 percent of Samoans and 46 percent of Tongans already live outside their countries.[130] However, the population must be tied to their land to ensure "a corporate feeling of common ownership" and independence, in contrast to a simple nomadic population.[131] Consequently, a requirement for "basic infrastructure at its disposal providing for the vital necessities of human life" is not necessary.[132] Even though this criterion may seem, at first glance, to describe only the abstract necessity of persons living permanently on a specific piece of land, the connection between peoplehood and self-determination is very close; therefore, it is of crucial importance in the context of the threatened disappearance of territory.[133]

The third requirement—the effective government—"is closely tied to the principle of territorial control," as well as the security and recognition in the international community.[134] It is thus subdivided into an internal and external dimension, "the authority with respect to the people and the independence with respect to other States".[135] However, this is why Statehood stands and falls with the effectiveness of government and is considered the most important criterion, "since all the others depend upon it".[136] Moreover, the criterion is closely linked

Change: How to deal with the disappearing islands in the exemplary case of the Atoll State Kiribati under the International Law, 2020, 19;

126 I. Brownlie and J. Crawford (note 30 in Chap. 2), 118.

127 J. McAdam (note 10 in Chap. 1), 131 et seq.

128 J. Grote Stoutenburg (note 132), 64; M. A. Brinker (note 133), 19.

129 J. McAdam (note 10 in Chap. 1), 131.

130 Ibid., 132.

131 Ibid., 131; *M. N. Shaw*, International law, 7th ed., 2014, 199; GA-Res. 2869 (XXVI) (1971).

132 J. Grote Stoutenburg (note 132), 64.

133 M. A. Brinker (note 133), 19.

134 S. Willcox (note 7 in Chap. 1), 180; J. McAdam (note 10 in Chap. 1), 132.

135 J. Grote Stoutenburg (note 132), 66.

136 J. McAdam (note 10 in Chap. 1), 132; *J. Crawford*, The creation of states in international law, 1979, 57.

to the criterion of permanent population, because the execution of effective government depends on the remaining "population nucleus," which, in turn, is a requirement for external recognition by the international community.[137]

The fourth criterion, the "capacity to enter into relations with other States," is closely intertwined with the criterion of government and independence.[138] According to the *Island of Palmas* case, it comprises two elements: "a separate existence within reasonably coherent borders, and not being subject to the authority of any other State".[139] Consequently, because the third criterion already includes the factual capacity—the government as the executive element—and the legal position—the pure recognition of the State as an entity—it is challenging to vitalize this criterion.[140] However, in particular, in the context of disappearing island States, where the government "in exile" cannot operate from its territory, this criterion may become more critical.[141] To say it with Hans Morgenthau:

> *"Intelligibility of any legal system depends on the recognition of such a set of fundamental ethical principles which constitute the ethical substance of the legal system and shed their illuminating light upon each particular rule of law."*[142]

In conclusion, the Montevideo Convention defines Statehood with its four criteria in a very straightforward and determined manner, but—in some opinions—too simply, *e.g.*, because of the missing link to democratic ideals such as "respect for the rights of minorities".[143] However, these requirements nowadays seem outdated and unsatisfactory, particularly given today's pressing problems, such as climate change. They can still be interpreted in a broader context.[144]

> *"The Convention includes elements that are not clearly prerequisite to Statehood, and it excludes elements that writers now widely regard as indispensable to a definition of the State. (…) It addresses a concept that had been in flux over the century leading up to*

---

137 J. Crawford (note 14), 57; M. A. Brinker (note 133), 20.

138 M. A. Brinker (note 133), 20.

139 J. McAdam (note 10 in Chap. 1), 133.

140 M. A. Brinker (note 133), 20.

141 J. McAdam (note 10 in Chap. 1), 134.

142 *H. J. Morgenthau,* Positivism, functionalism, and international law, American journal of international law (1940), 268; B. Knoll (note 88), 56.

143 *C. Blanchard,* Evolution or revolution? Evaluating the Territorial State-Based Regime of International Law in the Context of the Physical Disappearance of Territory Due to Climate Change and Sea-Level Rise, Canadian Yearbook of International Law 53 (2015), 76.

144 C. Blanchard (note 17), 75 et seq.

its framing and that continued to change thereafter. It posits a definition of Statehood highly contingent upon the history, politics, and legal thought of its moment. It is over-inclusive, under-inclusive, and outdated."[145]

In the context of the right to self-determination and the principle of permanent sovereignty over natural resources, we can explore new ways of interpretation to establish a solid basis for addressing present and future challenges of climate change.

3.1.3.2 Territorial Sovereignty of States

In contrast to the definition of the State, "sovereignty prescribes that ultimate and exclusive authority [in the political community] is maintained by each State within its territory"[146] or as a "monopoly of the legitimate use of physical force within a given territory".[147] This strict and straightforward concept is still based on "the central claim of the Westphalian order that the modern State must be or should be territorial."[148] Consequently, it "requires the full range of territorial rights that we normally associate with State Sovereignty".[149] In general, "territory" is understood as "the right of jurisdictional authority over a territorial or geographical domain", which includes "rights of jurisdiction, rights to control borders and resources".[150] This goes as far as that territory, as such is never a "neutral criterion or objective entity" but a "socially constructed form of spatial relations";[151] "an expression of underlying political relationships", on which political authority on the principle of territorial exclusivity is based.[152] Once again, we must note that sovereignty is "a classic term of European international law referring to the absolute and inviolate power of a nation to manage generally its own affairs."[153]

---

[145] C. Blanchard (note 151), 76., Grant, p. 453.

[146] *R. Adler-Nissen/T. Gammeltoft-Hansen*, in: R. Adler-Nissen/T. Gammeltoft-Hansen, Sovereignty games, 2008, 2; S. van Wyk (note 1 in Chap. 2), 78.

[147] L. W. Pauly and E. Grande (note 124), 7.

[148] A. Banai (note 81), 143; J. Agnew (note 12), 103.

[149] *M. Moore*, A Political Theory of Territory, 2015, 4.

[150] Ibid.

[151] *A. Meine*, in: A. Santos Campos/S. Cadliha, Sovereignty as value, 2021, 135.

[152] Ibid.

[153] *E. Charles-Newton/E. A. Kronk*, in: R. Abate, Climate change and indigenous peoples: The search for legal remedies, 2013, 64.

In the 16th and 17th centuries, Hobbes and Bodin saw the "supreme authority" resting in the "right of the State to command and to be obeyed".[154] However, both followed different ideas of the concept. While Hobbes supported the idea of removing all rights of the people and complete subjugation to the State, Bodin followed the concept of the so-called "social contract between the ruler and the ruled".[155] Grotius, regarding sovereignty as a property (see above Chap. 2, part A. I.), invented the "sovereignty of the people", basing this on "inalienable natural legal rights".[156] In the Era of Enlightenment, Rousseau, similarly to Locke, adopted the idea of a social contract from Bodin, considering the people as the only legitimate sovereign and the State as the result of the contract.[157] Not until the 19th century, when Kant and Montesquieu established the concept of the political organization in the three branches of state power— legislation, execution, and judiciary —and the delegation of power by the people, did the supremacy of the State as the unique holder of sovereignty come more and more into focus.[158]

Sovereignty is defined as "the supremacy and inviolability of a State's institutions, its unboundedness both internally and externally".[159] It encompasses power or control in political, economic, or symbolic terms, along with legitimacy and personality, to assert and fulfill the appropriate duties and obligations.[160] Moreover, sovereignty is exercised over the oceans and uninhabited land, allowing the State to expand its authority across a geographical domain until rival claims to the same territory are raised, extending sovereign rights up to the EEZ as "quasi-sovereignty".[161]

According to Judge Alvarez, former judge of the ICJ, "by sovereignty, we understand the whole body of rules and attributes, which a State possesses in its territory, to the exclusion of all other States, and also in its relation with other States."[162] Consequently, sovereignty was and is attributed to "an independent

---

[154] S. van Wyk (note 1 in Chap. 2), 78.

[155] Ibid., 78 et seq; *J. Bartelson*, in: R. Adler-Nissen/T. Gammeltoft-Hansen, Sovereignty games, 2008, 37.

[156] S. van Wyk (note 1 in Chap. 2), 79, G. Elian and A. Bantas (note 56), 2.

[157] S. van Wyk (note 1 in Chap. 2), 80.

[158] Ibid., 83; *F. H. Hinsley*, Sovereignty, 2nd ed., 1986, 1, 25–26.

[159] R. Adler-Nissen and T. Gammeltoft-Hansen (note 154), 3.

[160] Ibid.

[161] M. Moore (note 157), 4; *L. Elliot*, in: T. Jacobsen/C. J. G. Sampford/R. Thakur, Re-envisioning sovereignty: The end of Westphalia?, 2008, 199; C. Armstrong (note 46 in Chap. 2), 202.

[162] *D. Raič*, Statehood and the law of self-determination, 2002, 25.

territorial unit", often considered a "State".[163] Therefore, sovereignty is "a brief term for the State's attribute of more-or-less plenary competence".[164] Territorial sovereignty, as it was recognized in the *Isla de Palmas case*, involves, on the other hand, "the exclusive right to display the activities of a State", which means that it can, *e.g.*, exclude the activities of other States within this territory.[165] Consequently, the concept of sovereignty is a "relative sovereignty" or "limited sovereignty", because it is limited by the freedom of others and the constraints of international law.[166] In sum, the principle of sovereign equality is as important as the independence of the State because it represents the "touchstone for the relations, which should exist between all the States in the world".[167] This becomes increasingly important when new States attain independence, "wishing to participate in international relations on a footing of complete equality".[168] In conclusion, sovereign equality signifies "the right of every State to establish its own political, social and economic structure, without interference or intimidation from outside, in the best interests of its inhabitants", respecting and including "the right of its people to self-determination".[169]

Sovereignty, therefore, means independence, at least, regarding a portion of the globe; it stands for the "totality of international rights and duties recognized by international law".[170] In full range, sovereignty is

> *"the unique, full, and indivisible supremacy of State power within the limits of the territorial frontiers and the independence of this power, in relation to any other power, which is expressed in the State's exclusive and inalienable right to lay down and carry out its home and foreign policy independently, to discharge its functions, to implement the practical measures for organizing its social life at home and its foreign relations on the basis of respect for the sovereignty of other States, for the principles and norms of international law accepted of its own free will."*[171]

[163] Ibid., 25.

[164] Ibid., 26.

[165] I. Brownlie and J. Crawford (note 30 in Chap. 2), 138.

[166] S. van Wyk (note 1 in Chap. 2), 84; *F. X. Perrez*, Cooperative sovereignty, 2000, 16 et seq; G. Elian and A. Bantas (note 56), 8.

[167] A. Cristescu (note 10), 26, para. 164.

[168] Ibid., 26, para. 166.

[169] Ibid., 26, para. 170; J. Agnew (note 12), 103.

[170] I. Brownlie and J. Crawford (note 30 in Chap. 2), 138 et seq.

[171] S. van Wyk (note 1 in Chap. 2), 84 et seq.

To sum up, sovereignty is nowadays defined by five fundamental properties: territory, mutual recognition, autonomy against external interference, control of borders, and legitimacy.[172] This makes it one of the most essential principles in international law.[173] Its universal recognition as customary law symbolizes the "obvious entitlement to decide within the confines of international law, how to deal with the resources" within this territory.[174]

3.1.4 Territorial Sovereignty in the UNCLOS

The concept of territorial sovereignty and the exclusive control of Nation-States "over a band of adjacent waters", also extends to the Law of the Sea, historically based on the basic tenet of customary international law, later based on the rules of UNCLOS, today's "central element in the law of sea regime".[175] Grounded upon the principle of "the land dominates the sea,"[176] the coastal State enjoys sovereignty "within its land territory, internal waters, archipelagic waters, and the territorial sea," as defined in Articles 1 and 2 UNCLOS.[177] Moreover, according to Article 2, paragraph 2 UNCLOS, "this sovereignty extends to the airspace over the territorial sea as well as to its bed and subsoil", which found its identical origin in the source of Article 2 of the 1958 Territorial Sea Convention.[178] The archipelagic State, which has the same status as a coastal State, "enjoys the same sovereignty that the coastal State does."[179]

Sovereignty in the context of the UNCLOS comprises the whole range of "plenary powers upon the coastal State to regulate whatever happens in its territorial sea", which means the complete exclusion of other States or powers within

[172] L. Elliot (note 169), 195.

[173] S. Hobe (note 8 in Chap. 2), 11.

[174] Ibid.

[175] *M. S. Soroos*, Beyond sovereignty: Chap. 8: Ocean Resources—Negotiating a New Law of the Sea, 1986, 271; *I. U. Jakobsen/E. Johansen/P. P. Nickels*, in: I. U. Jakobsen/E. Johansen/S. V. Busch, The law of the sea and climate change: solutions and constraints, 2021.

[176] *North Sea Continental Shelf Cases (Federal Republic of Germany/ Denmark; Federal Republic of Germany/ Netherlands)*, para. 96; *S. V. Busch*, in: E. Johansen/S. V. Busch/Jakobsen Ingvild Ulrikke, The Law of the Sea and Climate Change, 2021, 313; compare Art. 5.

[177] *K. Aquilina*, in: D. J. Attard/M. Fitzmaurice/N. A. Martínez Gutiérrez, The IMLI Manual on International Maritime Law: Volume I: The Law of the Sea, 2014, 28.

[178] Ibid.

[179] Ibid.

these areas.[180] According to Tanaka "territorial sovereignty in international law [is] characterized by completeness and exclusiveness; the coastal State can exercise complete legislative and enforcement jurisdiction over all matters and all people in an exclusive manner unless international law provides otherwise".[181] It is worth to mention at that point, that this extension also includes "the exclusive right and exploitation of the living and non-living resources of the seabed and subsoil".[182] The sovereignty of coastal States finds its recognition, but also its limits, in Article 2, paragraph 3 UNCLOS, which recognizes as "exercised subject to this Convention and to other rules of international law", which refers primarily to customary rules and treaty obligations.[183] This bestowal of rights also involves the "entitlement to claim territorial waters if you want them", which means that also non-maritime States can claim territorial waters, if they wish to do so.[184] This occurred for the first time in the Anglo-Norwegian Fisheries case, where Norway was granted the exceptional right to draw its baselines with a series of artificial lines linking the outermost points of skerries off the Norwegian coast, rather than the regular classification of straight baselines, as later determined in Article 7(1) UNCLOS.[185] Moreover, one of the rights of every State, independent of its status as a coastal State or landlocked State, is the right of innocent passage, which represents one of the most important "duties"[186] or "a sort of universal servitude imposed on all coastal States".[187] In conclusion, "the maritime territory is an essential appurtenance of land territory" and is "an inseparable appurtenance of this land territory" as was already determined in the Grisbadarna Case in 1909.[188]

On the other hand, the further one moves beyond 12 nautical miles from the territorial sea, into the so-called EEZ above the continental shelf, the coastal State can exercise "sovereign rights", which are functionally limited compared to full

---

[180] Ibid., 29.

[181] *Y. Tanaka*, The International Law of the Sea, 2012, 84; K. Aquilina (note 185), 29.

[182] K. Aquilina (note 185), 29; *R. MacLean*, Public International Law Textbook, 16th ed., 1994, 250.

[183] K. Aquilina (note 185), 30; *D. J. Harris*, Cases and materials on international law, 7th ed., 2010, 325.

[184] K. Aquilina (note 185), 34.

[185] *Anglo-Norwegian Fisheries Case,* 18.12.1951, 130; *S. V. Busch*, in: E. Johansen/S. V. Busch/I. U. Jakobsen, The law of the sea and climate change: Solutions and constraints, 2021, 329.

[186] K. Aquilina (note 185), 49.

[187] Ibid., 38.

[188] Ibid., 34; Y. Tanaka (note 189), 84.

sovereignty under Article 56 of UNCLOS.[189] So, the EEZ does not belong to the coastal State's territory, as sovereignty would be, but is instead equated to a limited scope of rights, like *e.g.*, exploration and exploitation of resources explicitly determined in the Convention.[190] The invention of the EEZ extended the sovereign rights of coastal States beyond the territorial sea, whereas sovereignty before extended only to the territorial sea. Furthermore, the 1993 Convention on Biological Diversity constituted an even vaster range of sovereignty over plant and animal genetic resources.[191] After UNCLOS was signed, States claimed rights to over 50 percent of the Earth's surface, compared to less than 30 percent before.[192] In the High Seas, in contrast, the strict prohibition on claims of territorial sovereignty prevails for any State, based on Hugo Grotius' doctrine of *mare liberum.*[193] This zone is partially under the ISA's control, which explicitly governs the deep seabed and, consequently, its natural resources.[194] Therefore, this reveals a significantly different development, contrasting with the idea of the Westphalian Regime or the *uti possidetis juris*, which prioritizes restricting access for all States over granting further access to some States.[195]

Since its invention, the doctrine of *mare liberum* stood in a great doctrinal conflict with the concept of *mare clausum* by John Selden, who advocated in favor of an appropriation of the sea by States and, *e.g.*, considered the sea as exhaustible, foreseeing its exhaustion and exploitation by its owners.[196] In the end, Grotian's concept of the freedom of the seas persuaded more scholars, and it dominated the field for more than two centuries.[197] However, in modern history, the "territorial temptation" of the States has hollowed out the formerly predominant idea of *mare liberum.* A root of this evolution can be witnessed, *e.g.*, in the continental shelf regime, dating back to the Truman Proclamation in 1945, in which the

---

[189] K. Aquilina (note 185), 28, 31.

[190] *A. Proelß*, United Nations Convention on the Law of the Sea: A Commentary, 1st ed., 2017, Sec. 56, para. 9–10.

[191] L. Elliot (note 169), 199.

[192] C. Armstrong (note 46 in Chap. 2), 202.

[193] K. Aquilina (note 185), 33; *B. H. Oxman*, in: J. N. Moore, Common Resources—Law of the Sea, Outer Space, and Antarctica, 2018, 367 et seq. *H. 1.-1. Grotius*, The Freedom of the seas or the right which belongs to the Dutch to take part in the East Indian trade, 1916, 7.

[194] K. Aquilina (note 185), 29; *C. Prip*, in: E. Johansen/S. V. Busch/Jakobsen Ingvild Ulrikke, The Law of the Sea and Climate Change, 2021, 338; compare: Art. 117–120, 145, 207.

[195] B. H. Oxman (note 201), 368.

[196] K. Aquilina (note 185), 32 et seq; *H. Türk*, Reflections on the contemporary law of the sea, 2012, 7.

[197] H. Türk (note 204), 7.

United States secured "property rights" over resources in the seabed and water column of the continental shelf.[198] Consequently, the classical 3-mile limit as a demarcation of the territorial sea—the so-called cannon-shot rule[199] -, which was recognized as customary international law in the *Guinea/Guinea-Bissau Maritime Delimitation Case*[200] in 1909, was expanded to 12 miles during the elaboration of the 1958 Convention on the Territorial Sea and the Contiguous Zone.[201] However, this Convention is examined in vain for any definition of the coastal State's sovereign rights over seabed resources beyond the territorial sea.[202] In contrast to the "triumph of the territorial temptation," together with this unclear definition of the High Sea stood the weaker protection of natural resources.[203] The response to all these insecurities and inabilities concerning the "territorial temptation" was the invention of the UNCLOS. This Convention established the maximum limit of 12 miles for the territorial sea, as well as the maximum limit of 200 miles for the EEZ and the continental shelf, including the sovereign rights over natural resources (see above).[204] It generalized the regime of baselines, developed by the ICJ in the *Anglo-Norwegian Fisheries* case.[205]

However, the "territorial temptation" is far from resolved. Moreover, the Law of the Sea Convention is subject to constant change to "measure and balance the overall long-term interests" of the States.[206] The substantive balance is now more important than the geographical balance, as it addresses global problems such as environmental protection and climate change.[207] Considering that "the EEZ is already perceived in quasi-territorial terms", the coordination between

---

[198] B. H. Oxman (note 201), 367, 370; *V. A. Ventura*, Environmental Jurisdiction in the Law of the Sea: The Brazilian Blue Amazon, 2020, 145; H. Türk (note 204), 9.

[199] K. Aquilina (note 185), 32; J. A. Simmons (note 25), 188.

[200] Guinea/Guinea-Bissau Maritime Delimitation Case 77, ILR 636, 638, 1988, 25 ILM 251, 272, para. 43; M. N. Shaw (note 139), 569; *S. Oda*, Fifty Years of The Law of the Sea: With a Special Section on the International Court of Justice, 2003, 9–10, 14; H. Türk (note 204), 8.

[201] B. H. Oxman (note 201), 371; H. Türk (note 204), 10 et seq.

[202] B. H. Oxman (note 201); Convention on the Continental Shelf, 29.04.1958, Art. 1.: *"(...) to the seabed and subsoil of the submarine areas adjacent to the coast but outside the area of the territorial sea, to a depth of 200 metres or, beyond that limit, to where the depth of the superjacent waters admits of the exploitation of the natural reosurces of the said areas"*.

[203] B. H. Oxman (note 201), 373.

[204] Ibid., 376 et seq.

[205] Ibid.

[206] Ibid., 378.

[207] Ibid., 381.

foreign ministries, governments, and international organizations is highly complex.[208] Following the Stockholm Conference in 1972, this treaty has consistently maintained a high standard of protection and preservation of the marine environment, including rules for the exploitation of deep-sea bed resources, particularly deep-sea minerals.[209] Additionally, the treaty imposed on States the obligation to prevent, reduce, and control marine pollution to avoid harm to other States.[210] This well-known preventive principle, dating back to the 1972 Stockholm Conference and demonstrating the reciprocity of States' duties under UNCLOS, can be found in various Articles of UNCLOS.[211] Consequently, UNCLOS represents to this day "the strongest comprehensive environmental treaty now in existence or likely to emerge for quite some time", providing "a broad compulsory dispute-settlement system for environmental issues".[212]

3.1.5 Statehood as an Implementation of Self-Determination

Reviewing our considerations above, States are the "principal maker and subjects of international law," which implicates their privileges in standing before the ICJ and their membership in the United Nations.[213] "Only through the intervention of a State on its behalf" is it feasible to enforce rights and duties to individuals within the international community.[214] Consequently, Statehood is, in contrast to the right of self-determination, a very fixed notion of "a central

[208] Ibid., 381, 394.

[209] *J. I. Charney*, in: J. N. Moore, Common Resources—Law of the Sea, Outer Space, and Antarctica, 2018, 264.

[210] *A. Boyle*, in: M. C. Ribeiro, 30 Years after the Signature of the United Nations Convention on the Law of the Sea: The Protection of the Environment and the Future of the Law of the Sea: Proceedings of the International Conference, 2012, 365.

[211] Ibid., 365–366, 371; *e.g.*: Article 117, 192–194, 207, 212 UNCLOS.

[212] B. H. Oxman (note 201), 387; J. I. Charney (note 217), 262–263, 276–277; H. Türk (note 204), 29.

[213] *Compare:* Charter, 26.05.1945, Art. 4(1); Statute of the International Court of Justice, 26.05.1945, Art. 34(1).

[214] *G. J. Abhimanyu,* The 21st century atlantis: The International Law of Statehood and Climate Change-Induced Loss of Territory, Stanford Journal of International Law 50 (2014), 7.

organizing idea."[215] The legal figure of the State is probably the most desired of every legal personality the international law offers—represented in today's dominant UN practice –, because the "ticket of general admission to the international arena" is only granted to States.[216] However, we must bear in mind that the construct of a State is only "a vehicle", the feasible and preferred permutation of the abstract principle of the right of self-determination. [217] Whereas the State is only "one mode of implementation", the right of self-determination, as a "principle concerned with the right to be a State", can take many forms, beyond the State as the leading legal figure, namely, free association or integration within an independent State.[218] Generally, it represents the right to elect independence under international law.[219]

Without the right of self-determination, State autonomy cannot exist; therefore, we can conclude that "the positive aspect of State autonomy is expressed by the principle of self-determination," allowing for the construction of independent Statehood without interference or control by other States and entities.[220] Self-determination, in contrast to the other important cornerstone of Statehood—the principle of non-intervention—"looks behind the political order to the order of social, cultural, ethnic, linguistic groups" in order "to bring political boundaries into alignment with boundaries between groups".[221] We have come full circle, considering this was also the basis of the "moral personhood" mentioned above.

In the context of established statehood, the question arises of whether "self-determination refers to the population of a group"—"the people"—or to an independent government, which requires institutional responsibility on the part of the people.[222] These considerations demonstrate that the scope of "kind of independence" is significantly broader than Statehood, allowing for more extensive development and fully exploiting the range of freedom of association.[223]

---

[215] *N. Berman*, Sovereignty in Abeyance: Self-Determination and International Law, 1988b, 53.

[216] I. Brownlie and J. Crawford (note 30 in Chap. 2), 125.

[217] M. Moore (note 63), 149; *N. Berman*, Sovereignty in Abeyance: Self-Determination and International Law, 1988, 55, 69.

[218] J. Crawford (note 14), 107; I. Brownlie and J. Crawford (note 30 in Chap. 2), 139 et seq.

[219] I. Brownlie and J. Crawford (note 30 in Chap. 2), 130 et seq.

[220] C. R. Beitz (note 110), 92 et seq.

[221] Ibid., 93.

[222] Ibid., 95.

[223] Ibid., 95 et seq.

We must be aware that the State, as such, is also only a man-made idea, a legal construction, which is rooted and therefore also limited "in a grammar of fixed boundaries and identities".[224] Statehood "acquires a personhood that then underwrites its special status as the locus of sovereignty".[225] States, as well as persons, are formed "through the interaction and recognition of households, tribes, dynasties, social movements, and such."[226] Consequently, what creates the State as such is the mutual recognition, the net of "inter-state relations".[227] Creating the State as a "super-person" means establishing loyalty and backing among the population, followed by the legitimation of other States, the so-called "cross-mapping of nations with State".[228] These same ideas are found in the similar construction of internal and external self-determination.

Considering this, where does the State take the privilege to claim sovereignty? The claim of sovereignty by the State, or whatever other State-like construction, is an effort to establish "a relation as an institutional fact"—"the fact being the supreme and ultimate authority and an independent authority"- followed by a set of rights and responsibilities.[229] Seen at the beginning of nation-building in the later United States, the Philadelphia-States Union represented "a choice between different configurations of authority and institutional structure".[230] As Agnew formulates it:

> *"As a result, sovereignty is more than just a word, norm, or principle; it is all of these concurrently".*[231]

However, this privilege is not merely awarded to the State; Statehood is, like personhood, only a "subjectivity formed out of social interaction and mutual recognition."[232]

---

[224] J. Agnew (note 12), 132; *J. A. Camilleri,* The end of sovereignty?, 1992, 171.

[225] J. Agnew (note 12), 132.

[226] Ibid., 133.

[227] Ibid; A. Cristescu (note 10), 25, para. 169, 175.

[228] J. Agnew (note 12), 133.

[229] Ibid., 133 et seq.

[230] T. Biersteker and C. Weber (note 9), 230 (280).

[231] J. Agnew (note 12), 134.

[232] Ibid., 132 et seq.

Consequently, in today's steadily developing world, the entity of Statehood seems outdated—"the State is thus treated as a '(pre)given'"[233]—because "independence and nationality—so essential to the due growth and development of a people further advanced in improvement—are generally impediments to theirs".[234] Self-determination and sovereignty of States go hand in hand, forming the very basis of principles like international cooperation and sovereign equality, and, of course, the State itself.[235] In conclusion, the right of self-determination applies not only to groups of people sharing a common nationality but also to associations of diverse nationalities, thereby supporting the foundation of a multinational entity such as the European Union (EU).[236] In sum, "Europe is still at the center of discussions about the State, but it is also the center of discussion about the human potential for superseding traditional forms of States".[237]

3.1.6 Concluding Remarks: Rethinking the Concept of Territorial Sovereignty

In the last part, we reviewed the steady transformation of the definition of the State. The development began with fundamental differentiation between property rights and occupancy rights, followed by the creation of the Nation-State. This legal personality dominated the 19th century and was supposedly perfected in today's dominant definition of Statehood under the Montevideo Convention. However, this steady shift in understanding sovereignty—not only in individual treaties like UNCLOS but also in the broader context of territorial sovereignty—has led to a stubborn adherence to territoriality, which is becoming an increasingly significant problem.[238] As the former UN General Secretary Boutros Boutros-Ghali put it in a nutshell: "the time of absolute and exclusive sovereignty (…) has passed; it has, in particular, been eroded by globalization and liberalization.[239] The basic form ("Grundform") of sovereignty "is produced under crisis conditions wherein notions of time, space, and political identity are

233 Ibid., 132, 134.

234 C. R. Beitz (note 110), 99.

235 A. Cristescu (note 10), 25, para. 164.

236 C. R. Beitz (note 110), 112.

237 L. W. Pauly and E. Grande (note 124), 7.

238 A. Banai et al. (note 100), 99.

239 R. Adler-Nissen and T. Gammeltoft-Hansen (note 154), 3; T. Aqorau (note 221 in Chap. 2), 218.

subject to disruption (…) attempting to fix time, space, and identity within a social order".[240] In simple words: "Sovereignty is a tool of debate and conflict more than an actual condition".[241]

However, in a changing world facing economic interconnectedness, movement of goods and money, as well as interdependent environmental problems of climate change, the conveyance of power and competencies to other global players, mostly non-state actors, like supranational organizations, but also private companies or even individuals, raises the question of whether territoriality has lost its significance.[242] Moreover, as the "constructed character of territories' functionality" becomes visible, the instrumentality of territory begins to crumble.[243] Therefore, we have to consider "sovereignty regimes (…) neither inherently territorial nor (…) exclusively organized on a State-to-State basis".[244] The single territorial model, where the earth is subdivided into mutually exclusive and self-contained State units, has been and will continue to be "an important dimension of politics, law, power, and authority".[245] However, this "archetype of the territorial-sovereign Nation-State including a national, centralized State power within fixed geographical borders"[246] represents only one model of a "constellation of relationships between the three elements: (1) a piece of land; (2) a group of people residing on the land; and (3) a set of political institutions that govern the people within the geographical domain".[247] Moreover, the classical model of a Nation-State has to be overcome and replaced by a model of "debatable lands".[248] The creation of "territories in which nations coexist in conditions of fluid identities" has to be pushed forward, whereby international organizations not only administer territory as legal representatives but also assume legal responsibility for the territory.[249] The basis of nations has to change to a notion of "togetherness",

240 R. L. Doty (note 91), 123.

241 J. Agnew (note 12), 103.

242 A. Banai et al. (note 100), 99; R. L. Doty (note 91), 123.

243 A. Meine (note 159 in Chap. 2), 138.

244 A. Banai et al. (note 100), 100.

245 Ibid; S. van Wyk (note 1 in Chap. 2), 89.

246 A. Banai et al. (note 100), 101.

247 Ibid., 102.

248 Ibid.

249 I. Brownlie and J. Crawford (note 30 in Chap. 2), 132; B. Knoll (note 88), 92 et seq.; *1966 GA terminated the Mandate of South West Africa.*

a basis of shared morality, "independently of their origin, cultural or religious background, and affiliation":[250]

This seems to be of increasing importance, bearing in mind that the transformation from a Nation-State has always gone and, until this day, goes with "a crisis of national identity that called into question the boundaries of the political community."[251] Some scholars already speak of a complete failure when defining nationhood "because they try to fit historically novel, emerging, changing, and far-from-universal entities into a framework of permanence and universality".[252] Focusing more on the "identity of the people, who constitute the inside of nations and to whom national identities are attached" and stopping the "marginalization of group identities of diverse peoples" seems attractive to many scholars. [253] This, however, poses the question of "the identity of a people", which appears to be a "never-completed project" (see Chap. 3).[254]

Referring to the concept of sovereignty already described, the component that has held a Nation-State together is "the formation of valid legal commands constituting the highest manifestation of sovereignty".[255] However, in our globalized world, the "whole idea of a territorially fixed population forming the basis of the sovereign Nation-State" is highly questionable, and the debate of surrendering sovereignty to a supra-national organization is arising.[256]

In particular, referring to the new challenge of environmental protection, the "traditional role" of State sovereignty today has a bad reputation, as it is considered "an agent or accomplice in ecological devastation across the globe" and as an "obstacle" or "hindrance" to the effective response in international environmental law (see Chap. 4).[257] Hence, when the biosphere confronts the "sovereign domain" —the concept of separate areas within man-made boundaries, governed by separate governments —[this concept] cannot be reconciled with the "interrelated ecosystem of the Earth".[258]

Some scholars suggest that constructing another "enduring system" could be complex, without a territorial base, because the "modern State system has much

---

[250] C. Blanchard (note 151), 109.

[251] R. L. Doty (note 91), 124.

[252] Ibid., 125.

[253] Ibid., 126; D. Deudney (note 93), 315.

[254] R. L. Doty (note 91), 126.

[255] Ibid., 128.

[256] Ibid; S. van Wyk (note 1 in Chap. 2), 89.

[257] S. van Wyk (note 1 in Chap. 2), 91.

[258] Ibid., 91 et seq; J. A. Camilleri (note 232), 192.

to do with its territorial underpinnings."[259] It is evident that the current political order based on the "notion of territorial control", however, "is as dubious as to assume that territory and politics are about to be entirely uncoupled", considering, in particular, the nowadays "obvious shaking disjunctions between the political organization of the territory and the geography of economic, social, and political life".[260]

Other scholars view the erosion of sovereignty not as an urgent threat but as "part of the solution" to global issues, such as climate change, particularly through the implementation and enforcement of treaties.[261] That can be considered a translation of sovereignty into "operational" or "formal" sovereignty, in which the Nation-State can operate under international law.[262]

Consequently, the "growing interdependence of States and the ever-increasing trend towards democratization in international life" raises the question regarding the future social and political construct of human cohabitation.[263] We must bear in mind that the concept of an international order based on mutual recognition of States is relevant only to the Westphalian conception of guaranteeing and stabilizing the horizontal system of States.[264] As we can see in various models of authority, "equality of rights under modern international law is recognized as vesting not only in States but also in 'nations',[265] approaching independence".[266] Consequently, the international legal system, "once designed for sovereign States", seems less compelling, becoming increasingly "disaggregated and focused on sub-state actors".[267] Moreover, the "downplay of territorial sovereignty", while "the extraterritorial regulation as a highly appreciated figure of the world system gains in significance", presses us to rethink the traditional model of the Nation-State.[268] We have to bear in mind that "sovereignty is only one—not an exclusive one—of many identities that a State actor can take on" and

[259] A. B. Murphy (note 125), 109.

[260] Ibid.

[261] S. van Wyk (note 1 in Chap. 2), 93.

[262] Ibid.

[263] A. Cristescu (note 10), 25, para. 165.

[264] T. Biersteker and C. Weber (note 9), 284; S. van Wyk (note 1 in Chap. 2), 77; A. Meine (note 159 in Chap. 2), 139.

[265] *Meaning in this context „people"*

[266] A. Cristescu (note 10), 26, para. 171.

[267] *A. L. Parrish*, in: D. S. Margolies, The Extraterritoriality of Law: History, Theory, Politics, 2019, 172; A. Meine (note 159 in Chap. 2), 127.

[268] A. L. Parrish (note 275), 179; T. Biersteker and C. Weber (note 9), 280.

therefore not a necessary link between territory and sovereignty.[269] Consequently, the trend leads to a "more flexible, multilayered approach to political-territorial governance".[270] This "post-nationalist order" signified the "freedom from spatial constraints" expressed in the liberation from the "territorially bounded Nation-State". [271] These formations by allegiance and identity are reflected in a "re-or deterritorialized resource".[272]

What this possible new system might look like is highly speculative. *I.a.* a "variety of smaller-scale political territories with a specific range of governmental mandates", governed by a world order, is imaginable.[273] However, it becomes clear that "new meaning must be given to the concept of national sovereignty and State responsibility".[274] In conclusion, "[sovereignty as a contingent political effect suggests that] the social construction of sovereignty is always in process, and is a never-completed project whose successful production can be counted on totally".[275]

3.2 The Right of Self-Determination

As already realized in 1958 in Resolution 1314 (XIII), the right of self-determination or also called right to self-determination is the very basis of the principle of permanent sovereignty over natural resources.[276] It represents one of the pillars of this principle alongside the sovereignty of States. In this part of the Chapter, the research project will concentrate on the development and scope of the right of self-determination. We will begin with the historical context and the initial idea, examining the original scope of application of the "right". Later, we will investigate its legal status and review the importance of the principle in the present day and its much wider area of application.

---

[269] A. L. Parrish (note 275), 179; T. Biersteker and C. Weber (note 9), 280; A. Meine (note 159 in Chap. 2), 139.

[270] A. B. Murphy (note 125), 111; S. van Wyk (note 1 in Chap. 2), 94.

[271] *A. Ong*, Flexible citizenship, 1999, 15; A. Meine (note 159 in Chap. 2), 127.

[272] A. Ong (note 279), 15; A. Meine (note 159 in Chap. 2), 127.

[273] A. B. Murphy (note 125).

[274] S. van Wyk (note 1 in Chap. 2), 93.

[275] R. L. Doty (note 91), 143.

[276] Resolution A/RES/1314: Recommendations Concerning International Respect for the Rights of Peoples and Nations to Self-Determination, 12.12.1958; A/RES/1314; A. Cristescu (note 10), 12, para. 64.

3.2.1 The Idea of the Right of Self-Determination: Liberation From Colonial Domination

The then so-called principle of self-determination was first mentioned in the Declaration of Principles of 14 August 1941 (known as the "Atlantic Charter 1941").[277] President Roosevelt of the United States and Prime Minister Churchill of the United Kingdom announced that

> *"They desired to see no territorial changes that do not accord with the freely expressed wishes of the peoples concerned," and "they respect the right of all peoples to choose the form of government under which they will live, and they wish to see sovereign rights and self-government restored to those who have been forcibly deprived of them."*[278]

Later, this Charter inspired the San Francisco Conference of 1945 to draft some essential articles of the United Nations Charter (UN-Charter), which became "a legally binding norm for all member States".[279] For instance, Article 1 (2) of the UN Charter affirmed: *"to develop friendly relations among nations based on respect for the principle of equal rights and self-determination of peoples and to take other appropriate measures to strengthen universal peace"*. Article 55 of the UN Charter underscored compliance with the organization's goals and explicitly referenced the objective of development.[280] Moreover, Article 73 of the UN-Charter brought forward the idea of the application of the principle of self-determination in the context of colonies and dependent territories and the duties of the colonial powers, which result from the principle:[281]

> *"[M]embers of the United Nations which have or assume responsibilities for the administration of territories whose peoples have not yet attained full measures of self-government recognize the principle that the interests of the inhabitants of these*

---

[277] *D. Thürer/T. Burri*, Self-Determination, Max Planck Encyclopedias of International Law (2008), para. 5; *C. J. Iorns Magallanes*, Indigenous peoples and self-determination, Challenging State Sovereignty, Victoria University of Wellington Legal Research Papers (2017), 244; *B. Vukas*, in: H. P. Hestermeyer, Coexistence, cooperation and solidarity: Liber amicorum Rüdiger Wolfrum, 2012, 1544; F. Nawrot (note 118 in Chap. 2), 100, 107.

[278] The Atlantic Charter, 14.08.1941, Principle 2, 3.

[279] *K. Doehring*, in: B. Simma, The Charter of the United Nations—A Commentary, 2012, 57–58, para. 1; *W. G. Grewe*, in: B. Simma, The Charter of the United Nations—A Commentary, 2012, 10, para. 42.

[280] *N. Schrijver*, Self-determination of peoples and sovereignty over natural wealth and resources, 2013, 96; C. R. Beitz (note 110), 93.

[281] N. Schrijver (note 288), 96.

> *territories are* ***paramount****, and accept as a* ***sacred trust*** *the obligation to promote to the utmost, within the system of international peace and security established by the present Charter, the well-being of the inhabitants of these territories."*

Notably, in light of this paragraph, the colonial powers recognized one by one the broader interpretations of their duties and submitted, *e.g.*, more information about the political process to the United Nations according to Article 73 (e) UN Charter to bring forward dependent peoples to independence.[282]

Moreover, Chapter XII of the UN Charter, which contains the definition and basic objective of trusteeship, imposed the duty on the trustees in Article 76 (b) "*to promote (…) progressive development* [of the trust territories] *towards self-government or independence as may be appropriate to the particular circumstances of each territory and its peoples and the freely expressed wishes of the peoples concerned*".[283] While, the term "self-determination" was still not used, progress toward independence and self-government associated with "the peoples" for the first time.[284] There are also opinions, which read this Article, in particular the wording "progressive development" in a way that it set the incentive for the development of the principle of permanent sovereignty over natural resources.[285] In conclusion, the idea of a mandates system with a particular mandate to the administering States was created, in which these States had to be "accountable to the league for the well-being of the peoples involved as a sacred trust of civilization, as this latter idea was expressed in Article 22 of the Covenant".[286]

3.2.2 Self-Determination and Human Rights

The next step in developing "self-determination" was to recognize it not only as a legal obligation but also as a human right.[287] Initiated by the so-called "Declaration on Colonial Independence"[288] in 1960, this Resolution 1514 (XV) focused on the importance of the freedom of people, still in the context of the liberation of the colonial States, by emphasizing that,

---

[282] *R. Higgins*, Problems and process: International law and how we use it, 1994, 113.

[283] Ibid., 112.

[284] Ibid.; S. Willcox (note 7 in Chap. 1), 102.

[285] N. Schrijver (note 288), 96.

[286] *R. Falk*, in: W. Danspeckgruber, Self-determination and self-administration, 1997, 50.

[287] R. Higgins (note 290), 114.

[288] Resolution A/RES/15/1514: Declaration on the Granting of Independence to Colonial Countries and Peoples (note 2 in Chap. 2).

> *"All peoples have the right to self-determination; by virtue of that right, they freely determine their political status and freely pursue their economic, social, and cultural development."*

Moreover, it was underlined in paragraph 5 that *"immediate steps shall be taken, in Trust and Non-Self-Governing Territories or all other territories which have not yet attained independence, to transfer all powers to the peoples of those territories, without any conditions or reservations, in accordance with their freely expressed will and desire."* In conclusion, this Resolution already places greater emphasis on a broader application of self-determination. In contrast, Woodrow Wilson declared during the Peace Conference in 1945 that the "self" in self-determination would indicate "a race, a territorial area, or a community".[289] Meanwhile, the focus was continuously set on the process of decolonization. So, the principle of self-determination was given the status of a "counterpoint of colonialism".[290]

Meanwhile, the United Nations strove to identify the holder of the right of self-determination, focusing on developments in human rights. Only 24 hours after the adoption of Resolution 1514 (XV), Resolution 1541 (XV) for the first time defined the notion of "people" entitled to self-determination. Even though the focus still lay on the process of decolonization as set out in Article 76 of the UN Charter, the Resolution referred to territories that were then, in 1945, known as colonial territories. It stated that the obligation to report continues until "*a territory and its peoples attain a full measure of self-government.*"[291] However, the development of an independent State or another form of association was not only strengthened but also promoted further economic, social, and cultural development.[292]

This development was intensified by the adoption of the International Covenants in 1966, whose Article 1 articulated and supported the principles of

---

289 T. Gullberg (note 12), 40.

290 *H. Berman/O. Lyons/R. Falk,* Indigenous Peoples and the Right to Self-Determination, American Society of International Law (1993), 190; D. Thürer and T. Burri (note 285), para. 9.

291 Resolution A/RES/1541 (XV): Principles which should guide Members in determining whether or not an obligation exists to transmit the information called for under Article 73 e of the Charter, 15.12.1960; A/RES/1541 (XV); H. Hannum (note 63 in Chap. 2), 13.

292 *Compare*: Resolution A/RES/1541 (XV): Principles which should guide Members in determining whether or not an obligation exists to transmit the information called for under Article 73 e of the Charter, 15.12.1960; A/RES/1541 (XV), Annex, Principle VII; R. Higgins (note 290), 114.

self-determination, and by their establishment in Resolution 1514 (XV).[293] This integration of the principle of self-determination into a general international document was sufficient to confirm its status as a collective (human) right and to illustrate its significance to all States.[294]

The decisive step to the recognition as a "right" was manifested in adopting the Friendly Relations Declaration of 1970,[295] which also "expanded the scope of self-determination in a manner not earlier anticipated".[296] This resolution, adopted by consensus, created a comprehensive guideline and specification of the framework of this principle, which had already been adopted in the UN Charter. It included, on the one hand, the right of all people to "*the establishment of a sovereign and independent State, the free association or integration with an independent State or the emergence into any other political status* ***freely determined by a people*** *constitute modes of* ***implementing the right of self-determination by that people***," and on the other hand the duty of every State *"to respect this right in accordance with the provisions of the Charter."*[297]

This Declaration was safeguarded by other critical international documents, such as the Helsinki Final Act in 1975 and the African Charter on Human and Peoples' Rights in 1982, which "self-determination is articulated as a right, and that it is of general application".[298] The Helsinki Final Act determined in Article VIII:

---

[293] *Art. 1 (1): All peoples have the right of self-determination. By virtue of that right they freely determine their political status and freely pursue their economic, social and cultural development. (2) All peoples may, for their own ends, freely dispose of their natural wealth and resources without prejudice to any obligations arising out of international economic co-operation, based upon the principle of mutual benefit, and international law. In no case may a people be deprived of its own means of subsistence. (3) The States Parties to the present Covenant, including those having responsibility for the administration of Non-Self-Governing and Trust Territories, shall promote the realization of the right of self-determination, and shall respect that right, in conformity with the provisions of the Charter of the United Nations.*

[294] D. Thürer and T. Burri (note 285), para. 10.

[295] Resolution A/RES/2625(XXV): Declaration on Principles of International Law concerning Friendly Relations and Cooperation among States in accordance with the Charter of the United Nations., 24.10.1970; A/RES/2625(XXV); *J. Crawford*, in: P. Alston, Peoples' rights, 2001, 31 et seq; *A. Cassese*, in: T. Buergenthal, Human rights, international law and the Helsinki accord, 1979, 91.

[296] R. Falk (note 294), 53.

[297] D. Thürer and T. Burri (note 285), para. 11.

[298] Helsinki Final Act, 01.08.1975, Article VIII; African Charter on Human and Peoples' Rights, 27.06.1981; Banjul Charter, Art. 20 (1), J. Crawford (note 304), 31 et seq.

> *"The participating States will respect the equal rights of peoples and their rights to self-determination (...). By virtue of the principle of equal rights and self-determination of peoples, all peoples always have the right, in full freedom, to determine, when and as they wish, their* ***internal and external political status****, without external interference, and to pursue as they wish their political, economic, social, and cultural development."*

Even though this transparent and open formulation left little room for interpretation, the opinion prevailed, focusing narrowly on decolonization. In Eastern European States, the idea of the people's entitlement to "determine their own political and economic destiny" was frowned upon.[299] Mainly, because of the interpretation of Resolution 2625 (XXV), a majority of scholars believed that "self-determination is only about independence" and that this could only be "achieved through secession."[300] In contrast to this belief, the Committee on Human Rights adhered to the idea of the unending applicability of the principle of self-determination, while, for the first time, differentiating between external and internal self-determination, as already hinted at in the Helsinki Final Act.[301] In the *Western Sahara* case, it was similarly stated that the right of self-determination is "a right of due process" or "a right to have an act of free choice".[302]

In the following years, it became more and more apparent that the scope of application of "independence" was too short-sighted. Already Resolution 1541 (XV) opened a broader scope for exercising the right of self-determination "*through independence, free association, integration with an independent State or emergence into any other political status freely determined by a people*". For instance, at this time, there were other forms of independence: Puerto Rico allowed its people to choose between "independence", "association", or "51st State of the Union".[303] In the end, they remained associated with the United States. Moreover, in the *Western Sahara* Case, the ICJ made observations concerning the consultation of the inhabitants as right-holders of self-determination:

> *(...) In certain cases, the General Assembly has dispensed with the requirement of consulting the inhabitants of a given territory. Those instances were based either on the consideration that a certain population did not constitute a "people" entitled*

[299] R. Falk (note 294), 47 et seq.; R. Higgins (note 290), 116.

[300] R. Higgins (note 290), 117 et seq.; A. Cassese (note 304), 88 et seq.

[301] R. Higgins (note 290), 117.

[302] *Western Sahara,* 16.10.1975, para. 57; *R. Pitty,* Indigenous Peoples, Self-determination and International Law, The International Journal of Human Rights 5 (2001), 53.

[303] *W. M. Reisman*, Puerto Rico and the international process: New roles in association; a report for the Conference on "Puerto Rico and the Foreign Policy Process", 1975, 35, 51–53; J. Crawford (note 14), 626 et seq.; R. Higgins (note 290), 118.

> *to self-determination or on the conviction that consultation was unnecessary due to special circumstances.*[304]

Examples, such as referenda in Namibia and Zimbabwe, followed this decision.[305] In these cases, the United Nations could lend support with its expertise by organizing plebiscites or monitoring elections, which meant "*being able to contribute to the exercise of free choice that underlies self-determination*".[306] Today, it has its scope of application in the political autonomy of indigenous people, as well as in the emergence of the new Eastern European States, and as a support for Palestinian people living in the occupied Palestinian territories.[307] In conclusion, history showed that "*self-determination never simply meant independence, but free choice of peoples*".[308]

3.2.3 The Right of Self-Determination and Minorities

Is the contemporary right of self-determination, however, limited to the exercise of political rights? Does it play no role in the context of territorial integrity? This question leads us back to the original objective of self-determination — namely, decolonization — and to the question of maintaining the international principle of *uti possidetis.* The former colonial rulers created this principle in the administrative division of Latin America and Africa. It was intended to guarantee the territorial integrity of the colonial States.[309] Later, it found application in the national unity of independent States and the maintenance of borders drawn during colonization, becoming an integral part of international law.[310] The ICJ also affirmed the validity of the principle in the *Mali-Burkina Faso* case and called it "*an essential requirement of stability in order to survive, develop and gradually consolidate their independence in all fields*".[311] It is sometimes equated with the

---

304 *Western Sahara,* 16.10.1975, 25, para. 59.

305 R. Higgins (note 290), 120.

306 Ibid., 119.

307 *W. K. Barth,* On Cultural Rights: The Equality of Nations and the Minority Legal Tradition: Chapter 3: Minority Protection in the Era of Human Rights (2008), 87, 88.

308 R. Higgins (note 290), 119.

309 Ibid., 122.

310 D. Thürer and T. Burri (note 285), para. 15; *J. Castellino,* in: J. Castellino/N. Walsh, International Law and Indigenous Peoples, 2005, 100 et seq.

311 *Case Concerning the Frontier Dispute—Burkina Faso vs. Republic of Mali,* 22.12.1986, 16, para. 25.

right of self-determination, "in terms of conceptual genealogy", but it "bears no intrinsic relationship to the self-determination of peoples."[312]

However, there are also critical voices that consider the principle as "part of the hypocritical strategy on the part of majority elites in the seceding territories to augment the territory under their control"[313] or as "the capacity to reduce complexity".[314] Judge Abi Saab affirmed in his separate opinion to the *Mali-Burkina Faso* case that "[without the stability of frontiers], *it will be the inevitable fate of the principle of* uti possidetis *to operate as a mere fiction that jars with reality,*"[315] so that the application of self-determination is, in reality, a mirage.[316] In conclusion, does the right of self-determination end at the boundaries of the territory to respect the *uti possidetis* principle?

Does this not contradict the understanding of the right of self-determination as a human right, as such a right, in particular, should be applicable in the context of intense oppression? Does a desire for secession not represent one of the strongest expressions of self-determination? Thus, the key question becomes how to understand the term "people" in the context of self-determination. Does it only refer to the "entire people of a State," or does it also include individual groups regarding race, ethnicity, or religion?[317] In light of this conflict between two principles of international law, we must conclude that "people" in the sense of "the entire nation" have the right to self-determination.[318] Consequently, a minority as such is not entitled to the right of self-determination.

However, does this mean that minorities are unprotected? That is not the case, as we can see in Article 27 of the ICCPR, which explicitly gives minorities the right *"to enjoy their own culture, to profess and practice their own religion, and to use their own language."*[319] To harmonize the two principles, we have

---

[312] *Z. OKLOPCIC,* Populus Interruptus: Self-Determination, the Independence of Kosovo, and the Vocabulary of Peoplehood, Leiden Journal of International Law 22 (2009), 680.

[313] M. Moore (note 115), 171; Z. OKLOPCIC (note 321), 687.

[314] *A. Skordas,* Self-determination of peoples and transnational regimes: a foundational principle of global governance, 2007, 218; Z. OKLOPCIC (note 321), 690.

[315] *Case Concerning the Frontier Dispute—Burkina Faso vs. Republic of Mali,* 22.12.1986, p. 112, para. 14.

[316] *Case Concerning the Frontier Dispute—Burkina Faso vs. Republic of Mali,* 22.12.1986, 16, para. 23; R. Higgins (note 290), 123.

[317] R. Higgins (note 290), 124.

[318] Ibid.

[319] International Covenant on Civil and Political Rights (note 6 in Chap. 2), Art. 27: *In those states in which ethnic, religious or linguistic minorities exist, persons belonging to such minorities shall not be denied the right, in community with other members of their group,*

to summarize that, on the one hand, the right of self-determination does not permit minorities to secede and, on the other hand, the principle of *uti possedetis* does not prohibit the secession or formation of new States, it only ensures the acceptance of the inherited colonial boundaries by the States.[320] In conclusion, the international community agreed that "the 'self' in self-determination signifies in all circumstances the existing States constituting international society, and that the only acceptable exceptions to this norm of limitation relate to secession by agreement".[321]

Consequently, we have to conclude that minorities are recognized under the ICCPR but are not equated to "people" according to Article 1 ICCPR. Some minority groups are identified as "people" under the right of self-determination, such as the Inuit in Canada or the Saami in Scandinavia.[322] However, these groups cannot invoke their right to self-determination before the Committee on Human Rights, as in Article 1 of the Optional Protocol to the ICCPR.[323] As the wording of the Article already shows, this right to claim refers to individuals, not to "groups" or "people". However, as recognized in *Lubicon Lake Band vs. Canada* in 1984,[324] individuals can invoke Article 27 through this procedure, thereby establishing that minority rights are, in fact, individual rights.[325] This realization

to enjoy their own culture, to profess and practice their own religion, and to use their own language.

[320] R. Higgins (note 290), 85, 87.

[321] R. Falk (note 294), 47.

[322] R. Higgins (note 290), 126 et seq.

[323] International Covenant on Civil and Political Rights (note 6 in Chap. 2), Optional Protocol Art. 1: *A State Party to the Covenant that becomes a Party to the present Protocol recognizes the competence of the Committee to receive and consider communications from individuals subject to its jurisdiction who claim to be victims of a violation by that State Party of any of the rights set forth in the Covenant. No communication shall be received by the Committee if it concerns a State Party to the Covenant which is not a Party to the present Protocol.*

[324] *Lubicon Lake Band vs. Canada*„ Communication No. 167/1984, 26.03.1990, para. 32.1; *Communication No. 167/1984: While all peoples have the right of self-determination and the right freely to determine their political status, pursue their economic, social and cultural development and dispose of their natural wealth and resources, as stipulates in Article 1 of the Covenant, the question whether the Lubicon Lake Band constitutes a "people" is not an issue for the Committee to address a procedure under which individuals can claim that their individual rights have been violated. These rights are set out in Part III of the Covenant, article 6–27, inclusive.*

[325] R. Higgins (note 290), 127.

brings us full circle to the conclusion that the right of self-determination also applies to individual and group human rights pursuits.[326]

Consequently, we can conclude that—returning to the question of the territorial right—self-determination and its exercise represent an instrument of "fragile, somewhat arbitrary, doctrinal clarity".[327] In particular, the broader scope of the right nowadays "faces a new danger: that of being all things to all men".[328] Referring to the often-quoted phrase of Judge Dillard in his separate opinion in Western Sahara: "*it is for the people to determine the destiny of the territory and not the territory the destiny of the people.*"[329] This gave the "self-determination genie the possibility to open the doctrinal box of a statist world."[330] While representing an excellent opportunity, this is also an invitation to misuse. For instance, in the cases of *Gibraltar* and *the Falklands (Malvinas),* the United Kingdom used the plebiscites to enforce its dominant position in these territories.[331] A similar situation occurred recently in Crimea in 2014 and in Donetsk and Luhansk in 2022.[332] However, even though other parties in these cases, such as Spain and Argentina, or even the majority of Western States in the case of Crimea, Donetsk, and Luhansk, do not agree with the decision of the people, it must be accepted, according to the doctrine. In conclusion, the right of self-determination has a "state-shattering" effect because it is often not "reconcilable with the right of existing States to territorial integrity".[333]

---

[326] R. Falk (note 294), 54.

[327] Ibid., 47.

[328] R. Higgins (note 290), 128; R. Falk (note 294), 55; A. Cristescu (note 10), 39, para. 267–268.

[329] *Western Sahara,* 16.10.1975, 122.

[330] R. Falk (note 294), 55.

[331] R. Higgins (note 290), 127.

[332] *G. Pentassuglia,* Self-Determination, Human Rights, and the Nation-State, International Community Law Review 19 (2017), 459; I. Brownlie and J. Crawford (note 30 in Chap. 2), 132.

[333] *R. Lapidoth/H. Owada,* in: W. Danspeckgruber, Self-determination and self-administration, 1997, 55; G. Pentassuglia (note 341), 259 et seq.

3.2.4 Legal Status of the Right of Self-Determination

In this context, the legal status of self-determination arises. As already noted, the change from a "vague and malleable" principle to a "right" was gradual,[334] and comparable to "ebb and flow concerning the multiple reality of self-determination, but, cumulatively, a movement toward its legal acknowledgment and application across an expanded spectrum of circumstances".[335] First, only considered a "political aspiration" by the colonial powers, "the resistance to the idea of a legal right became more muted".[336] The UN Charter was once formulated as a principle,[337] and the change to the wording "right" emerged in the General Assembly in 1955.[338] Here, the Assembly finally decided on the expression of "right" because, even though a principle would have been a strong moral force, this would have constituted an obstacle to enforcing any mandatory and legal terms.[339] Therefore, already in this session, the Committee decided that self-determination was a collective right and that it was "therefore inappropriate for inclusion in an instrument which was attempting to lay down the right of individuals".[340] Consequently, the Friendly Relations Declaration of 1970, in which the "right" of self-determination was already awarded to "all people", the Helsinki Final Act of 1975, and the Vienna Declaration of 1993 perpetuated the wording of the "right" of self-determination.[341] The driving force behind this development was the Human Rights Committee, which proclaimed that "*self-determination is articulated as a right, and that it is of general application*".[342]

As mentioned above, Article 1(3) of the ICCPR also imposes obligations on States towards their inhabitants and vis-à-vis the people of other States, a facet of the external dimension of the right of self-determination. As stated in the Western Sahara case before the ICJ in 1975, people must also have the right to choose their political status in the international community —the "*freely expressed will*

[334] H. Hannum (note 63 in Chap. 2), 12; T. Gullberg (note 12), 40.

[335] R. Falk (note 294), 51 et seq.

[336] R. Higgins (note 290), 113.

[337] R. Falk (note 294), 51.

[338] A. Cristescu (note 10), 8, para. 46.

[339] Ibid.

[340] Ibid.

[341] Helsinki Final Act, 01.08.1975, Principle VIII; Vienna Declaration and Programme of Action, 25.06.1993, Principle 2.

[342] J. Crawford (note 304), 31 et seq.

of peoples."[343] This includes "*the establishment of a sovereign and independent State, the free association or integration with an independent State or the emergence into any other political status freely determined by a people*".[344]

Consequently, while after 1945 this "right" was "largely accepted as lex lata—as a precisely determined, formally settled principle of international law", in the context of decolonization, it remained *lex obscura* in a more general context, which means, contentious and conceptually incomplete.[345] However, the ICJ provided clarification in the *South West Africa* case of 1964, where the issue of self-determination in the context of decolonization was first discussed. In 1975, the court affirmed in the judgment of the *Western Sahara* Case that:

> *"The consultation of the people of a territory awaiting decolonization is an inescapable imperative. (…) Thus, even if integration of territory was demanded by an interested State, as in this case, it could not be without ascertaining the freely expressed will of the people – the very 'sine qua non' of all decolonization."*[346]

At this time, the principle gained vast importance as "a universally recognized right under contemporary international law, a legally binding principle enjoying universality and constituting a general rule of international law".[347] It reached this status mainly due to its recognition in various contexts, such as non-interference in domestic affairs, non-resort to the threat or use of force, and a broader context of maintaining international peace and security.[348] On the other hand, it was also applied to fostering cooperation among States and to economic, social, and cultural progress.[349] For instance, already in the 1980s, the right of

[343] *Western Sahara,* 16.10.1975, 33, para. 59.

[344] Resolution A/RES/2625(XXV): Declaration on Principles of International Law concerning Friendly Relations and Cooperation among States in accordance with the Charter of the United Nations., 24.10.1970; A/RES/2625(XXV), 4; *P. Alston (ed),* Peoples' rights, 2001, 292; *compare:* S. Willcox (note 7 in Chap. 1), 91, 95.

[345] S. Willcox (note 7 in Chap. 1), 92.

[346] *Western Sahara,* 16.10.1975, 25, para. 59; p. 81.

[347] A. Cristescu (note 10), 22, para. 136.

[348] Ibid; Resolution A/RES/2160 (XXI): Strict observance of the prohibition of the threat or use of force in international relations, and of the right of peoples to self-determination, 30.11.1966; Resolution A/RES/2936 (XXVII): Non-use of force in international relations and permanent prohibition of the use of nuclear weapons, 29.11.1972.

[349] Resolution A/RES/2925 (XXVII): Strengthening of the role of the United Nations with regard to the maintenance and consolidation of international peace and security, the development of co-operation among all nations and the promotion of the rules international law in relations between States, 27.11.1972.

self-determination represented "an important component of the nucleus of international law".[350] Moreover, it carried the title of customary law, in particular, due to the far-reaching importance of the already discussed Resolutions 1514 (XV) and 2625 (XXV), which substantiated the principles, as well as the International Law of Friendly Relations and Cooperation.[351]

However, the landmark decision for the development of the principle was the *East Timor* judgment of 1995, where the ICJ confirmed the *erga omnes* character of the right:

> *"In the Court's view, Portugal's assertion that the right of peoples to self-determination, as it evolved from the Charter and from United Nations practice, has an erga omnes character is irreproachable."*[352]

Although the Court did not explicitly affirm the *ius cogens* status of the right to self-determination,[353] this status is widely accepted.[354]

3.2.5 The Different Manifestations of the Right of Self-Determination

The differentiation between the two aspects of self-determination—"the collective struggle for national independence" and "the individual quest for human rights" leads us to the next element: the two different manifestations of self-determination.[355] The exercise of the right of self-determination not only means the attainment of independence but also the free choice of the people.[356] For

---

[350] A. Cristescu (note 10), 22, para. 136.

[351] Ibid., 23, para. 149–150.

[352] *East Timor Judgement,* 30.06.1995, para. 29; *Recognition of erga omnes in International Law: The Barcelona Traction, Belgium vs. Spain, 24.07.1964, para. 33.*

[353] *East Timor Judgement,* 30.06.1995, heading: *"Right of peoples to self-determination as right* erga omnes *and essential principle of contemporary international law—Difference between* erga omnes *character of a norm and rule of consent to jurisdiction".*

[354] S. Willcox (note 7 in Chap. 1), 95; *critical:* H. Hannum (note 63 in Chap. 2), 32; S. van Wyk (note 1 in Chap. 2), 45; N. Schrijver (note 1 in Chap. 2), 376.

[355] R. Falk (note 294), 54.

[356] S. Willcox (note 7 in Chap. 1), 95; *G. Abi-Saab,* in: M. Bedjaoui, International law: Achievements and prospects, 1991, 600; Resolution A/RES/15/1514: Declaration on the Granting of Independence to Colonial Countries and Peoples (note 2 in Chap. 2); Resolution A/RES/2625(XXV): Declaration on Principles of International Law concerning Friendly

instance, following this train of thought, the right also must include the entitlement to choose a government.[357] With this consideration in mind, we are already immersed in the narrow differentiation between the internal and external facets of self-determination.

During the sixth session of the General Assembly in 1952, the Assembly noticed that the right of people to self-determination had two different aspects: "from the domestic point of view, this signified the peoples' right to self-government and from the external point of view their independence."[358] Therefore, especially in its external dimension, it was determined to play a constructive role in ensuring international peace and security and fostering fruitful international cooperation.[359] Later, the Friendly Relations Declaration of 1970 divided these two facets of the right of self-determination into the internal and external rights of self-determination, as recognized to this day.[360]

Internal self-determination encompasses the ability to select the political representation for each member of society. This allows the population to choose the political and economic regime, as well as its leaders, and to participate in the political model that suits them.[361] In short, it can be determined as autonomy, the "group's ability to govern itself by adjudicating, legislating, and enforcing laws on its own".[362] Consequently, various configurations of human rights and democratic principles, such as the right to vote, the right to peaceful assembly, the freedom of association, and the freedom of expression, emerged from this branch of the right to self-determination. At the same time, acknowledging cultural identity and self-governed groups within a State, such as indigenous peoples, can be

---

Relations and Cooperation among States in accordance with the Charter of the United Nations. (note 353), Principle 5.

[357] R. Higgins (note 290), 120.

[358] Official Reports of the General Assembly; Sixth Session, Third Committee, 397th meeting, para. 5; A. Cristescu (note 10), 4, para. 32.

[359] A. Cristescu (note 10), 4, para. 32; Official Reports of the General Assembly; Sixth Session, Third Committee, 397th meeting, para. 22.

[360] *Compare:* Principle 5.1: „*By virtue of the principle of equal rights and self-determination of peoples enshrined in the Charter of the United Nations, all peoples have the right freely to determine, without external interference, their political status and to pursue their economic, social and cultural development, and every State has the duty to respect this right in accordance with the provisions of the Charter.*"

[361] J. Crawford (note 304), 25.

[362] *J. Ödalen,* Underwater Self-determination: Sea-level Rise and Deterritorialized Small Island States: Underwater Self-determination: Sea-level Rise and Deterritorialized Small Island States, Ethics, Policy & Environment (2014), 229.

included in this facet.[363] In sum, the internal aspect of self-determination consists of "bundles of individual rights and group rights, [which serve as] an instrument to achieve [and exercise] self-determination".[364]

On the other hand, the external facet concerns "friendly relations and cooperation among States."[365] Consequently, this dimension of the right of self-determination also imposes extraterritorial obligations upon States.[366] These obligations are double-sided: on the one hand, the negative duty to "respect" the right to external self-determination; on the other, the positive duty to "promote" its realization, particularly through diplomatic and non-military measures.[367] In other words, it can also be understood as "independence", or the capacity of a group to exercise "political control independent of higher or foreign political units to which the group's self-made laws are subject to being overridden or revoked."[368] In jurisdiction, self-determination was recognized as a concern of all States and a source of "obligations…towards the international community as a whole".[369] However, already in the discussion of the reorganization of the former Yugoslavia and the foundation of new States in this region, some scholars criticized the external dimension as "inoperative" because of the lack of applicability and enforceability in these particular cases and denied the "single, overarching" character of the "principle of territorial reconstructions".[370] Therefore, in this context, it represents a "multidimensional goal, not a single right".[371]

---

[363] *J. Crawford*, State practice and international law in relation to sucession, 1998, 117; *compare: G. Pentassuglia,* Evolving Protection of Minority Groups: Global Challenges and the Role of International Jurisprudence, International Community Law Review 11 (2009), 207.

[364] *A. E. Buchanan,* The Right of Self-Determination: Analytical and Moral Foundations, Arizona Journal of International and Comparative Law (1991), 44; *J. Ödalen,* Underwater Self-determination: Sea-level Rise and Deterritorialized Small Island States: Underwater Self-determination: Sea-level Rise and Deterritorialized Small Island States, Ethics, Policy & Environment (2014), 230.

[365] A. Cristescu (note 10), 25, para. 164.

[366] S. Willcox (note 7 in Chap. 1), 95.

[367] Resolution A/RES/2625(XXV): Declaration on Principles of International Law concerning Friendly Relations and Cooperation among States in accordance with the Charter of the United Nations. (note 353); *Israeli Wall,* 09.07.2004, para. 159–160.

[368] J. Ödalen (note 373), 229.

[369] *Compare*: *East Timor Judgement,* 30.06.1995, *Israeli Wall,* 09.07.2004, *Case Concerning Military and Paramilitary Activities in and against Nicaragua—Nicaragua v. U.S.,* 26.11.1984.

[370] Z. OKLOPCIC (note 321), 679.

[371] Ibid., 680.

The internal dimension of the right of self-determination aligns more closely with the human rights regime and the inherent rights of individuals and groups within a community.[372] Internal self-determination thus constitutes the capacity to actively participate in society and policy, and to stand up for one's rights, for example, as a minority.[373] In consequence, it represents the "rights of individuals and rights of peoples buttress and sustain each other".[374] This aspect is also affirmed in Article 25 of the ICCPR, which includes the free expression of the will of the electors in universal and periodic elections.[375] For instance, the limitation on a four-party system, as it was intended in Zaire in 1990, violated the right of self-determination in its internal facet and, so, the ongoing choice of the people as to their governance and, going a step further, resulting from that, their economic, social, and cultural development.[376]

Returning to the question mentioned above — whether self-determination ends at the boundaries of the State — we can now answer it in the negative. In the case of external self-determination, this is evident in its international context. However, internal self-determination must be understood as being free from territorial borders. As Banai noticed, "boundaries of States (or other self-determining political units) are normatively relevant for and overlap with the scope of duties of distributive justice and rights to democratic participation".[377] Hannum expressed this thought more drastically, as he views "self-determination as a code word for ethnic supremacy or the assertion of increasingly vague "sovereignty".[378]

3.2.6 The Right of Self-Determination Today

One of the most recent steps in the development of the right of self-determination, besides the aforementioned broadening of its scope to non-colonial foreign occupation and the dissolution of States,[379] was the adoption of the UN Declaration

---

[372] S. Willcox (note 7 in Chap. 1), 96.

[373] *A. Banai,* Political Self-Determination and Global Egalitarianism: Towards an Intermediate Position, Social Theory and Practice 39 (2013), 46 et seq.

[374] *P. Thornberry,* in: C. Tomuschat, Modern law of self-determination, 1993, 137; S. Willcox (note 7 in Chap. 1), 96,

[375] R. Higgins (note 290), 120 et seq.

[376] Ibid., 120.

[377] A. Banai (note 382), 46.

[378] H. Hannum (note 63 in Chap. 2), 64.

[379] *R. McCorquodale,* in: M. Evans, International law, 2018, 274; S. Willcox (note 7 in Chap. 1), 94.

on the Rights of Indigenous Peoples (UNDRIP).[380] Here, the right was not only incorporated into Article 4 of the UNDRIP but also served as the foundation for strengthening the rights of indigenous peoples in the international community, constituting the cornerstone of "*the right to autonomy or self-government*" for indigenous peoples. Considering the above-mentioned distinction between the human right of internal self-determination for individuals and minorities and the right of people to self-determination, or external self-determination, the classification of the rights set out in the UNDRIP is challenging.

Due to the unclear use of the term, the question of a broader application scope for the right of self-determination arose. Not only the question of the possible "full dignity of the status of indigenous peoples as a people." [381] Now, even potential applications in the context of environmental pollution and climate change have been discussed.[382] As expected, some take a critical stance toward this "patchwork of rights to self-determination".[383] They want to "limit the relevance [of the right of self-determination] in the postcolonial setting to its human rights role of empowering individuals to act within existing State structures of authority".[384] However, the development of the right has already reached a dimension where it is "too late to put the genie of self-determination back in its colonialist bottle".[385] Furthermore, the right of self-determination today eclipses beyond the framework of "an exclusive, territorially bounded, one-off right to freedom from violent oppression" and constitutes a "much more complex and multilateral case situation, in which the international community is as a whole responsible for the harms of, *e.g.*, Climate Change".[386]

Consequently, we have to quarry for the very essence of self-determination. Considering all the approaches examined above, it has become apparent that the right is applicable when someone is "confronted with problems concerning the

---

[380] Declaration on the Rights of Indigenous Peoples (UNDRIP), 13.09.2007a; A/RES/61/295, Art. 3–4.

[381] R. Falk (note 294), 49; S. Willcox (note 7 in Chap. 1), 98.

[382] R. Falk (note 294), 49; S. Willcox (note 7 in Chap. 1), 98.

[383] *M. Craven/R. Parfitt*, in: M. Evans, International law, 2018, 208 et seq.; S. Willcox (note 7 in Chap. 1), 97.

[384] R. Falk (note 294), 49. M. Craven and R. Parfitt (note 392).

[385] R. Falk (note 294), 49.

[386] *S. Atapattu,* Climate change, human rights and forced migration: Implications for International law, Wisconsin International Law Journal (2009), 610; S. Willcox (note 7 in Chap. 1), 100.

destiny of a people".[387] The same connection to the people is found in the definition of Brownie, who stated that it is "a right of cohesive national groups (peoples) to choose for themselves a form of political organization and their relation to other groups".[388] In conclusion, as already determined in the Resolutions of the General Assembly, the context of the use of the right may change, but the core statement—the free and voluntary choice by the people of the territory concerned—does not.[389]

Bearing in mind the various contexts in which the right of self-determination has already found application, it appears as a logical extension that the right intervenes in any case in which a significant threat to the destiny of the peoplehood appears.[390] Consequently, the question of whether the right can be generalized to apply to other possible threats is well justified.

In sum, it seems that whenever the "destiny of the people" is limited in any way, the right sets out a general and "fundamental standard of behavior".[391] After its initial focus on the narrow aim of decolonization, the scope of application has broadened.[392] It first has the task of securing international peace, stability, and security, as Article 1(2) of the UN Charter prescribes, which states, "promotes friendly relations and cooperation among States."[393] However, this cannot be the primary aim of the right of self-determination, as this only shows the narrowest possible scope of this right. To give full effect to the importance and potential, the right must apply to every situation where someone is "confronted with problems concerning the destiny of a people".[394]

---

[387] *A. Cassese*, Self-determination of peoples: A legal reappraisal, 1st ed., 1995, 319 et seq.; S. Willcox (note 7 in Chap. 1), 104.

[388] I. Brownlie and J. Crawford (note 30 in Chap. 2), 595.

[389] Resolution A/RES/2625(XXV): Declaration on Principles of International Law concerning Friendly Relations and Cooperation among States in accordance with the Charter of the United Nations. (note 353), 4; Resolution A/RES/1541 (XV): Principles which should guide Members in determining whether or not an obligation exists to transmit the information called for under Article 73 e of the Charter (note 300), Principle VII; S. Willcox (note 7 in Chap. 1), 103.

[390] S. Willcox (note 7 in Chap. 1), 104; P. Alston (note 41), 272.

[391] *A. Cassese*, International law in a divided world, 1986, 126.

[392] P. Alston (note 353), 291 et seq.; *K. Knop*, Diversity and self-determination in international law, 1st ed., 2002, 68; S. Willcox (note 7 in Chap. 1), 91.

[393] Resolution A/RES/2625(XXV): Declaration on Principles of International Law concerning Friendly Relations and Cooperation among States in accordance with the Charter of the United Nations. (note 353).

[394] A. Cassese (note 396), 319; S. Willcox (note 7 in Chap. 1), 104, 112.

3.2.7 Modern Scope of Application

As previously discussed, the right has been affirmed in various contexts regarding secession from an unlawful regime.[395] Therefore, the right of self-determination is not only applicable in the context of the liberation of "non-self-governing territories," as mentioned in the *South West Africa* Decision of the ICJ,[396] based on Article 73 of the UN Charter.[397] The development also extends to the "integration with an independent State."[398] Following these considerations, the right applies in the context of a conflict over one territory and in the case of losing territory.[399]

The internal aspect of the right, which protects against grave violations, is of great importance in the context of political participation or of minority rights harmed, as mentioned above.[400] In summary, protecting individual human rights within the internal facet of self-determination, such as political participation and

[395] J. Crawford (note 372), 86.

[396] *South West Africa Cases,* 21.12.1962, 338, para. 23.

[397] *Compare*: Charter, 26.05.1945, Art. 73*: Members of the United Nations which have or assume responsibilities for the administration of territories whose peoples have not yet attained a full measure of self-government recognize the principle that the interests of the inhabitants of these territories are paramount, and accept as a sacred trust the obligation to promote to the utmost, within the system of international peace and security established by the present Charter, the well-being of the inhabitants of these territories, and, to this end: (...).*

[398] J. Crawford (note 372), 89.

[399] S. Willcox (note 7 in Chap. 1), 114.

[400] *Compare:* Vienna Convention on the Law of Treaties, 23.05.1969, Art. 2, Chapter 1: *All peoples have the Right of Self-Determination. By virtue of that right they freely determine their political status, and freely pursue their economic, social and cultural development. Taking into account the particular situation of peoples under colonial or other forms of alien domination or foreign occupation, the World Conference on Human Rights recognizes the right of peoples to take any legitimate action, in accordance with the Charter of the United Nations, to realize their inalienable right of Self-Determination. The World Conference on Human Rights considers the denial of the right of Self-determination as a violation of human rights and underlines the importance of the effective realization of this Right. In accordance with the Declaration on Principles of International Law concerning Friendly Relations and Cooperation Among States in accordance with the Charter of the United Nations, this shall not be construed as authorizing or encouraging any action which would dismember or impair, totally or in part, the territorial integrity or political unity of sovereign and independent States conducting themselves in compliance with the principle of equal rights and Self-Determination of peoples and thus possessed of a Government representing the whole people belonging to the territory without distinction of any kind.*

the protection and involvement of minorities, is equally important as the initial application in the context of decolonization.[401]

In the broader scope of application, the question must be raised again: in which context does the destiny of the people play a role? As already shown, under Articles 1 of the ICCPR and the ICESCR, people must have the capacity to "determine freely the political status and economic, social and cultural development". Consequently, the people must enjoy autonomy—the ability to make their own legal structure—as well as independence—the freedom from external control.[402] In conclusion, the right of self-determination has the task of "protecting peoples' collective interest in autonomy and independence against grave (external or internal) threats over which they have little control."[403]

Banai argues similarly, as he examined the principle from the political angle and came to the conclusion that the borders of States nowadays are too narrow for the dimension of self-determination, so that today's "rights of political participation [can] correspond to the borders of States", however, in most cases, "overlap with them".[404] Leaving the strict definition based on territory and State aside, the moral aspect of this right is personal autonomy, according to which "individuals are entitled to form and pursue their own conceptions of what makes life worth living".[405] That often includes a political element—namely, a political identity.

Hannum expresses this new form of self-determination as "functional sovereignty", detached from Statehood and independence.[406] It would include an allocation to "sub-state groups the powers necessary to control political and economic matters of direct relevance to them while bearing in mind the legitimate concerns of other segments of the population and the State itself."[407] In conclusion, the capacity of self-determination, in the same way international law in general, is in constant evolution and "is capable of embracing much more nuanced interpretations and applications, particularly in an increasingly interdependent world in which the formal attributes of Statehood mean less and less."[408] He furthermore underlined that "human rights norms expand to include

[401] S. Willcox (note 7 in Chap. 1), 114.

[402] R. Jennings et al. (note 126), 382–394.

[403] S. Willcox (note 7 in Chap. 1), 116; P. Alston (note 353), 292.

[404] A. Banai (note 382), 47.

[405] Ibid., 49.

[406] H. Hannum (note 63 in Chap. 2), 66.

[407] Ibid.

[408] Ibid., 63.

political participation and protection of identity (within a larger context of continuing protection for the individual members of both minorities and majorities), self-determination can be more meaningfully and readily exercised (…)".[409]

In conclusion, "the post-colonial norm of self-determination includes the right to be different and to enjoy a meaningful degree of control over one's own life, individually and collectively, as well as the right to participate in the affairs of the larger State".[410] In addition, Crawford indicates, "the continuing vitality and potential for expansion of the principle of self-determination should not be underestimated".[411] Self-determination "introduced a highly dynamic factor of change that deeply undermine(s) the status quo" and already reached several milestones in international law, recognizing collective rights to identity and autonomy.[412] As Hannum summarized, "self-determination postulates the right of a people organized in an established territory to determine its collective political destiny in a democratic fashion and is therefore at the core of the democratic entitlement".[413]

3.2.8 The Economic Self-Determination

In addition to the newly developed political and recessionary dimensions of the right of self-determination, economic self-determination is often used interchangeably with the principle of permanent sovereignty over natural resources. Consequently, the right of permanent sovereignty over natural resources is a fundamental element in the right to self-determination.[414] Therefore, we will shed light on this dimension of this right.

As noted above, the principle of permanent sovereignty over natural resources was long recognized as a right of the people. Hence, the "self-determination of people gives rise to the people's right of economic self-determination in terms of PSNR".[415] Therefore, the right to control natural resources is applicable within

[409] Ibid., 66.

[410] Ibid., 68.

[411] J. Crawford (note 304), 65; S. Willcox (note 7 in Chap. 1), 93.

[412] A. Cassese (note 396), 316.

[413] H. Hannum (note 63 in Chap. 2), 9.

[414] A. Cristescu (note 10), 78, para. 464.

[415] S. van Wyk (note 1 in Chap. 2), 292.

State borders.[416] Considering this, it is not far-fetched to conclude that economic self-determination also belongs to people, not States.[417] This conclusion is also affirmed in the Banjul Charter, where Article 21 (5) determined that "*peoples* [should be] *able to fully benefit from the advantages derived from their national resources*".[418]

However, this was not always self-evident. For instance, during the adoption of the International Covenants on Human Rights, the inclusion of the permanent sovereignty over natural resources in Article 1 (3) was rejected, because "a right of people was seen as contradicting the established international law position that States were to exercise permanent sovereignty over natural resources".[419] Consequently, despite the wording of Article 1(2) of the UN Charter and Article 1(1) of the International Covenants on Human Rights, as well as the various references to the people as right-holders in UNGA Resolutions, PSNR was originally a more state-centric than people-centric principle.[420] This interpretation starkly contrasted with the undisputed source of this principle—the right of self-determination—which included "the simple and elementary principle that a nation or people should be master of its own natural wealth or resources."[421]

On the other hand, the Covenants recognized the principle of permanent sovereignty over natural resources as an "inherent right of all people to enjoy and utilize fully and freely their natural wealth and resources".[422] Consequently, the

---

[416] *A. Farmer,* Towards a Meaningful Rebirth of Economic Self-Determination: Human Rights Realization in Resource-Rich Countries, International Law and Policies 39 (2006), 441.

[417] Ibid., 452; S. van Wyk (note 1 in Chap. 2), 294; A. Cristescu (note 10), 71, para. 71.

[418] African Charter on Human and Peoples' Rights, 27.06.1981c; Banjul Charter, Art. 21(5): "*States parties to the present Charter shall undertake to eliminate all forms of foreign economic exploitation particularly that practiced by international monopolies so as to enable their peoples to fully benefit from the advantages derived from their national resources.*"

[419] *J. Gilbert,* The Right to Freely Dispose of Natural Resources, Netherlands Quarterly of Human Rights 31 (2013), 322; S. van Wyk (note 1 in Chap. 2), 297.

[420] S. van Wyk (note 1 in Chap. 2), 344; A. Cristescu (note 10), 72, para. 439–440.

[421] Annotations on the text of the draft International Covenants on Human Rights, 1955; A/ 2929, 15, para. 21.

[422] International Covenant on Economic, Social and Cultural Rights (note 6 in Chap. 2), Art. 25, International Covenant on Civil and Political Rights (note 6 in Chap. 2), Art. 47: *Nothing in the present Covenant shall be interpreted as impairing the inherent right of all peoples to enjoy and utilize fully and freely their natural wealth and resources.*

link between self-determination and natural resources was already established.[423] This link became much more evident in the Declaration on the Right to Development of 1986,[424] where Article 1 (1) declared "the right to development and the right to self-determination belong to 'all people', followed by Article 1 (2), where the link to the principle of permanent sovereignty over natural resources was made clear.[425] The Banjul Charter, with the precise wording of its Article 21, falls into the same period.

In conclusion, PSNR is a right of States and people; therefore, the State can exercise this right on behalf of people, without excluding people from exercising it.[426] At least, it is agreed, that the people are the primary beneficiaries of the exploitation of natural resources, so they have to be enshrined as the right-holders of economic self-determination, otherwise "the deep connection between internal self-determination and economic self-determination is void".[427]

However, the dichotomy of this conclusion can be resumed in a simple question: "Does the inalienable right to permanent sovereignty over natural wealth and resources, a right which is vested in peoples, permit the existence and exercise of acquired rights by foreign interests in the exploration and exploitation of these resources, and if so, to what extent?"[428] This question becomes even more critical, given the current trend in which raw materials and energy, linked to the concept of permanent sovereignty over natural resources, are gaining significance for the future of human civilization and, consequently, for people.[429] However, the developing countries are still anxious to prevent foreign investors

---

[423] *F. X. Perrez,* The Relationship Between "Permanent Sovereignty" and the Obligation not to cause transboundary environmental damage, Environmental Law (1996), 1190; G. Abi-Saab (note 365), 600., N. Schrijver (note 1 in Chap. 2), 49 et seq., S. van Wyk (note 1 in Chap. 2), 298.

[424] A/RES/41/128: Declaration on the Right to Development, 04.12.1986; A/RES/41/128.

[425] Ibid., Art. 1: *The right to development is an inalienable human right by virtue of which every human person and all peoples are entitled to participate in, contribute to, and enjoy economic, social, cultural and political development, in which all human rights and fundamental freedoms can be fully realized. The human right to development also implies the full realization of the right of peoples to self-determination, which includes, subject to the relevant provisions of both International Covenants on Human Rights, the exercise of their inalienable right to full sovereignty over all their natural wealth and resources.*

[426] *E. Duruigbo,* Permanent Sovereignty and Peoples' Ownership of Natural Resources in International Law, The George Washington International Law Review 38 (2006), 49; S. van Wyk (note 1 in Chap. 2), 300.

[427] A. Farmer (note 425), 445.

[428] A. Cristescu (note 10), 71, para. 435.

[429] Ibid., 71, para. 436.

and wish to take the responsibility for their own destiny, as well as "affirm their national interests in the exploitation of these resources".[430] Following this idea, the "struggle for economic independence" lies in the complex interplay among economic, legal, and technical aspects that developing countries and their people must address.[431] Consequently, "economic independence cannot be guaranteed unless peoples enjoy the right to possess, use, and develop their natural wealth and resources in their own interest; however, without that enjoyment, sovereign political independence cannot be maintained".[432] In conclusion, economic self-determination has to be brought "out of the shadows and employ it as a powerful tool for human rights advocacy related to the distribution of wealth,"[433] because without equal access to the right of development, "it no longer makes sense to speak of a human right".[434]

3.2.9 Concluding Remarks

In this part of the Chapter, we illustrate the development of the right to self-determination, beginning with the Atlantic Charter and the UN Charter, reviewing various UN Resolutions, and concluding with the UN Declaration on the Rights of Indigenous Peoples. We observed that not only has the wording of the right to self-determination changed, but also its scope of application. Initially, it represented the classical application in the context of decolonization. Still, nowadays, it has expanded to encompass a much broader scope of application, particularly in relation to indigenous peoples and climate change. Consequently, the development from a principle to a right occurs alongside the elaboration of various rules governing internal and external self-determination, highlighting their significance in distinct areas of international law. Ultimately, the approach to economic self-determination was demonstrated, focusing on the principle of permanent sovereignty over natural resources, a key aspect of the right to self-determination.

In conclusion, "international law is said to have created a patchwork of rights to self-determination", including "right to democracy, women's rights, indigenous rights, and minority rights, it is predominantly understood as a right associated

[430] Ibid.

[431] Ibid., 71, para. 437.

[432] Ibid., 78, para. 464.

[433] A. Farmer (note 425), 419.

[434] *A. Carty*, in: S. R. Chowdhury/E. M. Denters/P. de Waart, The right to development in international law, 1992, 44.

with the foreign occupation of a people, of which colonialism is a paradigmatic example," as well as tendencies of secession like new States the former Yugoslavia.[435] However, to this day, low acceptance and vague language are signs of the "impossibility of pinning down the acceptable limits of plausible legal claim". However, nowadays, self-determination is recognized in a broad context as "one of the essential principles of contemporary international law"[436] and the "basic, overarching guideline, that identifies the essence of self-determination".[437]

[435] G. Pentassuglia (note 341), 458; S. Willcox (note 7 in Chap. 1), 97; *H. Charlesworth*, The boundaries of international law, 1st ed., 2000; S. *J. Anaya*, Indigenous peoples in international law, 2nd ed., 2004, 97 et seq.; *P. Thornberry*, in: M. Suksi, Autonomy: Applications and implications, 1998, 97 et seq.

[436] S. Willcox (note 7 in Chap. 1), 91.

[437] A. Cassese (note 396), 319 et seq; N. Schrijver (note 288), 95.

Subjects of the Principle of Permanent Sovereignty over Natural Resources

4

In the kind of world for which we fight, there must cease to exist any need for the use of that accursed term "racial or religious minority" (W. K. Barth (note 316 in Chap. 3), 72)

(Summer Welles, American Undersecretary of State, 31 May 1943)

Having already analyzed the concept of permanent sovereignty over natural resources and its two main pillars—state sovereignty and the right of self-determination—we will take a closer look at the subjects of this principle in the following sections. After the development of the concept of Statehood, it might be evident that the State as such is the right-holder, or rather, principle-holder, of this principle. However, as we have already analyzed, State sovereignty is only a legal fiction, created and developed on the basis of theories of property and occupancy. Consequently, there must be a starting point at which the State's sovereignty was created. In the following, we will examine the type of construct that existed before the idea of the State. We can find this conflict of "the interests and rights of indigenous peoples relating to their lands, as well as their rights related to the exploitation of natural resources, such as fishing and herding rights, which [nowadays] often is resolved by property rights".[1] However, as Elian already noticed, "sovereignty is a faculty, an attitude of a people to shape their fate a destiny freely".[2]

---

[1] *S. Iglesias Sánchez,* in: E. Conde Pérez/S. Iglesias Sánchez, Global challenges in the Arctic region, 2017, 222.

[2] G. Elian (note 98 in Chap. 2), 5.

M. A. Brinker, *The Principle of Permanent Sovereignty over Natural Resources as an Anchor in Times of Sealevel Rise*, https://doi.org/10.1007/978-3-658-50527-1_4

Consequently, this chapter will try to find an answer to the question of whether the State is the predominant right-holder of the principle of permanent sovereignty over natural resources, as the prevailing opinion takes this point of view, or if it is in any way possible to view the people as right- or rather principle-holder (in the following "right-holder"). The following chapter will analyze the concept of people and their development, examining their connection to natural resources. After all, this will be the decisive question of analysis on the subject of the principle of permanent sovereignty over natural resources.

4.1 The State as Predominant Right-Holder

At first glance, we might conclude, considering that the main attributes of Statehood are sovereignty, territory, and the concept of permanent sovereignty, that this principle must be irrevocably connected to Statehood.[3] In other words, "States enjoy exclusive rights concerning the control and use of natural resources within their territories."[4] However, as we concluded in the previous chapter, the principle of permanent sovereignty over natural resources rests on two pillars: state sovereignty and the self-determination of the people.[5] The conclusion we can draw from this is that the right-holders of permanent sovereignty over natural resources are States and the people in equal parts. However, today's reality looks quite different. The predominant view, which also reflects the practice in international law, is that "permanent sovereignty over natural resources serves to safeguard State sovereignty in use, exploitation, and disposal of natural resources".[6] In particular, during the 1970s, the concept of the people as an entity lost its significance as a right-holder of the principle of permanent sovereignty over natural resources.[7] As we saw in Chap. 2 above, after decolonization, the role of people as independent actors in international law was pushed back further and further, so that, in the end, the State remained the sole actor in international law. This is most evident in the United Nations Convention on the Law of the

[3] Y. Tyagi (note 15 in Chap. 2), 588–589.

[4] *O. Angeli,* Self-Determination and Sovereignty over Natural Resources, Ratio Juris (2017), 290.

[5] F. Nawrot (note 118 in Chap. 2), 99 et seq.

[6] S. van Wyk (note 1 in Chap. 2), 23.

[7] F. Nawrot (note 118 in Chap. 2), 100.

Sea, where people as actors are not even mentioned.[8] Furthermore, the Convention repeatedly stresses, "*States have the sovereign right to exploit their natural resources*".[9] For a more socialistic view of the matter, we can quote Marx:

> *"The people's sovereignty is only an abstraction if one fails to identify the class which represents the people at a certain period of development of the State."*[10]

Consequently, the self-determination of people, once described as one of the main pillars of the principle of permanent sovereignty over natural resources, can only be considered the stepping stone for the State to reach absolute sovereignty over natural resources again, as it is exculpated by the simple explication that

> *"The sovereignty of the (...) State represents the peoples' sovereign right to determine their own fate by themselves, to ensure the development necessary to the new State's power, to ensure the exercise of the right to independence in relationships with other States."*[11]

In the following, some scholars even argued that permanent sovereignty over natural resources was not even the combination of two equal principles, but misrepresented the interplay between them:

> *"Territorial sovereignty has as its corollary the right of States freely to dispose of their natural wealth and resources. (...) by virtue of this right, any State may reintegrate natural wealth and resources into the national assets and use them in the interests of its peoples."*[12]

Thus, the empowerment of people in creating the principle was considered only a necessary intermediate step to guide developing States and their people toward the highest level of self-government: the State.[13] Consequently, the debate on

---

[8] *I. Papanicolopulu,* The Law of the Sea Convention: No place for persons?, International Journal of Marine and Coastal Law (2012), 868.

[9] Convention on the Law of the Sea 1982 (note 194 in Chap. 2), Art. 193; *compare:* Convention on the Law of the Sea 1982 (note 194 in Chap. 2), Art. 56(1)(a); 77(1), (2); 79 (2); 193(3)(c); 246(5)(a).

[10] G. Elian and A. Bantas (note 56 in Chap. 3), 4.

[11] Ibid., 4 et seq.

[12] A. Cristescu (note 10 in Chap. 3), 25, para. 176.

[13] J. Crawford (note 14 in Chap. 3), 621 et seq.

sovereignty over natural resources increasingly shifted toward the "developmental dimension" and expansion, rather than focusing on the proper representation and integration of self-determining people.[14] Hence, it was a popular line of reasoning in the 1980s that the developed countries had to do everything in their power

> *"to assist the developing countries in bridging the gap between the two groups of countries, to fully respect the principle of the sovereignty of every State."*[15]

This thesis remains the leading rationale in many international judgments, including the recently concluded South China Sea case.[16] Already before the case, in which China did not participate, China based its claims for an expansion of maritime territorialization, also for maritime resources, on a "vernacular perspective of territoriality", considering the South China Sea as a "maritime province" and referring to their "historical bases of sovereignty fundamentalism".[17] In conclusion, specific modalities of state sovereignty were more often the subject of the "permanent sovereignty debate" than the self-determination of people was even considered in this context.[18]

However, in recent times, the rights of people—particularly in the context of self-determination—have increasingly come to the fore. Initially, particularly due to the expanding scope of State sovereignty—for example, the pursuit of the well-being of the people –, the self-determination of people as an equal and fully adequate principle compared to State sovereignty gained new significance.[19] In the following, we will take a look at the quality of the people as the subject of the principle of permanent sovereignty over natural resources, while trying to answer some questions: what are the people as such, how are they defined in international law, and can they be the main principle-holder of the permanent sovereignty over natural resources?

---

[14] S. Hobe (note 8 in Chap. 2).

[15] A. Cristescu (note 10 in Chap. 3), p. 25, para. 176.

[16] *The South China Sea Arbitration,* PCA Case No. 2013–19, 12.07.2016.

[17] *R. Strating/J. Wallis,* Maritime sovereignty and territorialisation: Comparing the Pacific Islands and South China Sea, Marine Policy (2022), 5.

[18] N. Schrijver (note 8 in Chap. 2), 22.

[19] Ibid.

4.2 The People as the Right-Holder

As already noted, defining people as the right-holders of the principle of permanent sovereignty over natural resources is one of the essential determinants of the further course of this research project. However, defining people is difficult. Even though the term "people" as the right-holder of the principle appeared as early as Resolution 626 (VII) in 1952, we can find no definition of the term.[20] Moreover, the search for the definition appears tricky due to the different branches of interpretation of the expression "people". On the one hand, we can describe a country's population in terms of its people.[21] However, there is also the possibility of limiting the expression "people" to a specific group within a State's population, such as minorities or indigenous peoples.[22] These two understandings must already be strictly separated. Therefore, this chapter will take a closer look at the different groups within a population, which must be considered the right-holders of the term "people." It will conclude with an attempt to define and question the "correct" right-holders for the principle of permanent sovereignty over natural resources.

4.2.1 The Importance of People's Rights

Before we define the people, we must be aware of the importance of people's rights, particularly in comparison to the rights of States and human rights. The transition between the rights of States, the groups' or the peoples' rights, and, consequently, human rights is fluent. Therefore, their differentiation is significant, particularly considering the essential role of group rights in this research project. This differentiation becomes particularly apparent in the Banjul Charter, where human and peoples' rights appear in the title.[23]

---

[20] Resolution A/RES/626 (VII): Right to Exploit Freely Natural Wealth and Ressources (note 2 in Chap. 2), para. 3: *"Remembering that the right of peoples freely to use and exploit their natural wealth and resources in inherent in their sovereignty and is in accordance with the Purposes and Principles of the Charter of the United Nations."* C. J. Iorns Magallanes (note 285 in Chap. 3), 287; H. Hannum (note 63 in Chap. 2), 16.

[21] *N. Schrijver*, in: I. Boerefijn/C. Flinterman, Changing perceptions of sovereignty and human rights: Essays in honour of Cees Flinterman, 2008, 88.

[22] Ibid.

[23] African Charter on Human and Peoples' Rights (note 427 in Chap. 3); *R. Kiwanuka,* The Meaning of "People" in the African Charter on Human and Peoples' Rights (1988), 82.

Similarly, the Assembly of Heads of State and Government of the Organization of African Unity (OAU) addressed the topic, emphasizing the distinction between the individual and the group in relation to the State.[24] This "African" approach stands in stark contrast to the typical Western perspective, which maintains a clear division between the State and the individual and does not consider the autonomous concept of groups' rights vis-à-vis the State.[25] We can also find this idea of "people as a contradistinction to the State" in other African Declarations, such as the Algiers Declaration.[26] Of course, this concept carries the potential for conflict, especially given the divergence between the state's and the people's interests.[27] However, we can say that—in the international context—governments cannot [always] be entrusted with the role of guardians of fundamental human rights, as demonstrated by government-led organizations in their efforts to protect and represent people's interests.[28]

In this context, clearly distinguishing between individual rights and people's rights is crucial for advancing this research project. According to Rich, three significant guidelines can be used in the coining of a more precise definition: (1) the individual remains the primary subject of international human rights law; (2) international human rights law recognizes the existence of groups; (3) the enjoyment of individual human rights requires certain human rights to be delegated directly upon groups.[29]

These three aspects have already highlighted the challenges faced by people as rights-holders. Hence, if we accept that human rights can also be bestowed upon groups, making people the right-holders of human rights, the question arises: "Can human rights be vested in States?"[30] Indeed, an overwhelming majority will deny this, arguing that "human rights are always vested in the individual"

---

[24] Rapporteur's Report, 1981; CM/1149 (XXXVII), Annex 1, para. 13: *Nothing that in Africa, Man is part and parcel of the group, some delegations concluded that individual rights could be explained and justified only by the rights of the community. Consequently, they wished that the Draft Charter made room for the Peoples' Rights and adopt(ed) a more balanced approach to economic, social and cultural rights on the one hand and political and civil rights on the other.*

[25] R. Kiwanuka (note 32), 82.

[26] Ibid., 83.

[27] Ibid.

[28] *R. A. Falk*, Human rights and state sovereignty, 1981, 189 et seq.

[29] *R. Rich*, The right to development: A right of peoples?, 1988, 43.

[30] R. Kiwanuka (note 32), 86; P. Alston (note 353 in Chap. 3), 290.

and that collective human rights, such as the right to freedom of association, are ultimately destined for individuals.[31]

Therefore, recognizing collective rights as *sui generis*, belonging to groups, communities, or peoples with individuals as the beneficiaries, seems an adequate approach.[32] Thus, collective rights play a more critical role in international law than in classical public law disputes, where the counterparts are the State and the individual. In conclusion, individual human rights are essential within a state entity, whereas collective rights serve as their counterparts in the international context.[33] Therefore, it is worthwhile to examine the idea of people as rights-holders.

4.2.2 Definition of People

The definition of the term "people" is one of the most difficult in international law. People were defined over centuries as depending on the State. According to a broad majority of scholars, the State has to be understood as "the plenipotentiary or international dimension of peoples".[34] In this statement, the dichotomy in defining people dependent on the State becomes apparent. At the beginning of international law, in the Peace of Westphalia in 1648, an attempt was made to define sovereignty for the first time.[35] During this process, the distinction between the so-called "communities" and "societies"—the then-standard terms, now replaced by the modern concepts of "nation" and "people"—was established.[36] The same differentiation still exists in the "United Nations".[37] As we can see, even in this early stage of sovereignty creation, these two aspects of sovereignty have gone hand in hand, and to this day, we cannot consider them separately. Therefore, defining people as completely isolated from the State provokes many complications in international law.

---

[31] R. Kiwanuka (note 32), 85; P. Alston (note 353 in Chap. 3), 290.

[32] R. Kiwanuka (note 32), 85; S. Iglesias Sánchez (note 10), p. 218–219; *G. Otis/A. Laurent,* Indigenous land claims in Europe, Arctic Review on Law and Politics 4 (2013), 166.

[33] R. Kiwanuka (note 32), 86.

[34] S. Willcox (note 7 in Chap. 1), 106.

[35] S. J. Anaya (note 6), 156; *J. Anaya,* International Human Rights and Indigenous Peoples (2009), 40.

[36] G. J. Abhimanyu (note 222 in Chap. 3), 6 et seq; *R. Nicholson,* Statehood and the State-Like in International Law, 2019, 1 et seq.

[37] G. J. Abhimanyu (note 222 in Chap. 3), 6 et seq; R. Nicholson (note 45), 1 et seq.

According to the analysis of Cristescu, who compared the use of the words "State", "nation", and "people" in international documents, *e.g.*, of the technical committee, the word "State" is often found in the context of determining functions of organizations, concerning security or non-security fields, or in the distinction between member and non-member.[38] Contrary to its colloquial use, the term "nation" often refers to a broader, non-political sense, encompassing colonies, mandates, protectorates, quasi-states, and the States themselves.[39] By contrast, the notion of "people" is emphasized in the context of speaking about the idea of "all mankind" or "all human beings".[40]

By contrast, Cassese defined the people as "conglomerates of individuals whose wishes and aspirations must be taken into account and given as much legal force as possible."[41] While this attempt is praiseworthy, it does not yield a satisfactory result. What initially seems like a purely philosophical approach must be set in a "collectively organized" context.[42] Consequently, Cassese could not determine "the people" completely detached from the State or another type of "structural organization".[43]

Other attempts at definition seem too narrow for the inevitable state of flux to which this expression is submitted. Exemplary is the approach of the International Meeting of Experts of the UNESCO in 1989, which argued that "the people" is "a group, which shares some form of collective identity—like a common history, race or ethnicity, language, culture, religion, ideology, attachment to land or economic life; meet some minimum population requirement; hold some collective will or consciousness as a people; and share institutions that express some form of collective identity".[44] Similarly, Crawford defines "peoples" as relating to "a specific type of human community sharing a common desire to establish an entity to ensure a common future".[45]Also Hannum's definition refers to the "self" of "self-determination" consisting of subjective and objective components, including

---

[38] A. Cristescu (note 10 in Chap. 3), 38, para. 262.

[39] Ibid.; C. J. Iorns Magallanes (note 285 in Chap. 3), 238.

[40] A. Cristescu (note 10 in Chap. 3), 38, para. 262.

[41] *A. Cassese*, in: V. Lowe/M. Fitzmaurice, Fifty years of the International Court of Justice, 1996, 361.

[42] S. Willcox (note 7 in Chap. 1), 106.

[43] *Compare*: Discussion about *Western Sahara,* 16.10.1975: A. Cassese (note 50), 360; S. Willcox (note 7 in Chap. 1), 106.

[44] *International Meeting of Experts on Further Study on the Concept of the Rights of Peoples; Final Report and Recommendations,* SHS-89/CONF.602/7, 27.11.1989, para. 22–23.

[45] C. J. Iorns Magallanes (note 285 in Chap. 3), 288; *J. Crawford (ed),* The rights of peoples, 1988, 169 et seq; C. Nine (note 38 in Chap. 1), 50, 59.

ethnical, linguistic, historical and religious differentiator.[46] This vague and broad approach risks including groups with no connection to the legal concept of self-determination or permanent sovereignty over natural resources, such as football or tennis clubs, which, as everyone will agree, cannot be rightful holders of the right to self-determination.[47] Others see the problem of such a broad definition in drawing the line between people and ethnic groups, insisting on their opinion that ethnic groups only enjoy minority rights, and thereby denying the right of self-determination for indigenous people.[48] Moreover, this approach harbors the risk of introducing further uncertainties, particularly regarding definitions such as race and ideology.[49]

Therefore, many scholars argue that the definition should follow a case-by-case approach, so that "peoples" are defined according to particular groups for which the right to self-determination has already been acknowledged. According to this opinion, people are (a) a population of trust or non-self-governing territories, (b) a population that is subject to foreign occupation or subjugation, and (c) racial minority groups that are denied fair access to political institutions. However, this approach appears outdated and only partially aligns with the concept of political self-determination.[50] This approach focuses solely on the internal aspect of self-determination and does not address the PSNR topic in this research project. However, we can infer that all these groups are "facing a handful of threats identified in international law as warranting the protection of a right to self-determination".[51]

Furthermore, what many scholars have in common in their attempts at definition is the link to the territory, particularly in the context of dis- or replacement of the people from their "homeland".[52] For instance, Cristescu stressed that "people" are defined by their relationship to a territory, rather than as a social entity. He underlined expressively that people should not be confused with ethnic, religious, or linguistic minorities in contrast to Article 27 ICCPR.[53] Even though

---

[46] H. Hannum (note 63 in Chap. 2), 16, 35.

[47] S. Willcox (note 7 in Chap. 1), 107; R. Kiwanuka (note 32), 85.

[48] R. Lapidoth and H. Owada (note 342 in Chap. 3), 64; D. Miller (note 83 in Chap. 3), 164 et seq.

[49] *I. Brownlie*, in: J. Crawford, The rights of peoples, 1988, 104, 107–108; R. Kiwanuka (note 32), 87.

[50] R. Kiwanuka (note 32), 89.

[51] S. Willcox (note 7 in Chap. 1), 107.

[52] A. Skordas (note 323 in Chap. 3), 219; *M. Moore,* Place-related attachments and global distributive justice, Journal of Global Ethics 9 (2013), 218.

[53] A. Cristescu (note 10 in Chap. 3), 12, para. 279.

this Article does not emphasize the connection between cultural rights and land rights,[54] the territorial link appears to be one of the few areas of agreement among the numerous opinions on the definition of people. This is particularly true when discussing minorities or indigenous peoples, which will be addressed at a later point.[55]

4.2.2.1 People as the Whole Population of a State

Starting with the classical view of people as the population of the State, we must return to the definition of a State. Article 1 of the Montevideo Convention on the Rights and Duties of States of 1933 sets out four requirements for defining a State: a permanent population, a defined territory, a government, and independence, which can be equated with the capacity to enter into relationships with other States.[56] This regional convention defines the State in this manner for the first and only time in an international treaty, based on Jellinek's philosophical theory of a State, which is extended to include another criterion: the capacity to enter into relationships with other States.[57]

In the case of this definition, the population complies with the functional requirement that the territory had to be settled, similar to the differentiation between an island in Article 121 (1) UNCLOS and a rock, which cannot sustain human habitation or economic life of its own, according to Article 121 (3) UNCLOS.[58] Consequently, the permanent population, as defined in this sense, represents a collective settlement or a stable community.[59] The definition requires a population, but a few people are sufficient to qualify as a State.[60] Moreover,

---

[54] *J. Gilbert,* Land Rights as Human Rights: The case for a specific Right to Land, International Journal on Human Rights (2013), 119.

[55] R. Kiwanuka (note 32), 87 et seq.; H. Hannum (note 63 in Chap. 2), 36.

[56] Montevideo Convention on Rights and Duties of States, 26.12.1933, Art. 1: "*The state as a person of international law should possess the following qualifications: a. a permanent population; b. a defined territory; c. government; and d. capacity to enter into relations with the other States.*"

[57] *H. Sodan/J. Ziekow,* Grundkurs Öffentliches Recht: Staats- und Verwaltungsrecht, 10th ed., 2023, Sec. 4, para. 1–2.

[58] *J. Grote Stoutenburg,* in: M. B. Gerrard, Threatened Island Nations, 2013, 64.

[59] I. Brownlie and J. Crawford (note 30 in Chap. 2), 118.

[60] Resolution A/RES/2869(XXVI): Question of American Samoa, Bahamas, Bermuda, Brithish Virgin Islands, Brunei, Cayman Islands, Cocos (Keeling) Islands, Gilbert and Ellice Islands, Guam, Montserrat, New Hebrides, Pitcairn, St.Helena, Seychelles, Solomon Islands, Turks and Caicos Islands and the United States Virgin Islands, 29.12.1971; A/RES/2869(XXVI).

the corporate feeling of living together has to bond the population.[61] Therefore, it is considered insufficient that a "basic infrastructure at its disposal providing for the vital necessities of human life" exists.[62] Consequently, we can note that this very technical definition also includes the idea of a standard tie within the population.

Therefore, according to the definition of Statehood, the population of an existing State is considered the people.[63] That complies with the other criterion of Statehood under the Montevideo Convention, which requires an operating governmental system. Consequently, following the traditional theory of a "legitimate State", the definition of an "initially unconnected group of citizens may be made into a 'people' by cooperating in the shared institutions" is predominant.[64] Therefore, political identity is the foundation of a sense of belonging.[65] The ICJ reached a similar conclusion in the Western Sahara case, where it determined that "common institutions or organs" are decisive in deciding questions of sovereignty and self-determination.[66] However, people do not comply with the definition if they adopt only a passive role within the State's structure. There is a mutual obligation between the "members of a people" and the State. On the one hand, the State has to maintain an effective system of law "that rules in the name of the people" and is "responsive to their values".[67] On the other hand, the people have to be "engaged in shaping and sustaining their common institutions of Statehood". The Administrative Court of Cologne affirmed "a population is not merely an association for tax or commercial purposes but a dynamic, flourishing community with shared institutions and a common life or 'destiny'".[68]

However, only the tie of a shared political system can hold individuals together and determine them as "members of a people".[69] In particular, in the case of undemocratic, totalitarian regimes, there is agreement among scholars that

---

61 J. Grote Stoutenburg (note 67), 64.

62 *Case "Sealand"*, 9 K 2565/77, 03.05.1978, 511 et seq.; J. Grote Stoutenburg (note 67), 64.

63 S. Willcox (note 7 in Chap. 1), 108.

64 *A. Stilz,* Nations, States, and Territory, Ethics 121 (2011), 579 et seq.; S. Willcox (note 7 in Chap. 1), 108.

65 A. Banai (note 382 in Chap. 3), 50.

66 *Western Sahara,* 16.10.1975, 55, para. 149.

67 A. Stilz (note 73), 587 et seq.; S. Willcox (note 7 in Chap. 1), 108.

68 *Case "Sealand"*, 9 K 2565/77, 03.05.1978, 688; S. Willcox (note 7 in Chap. 1), 109.

69 A. Stilz (note 73), 597.

the capacity for collective autonomy is in abeyance, or, in other words, "people share political bonds even when their history is undemocratic".[70] Similarly, the definition supported by Hannum suggests "a people consists of a community of individuals bound together by mutual loyalties, an identifiable tradition, and a common cultural awareness, (…)".[71] Banai indicates that national self-government and identity must be built on "other values such as trust and social justice".[72] In conclusion, already in the State of annexation or dissolution, the people "may continue to hold a residual right to self-determination for a certain time."[73] However, they are turning, to say it in the words of Kant, into a "moral person".[74] Consequently, Kant argued "the State is a collectivity of individuals, and that no one but the individuals themselves can make decisions concerning their lives".[75]

Moreover, numerous examples show that a State need not "be composed of only a single people".[76] To name a few, the Swiss, Indians, Nigerians, and Guatemalans already unite a variety of different "people" within a single State and therefore represent multinational States.[77] All these issues show us that the equalization between the population of a State and "the people" does not adequately describe the people as such. Especially taking into account that the right

[70] A. Stilz (note 73), 592.

[71] H. Hannum (note 63 in Chap. 2), 36.

[72] A. Banai (note 382 in Chap. 3), 51.

[73] S. Willcox (note 7 in Chap. 1), 110; A. Stilz (note 73), 575.

[74] *I. Kant,* Zum ewigen Frieden (1795), 20.687: *Was das Völkerrecht betrifft.—Nur unter Voraussetzung irgend eines rechtlichen Zustandes (d.i. derjenigen äußeren Bedingung, unter der dem Menschen ein Recht wirklich zu Teil werden kann) kann von einem Völkerrecht die Rede sein; weil es, als ein öffentliches Recht, die Publikation eines, jedem das Seine bestimmenden, allgemeinen Willens schon in seinem Begriffe enthält, und dieser status iuridicus muss aus irgend einem Vertrage hervorgehen, der nicht eben (gleich dem) woraus ein Staat entspringt, auf Zwangsgesetzte gegründet sein darf, sondern allenfalls auch der einer fortwährend—freien Assoziation sein kann, wie (…) der Föderalität verschiedener Staaten. Denn ohne irgend einen rechtlichen Zustand, der die verschiedenen (physischen oder moralischen) Personen tätig verknüpft, mithin im Naturstande, kann es kein anderes als bloß ein Privatrecht geben.* Kant, Perpetual Peace, 8:344: *For a state is not (like the land on which it resides) a belonging (patrimonium): it is a society of human beings that no one other than itself can command or dispose of. Like a trunk, it has its own roots, and to annex it to another state as a graft is to do away with its existence as a moral person and to make a moral person into a thing, and so to contradict the idea of the original contract, apart from which no right over a people can be thought.*

[75] T. Gullberg (note 12 in Chap. 3), 36.

[76] H. Hannum (note 63 in Chap. 2), 36.

[77] Ibid.

of self-determination is considered a human right, people "may include a portion of the population of an existing State", but not the whole population.[78] Therefore, the majority of scholars argue that "the traditional tools (…) for managing the system may have to be reexamined and reconstituted in the light of this novel situation", considering also ethnical groups or indigenous peoples as right-holders of the right of self-determination and PSNR.[79] It is also likely that we need to consider a broader definition of the people than just the population of a State. Even though the State claims to be both the legal and the moral authority in the modern political understanding, this does not include, in many cases, the aspect of Kant's "moral person".[80]

4.2.2.2 The "Peoplehood"

While bearing this idea in mind, another interesting approach to defining "peoplehood" warrants mention. The notion is derived from the biblical context, referring to the Jewish people and other groups.[81] However, it has also arisen in the setting of international law, for the first time during the World Council of Indigenous Peoples (WCIP) 1975, where the first General Assembly included it in the Declaration:[82]

> *"Now, we come from the four corners of the earth,*
>
> *We protest before the Concert of Nations,*
>
> *that, 'we are the indigenous peoples,*
>
> *we who have a consciousness of culture and peoplehood…'*
>
> *We vow to control again our own destiny and*
>
> *recover our complete humanity and*
>
> *pride in being indigenous people."*[83]

---

[78] G. Pentassuglia (note 341 in Chap. 3), 465.

[79] R. Lapidoth and H. Owada (note 342 in Chap. 3), 65, 69.

[80] J. A. Simmons (note 15 in Chap. 3), 301.

[81] Merriam Webster Dictionary, https://www.merriam-webster.com/dictionary/peoplehood.

[82] *J. Castellino,* International Law and Indigenous Peoples: Part I—Human Rights Instruments and Indigenous Peoples (2005), 74.

[83] *Extract from* Declaration from the First General Assembly, Port Albemi, BC Canada, 10.1975.

The notion is also found in other contexts and can be related to the following attributes: "the commonality of interests, group identity, distinctiveness, and a territorial link".[84] Stilz defined peoplehood as the counterpart to a nation, meaning "a self-determining group need not share cultural features but is defined by some other tie."[85] As already noticed above, this definition not only allows the subsumption of minority groups or indigenous people, but it also could include "a group of persons within a specific geographical entity, as well as all the persons within that entity".[86] This suggests that peoplehood and the right of self-determination cannot be confined "within the straitjacket of an independent Statehood", so we have to think outside the box.[87]

Numerous examples in the history of international law illustrate various approaches to recognizing peoplehood within the framework of the State.[88] One example is the Good Friday Agreement of 1998 between Britain and Ireland, which recognizes the exercise of self-determination by the people of Ireland in both the North and the South.[89] This case shows that "behind state sovereignty is a notion of shared peoplehood, evident in different forms of succession", *e.g.*, in Hong Kong, Germany, or the former Yugoslavia.[90] For instance, the National Assembly of Kosovo declared its independence on 17 February 2008, invoking "the call of the people to build a society that honors human dignity [and to reflect the] will of [the] people".[91] In sum, there must be an entity, which might be called "peoplehood," and which must be differentiated from the State's institutional structure.[92] However, we cannot reduce peoplehood—as opposed to Statehood—to the relational tie between the persons. Relational values, which

[84] R. Kiwanuka (note 32), 87 et seq.

[85] A. Stilz (note 85 in Chap. 2), 28.

[86] R. Kiwanuka (note 32), 88.

[87] Ibid., 92.

[88] *J. Summers*, Peoples and international law, 2014, 474.

[89] Good Friday Agreement, 10.04.1998; GFA, Art. 1(II): *recognize that it is for the people of the island of Ireland alone, by agreement between the two parts respectively and without external impediment, to exercise their right of self-determination on the basis of consent, freely and concurrently given, North and South, to bring about a united Ireland, if that is their wish, accepting that this right must be achieved and exercised with and subject to the agreement and consent of a majority of the people of Northern Ireland...*

[90] J. Summers (note 98), 480.

[91] Declaration of independence, 17.02.2008; Z. OKLOPCIC (note 321 in Chap. 3), 677.

[92] A. Stilz (note 73), 575, 594.

extend beyond the state's non-relational interests, play a significant role in defining peoplehood.[93] However, "peoplehood is not a voluntary association" in the sense that a friendship is.[94] According to Moore, in contrast to the "shared we" in a sense of a social group or type of collective agent, "peoplehood" unites the shared aspiration to exercise collective self-government.[95]

The opinions remain divided. On the one hand, scholars like Crawford argue that "people" can or even have to exist before a predetermined unit later founded as, *e.g.*, a State: "the people are nothing more than a *terminus technicus* that international law uses to describe a phase in a process of polity formation."[96] Similarly, Jennings' famous words state, "[the idea of self-determination of People is] ridiculous, because the people cannot decide until somebody decides who the people are."[97] Koskenniemi also, in picking up the "civil idea of self-determination," concluded "the people are artificial communities, collections of individuals which exist only by belonging to the same constitutional order".[98] A close relative of this idea is the "legitimate State theory" by Stilz, who recognizes the "residual claim of the people to reconstitute themselves as a legitimate State", but deprives them of the status of "a cultural group" and only considers them as "simply [as] the collective subject of a prior State".[99]

All these approaches raise the question of whether people can exist without a State. This allows us to revisit the early ideas of statehood by Thomas Hobbes and Jean-Jacques Rousseau, considered the progenitors of the principle of self-determination.[100] Hobbes recognized the notion of self-determination, arguing that "commonwealth is said to be instituted when a multitude of men agree and covenant, everyone with everyone".[101] Rousseau, in contrast, argued

93 Ibid., 596.

94 Ibid.

95 M. Moore (note 157 in Chap. 3), 50; A. Stilz (note 85 in Chap. 2), 29.

96 J. Crawford (note 144 in Chap. 3), 100; Z. OKLOPCIC (note 321 in Chap. 3), p. 682.

97 *I. Jennings*, The approach to self-government, 1958, 56; Z. OKLOPCIC (note 321 in Chap. 3), p. 682.

98 *M. Koskenniemi*, National self-determination today: Problems of legal theory and practice, 1994, 249; Z. OKLOPCIC (note 321 in Chap. 3), 682.

99 A. Stilz (note 73), 575.

100 Z. OKLOPCIC (note 321 in Chap. 3), 682.

101 *T. Hobbes*, Leviathan, 1651, 133, para. 88; *T. Hobbes*, Leviathan., 2000, 79; Z. OKLOPCIC (note 321 in Chap. 3), 682.

that "the people are created when each one of us puts [his person] into the community...and under the supreme direction of the general will".[102] Both theories suggest the concept of peoplehood before the establishment of unity. In addition, Rousseau's idea of the installation of the territory suggests that "lands of private persons when they are united and contiguous become public property".[103] We can also find references to a predetermined geographical area in Hobbes' Leviathan.[104]

Consequently, we can say that individuals existed before the State existed. Only to what extent are they already "united as a people"? There are three theories today elaborating on the question of external self-determination and, in extension of this thought, the importance of peoplehood within this principle. The first one, the so-called "choice theory", is equivalent to the approach of Rousseau of an "aggregate of individual rights", which is to say that a "new polity is legitimate, if there is a sufficient number of individuals desiring to create their own polity".[105] The second theory, the nationalist theory, aligns with the legitimate State theory and requires individuals or minorities who wish to create a new State to "belong[ing] to a nation."[106] This requirement should avoid the unwanted situation in which militant groups or guerrillas could invoke the right to self-determination.[107] Consequently, drawing boundaries around groups would enable the collective autonomy of the "nation" or "people."[108] Both theories entail the risk that a national majority could abuse the principle of *uti possidetis* "to promote its culture and perpetuate its way of life."[109] The third theory gives the right of secession to people who are suffering grave injustices by the

---

[102] *J.-J. 1.-1. Rousseau,* An inquiry into the nature of the social contract, 1791, 61; Z. OKLOPCIC (note 321 in Chap. 3), 682.

[103] J.-J. 1.-1. Rousseau (note 112), 67; Z. OKLOPCIC (note 321 in Chap. 3), 684.

[104] T. Hobbes (note 111), 81: Chapter XVIII: *"because the major part hath by consenting voices declared a sovereign, he that dissented must now consent with the rest; that is, be contented to avow all the actions he shall do, or else justly be destroyed by the rest. If he does not follow through, then (he) must...be left in the condition of war he was in before"*; Z. OKLOPCIC (note 321 in Chap. 3), 684.

[105] Z. OKLOPCIC (note 321 in Chap. 3), 687.

[106] Ibid.

[107] Ibid., 688; M. Moore (note 115 in Chap. 3), 171.

[108] Z. OKLOPCIC (note 321 in Chap. 3), 688; M. Moore (note 115 in Chap. 3), 199 et seq.

[109] M. Moore (note 115 in Chap. 3), 157; Z. OKLOPCIC (note 321 in Chap. 3), 688; *J. Castellino and N. Walsh (eds),* International Law and Indigenous Peoples, 2005, 92.

State they live in, like genocide or discrimination.[110] However, drawing the line to determine the seriousness of injustice appears problematic.

All these theories acknowledge people who are unwilling or unable to unite into a State. As a result, Skordas considers self-determination to be an interplay among the *pouvoir constituant*, the people, and external actors.[111] According to him, the "self" will be determined by two factors: the constituent power of a military group or radical political parties and the external recognition by other States.[112] In sum, people choose the status of a unit once external actors have designated it as a candidate for independent statehood.[113] Consequently, the international community's external power plays a decisive role in recognizing people and establishing statehood.

In conclusion, to gain a more precise understanding of self-determination, the concept of peoplehood can serve as a "goal to be sought, never attainable, always receding, but approachable and worth approaching."[114] Moreover, we can conclude that self-determination can strengthen the sense of civic solidarity —the sense of "being in it together" —in a territorial political project that goes further than mere "ethno-nationalist" group interests.[115] In particular, in today's ideals of political involvement, invoking "the people" is "particularly well suited for contemporary societies and temperaments".[116] Therefore, we can summarize the idea of peoplehood independently of the State, particularly within the concepts of an already existing structure or the separation of a State.

4.2.2.3 History and Development of Minorities

In considering the process of recognizing peoplehood, let us examine the development of minority rights, which are likely among the first groups to be identified. After World War II, with its fatal consequences and discrimination against groups viewed as separate and different from the majority, the clamor for a strengthening of minority rights arose.[117] However, this did not seem as self-evident as it

---

[110] Z. OKLOPCIC (note 321 in Chap. 3), 688; W. K. Barth (note 316 in Chap. 3), 88.

[111] Z. OKLOPCIC (note 321 in Chap. 3), 690.

[112] Ibid.

[113] Ibid., 696.

[114] *E. S. Morgan*, Inventing the people: The rise of popular sovereignty in England and America, 1988, 306; Z. OKLOPCIC (note 321 in Chap. 3), 700.

[115] Z. OKLOPCIC (note 321 in Chap. 3), 699.

[116] *W. E. Connolly*, The ethos of pluralization, 1995, XX–XXI; Z. OKLOPCIC (note 321 in Chap. 3), 700.

[117] W. K. Barth (note 316 in Chap. 3), 69 et seq.; G. Pentassuglia (note 372 in Chap. 3), 187 et seq.

should have been because already during the discussion in the UN Human Rights Commission in 1947, the Americans postulated, for the fear of a reinvigoration of the Native Americans, that:[118]

> *"The aim of States was to assimilate and absorb large foreign groups and to make them part of the nation. (...) Minority questions did not exist on the American Continent. (...) The United States' experience with foreign groups residing within its borders has been positive, emphasizing assimilation throughout. (...) Provisions relating to minorities had no place in a declaration of human rights."*[119]

Even though there was a strong opposition, here represented by the President Benes of Czechoslovakia, by the statement:

> *"Minorities in individual States must never again be given the character of internationally recognized political and legal units, with the possibility of again becoming sources of disturbance."*[120]

The first Resolution of the UN General Assembly determined that

> *"The United Nations could not remain indifferent to the fate of minorities, but (...) decides not to deal in a specific provision with the question of minorities in the text of [the] Declaration."*[121]

One of the first steps of inclusion of minorities was the Genocide Convention in 1948, where the crime of genocide was created in international criminal law to avoid further crimes against other ethnic or minority groups.[122] This was followed by Article 27 of the ICCPR in 1966,[123] which recognized minority rights

[118] W. K. Barth (note 316 in Chap. 3), 74.

[119] Ibid., 73.

[120] Ibid., 71; E. Charles-Newton and E. A. Kronk (note 161 in Chap. 3), 67 et seq.

[121] Resolution 217 A (III): Universal Declaration of Human Rights, 10.12.1948; A/RES/3/217 A; W. K. Barth (note 316 in Chap. 3), 78.

[122] W. K. Barth (note 316 in Chap. 3), 78 et seq.; *J. Gilbert,* Indigenous Rights in the Making: The United Nations Declaration on the Rights of Indigenous Peoples, International Journal on Minority and Group Rights 14 (2007), 223; J. Crawford (note 54), 171; T. Aqorau (note 221 in Chap. 2), 218.

[123] International Covenant on Civil and Political Rights (note 6 in Chap. 2), Art. 27: *In those States in which ethnic, religious or linguistic minorities exist, persons belonging to such minorities shall not be denied the right, in community with the other members of their group, to enjoy their own culture, to profess and practice their own religion, or to use their own language.*

as human rights for the first time.[124] However, until the early 1980s, the dominant approach was "that there was no alternative to assimilation within other societies".[125] The UN standards of human rights were adopted by the Council of Europe's Framework Convention for the Protection of National Minorities in 1995.[126] This development is closely linked to the adoption of the ILO Convention 169 in 1989, which included a proposal to strengthen the rights of Indigenous Peoples. However, only ten States ultimately ratified it.[127] Finally, UNDRIP was adopted in 2007.[128]

However, all these efforts were based on the premise that States uphold the standards of the minority, derived from the individualistic approach to human rights, thereby defending "nation-state-based sovereignty."[129] The connection between minority rights and the international human rights regime raises questions about States' legally binding obligations and the recognition of minority societies.[130] The human rights approach developed a "hybrid character", which demonstrated once again, "the incompatibility of group-based rights with the liberal theory" and, therefore, "a political compromise between claims by national groups with Nation-States that fetter minority group secession".[131] The strengthening of minority rights always signifies an interference in and limitation of the State's leeway, and, therefore, States, in particular, autocratic States, try to suppress minority rights.[132] The reaffirmation of minority rights as a basic standard of social and political stability, diversity, and the enhancement of democracy and respect for human rights in various UN Declarations at the beginning of the new millennium is a symptom of this development.[133] All of these attempts were

---

[124] G. Pentassuglia (note 372 in Chap. 3), 188 et seq.; W. K. Barth (note 316 in Chap. 3), 79.

[125] R. Pitty (note 311 in Chap. 3), 45.

[126] G. Pentassuglia (note 372 in Chap. 3), 189.

[127] *Ratification by the States: Denmark, Norway, Bolivia, Costa Rica, Guatemala, Honduras, Mexico, Paraguay, Peru;* ibid., p. 189; *A. Kuper,* The Return of the Native, Current Anthropology 44 (2003), 390; G. Otis and A. Laurent (note 41), 163.

[128] G. Pentassuglia (note 372 in Chap. 3), 189.

[129] Ibid., 190; *S. Young,* Re-historicising dissolved identities: Deskaheh, the League of Nations, and international legal discourse on Indigenous peoples, London Review of International Law 7 (2019), 396.

[130] G. Pentassuglia (note 372 in Chap. 3), 190.

[131] W. K. Barth (note 316 in Chap. 3), 95; *compare:* J. A. Simmons (note 15 in Chap. 3), 301.

[132] G. Pentassuglia (note 372 in Chap. 3), 201.

[133] Ibid., 193, 201; A/RES/55/2: United Nations Millennium Declaration, 18.09.2000; A/RES/55/2; Report of the High-Level Panel on Threats, Challenges and Change on a more

criticized because "real democracy is absent", which would safeguard the rights, interests, and, in particular, the voices of minorities.[134]

Suppose the legislative or executive power is absent. In that case, the decisive step comes from judicial decisions, specifically from international courts and institutions and their landmark cases concerning minority and indigenous rights.[135] The starting point is the *Awas Tinkni* case in Nicaragua[136] or the *Nanuvut*[137] case in Canada, but the *Saramaka People vs. Suriname* in 2007[138] showed a new jurisprudence perspective. What all these cases have in common is that they were brought to court by minorities or indigenous peoples as a group and not as individuals. In the Saramaka case, even though the Saramaka People do not meet the classical requirements of indigenous peoples, as they are descendants of African slaves brought to South America during the colonization period, the Court awarded them the status of indigenous peoples concerning specific rights.[139] Consequently, they not only exercised their right to participate but also claimed party status, becoming active members of the proceeding.[140] Therefore, the question of the Saramaka people as a juridical personality was resolved, and their group identity acknowledged.[141] This angle based on juridical fiction opens access to claims before international and domestic bodies, thereby "expanding the avenue to the four dimensions of international law, recognition, elaboration, mediation, and access to justice."[142] Finally, the Court recognized the collective dimension of reparations under Article 63 (1) of the American Convention on Human Rights (ACHR).[143] In conclusion, the classical approach to minorities has been superseded, and the right to participate has been affirmed as an expression of internal self-determination, through third-party intervention, based, inter

secure World: Our shared Responsibility, 02.12.2004; A/59/565; 2005 World Summit Outcome; A/RES/60/1.

[134] G. Pentassuglia (note 372 in Chap. 3), 194.

[135] Ibid., 196.

[136] J. Gilbert (note 132), 210.

[137] *N. Loukacheva,* Arctic indigenous peoples' internationalism: in search of a legal justification, Polar Record 45 (2009), 54 et seq.

[138] *Case of Saramaka People vs. Suriname,* No. 172, 28.11.2007.

[139] G. Pentassuglia (note 372 in Chap. 3), 193; J. Anaya (note 44), 293.

[140] *Case of Saramaka People vs. Suriname,* No. 172, 28.11.2007, para. 188–189; J. Anaya (note 44), 304, G. Pentassuglia (note 372 in Chap. 3), 200.

[141] G. Pentassuglia (note 372 in Chap. 3), 200; J. Anaya (note 44), 292 et seq.

[142] G. Pentassuglia (note 372 in Chap. 3), 200.

[143] Ibid., 204; G. Otis and A. Laurent (note 41), 166.

alia, on Article 27 of the ICCPR, as well as their external self-determination.[144] This development could be observed not only through direct minority participation, as in the case of the Saramaka people, but also through the intervention of Non-Governmental Organizations (NGOs).[145] In conclusion, the affirmation outshone the classical human rights approach and reached "dimensions of recognition and access to justice".[146] Consequently, several human rights supervisory organs, including the HRC, CERD, and the Inter-American and African systems, revised their jurisprudence and rules of procedure regarding *locus standi* to reflect the group's perspectives better.[147] These approaches have also found their way into regional and national jurisprudence.[148]

Contemplating the case *Saramaka People vs. Suriname*, where the descendants of African slaves were considered indigenous peoples, we must differentiate between minorities and indigenous peoples. [149] International courts also struggled to separate these terms. For instance, while the Inter-American Court of Human Rights (IACHR) affirmed the status of the Saramaka people as indigenous peoples contrary to the classical definition of indigeneity as "first people", the domestic court of Japan recognized the Ainu, one of the aboriginals of Japan, only as a minority group in the case *Kayano et al. vs. Hokkaido Expropriation Committee.*[150]

There are indeed some similarities between minorities and indigenous peoples, *e.g.*, the marginalization of these two groups. Some scholars already consider that concerning "the issues of self-determination, the treatment of minorities and the status of indigenous populations" are "in principle the same".[151] However, there are some pivotal differences, in particular concerning the aims of the two groups, so that indigenous people cannot be viewed as "just another minority

[144] G. Pentassuglia (note 372 in Chap. 3), 201; N. Schrijver (note 30), 92; *applicable for indigenous peoples for the recognition of their culture.*

[145] G. Pentassuglia (note 372 in Chap. 3), 205.

[146] Ibid., 203.

[147] *Case of Saramaka People vs. Suriname,* No. 172, 28.11.2007, para. 204; J. Anaya (note 44), 312 et seq.; G. Pentassuglia (note 372 in Chap. 3), 204.

[148] *Compare*: *Maya indigenous communities of the Toledo District vs. Belize,* OEA/Ser.L/V/II.122, doc. 5 rev. 1 (2004), 11.10.2004, para. 85, 111–119; G. Pentassuglia (note 371 in Chap. 3), 210.

[149] *Case of Saramaka People vs. Suriname,* No. 172, 28.11.2007; G. Pentassuglia (note 372 in Chap. 3), 198.

[150] *The Nibutani Dam Decision, Kayano et. al. vs. Hokkaido Expropriation Committee,* 27.03.1997; G. Pentassuglia (note 372 in Chap. 3), 203.

[151] I. Brownlie (note 58), 16; R. Pitty (note 311 in Chap. 3), 54.

group".[152] The greatest differentiations carved out by the UN's Working Groups on Minorities can be represented by the following comparison: minorities seek more institutional integration, not more institutional separateness, as seen in the case of indigenous peoples; they seek to exercise individual rights, not collective rights; and they seek non-discrimination, not self-government.[153] All these properties signify a minus to the demands of the indigenous peoples, who claim "the right to define their own membership".[154] Hence, non-discrimination signifies the recognition of "validity of diverse language, culture, and religion positively and directly, but rather by implication from an imaginatively interpreted standard".[155] In conclusion, the minorities have already internalized the doctrine of the colonial powers, or rather follow the course of assimilation and adaptation in favor of a dominant identity, while the indigenous peoples pursue the goal of separation.[156] In short: "the ultimate goal of their colonizers would be achieved by referring [the indigenous people] to minorities".[157]

Consequently, we can ascertain that the differentiation between the two groups is the distinctiveness of the indigenous peoples, "whereas minority rights aim at ensuring a space for pluralism in togetherness."[158] While both groups seek "the right to live without adverse discrimination", only indigenous peoples are currently recognized regarding political identity and self-government as a "matter of international law".[159] In other words, the distinction between indigenous peoples and minorities "is the status of individual and collective rights",[160] because the indigenous people always seek "a higher degree of autonomous development".[161]

---

[152] R. Pitty (note 311 in Chap. 3), 54.

[153] Prevention of Discrimination Against and the Protection of Minorities, 19.07.2000; E/CN.4/Sub.2/2000/10, U.N. cited in *W. Kymlicka,* The Internationalization of minority rights, International Journal of Constitutional Law (2008); *R. Shrinkhal,* Problems in Defining Indigenous Peoples unter International Law, Chotanagpur Law Journal (2014), 194; *compare:* R. Pitty (note 311 in Chap. 3), 57.

[154] H. A. Northcott (note 19 in Chap. 3), 77.

[155] W. K. Barth (note 316 in Chap. 3), 75.

[156] Ibid., 73.

[157] *P. Thornberry,* International law and the rights of minorities, 1991, 331; R. Shrinkhal (note 163), 194.

[158] R. Pitty (note 311 in Chap. 3), 56.

[159] Ibid., 56 et seq.

[160] Ibid., 57.

[161] Ibid., 56.

4.2.2.4 Indigenous Peoples as People

In exploring whether indigenous peoples are recognized as people, we must first define what it means to be recognized. We must first determine what constitutes indigenous peoples. Then, the question of the right of self-determination for indigenous peoples can be answered. The definition of indigenous peoples is an essential consideration for this research project for two key reasons: first, indigenous peoples are among the few remaining closed entities that still represent a prototype of community, and second, the inhabitants of disappearing islands are also considered indigenous peoples.

4.2.2.4.1 The Definition of Indigenous Peoples

First, we need to define the term "indigenous peoples" compared to the "population", as they do not view themselves as part of the latter. The definition of indigenous peoples is of equal importance to the correct use of the phrasing "indigenous peoples" in contrast to "indigenous people" or "indigenous populations", as many States continue to do to this day.[162] As opposed to the word "peoples", it "implies [neither] the right to full self-determination in international law" nor the claim to "Statehood or independence or any sort of secession".[163] According to the legal discourse, "indigenous" is to be understood in the sense of "native" or "originating or occurring naturally".[164] At the same time, terms like "Aboriginal" and "Indians" were rejected because of their negative historical context.[165] However, due to the lack of an official definition, there is no consensual definition of the term among the scholars, also because "the definition of indigenous populations "by themselves and their definition by others is a false dichotomy.[166] However, some similarities are found in many existing definitions. Nietzsche formulated one of the first types of genealogical examination:

---

[162] C. J. Iorns Magallanes (note 285 in Chap. 3), 212; S. Young (note 139), 391; R. Pitty (note 311 in Chap. 3), 46; *.R. Stavenhagen,* How Strong Are the Rights of Indigenous Peoples?, Journal of Human Rights 10 (2011), 418; S. *Oeter*, in: H. P. Hestermeyer, Coexistence, cooperation and solidarity: Liber amicorum Rüdiger Wolfrum, 2012, 481.

[163] C. J. Iorns Magallanes (note 285 in Chap. 3), 215.

[164] R. Shrinkhal (note 163), 188.

[165] H. Berman et al. (note 298 in Chap. 3), 195.

[166] I. Brownlie (note 58), 6.

> *"Line of descent that can be continuously traced from a common ancestor and that would enable us to trace moral notions and legal practices back to a natural, single, and fixed origin."*[167]

For instance, Anaya defines indigenous peoples as "the living descendants of preinvasion inhabitants of lands now dominated by others", who are "culturally distinct groups that find themselves engulfed by settler societies born of the forces of empire and conquest".[168] The ILO Convention 169[169], as well as José R. Martínez-Cobo, United Nations Special Rapporteur, determined that "indigenous communities, peoples and nations" adhere to criteria like non-dominance, distinctive culture, and determination to preserve, and they strive to develop and convey ethnic identity and the bond to ancestral territories to future generations.[170]

Some voices nowadays define the main characteristics of indigenousness as rooted in an association with a particular place, its territory.[171] Hence, the concept of indigenous peoples originated from their ties to a territory, a notion also affirmed by the IACHR.[172] Mostly, they are not only the erstwhile societies and first inhabitants of the given territory, but this territory also represents a "fundamental and multidimensional space" for them, "for the creation and recreation of the ecological, economic, and cultural practices of communities".[173] As it was declared in the 2002 Kimberly Declaration, where the indigenous peoples proclaimed:

---

[167] *C. Diethe/F. Nietzsche,* Introduction: on Nietzsche's critique of morality. Friedrich Nietzsche: On the Genealogy of Morality, XX; S. Young (note 139), 389.

[168] J. Anaya (note 44), 56.

[169] *C169—Indigenous and Tribal Peoples Convention,* C169, 27.06.1989.

[170] R. Shrinkhal (note 163), 188 et seq.

[171] *A. Mühlebach,* "Making Place" at the United Nations: Indigenous Cultural Politics at the U.N. Working Group on Indigenous Populations (2001), 416.

[172] *Compare*: R. Shrinkhal (note 163), 195: *"the indigenous population is structured on the basis of its profound relationship with the land (...) land, for indigenous peoples, is a condition of individual security and liaison with the group (...) the recovery, recognition, demarcation, and registration of the lands represents essential rights for cultural survival and for maintaining the community's integrity."*

[173] *A. Escobar,* Whose Knowledge, Whose nature? Biodiversity, Conservation, and the Political Ecology of Social Movements, Journal of Political Ecology (1998), 69; A. Mühlebach (note 181), 417.

> *"Our land and territories are at the core of our existence – we are the land and the land is us (...) we are the original peoples tied to the land by our umbilical and the dust of our ancestors."*[174]

As this quote shows, the indigenous peoples have a different understanding of their land; they not only see themselves as the "first people" with an entitlement to the land, but also see the relationship to the land as "inherently moral, non-destructive".[175] This morality is, according to some scholars, the very basis of the entitlement to the land because "States have no moral basis on which to argue for their rights to their present territories".[176]

At the same time, this means that when any subsequent society arrived, a dominant societal group was already in place, and both groups exhibited cultural diversity.[177] Kingsbury considered four criteria for the definition: delimitation from a distinct ethnic group, the experience of severe disruption or exploitation, a significant historical connection with a particular territorial unit, and the wish to retain its distinctive identity.[178] He also considered this approach "coming from five different directions: non-discrimination, minority rights, self-determination, historical sovereignty, and *sui generis* claims".[179]

The UNDRIP itself does not define the term indigenous people.[180] That may seem remarkable, but it reveals the problem with an official definition: a rigid definition of indigenous peoples could limit the indigenous group's ability to exercise its fundamental right to self-determination and would hardly be open to modification.[181] However, the scope of application is somewhat vague within the

---

[174] International Indigenous Peoples Summit on Sustainable Development Khoi-San Territory Kimberly, South Africa, 20.08.2002; The Kimberly Declaration; R. Shrinkhal (note 163), 195.

[175] A. Mühlebach (note 181), 426.

[176] C. J. Iorns Magallanes (note 285 in Chap. 3), 332; A. Mühlebach (note 181), 428.

[177] *P. Thornberry*, Indigenous peoples and human rights, 2002, 39; R. Shrinkhal (note 163), 190.

[178] *B. Kingsbury*, "Indigenous peoples" in international law: A constructuvist approach to the Asian controversy, 1998, 453; R. Shrinkhal (note 163), 190; *similar more general approach:* M. Moore (note 157 in Chap. 3), 59 et seq.; *critical to this anthropological approach:* A. Kuper (note 137), 396: "*the definition of indigenous and the authentic images of indigenous peoples are based on the assumption of ties of blood and soil derived from the Euro-American essentialist or nationalist ideology of culture and identity (...) constructed regardless of the reality of indigenous peoples' societies*".

[179] J. Gilbert (note 132), 210; *B. Kingsbury*, in: P. Alston, Peoples' rights, 2001, 109.

[180] R. Shrinkhal (note 163), 194 et seq.; J. Gilbert (note 132), 216.

[181] R. Shrinkhal (note 163), 191.

international community.[182] Moreover, it can lead to the absurdity that indigenous peoples have to prove their "indigeneity" based on their cultural traditions, *e.g.*, in the case of *Ivan Kitok vs. Sweden.*[183] Similarly, the Canadian Case *Lovelace vs. Canada* shows that, based on the human rights approach, the individual has to act "for the continued viability and welfare of the minority as a whole".[184] They have to "reformulate their ethnic identities to get access to resources", which seems absurd, because *e.g.* "no one expects '*the English*' to perform their Englishness, which means that being English allows one both to be '*modern*' and to make claims on an idealized English past of kings and queens, castles, medieval villages, and pastorals landscapes".[185] Thus, it shows the controversy, which is woven around the question of the recognition of the legal concept of "indigenous peoples", in contrast to a mere anthropological approach to indigenous peoples far away from international and domestic law.[186] However, integrating indigenous peoples into the legal framework is crucial to giving them a voice in the international community.[187]

4.2.2.4.2 Right of Self-Determination for the Indigenous Peoples

This highlights one of the main problems in recognizing indigeneity, which can be traced back to the so-called "saltwater decolonization" theory.[188] This theory emerged from the idea that during the decolonization process in the 1960s, nearly all countries abroad, geographically located across the sea from the administering power, gained independence. However, people with a different identity within the territories of the leading colonial powers were not granted this right.[189] They remained "enclosed within States", whose frontiers had been established based on the *uti possidetis* principle, "without their consent".[190] In conclusion, the theory is

[182] Ibid., 194 et seq.

[183] *Ivan Kitok vs. Sweden, Communication No. 197/1985,* CCPR/C/33/D/197/1985, 02.12.1985*; A. Kuper*, in: A. Cook/J. Sarkin, Who is indigenous?: Indigenous rights globally, in Africa, and among the san in Botswana, 2009, 113 oder 17, 20; R. Shrinkhal (note 163), 191.

[184] W. K. Barth (note 316 in Chap. 3), 97.

[185] A. Kuper (note 137), 391, 398; R. Shrinkhal (note 163), 191.

[186] *Affirming:* S. Young (note 139), 398; *Rejecting:* A. Kuper (note 137), 395, 400.

[187] S. Young (note 139), 400.

[188] C. J. Iorns Magallanes (note 285 in Chap. 3), 254; S. Willcox (note 7 in Chap. 1), 98.

[189] *C. Oguamanam,* Rio + 20: Indigenous Knowledge and Intellectual Property in Coastal and Ocean Law, Ocean Yearbook 27 (2013), 121 et seq., R. Shrinkhal (note 163), 192; T. Gullberg (note 12 in Chap. 3), 40.

[190] H. Berman et al. (note 298 in Chap. 3), 190.

based on the idea that the "right of self-determination is restricted to those non-self-governing territories separated by salt-water from the administering power and denied to those peoples engulfed by the contiguous territory of a metropolitan State".[191] It particularly concerns the American, Arctic, and Australasian regions, including the islanders in the South Pacific.[192] Consequently, these people could and still cannot adequately exercise their right to self-determination or, more precisely, not in the manner traditionally intended for the right of self-determination, namely "as a counterpoint to colonialism."[193]

However, a more modern approach to self-determination for indigenous peoples can be considered, one that is not based on the classical interaction between dominant and dominated powers. This theory postulates a functional approach to self-determination for the indigenous peoples, enabling them to "control their institutions, territories, resources, social orders and cultures without external domination or interference", while supporting interaction and exchange "with the dominant society"[194] through active participation.[195] The UNDRIP is based on this idea, namely the realization of self-determination, as set out in Article 1 of both the International Covenants on Human Rights and the International Covenant on Economic, Social and Cultural Rights, and on the assurance of the right of self-control over governance, lands, resources, social relations, and culture.[196] For instance, the idea of self-determination and self-autonomy is found in Article 1 of the UNDRIP, the right to political participation in Articles 13 and 20, and the right to self-autonomy regarding their own internal and local affairs in Article 4, which is further discussed in Articles 25 to 27. Moreover, the indigenous peoples have the right to participate in the adoption of treaties with States in Articles 35 and 37.[197] Although the UNDRIP does not have a binding effect on States, it has already had some effects.

Since the adoption of the UNDRIP in 2007, indigenous peoples have sought to increase their involvement with the international community to assert their interests, particularly in relation to their homelands.[198] We are already beyond the

[191] *J. T. Paxman*, Minority indigenous populations and their claims for self-determination, 1989, 185, 198; R. Shrinkhal (note 163), 192.

[192] R. Shrinkhal (note 163), 192.

[193] H. Berman et al. (note 298 in Chap. 3), 190 et seq.

[194] Ibid., 191.

[195] S. Young (note 139), 387.

[196] H. Berman et al. (note 298 in Chap. 3), 191; S. Young (note 139), 394.

[197] H. Berman et al. (note 298 in Chap. 3), 192; J. Gilbert (note 132), 221 et seq.

[198] N. Loukacheva (note 147), 51.

passive recognition of indigenous peoples in the international framework in light of the past colonial practices.[199] Instead, we have already reached a level of active participation and representation of indigenous actors in international diplomacy, transnational networks, and international bodies.[200] This development is particularly present in the Arctic, where the Saami and Inuit, as indigenous peoples, have growing political influence in the global and regional political transactions, for instance, in the Arctic Council, the UN Permanent Forum on Indigenous Issues (PFII), or with the successful Inuit Petition before the IACHR.[201] Here, external forces, like globalization and growing networks, "served as a catalyst for constructing a political agency among indigenous peoples," "increased the visibility of indigenous peoples, and amplified indigenous peoples' collective voices".[202] Consequently, this supported the growing global awareness of the situation of indigenous peoples, despite their limited influence in decision-making processes related to culture and cultural heritage.[203]

This leads us to another phenomenon closely linked to the actual development, the self-identification of indigenous peoples, which is based on the idea of "indigenous morality".[204] Various international human rights lawyers applied indigenous peoples' rights.[205] However, this concept "goes beyond universal human rights and existing regimes of minority rights, [what is also] one of the objectives of the international indigenous peoples' movement".[206] Even in this context, assigning political participation to issues that transcend State

[199] Ibid.

[200] Ibid.

[201] Ibid., 52; S. Iglesias Sánchez (note 10), 218, 223 et seq; *I. L. Stoyanova*, in: R. Abate, Climate change and indigenous peoples: The search for legal remedies, 2013, 306 et seq; *H. M. Osofsky*, in: H. M. Osofsky/W. C. G. Burns, Adjudicating climate change: State, national, and international approaches, 2009, 272 et seq.

[202] *E.-I. Daes*, in: S. Jentoft/H. Minde/R. Nilsen, Indigenous peoples: Resource management and global rights, 2005, 68; N. Loukacheva (note 147), 52.

[203] N. Loukacheva (note 147), 52; A. Mühlebach (note 181), 423 et seq.

[204] A. Mühlebach (note 181), 417.

[205] N. Loukacheva (note 147), 55: *e.g.* S. J. Anaya (note 6).

[206] N. Loukacheva (note 147), 53; B. Kingsbury (note 189), 102; *B. Kingsbury,* Reconciling Five Competing Conceptual Structures of Indigenous Peoples' Claims in International and Comparative Law, New York University Journal of International Law and Politics (2001), 237.

boundaries is considered a dimension of the external aspect of the right to self-determination.[207] The youngest expression of this phenomenon is Article 19 of the Nordic Saami Convention, which stipulates the representation of Saami in international institutions.[208] Consequently, once again, the external influence of the international community is evident in the definition of indigenous people, as noted above (compare Chap. 3.2).

The so-called "free-rider problem" refers to the unlimited right of indigenous peoples to self-identify, which allows them to claim certain benefits and advantages compared to other individuals or citizens of a State.[209] This leads to the phenomenon, for example, in Namibia and South Africa, where other minorities or ethnic groups aspire to the "indigenous status" to obtain the benefits typically afforded to indigenous peoples.[210] Hence, they have realized that "specifically indigenous identity" serves "as a viable and long-run strategy for liberation, equally viable but distinct from class-consciousness." [211] Therefore, this tendency of indigeneity represents a pioneering role for a minority.[212]

Considering a completely different concept of land ownership as it represents a unique spiritual, cultural, social, political, and economic relationship, already the approach to the right of property in Article 21 of the American Convention on Human Rights, according to IACHR in its jurisdiction concerning the *Awas Tingni* and the *Saramaka People,* seems prejudiced.[213] Indigenous peoples require recognition of collective land rights, which is far from the traditional understanding of individual land ownership.[214] This phenomenon was discussed during the drafting of the UNDRIP, in line with the already mentioned Genocide Convention

---

[207] *J. B. Henriksen,* Implementation of the Right of Self-Determination of Indigenous Peoples, Indigenous Affairs (2001), 10; N. Loukacheva (note 147), 53.

[208] Nordic Saami Convention, 16.11.2005, Art. 19: *"The Saami parliaments shall represent the Saami in intergovernmental matters. The states shall promote Saami representation in international institutions and Saami participation in international meetings"*; N. Loukacheva (note 147), 53.

[209] *M. Olson,* The logic of collective action, 2nd ed., 1971; *E.-I. A. Daes,* Working Paper by the Chairperson-Rapporteur, Mrs. Erica-Irene A. Daes, on the concept of "indigenous people", http://www.derechos.org/nizkor/bolivia/doc/daes.html (last reviewed Oct. 9, 2025), 1996; R. Shrinkhal (note 163), 192; E.-I. A. Daes (note 219).

[210] R. Shrinkhal (note 163), 192.

[211] A. Mühlebach (note 181), 420.

[212] Ibid.

[213] J. Gilbert (note 132), 210, 226; J. Anaya (note 44), 290 et seq.; J. Gilbert (note 63), 119.

[214] J. Gilbert (note 132), 223.

of 1948 and the concept of ethnocide, and is reflected in Article 8, paragraph 2(b), and the Preamble of this UN Declaration.[215]

> *"Land was a key component of indigenous culture, and dispossession of land was paramount to ethnocide."*[216]

Consequently, exercising the already mentioned collective or group rights is of great importance to the indigenous peoples "not only for indigenous spirituality but also to maintaining the inter-generational nature of all our social, cultural, economic and political rights".[217] The international jurisprudence has already acknowledged the collective nature of property rights, *e.g.*, in the *Awas Tingni* case, where the right to property in lands for "*members of indigenous communities within the framework of commonality of possession (...)*" was affirmed.[218] The IACHR implemented in this case:

> *Indigenous groups, by virtue of their very existence, have the right to live freely in their own territory; the close ties of indigenous peoples to the land must be recognized and understood as the fundamental basis of their cultures, their spiritual life, their integrity, and their economic survival. For indigenous communities, relations to the land are not merely a matter of possession and production but a material and spiritual element, which they must fully enjoy to preserve their cultural legacy and transmit it to future generations.*[219]

However, a collective right was not explicitly included in the UN Declaration; it was instead implied only in Article 26, paragraph 2.[220] Additionally, the Human

---

[215] Ibid., 223 et seq; Declaration on the Rights of Indigenous Peoples (UNDRIP), 13.09.2007b; A/RES/61/295, Art. 8, para. 2(b); *States shall provide effective mechanisms for prevention of, and redress for: any action which has the aim or effect of dispossessing them of their lands, territories or resources.*

[216] J. Gilbert (note 132), 224; Report of Working Group for Draft United Nations declaration on the Rights of Indigenous Peoples, 15.03.2002; E/CN.4/2002/98, 18.

[217] J. Gilbert (note 132), 224 et seq; Report of Working Group for Draft United Nations declaration on the Rights of Indigenous Peoples, 15.03.2002; E/CN.4/2002/98, Annex II, 28.

[218] Report of Working Group for Draft United Nations declaration on the Rights of Indigenous Peoples (note 227), Annex II, 28; J. Anaya (note 44), 283; J. Gilbert (note 132), 225.

[219] *The Mayagna (Sumo) Awas Tingni Community vs. Nicaragua*, No. 79, 31.08.2001, para. 149; J. Gilbert (note 63), 119.

[220] Declaration on the Rights of Indigenous Peoples (UNDRIP) (note 225), Art. 26, para. 2: *Indigenous peoples have the right to own, use, develop and control the lands, territories and*

Rights Council's reluctant approach, affirming that "States shall give legal recognition and protection to these lands, territories, and resources [of the indigenous peoples]," reveals the States' fear of losing control over their territories by granting these rights to indigenous peoples.[221] This fear stems from the notion that self-determination would foster discontent, disorder, and rebellion.[222] Therefore, the "inextricable linkage between peoples and places" increasingly forces the indigenous peoples to come to the fore, to "erode the commonplace notion of the 'sacrosanct' Nation-State as a territorially integrated entity."[223] The fact is that the "traditionally individualistic approach to property rights can be challenged" in the context of the rights of indigenous peoples, and that this approach is "not sufficient [for them] as they do not integrate their specific cultural attachment to their traditional territories".[224] Thus, the example of the Saami shows that they have already reached a new level of recognition beyond the borders of the State because "for indigenous peoples self-determination is not only about Statehood and secession, [...] [but] about free control, choice and way of life."[225]

4.2.3 People as the Right-Holder of Self-Determination and the Principle of Permanent Sovereignty over Natural Resources

After an extensive search for the correct definition of people and the differentiation between their various facets, we will now take a closer look at the relevant question: whether the people are the right-holders of the essential principles of international law, the right of self-determination, and consequently, the principle of permanent sovereignty over natural resources.

4.2.3.1 Moral Attachment of People

The question is, if the people are nowadays the right-holders of the right of self-determination, or rather, "principle-holders" of the principle of permanent

resources that ***they possess*** *by reason of traditional ownership or other traditional occupation or use, as well as those which they have otherwise acquired;* J. Gilbert (note 132), 225.

[221] J. Gilbert (note 132), 226.

[222] *R. Lansing*, The peace negotiations: A personal narrative, 1921, 87; S. Willcox (note 7 in Chap. 1), 97.

[223] A. Mühlebach (note 181), 417; J. Gilbert (note 132), 223.

[224] J. Gilbert (note 63), 121.

[225] J. Gilbert (note 132), 220.

sovereignty over natural resources. Consequently, if they are entitled to this principle and also addressed to this principle. The idea of the people as representatives of the "moral person" seems logical, particularly because "States have no moral basis on which to argue for their rights to their present territories, that existing distribution of territory and resources is *completely morally arbitrary*".[226] In other words:

> *"The distribution of natural resources is entirely arbitrary from a moral point of view; it has, at any rate, the kind of fairness displayed by a lottery. That is presumably better than a situation in which the weak are despoiled of their prizes by force and fraud."*[227]

Therefore, we must discuss the theory of "the attachment of specific peoples to specific pieces of land", as this so-called people-based account "is superior to two main alternatives—the nation-centered and state-centered accounts".[228]

Already, Hobbes and Kant argued, in their development of the idea of a State based on their legitimate theories, that "people have a right to a place, within which our projects and relationships and pursuit of life are typically attached".[229] However, how can we pinpoint this "attachment problem" in the juridical structure?[230] Some scholars search for "the right of occupancy" to define a "morally adequate" allocation or occupation of territory.[231]

As mentioned (see Chap. 3), the right of occupancy cannot be equated to the right of property, but instead describes the moral attachment to a country or land depending on the "cultural and institutional context in which people live".[232] The equation between property rights and land attachment by people is one of the major mistakes in the definition of the right of occupancy, evident in jurisdictions to the present day. It is based on the long-lasting and "spurious legal expression *terra nullius*"—the concept of ownerless land before the arrival of the European settlers.[233]

---

[226] C. J. Iorns Magallanes (note 285 in Chap. 3), 332; A. Mühlebach (note 181), 428; D. Miller (note 83 in Chap. 3), 165, *Compare*: *E. Özmen*, in: H. Hahn/R. Mosayebi, John Rawls: Das Recht der Völker, 2019, 13 et seq; C. Armstrong (note 46 in Chap. 2), 93.

[227] *O. Angeli,* Self-Determination and Sovereignty over Natural Resources, Ratio Juris (2017), 290 et seq.

[228] A. Banai et al. (note 100 in Chap. 3), 102; A. Meine (note 159 in Chap. 3), 136.

[229] M. Moore (note 61), 217; C. Nine (note 38 in Chap. 1), 96, 105.

[230] A. Banai et al. (note 100 in Chap. 3), 102.

[231] M. Moore (note 61), 217.

[232] Ibid., 218.; A. Stilz (note 85 in Chap. 2), 249.

[233] R. Pitty (note 311 in Chap. 3), 51; R. Stavenhagen (note 172), 419.

It was first criticized by Judge Gros in the *Western Sahara* case for promoting the better and "far-reaching significance of an autonomous world."[234] Consequently, even though the expression "collective ownership" is often misused in this context, courts frequently use it to confer these rights on people, *e.g.*, in *Saramaka people v. Suriname.*[235] In this case, the court awarded the Saramaka people "communal property", recognizing the "ownership of the land centered on the group and its community".[236] The crux of the matter is that ownership and property rights, to which minorities refer, are individual human rights, whereas indigenous peoples, such as the *Saramaka people*, strive for collective rights, for the "rights of peoples."[237] Moreover, the ILO Convention 169 takes up a similar stance by adopting the idea of the right of people "to participate in the use, management, and conservation of these resources" and to own and possess the land they occupy.[238] However, the claim of the indigenous peoples goes beyond this right; they wish "to own, develop, control and use the lands and territories, including the environment of the lands, air, waters, coastal seas, sea-ice, flora and fauna and other resources which they have traditionally owned or otherwise occupied or used".[239] However, the Human Rights Committee has never recognized the sovereign right of indigenous peoples to control and manage their natural resources; instead, it has always regarded the State as the primary right-holder, obliged to consult and cooperate with indigenous peoples.[240] Moreover, in recent decisions of international courts, the rights of indigenous peoples have been recognized as participatory rather than sovereign rights.[241] Furthermore, none of the international environmental treaties mentioning indigenous peoples recognizes a

---

[234] R. Pitty (note 311 in Chap. 3), 51; *Western Sahara,* 16.10.1975, Judge Gros, para. 11.

[235] *Compare: Case of Saramaka People vs. Suriname,* No. 172, 28.11.2007, para. 87–88.

[236] *Case of Saramaka People vs. Suriname,* No. 172, 28.11.2007, para. 87–89.

[237] R. Pitty (note 311 in Chap. 3), 56, *compare: „ Könkämä and 38 other Saami villages vs. Sweden, No. 27033/95, 25.11.1996* ": S. Iglesias Sánchez (note 10), 218–220; G. Otis and A. Laurent (note 41), 170 et seq.

[238] *C169—Indigenous and Tribal Peoples Convention,* C169, 27.06.1989, Art. 14, 15(1); H. A. Northcott (note 19 in Chap. 3), 79; N. Schrijver (note 30), 93.

[239] Declaration on the Rights of Indigenous Peoples (UNDRIP) (note 225), Art. 26(2), Draft; J. Gilbert (note 132), 227.

[240] N. Schrijver (note 30), 94 et seq; Concluding observations: Suriname, 04.05.2004; CCPR/CO/80/SUR, para. 21; Concluding Observation: Sweden, 24.04.2002; CCPR/CO/74/SWE, para. 15; Concluding Observations: Guyana, 25.04.2000; CCPR/C/79/Add. 121, para. 21.

[241] N. Schrijver (note 30), 96; *The Mayagna (Sumo) Awas Tingni Community vs. Nicaragua,* No. 79, 31.08.2001; *Case of Saramaka People vs. Suriname,* No. 172, 28.11.2007.

sovereign right of indigenous peoples to control and exploit natural resources.[242] Consequently, indigenous peoples cannot be equated with "people" in the sense of the "principle-holder" of the permanent sovereignty over natural resources.[243]

Therefore, the matter of a moral right of occupancy for the people seems one of the key issues in answering the question of the people as "principle-holder" of the permanent sovereignty over natural resources.[244] Nowadays, the moral right of occupancy can be deduced from the interpretation of self-determination, or rather, both are regarded as mutually dependent because "possession of land [or better, the attachment of land] is instrumentally necessary to the realization of robust forms of self-determination".[245] Realizing this, self-determination can also "postulate the right of a people in an established territory to determine its collective political destiny in a democratic fashion and is therefore at the core of the democratic entitlement".[246]

Consequently, does not this conclusion imply that occupancy rights or whatever we call the entitlements of people to the land also include the rights to resources? For the indigenous peoples, for instance, "the unique importance of rights to land and natural resources" is deduced from the rights of peoples.[247] Therefore, control over resources is also an essential dimension of collective self-determination.[248] Following this idea, the demand of indigenous people for "territorial autonomy including a considerable degree of self-management and control over land and other natural resources" is understandable.[249] Furthermore, the cultural and ideological dimensions of land adhere to different rules and, therefore, require a different definition of resources.[250] Hence, for many indigenous cultures, resources are considered a kind of gift of *Mother Nature*—for indigenous peoples in South America, *"Pachamama"*—consequently, their exploitation is "deeply arbitrary from the moral point of view".[251] They consider

---

[242] N. Schrijver (note 30), 97; Convention on Biological Diversity, 22.05.1992a; CBD; International Tropical Timber Agreement, 01.02.2006; ITTA.

[243] N. Schrijver (note 30), 98.

[244] M. Moore (note 61), 217.

[245] Ibid., 216.

[246] *T. M. Franck,* The emerging right to democratic governance, The American Journal of International Law (1992), 52; J. Gilbert (note 132), 220.

[247] R. Pitty (note 311 in Chap. 3), 56.

[248] M. Moore (note 61), 221.

[249] R. Pitty (note 311 in Chap. 3), 56.

[250] M. Moore (note 61), 221.

[251] Ibid., 220; D. Deudney (note 93 in Chap. 3), 316 et seq.

the relationship of human beings to the natural world based on "ethics of respect and reciprocity," better explained as a "model of stewardship, rather than the Western property-based notion of dominion."[252]

For instance, the *Lakota Sioux* did not consider the Black Hills as mining grounds because they were sacred to them.[253] Given their deliberately open definition, natural resources are anything derived from the environment that is instrumental in satisfying human wants and needs.[254] However, when defining resources, we must also recognize that the social context determines what constitutes a resource and what value it holds.[255] Similarly, the definition by Nine viewed a "resource" as "a naturally occurring non-human thing" that may be of use or value to persons, while "value" has to be understood in many different, culturally or non-culturally specific ways.[256] Consequently, whether we are discussing the indigenous cultural or religious understanding of their relationship to their land, or the attachment of a nation to its national identity and its ability to be self-determining, both are grounded in the right to territorial control.[257] Even though people do not have a strong attachment to their natural resources, they are connected to certain things or ways of life that provide a basis for identification with this territory.[258] Consequently, the justification is that we would probably not find a "national property-like right", but rather in the "right to reasonable control",[259] which can comply with the equivalent "principle"-holdership.

4.2.3.2 Contradiction to the Nation-State?

However, does this concept not stand in stark contrast to the idea of the sovereignty of Nation-States and their territorial rights?[260] As we developed above, the modern State bases this entitlement over the territory on the triad of State sovereignty; the rights to jurisdictional authority (1)—*the right over subjects* –, a right to control entry and exit of goods and people (2)—*the right*

---

[252] *R. Tsosie*, in: R. Abate, Climate change and indigenous peoples: The search for legal remedies, 2013, 84.

[253] M. Moore (note 61), 220; *M. Moore,* Natural Resources, Territorial Right, and Global Distributive Justice, Political Theory (2012), 88.

[254] M. Moore (note 263), 87.

[255] Ibid., 93, 98.

[256] C. Nine (note 38 in Chap. 1), 117.

[257] J. A. Simmons (note 25 in Chap. 3), 202.

[258] Ibid., 203.

[259] Ibid.

[260] M. Moore (note 61), 219.

against aliens –, and a right to control, extract and tax resources within the territory (3)—*the right over territory.*[261] Nowadays, it is assumed that the legitimate political order that makes decisions concerning the extraction, control, sale, and use of natural resources within the territory depends on the territory's legitimate sovereignty.[262] However, primarily in the case of control over natural resources, this legally constructed sovereignty confers an undeserved advantage on the State because, based on this legal authority, it can also claim moral authority.[263] However, we must bear in mind that these States' claims over natural resources are only legitimized by the need for "the State's performance of its morally mandated functions".[264] Consequently, it is a vicious circle of argumentation, based upon which we justify the State's right over natural resources.

The question remains whether this principle is compatible with the people's right of occupancy. In this context, Locke's concept of "the tragedy of the commons" comes to mind, suggesting that land is held for general use and, without authoritative rules governing its use, becomes a common resource.[265] Notably, this jurisdictional authority does not stand in contrast to the exercise of collective self-determination; on the contrary, this theory does not exclude the possibility that people can have control over natural resources.[266] Instead, within the legitimate political order, a jurisdictional authority shall ensure the use of natural resources that align with the common good.[267] Consequently, establishing adequate control over resources in line with robust collective self-determination involves creating rules concerning the acquisition, transfer, and use of natural resources, ultimately established by a jurisdictional authority.[268] Consequently, it is not unlikely that using and improving natural resources for collective purposes can establish collective rights of people over these resources.[269]

However, this theory is called "the tragedy" because it assumes that the idea of the common good is a utopian fantasy, as we can see in the traditional concept of a territorial State. In the words of Angeli:

---

[261] J. A. Simmons (note 15 in Chap. 3), 300, 305–306.; M. Moore (note 263), 85.

[262] M. Moore (note 61), 219.

[263] M. Moore (note 263), 85 et seq.; J. A. Simmons (note 15 in Chap. 3), 301, 303.

[264] J. A. Simmons (note 25 in Chap. 3), 204.

[265] M. Moore (note 263), 86; J. A. Simmons (note 15 in Chap. 3), 301, 303.

[266] M. Moore (note 263), 87–88, 95.

[267] Ibid., 87.

[268] Ibid., 88 et seq.

[269] J. A. Simmons (note 25 in Chap. 3), 205.

> *"If each State pursues its national interests (...) in using the territory and resources as it will, planetary resources are drawn down, and environmental integrity is compromised not simply within the State but across borders."*[270]

The territorial State is not "an unalterable feature of the human condition"; rather, it is one form of appearance of "organized, law-governed human association".[271] As already explained, today's Nation-State is based on the "limited European idea of civilization", where the "State-sanctioned rights acquired by political organizations" replaced "individual natural law rights inherent in different peoples".[272] Consequently, there is room for new forms of "organized, law-governed human association" independent from the traditional shape of a territorial State.

Hence, we can conclude that the States have "a morally legitimate interest in maintaining their territorial integrity", but that does not automatically entail that the State has a *right* to its territory.[273] Even though it is morally legitimate, an interest does not automatically result in a right.[274] The Lockean voluntarist theory or the Kantian theories can only justify limited State authority over resources "radically different from the full conception of resource rights" as they are hardly able to include "rights over undiscovered goods, over goods not owned by the State's citizens, goods held by the collective in common or goods held in a trusteeship for future generations".[275] Thus, as seen in Chap. 3, it can be affirmed that "State territorial jurisdiction is strongly analogous to private ownership from an international point of view", [276] while considering the different shapes[277] of

---

[270] O. Angeli (note 237), 291.

[271] J. A. Simmons (note 15 in Chap. 3), 303.

[272] R. Pitty (note 311 in Chap. 3), 49; *P. Keal,* European Conquest and the Rights of Indigenous Peoples: The moral backwardness of international society (2003), 137.

[273] C. J. Iorns Magallanes (note 285 in Chap. 3), 332.; J. A. Simmons (note 15 in Chap. 3), 312.

[274] J. A. Simmons (note 15 in Chap. 3), 312.

[275] J. A. Simmons (note 25 in Chap. 3), 207; C. Nine (note 38 in Chap. 1), 126 et seq.

[276] *H. Sidgwick,* The elements of politics, 2nd ed., 1897, 252; J. A. Simmons (note 15 in Chap. 3), 317; J. A. Simmons (note 25 in Chap. 3), 209.

[277] *According to N. Schrijver (note 1 in Chap. 2), 391.: a right to possess, use, and "freely dispose" of the natural resources within its territory; a right to freely determine and control the exploration, development, and disposition of these resources; a right to manage natural resources in accordance with national developmental and environmental policies; a right to regulate foreign corporations and investors in their activities regarding these resources; and a right to nationalize or expropriate property in resources, subject to the requirement to pay appropriate compensation.*

the legal doctrine of permanent sovereignty.[278] Some scholars even argue that fewer rights to natural property are included in State jurisdiction.[279] However, suppose there is nothing more than the legitimate interest analogous to private ownership. In that case, the entitlement of a territory can also give rise to the people referring to their "national homelands".[280] Therefore, we can conclude that the State does not have an inherent right to a territory. In contrast, the peoples are ascribed rights because of the moral links they hold and because of "the right of self-determination as an inherent right of peoples to control their own destiny".[281] Moreover, we can say that to remain self-determining and to justify a right of self-determination over a considerable territory, the ownership—or, in the application of the preferred model of respect and reciprocity, "the stewardship"—of the natural resources on and around this particular territory is essential.[282]

In sum, we close with the notion that the right and control over natural resources are in the better hands of the "peoples", in the assumption that the distribution of natural resources reflects the moral attachment to a piece of land in a better way. This concept not only complies with the people's demand for "some degree of territorial autonomy", involving "a considerable degree of self-management and control over land and other natural resources",[283] but also can support the idea of a better and fairer distribution of natural resources. This corresponds to the principal values of self-determination, which do not target "the welfare of individuals within different political communities, but the self-determination of political communities themselves".[284] This idea focuses more on an "egalitarian view of resources as directly instrumental to the satisfaction of people's needs (…) and can be directly applied to ensure that people's basic rights to subsistence are met" to deliver "natural resource justice".[285]

---

[278] A. Stilz (note 85 in Chap. 2), 227.

[279] J. A. Simmons (note 15 in Chap. 3), 317.

[280] Ibid., 319; S. Oeter (note 172), 484; Art. 14–15 of ILO Convention 169; Art. 26 para. 2 of the UNDRIP.

[281] C. J. Iorns Magallanes (note 285 in Chap. 3), 307.

[282] J. A. Simmons (note 25 in Chap. 3), 202; R. Tsosie (note 262), 84.

[283] R. Pitty (note 311 in Chap. 3), 56.

[284] M. Moore (note 263), 98.

[285] Ibid., 99; C. Armstrong (note 46 in Chap. 2), 18.

4.3 Conclusion

Following the purpose of this chapter, we have to find an answer to the question of who the right-holder of the principle of permanent sovereignty over natural resources is and, in the following, whether one of these two possibilities is the better one.

4.3.1 The State as the Predominant Right-Holder of Natural Resources

As already concluded in Chaps. 3 and 4, the States are considered the absolute right-holders or principal holders of the natural resources in their territory. While this was highly controversial in the 1950s and 1960s, at last in the 1970s, it finally became the predominant "status quo of the contemporary world order" in the 1970s,[286] that "individual Nation-States enjoy an extensive and essential exclusive set of rights over the resources within their territories", breached by the concession of voluntary treaty making.[287] While the historical development was already illuminated in Chap. 2, the question arises as to which entitlement the Nation-States base their claims on natural resources, and if there is a considerable justification.

Natural resources are defined as "natural assets (raw materials) occurring in nature that can be used for economic production or consumption."[288] The German equivalent "Rohstoff" captures the significance of natural resources even better: "natural resources are the raw materials we are confronted with in coming into existence in the world, with which we can potentially support our various (and competing) human projects".[289] We can deduce from this definition that a connection to the land is not needed, even though economic theories list it as a factor of production, alongside land, labor, and capital.[290] However, it becomes clear that a fixed connection to the land or territory is not mandatory when defining natural resources.[291] We must be aware that natural resources are separable

---

286 C. Armstrong (note 46 in Chap. 2), 133; A. Stilz (note 85 in Chap. 2), 219.

287 *C. Armstrong,* Against "Permanent Sovereignty" over Natural Resources, Politics, Philosophy and Economics (2015), 130–131.

288 Ibid., 133; C. Armstrong (note 46 in Chap. 2), 11.

289 C. Armstrong (note 46 in Chap. 2), 11.

290 C. Armstrong (note 297), 134.

291 Ibid.

from the land because they are removable.[292] Therefore, it remains questionable why the Nation-State, whose definition and existence depend on territory and land, claims exclusive rights over natural resources. Stilz regarded it as an "open question" why the connection between jurisdiction over territory, membership, and resources appears immutable.[293]

Consequently, we identify the specific claims to a resource, divided into direct and indirect claims, which go hand in hand with the rights associated with that resource.[294] Direct claims include the prima facie claim to control, access, and constrain others' access to the resource solely on the basis of the relationship with that resource.[295] Indirect claims involve actions derived from others who hold the direct rights, making these claims more unstable and "fugacious".[296] Direct claims, by contrast, remain intact as long as the resource remains intact, regardless of accessibility, and do not depend on a specific geographical site, making them more durable.[297] The rights to natural resources, however, include access, withdrawal, alienation, and the derivation of income from their use.[298] These branches of specific exercise of rights probably remind us of another, more common right: ownership.[299] At this point, it becomes apparent that ownership is not, and has never been, a genuine right of the Nation-State (see above, Chap. 3).

Consequently, the questions remain: Is a connection between natural resources and the territory unnecessary, and if the state is not the rightful owner, who is entitled to claim rights over natural resources? Two theories seek to explain the relationship between the State and natural resources. The first one—the improvement-based national claims—is based on the idea that "the national communities may invest a good deal of care and work in a territory or its resources." The second one—the attachment-based national claims—is based on their claims regarding the attachment of national communities to their respective lands.[300]

Examining the first theory, there are several reasons to doubt its validity. Even though the "nation"—represented by its people—improves a territory through

---

[292] Ibid., 134.

[293] Ibid; A. Stilz (note 73), 572 et seq.

[294] C. Armstrong (note 297), 134.

[295] O. Angeli (note 237), 300 et seq.

[296] C. Armstrong (note 297), 134 et seq.

[297] Ibid., 135.

[298] Ibid., 135 et seq; S. van Wyk (note 1 in Chap. 2), 225 et seq; C. Armstrong (note 46 in Chap. 2), 22 et seq; O. Angeli (note 237), 300.

[299] C. Armstrong (note 297), 136.

[300] Ibid., 137 et seq.

investments like, *e.g.*, the cultivation of land and the construction of infrastructure, it is questionable whether these measures can justify a doctrine of permanent sovereignty.[301] In particular, in a time of globalization, where improvement often comes from outsiders, such as multinational corporations or Chinese companies investing in African infrastructure to extract resources for the global market, the involvement of the own Nation-State becomes increasingly questionable.[302] Moreover, the improvement argument applies only to improvable resources, and therefore, its feasibility varies from resource to resource.[303] However, the most crucial point of criticism is the legitimacy of a Nation-State's claim to enhanced value if the entitlement is based solely on property-like claims.[304] Bearing in mind that improving a resource is one of the attributes in defining property, consequently, one leads to the other, and vice versa.[305] As Miller clarified, the guarantee that a group can continue to enjoy its values exists only when the group is adequately represented.[306] This point is highly doubtful, given that only a small group is likely directly concerned with improving the land. Therefore, this does not align with the concept of the entitlement of a whole Nation-State. Before the regime of permanent sovereignty is bestowed upon the Nation-State, it remains in its earlier form, ownership, and, consequently, in the hands of the individuals and the peoples.[307]

The second theory—the attachment-based national claims—argues for attachment as a basis for the permanent sovereignty of peoples, rather than that of Nation-States, because only communities, as collectives of people, can live in a close relationship with the land.[308] Examples of this relationship can be found in most indigenous land claims, such as the Saami people's claim. [309] These cases are distinguished, in particular, by the fact that they are claims *against* Nation-States.[310] They are often resolved by the "traditional interpretation of the

[301] Ibid., 138.

[302] Ibid., 139; C. Armstrong (note 46 in Chap. 2), 103 et seq.

[303] C. Armstrong (note 297), 139.

[304] Ibid., 140 et seq.

[305] C. Armstrong (note 46 in Chap. 2), 96 et seq.

[306] C. Armstrong (note 297), 141; D. Miller (note 100 in Chap. 3), 218.

[307] C. Armstrong (note 297), 142.

[308] Ibid., 143.

[309] Ibid., 143 et seq; C. Armstrong (note 46 in Chap. 2), 137, 145. *Compare: the Lakota Sioux, cultural minorities in New Zealand and Papua New Guinea.*

[310] C. Armstrong (note 297), 143 et seq; C. Armstrong (note 46 in Chap. 2), 137, 145. *Compare: the Lakota Sioux, cultural minorities in New Zealand and Papua New Guinea.*

property right," which concerns their interests in land and in rights to exploit natural resources, such as fishing and herding.[311] Consequently, it is much more likely that people living in a territory will be interested in exercising control over the territory and its resources, including preserving them for future generations.[312]

Moreover, as with the first theory, it seems nearly impossible for a Nation-State to be attached to all the resources within its territory. This attachment theory is therefore applicable only to a limited subset of resources.[313] Similarly, resources are naturally distributed across the territory in a "patchy and uneven" manner.[314] Consequently, nowadays, this argument pleads more for a right-holdership of peoples, especially of specific indigenous peoples, or at least implies a weaker form of "ownership," such as property rights.[315]

However, in many ways, the model of ownership does not adequately reflect the relationship between peoplehood and their land, considering only the absoluteness of property.[316] Consequently, ownership of States over natural resources, as well as the ownership of people, can be distinguished, so that only one of these actors can dispose of them.[317]

Focusing on property rights, we have to consider the "commonplace claim", which is defended by the argument that "assets will deteriorate in value unless they are '*owned*' or controlled by a single, specified agent"—in this context, the State.[318] According to Rawls in *The Law of Peoples*, comparable with property, the State, "a definite agent, is given responsibility for maintaining the territory and its environment".[319] Referring to the already mentioned "tragedy of the commons", he argued that to combine the interests of unspecific parties and conserving resources, the State must be considered a "good custodian" and adequate in its acts.[320] However, these arguments are not convincing because they assume that individual ownership requires communal control by a superior power —the State. [321] After all, the alternative of communal ownership is economically

[311] S. Iglesias Sánchez (note 10), 222.

[312] O. Angeli (note 237), 302.

[313] C. Armstrong (note 46 in Chap. 2), 137.

[314] Ibid.

[315] C. Armstrong (note 297), 145 et seq.

[316] A. Stilz (note 85 in Chap. 2), 236.

[317] Ibid.

[318] C. Armstrong (note 46 in Chap. 2), 139.

[319] *J. Rawls*, Das Recht der Völker, 2002, 8, 38–39; C. Armstrong (note 46 in Chap. 2), 139.

[320] J. Rawls (note 329), 38 et seq; C. Armstrong (note 46 in Chap. 2), 139.

[321] C. Armstrong (note 46 in Chap. 2), 140.

ineffective.[322] However, in reality, we experience that all challenging projects of exploitation and conservation of natural resources "span State borders", where "untrammeled State control is destined to fail".[323] Regardless of the Nation-State's political power to make and enforce binding agreements, national-level resource management seems hardly intelligible or effective, given the varying sizes and population densities of States.[324]

Are there thus any strong arguments that the permanent sovereignty over natural resources must be in the hands of Nation-States? The functionalist view holds that the State is the best right-holder because it always acts in the interests and "for the basic needs" of its subjects —the people.[325] However, can this argument be generalized and applied to all resources? Would it not be preferable to focus on the resources necessary to meet fundamental rights, rather than to apply this concept to all resources within a territory?[326] Naturally, there is a specific limitation between the various rights and duties of the State concerning sovereignty over natural resources, such as the duty to respect the rights and interests of indigenous peoples or the duty to share equitably in transboundary natural resources, so that a generalization of permanent sovereignty is not intended to be absolute.[327] However, under the two theories of claims, absolute territorial State jurisdiction does not align with basic needs: some resources will be abundant within the territory, while others will be in short supply.[328] Furthermore, there is no feasible argument against the theory that other institutions can protect resources than a State as the "single agent".[329]

Another argument in this context is that the State can provide the ideal platform and conditions to utilize resources, enabling its subjects to enjoy them.[330] Here, we come back to the idea of common ownership, which, as we notice above, can be perfectly appropriated by the people rather than the State as a single agent.[331] Reviewing the current system of natural resources, we recognize that

---

322 Ibid.

323 Ibid.

324 Ibid., 141.

325 C. Armstrong (note 297), 147; C. Nine (note 38 in Chap. 1), 41 et seq; A. Stilz (note 85 in Chap. 2).: *"basic rights"*.

326 C. Armstrong (note 297), 149.

327 Ibid; S. van Wyk (note 1 in Chap. 2), 225 et. seqq.

328 C. Armstrong (note 297), 150; C. Armstrong (note 46 in Chap. 2), 143.

329 C. Armstrong (note 297), 151.

330 Ibid.

331 Ibid., 152; A. Stilz (note 85 in Chap. 2), 227.

these resources are already owned and managed by individuals, and that national control is therefore redundant.[332] The still predominant system of State law as the only formal source of rights over land and resources continues to promote the State to dispose of the "unfettered rights to control, use, and manage "its" natural resources."[333]

Considering the global—*e.g.*, environmental—issues facing us in the present and future, this stands in contrast to the "morally legitimate interest of States to maintain territorial integrity".[334] Beyond the aforementioned duties of the States, more specific ones related to environmental challenges have emerged, such as the duty to respect the rights of future generations and refrain from causing significant harm to the environment and its natural resources.[335] The State can only fulfill these duties as a guardian of the public interest, focusing on the well-being of the population and supporting its people.[336] Therefore, a concept of "trans-national proprietorship" or a restricted interpretation of resource sovereignty rather than ownership could be a better solution, especially with the "long-term sustainability of the planet" in mind.[337]

4.3.2 Are the People the Better Right-Holder of Natural Resources?

Considering people as rights-holders, we first identified the differences between group and individual rights. Then, focusing on the definition, we examined different approaches to the term "people". In the beginning, we pursued the definition of "people", after which we passed on to the development of the expression "peoplehood" and took a quick look at the definition of minorities and indigenous peoples, contemplating, in particular, the most recent developments in the jurisdiction of international courts regarding indigenous peoples. Finally, we examined the pivotal question of the people's moral right to territorial occupancy, including their "right-holdership" over the territory and its natural resources.

[332] C. Armstrong (note 297).

[333] Ibid., 153; A. Stilz (note 85 in Chap. 2), 219; G. Otis and A. Laurent (note 41), 158; O. Angeli (note 237), 300.

[334] J. A. Simmons (note 15 in Chap. 3), 312.

[335] N. Schrijver (note 30), 89; A. Stilz (note 85 in Chap. 2), 238 et seq.

[336] N. Schrijver (note 30), 89.

[337] A. Stilz (note 85 in Chap. 2), 219 et seq.

Do all these considerations mean better protection of the natural resources under the people as right-holders or "principle-holders" of the principle of permanent sovereignty over natural resources? We can say that the view of strengthening collective rights over natural resources is gaining popularity; some scholars are already advocating for inter-state management of natural resources and reparations for "States' historical misuse of resources."[338] For instance, this idea has already found its way into national rules, *e.g.*, in paragraph 27 of the Pennsylvania Constitution:

> *"Pennsylvania's natural resources are the common property of all the people, including generations yet to come. As trustee of these resources, the Commonwealth shall conserve and maintain them for the benefit of the people."*[339]

Natural resources and biodiversity are considered common property resources, held under a mix of property arrangements, including open access, private property, communal property, and State control.[340] It is argued that the concept of "Nation-States emulating the European model" seems out of fashion, given the increasingly strong claim by people "to control their own political and economic development".[341] Consequently, we can observe that the indigenous peoples in their pioneer role not only claim to have been treated inadequately regarding their issues, but that it was argued that, seeing as it was "a private domestic matter for the State, the State denied them Statehood and the rights to make international law".[342] However, not only among the indigenous peoples, we can detect a growing dissatisfaction so that the "dominant conception of the international community as a society of States" seems to have fallen out of time.[343]

Contrary to that development, another theory suggests completely abandoning the doctrine of permanent sovereignty and returning to the famous speech of the Maltese diplomat Arvid Pardo. This approach would enforce and expand the CHM to encompass more natural resources beyond the high seas, the seabed,

---

338 *C. Nine*, Water Crisis Adaptation: Defending a Strong Right Against Displacement from the Home, Res Publica 22 (2016), 36.

339 P. H. Sand (note 202 in Chap. 2), 195.

340 *M. A. L. Miller*, in: K. T. Litfin, The greening of sovereignty in world politics, 1998, 177.

341 A. Mühlebach (note 181), 422; *F. Wilmer*, The indigenous voice in world politics, 1993, 2.

342 R. Pitty (note 311 in Chap. 3), 49.

343 A. Mühlebach (note 181), 423; R. Pitty (note 311 in Chap. 3), 49.

and areas beyond national jurisdiction.[344] Considering, in particular, the natural resources of worldwide significance, such as the rainforest in Brazil or the ice in the Arctic, these thoughts seem adequate and of "greater equality" in relation to international principles like intergenerational justice.[345] Moreover, this idea addresses the potential injustice of resource distribution more effectively, recognizing that resources would be unequally distributed under the concept of people's rights over them.[346] In sum, at the very least, it seems convenient for the earth's unoccupied regions to establish a regime, in international conventions, as the relevant authority.[347]

Aside from this development, it is worth noting that the principles of self-determination are increasingly "used as a basis for claims to political autonomy and natural resources", specifically, by indigenous groups.[348] For instance, in the aftermath of the *Western Sahara* case, the indigenous peoples of Western Sahara, the Saharawi people, managed to conclude the Fisheries Partnership Agreement with both the EU and Morocco, revealing the penetrating power and the "important role of natural resources in the self-determination of people".[349] Even though the international law community criticized the lack of compliance and provisions for the Saharawi people's sovereignty to natural resources, to "ensure the consent and benefit of the Saharawi people's sovereignty", the strong promotion of human rights was praised, so that it "counts for something in the face of a stalled self-determination process".[350]

However, the question remains whether these increasing tendencies of self-determination are enough to "elevate the individual, as well as qualified group, to have legal personality as well as standing."[351] For instance, Moore argues that, even though she affirms the cultural identity of distant groups to the people, she determines that the next step to "exercise jurisdictional rights" depends on the individual "group's capacity", which can also lead to a limited range of territorial

---

344 *Compare:* Convention on the Law of the Sea 1982 (note 194 in Chap. 2), Art. 137(1); A. Stilz (note 85 in Chap. 2), 229; C. Armstrong (note 46 in Chap. 2), 205 et seq; M. Dervovic (note 202 in Chap. 2), 310.

345 A. Stilz (note 85 in Chap. 2), 229; C. Armstrong (note 46 in Chap. 2), 19, 214–215.

346 A. Stilz (note 85 in Chap. 2), 233.

347 Ibid.

348 W. K. Barth (note 316 in Chap. 3), 87.

349 *J. Smith,* Fishing for Self-Determination: European Fisheries and Western Sahara—The Case of Ocean Resources in Africa's Last Colony, Ocean Yearbook 27 (2013), 288.

350 Ibid., 289.

351 W. K. Barth (note 316 in Chap. 3), 87.

rights dependent upon the restricted forms of self-determination.[352] Consequently, it can be assumed that, while "[national groups, cultural groups, and indigenous groups, dependent] on which peoplehood can be based, (...) are potential territorial right-holders",[353] this does not mean that they have the "right of the full stream of benefit from resources and the right to control over resources".[354] However, it seems much more appropriate to consider a "limited, conditional claim to natural resources" focused on "a principle of jurisdiction", at least for the State as a right-holder.[355] This would address the basic needs of people, such as essential material support for key life activities, and ensure fair use, allowing local communities to control and manage the natural resources critical to their everyday lives.[356] In conclusion, the option for individuals and groups "to break free of the so-called iron cage of State sovereignty and file a minority" exists; it is, however, highly dependent upon the individual group itself.[357]

Consequently, recognizing that the State is not a fixed legal personality but merely the prevailing form of self-determination leads to the notion that a people and a State are virtually interchangeable.[358] In the same way, sovereignty over natural resources is not "a static and absolute phenomenon, but one which has been constrained by the partial sharing of sovereignty over resources between States and by the parallel growth in duties under international law".[359] Therefore, the State does not have the monopoly to award people rights at its discretion, but as sovereignty "is not a gift from States, rather, it can only be a joint creation, something that is the product of participation at all stages by (...) peoples in a changing international system".[360] Therefore, it is the task of the international community to support and protect minorities and indigenous peoples by strengthening and enforcing their right to self-determination and their territorial rights.[361] In conclusion, we have to change our way of considering "natural resources as an undifferentiated class of goods which we can blithely move around the planet to maximize utility or satisfy equality" completely neglecting their social

---

352 M. Moore (note 157 in Chap. 3), 61.

353 Ibid.

354 M. Moore (note 263), 85.

355 A. Stilz (note 85 in Chap. 2), 235.

356 Ibid., 228 et seq., 234, 237.

357 W. K. Barth (note 316 in Chap. 3), 90.

358 R. Pitty (note 311 in Chap. 3), 55.

359 C. Armstrong (note 46 in Chap. 2), 143.

360 R. Pitty (note 311 in Chap. 3), 55.

361 Ibid.

context because for many people, "they are much more than mere interchangeable sources of benefit."[362] Because, "although nations may possess some good claims over natural resources, the institution of permanent sovereignty is a legal sledgehammer sent to crack a moral nut".[363] Consequently, we should appreciate and strengthen the attachment of people to their natural resources and "exempt them from principles which would seek to advance some pattern or other of resource allocation" to get a morally adequate distribution of natural resources and power.[364] Because "the people-oriented character of the [principle of permanent sovereignty over natural resources] has shown its potential to outshine its State-centric nature"[365]

[362] C. Armstrong (note 46 in Chap. 2), 17.

[363] Ibid., 146.

[364] Ibid., 17.

[365] Y. Tyagi (note 15 in Chap. 2), 588.

5 New Tendencies in International Law Regarding Climate Change in General and the Permanent Sovereignty over Natural Resources in Particular

The ascription of full status and participation rights usually reserved for "traditional" States to genuinely non-territorial entities would require the greatest structural transformation international law has seen since the establishment of the so-called Westphalian order. (J. Grote Stoutenburg (note 67 in Chap. 4), 87)

In this chapter, we will focus on the question already raised in the chapters above: the change in the two main pillars of the principle of permanent sovereignty over natural resources—sovereignty of States and the right of self-determination. First, we will take a closer look at the "evanescent" State sovereignty, particularly in the context of climate change and environmental degradation. Here, we can observe an increasing "erosion and perforation of operational sovereignty," which strengthens people through better representation across all three State powers, with this thesis focusing on the juridical power.[1]

The next part will focus on the reinterpretation of the right to self-determination, not only on climate change in general but also on the specific case of inundations induced by climate change in the South Pacific.

The final part is dedicated to the most pertinent question for the research project: how the principle of permanent sovereignty over natural resources is reinterpreted as a deduction from its two central pillars.

[1] *P. H. Sand*, in: G. Winter, Multilevel governance of global environmental change, 2006, 194.

M. A. Brinker, *The Principle of Permanent Sovereignty over Natural Resources as an Anchor in Times of Sealevel Rise*, https://doi.org/10.1007/978-3-658-50527-1_5

5.1 The Questioning of the Absolute Sovereignty of States

The absolute sovereignty of States is an illusion, as we already noted above. However, how can we prove this hypothesis? Over the last 50 years, we have particularly observed a decline in the power of State sovereignty, as evidenced by processes of internationalization and globally challenging problems, such as climate change. In unravelling this phenomenon, we will focus on the main pillars of the absolute sovereignty of States, on the one hand, and the growing power of people's voices, on the other, as they relate to climate change.

5.1.1 The Climate Change Regime After the 2002 Johannesburg Declaration

As already mentioned in Chap. 2, the idea of a "State-centered" world was first articulated in the Rio Declaration, which finalized the concept of the absolute sovereignty of States across all disciplines. Sovereignty has been and remains "a classic term of European international law referring to the absolute and inviolate power of a nation to manage generally its own affairs."[2] It would appear that after this fundamentally important declaration, no one would ever doubt the principle of the absolute sovereignty of States. However, during the WSSD in Johannesburg in 2002, it became apparent that the State, as an institution, could not face the imminent challenge of climate change alone.[3] The three main pillars of sustainable development—environmental protection, economic development, and social development—were outlined in the 2002 Johannesburg Declaration on Sustainable Development, marking a milestone in this pursuit. It soon became clear that these three goals could easily be undermined by the new global challenge: climate change.[4] Consequently, this summit revealed that the once-celebrated absolute sovereignty of States is a utopia, and international cooperation is the new dictum.[5] The presence of several NGOs during the conference, which began slowly, already foreshadowed the start of a new century: a century of cooperation

[2] E. Charles-Newton and E. A. Kronk (note 161 in Chap. 3), 64.

[3] F. Venter (note 18 in Chap. 3), 82.

[4] S. Atapattu (note 395 in Chap. 3), 608; *A. Gonzalez Arreaza,* Natural resource sovereignty and economic development in the WTO in light of the recent case law involving raw materials and rare earths, Review of European, Comparative & International Environmental Law (2017), 269.

[5] G. J. Abhimanyu (note 222 in Chap. 3), 608; F. Venter (note 18 in Chap. 3), 82.

among the international community of States, individual governments, international supranational institutions and organizations, multinational corporations, and NGOs.[6] It became increasingly clear that

> *"Sovereignty is a changing phenomenon. The field of environmental governance provides a useful demonstration that the State and its role, functions, and authority are steadily changing."*[7]

However, following the Rio Conference in 1992, Agenda 21—adopted as a "non-binding action plan for governments and NGOs" during the Conference—initiated a shift.[8] The protection of the oceans and their living resources sparked a newfound interest, and the inclusion of indigenous peoples was also initiated.[9] For the first time, indigenous knowledge regarding natural resources and the environment was acknowledged and incorporated, allowing it to be reflected in an international treaty, specifically the CBD.[10] Even though the CBD is regarded as the first "key influential instrument for the protection of indigenous knowledge", it represents "the link between indigenous knowledge and sustainable environment development, especially through biodiversity conservation, which includes marine and coastal biodiversity".[11] However, this treaty is still dominated by State sovereignty, because—of course—it was negotiated and adopted by States. This can be recognized in the preamble and Article 3, as they repeatedly emphasize the "sovereignty of States over their own biological resources".[12] Venter put this sobering realization in a nutshell:

> *"In effect, this preservation of the sovereignty of the States Parties means that the rest of the world has to depend on the comity of the individual State for its compliance with the Convention."*[13]

Hence, even though some scholars already consider State sovereignty as a "discretionary power within areas delimited by the law", and while "contemporary law

---

[6] N. Matz-Lück and L. Christiansen (note 21 in Chap. 2), 526; F. Venter (note 18 in Chap. 3), 66.

[7] F. Venter (note 18 in Chap. 3), 66.

[8] N. Matz-Lück and L. Christiansen (note 21 in Chap. 2), 524.

[9] C. Oguamanam (note 199 in Chap. 4), 123.

[10] Ibid., 125.

[11] Ibid., 125 et seq.

[12] F. Venter (note 18 in Chap. 3), 69.

[13] Ibid.

[has] evolved [it] still operates on the assumption that the State is the sovereign and that it exists for the benefit and protection of its "nation" and the associated legal system".[14] So, even as the clamor for a "perforation" of sovereignty, especially in response to transnational environmental problems, grew louder in the post-Rio period, international law revealed a different reality: the expansion of State sovereignty through national jurisdiction, most recently seen in UNCLOS with the introduction of the EEZ.[15]

However, the previously mentioned process does not demonstrate a focus on sovereignty, which in this case is likely "absolute sovereignty." The trends of the last years and developments in international law have, instead, resulted in an "unbundling of sovereignty", which allows us "to explore the status and content of sovereign rights".[16] This chapter aims to unbundle sovereignty in the context of environmental degradation and climate change. Furthermore, we will take a closer look at the role of "the people" in climate change, which first emerged in climate change litigation as the "voice of the people". Moreover, we will focus on the right to self-determination in the context of climate change and question whether it is applicable. In the final step, we will challenge the principle of permanent sovereignty over natural resources and dare to reinterpret it in the context of climate change.

5.1.2 Absolute State Sovereignty in the Context of Climate Change?

As already stated above, climate change and the environmental development it entails are currently challenging State sovereignty like no other threat and questioning the historical understanding of the regime of absolute sovereignty. In this context, absolute sovereignty as a "discretionary power within areas delimited by the law" gains new significance.[17] This becomes particularly apparent in "confronting a natural world which recognizes no human sovereignties".[18] As Camilleri and Falk put it in a nutshell:

---

[14] I. Brownlie and J. Crawford (note 30 in Chap. 2), 432; F. Venter (note 18 in Chap. 3), 66, 76–77, 88.

[15] P. H. Sand (note 202 in Chap. 2), 194.

[16] *V. Ward*, in: K. T. Litfin, The greening of sovereignty in world politics, 1998, 81 et seq.

[17] I. Brownlie and J. Crawford (note 30 in Chap. 2), 432; V. A. Ventura (note 206 in Chap. 3), 88.

[18] V. Ward (note 27), 79.

"If the world is entirely composed of sovereign States, then the boundaries of each domain are not only fixed and immutable in space, they are also fixed and immutable in time. Sovereignty is not just a theory about the past and present, but a never-ending prescription for an eternal future."[19]

A similar assumption is made by Karkkainen, who postulates the theory that environmental regulation is still based on a model of "rule-based and rule-bound", also known as "command and control"[20].This was established in the 1960s:

"It sought to solve environmental problems by imposing and enforcing fixed uniform rules, binding commands of the State to which all subject to its sovereignty must conform. This approach assumes that an expert decision-maker – the regulator, an arm of the State – would identify the key environmental problems, gather expert information, prescribe effective solutions with sufficient specificity to translate into legally binding commands and enforce those rules, backed by the coercive power of the State. This model approaches complex problems by fragmentation, carving the larger puzzle into smaller pieces that can be isolated and controlled through categorical commands."[21]

The problems with this outdated model are multifaceted and particularly apparent in environmental protection. The rules are often criticized as "crafted under necessarily fragmentary and incomplete information, costly, ineffective, rigid, underinclusive, overinclusive, or at cross purposes with other rules", while no progress can be seen. Others view the provisions as narrow and isolated, while it can be determined that "ecosystems continue to be fragmented and degraded."[22] Consequently, Ruhl underlined:

"Climate change…will also exert tremendous structural pressure on the very design and implementation of law itself."[23]

However, why do these weaknesses of the concept of State sovereignty become so evident in the context of environmental protection? In no other context—and that

---

[19] J. A. Camilleri (note 232 in Chap. 3), 171.

[20] *C. van der Lugt*, in: F. Biermann/R. Brohm/K. Dingwerth, "Global environmental change and the nation state", 2002, 230.

[21] *B. C. Karkkainen*, in: F. Biermann/R. Brohm/K. Dingwerth, "Global environmental change and the nation state", 2002, 207.

[22] Ibid.

[23] *J. B. Ruhl,* Climate Change Adaptation and the Structural Transformation of Environmental Law: Climate Change Adaptation and the Structural Transformation of Environmental Law (2010), 377; *M. Burkett,* The Nation Ex-Situ: On Climate Change, Deterritorialized Nationhood and the Post-Climate Era, Climate Law (2011), 373.

does not mean only in the here discussed, very vivid example of the disappearing islands—"the State, as a spatial unit, is irrelevant".[24] The "theoretical construct" of a Nation-State is based on five main pillars,[25] which are also "linked with (...) inextricably:"[26] territory, (mutual) recognition, autonomy against external interference,[27] control of borders, and legitimacy. These pillars have been challenged by "environmental degradation" in specific ways.[28] We will look further at each condition of sovereignty and the challenges they have faced so far.

5.1.2.1 Transgression of Borders

As we have already noted, environmental progress does not respect state borders.[29] The striking and shocking example of the Chernobyl accident in 1986, where "fixed boundaries of the national domain were effortlessly disregarded by the drifting clouds of radioactive gas",[30] is only one of a long series of serious transboundary accidents, which have questioned the simple and effective system of "the containers of sovereign States".[31] This type of incident prevents States from exercising the full scope of their internal sovereignty. Remembering the former intention of the State's territorial integrity, the establishment of internal social order, and the promotion of a population's general welfare protected by a "demarcated hard-shell", [32] the problem lies in the fact that environmental harm is not "territorial[ly] contained" and outside effects influence the "inside" of the State territory.[33]

However, not only are the cross-border effects problematic, but the lack of liability and uncertainty about the identity of the polluter are also issues.[34] Unlike the Chernobyl case, most environmental degradation is not caused by a single

---

[24] V. Ward (note 27), 79; *A. Linklater*, Critical theory and world politics, 1st ed., (1949) 2007, 92.

[25] J. A. Camilleri (note 232 in Chap. 3), 171.

[26] *M. Williams*, in: E. Kofman, Globalization: Theory and practice, 2003, 118.

[27] V. A. Ventura (note 206 in Chap. 3), 87, 91.

[28] L. Elliot (note 169 in Chap. 3), 195; J. A. Camilleri (note 232 in Chap. 3), 177 et seq; *P. Wapner*, in: K. T. Litfin, The greening of sovereignty in world politics, 1998, 277; C. Blanchard (note 151 in Chap. 3), 74; *T. Inoguchi/P. Bacon,* Sovereignties: Westphalian, liberal and anti-utopian, International Relations of the Asia-Pacific (2001), 288.

[29] M. Bothe (note 125 in Chap. 2), 542.

[30] J. A. Camilleri (note 232 in Chap. 3), 177; *U. Beck*, World risk society, 1999, 23.

[31] L. Elliot (note 169 in Chap. 3), 196.

[32] *R. J. Harknett*, in: E. Kofman, Globalization: Theory and practice, 2003, 140.

[33] L. Elliot (note 169 in Chap. 3), 196.

[34] M. Bothe (note 125 in Chap. 2), 541.

actor or factor, but rather by the combined effects of many influences on the ecological system.[35] Pollutants and waste are transmitted over long distances; land-based sources mainly cause oceanic and coastal pollution; and economic globalization has significant impacts on the environment of other States and the so-called global commons—areas beyond national jurisdiction.[36] Consequently, environmental law principles, such as the preventive principle, which was initially invented for disputes between neighboring States, did not have any effect in these cases, even though it had already been adopted in international environmental treaties.[37] Whereas the doctrine *sic utere tuo ut alienum non laedas* and the principle of good neighborliness are acclaimed to be "the heart of contemporary conception of sovereignty and environmental protection", it is completely neglected that they are only auxiliary constructions to find a balance between the contradictory ideas of sovereignty and environmental protection.[38] The often quoted and copied Principle 21 of the Stockholm Declaration, once celebrated as a "triumph of diplomatic compromise," is nothing but this: a "diplomatic compromise" or, in other words, a description of the status quo: the attempt to fit environmental protection into the long-lasting doctrine of sovereignty.[39]

To make matters worse, the weakest and often poorer States are not supported in any way by "upholding sovereignty in the international sphere" and by the "long and established tradition of respecting State sovereignty". Consequently, their development is constrained by their inability to address the growing problems of pollution and environmental degradation.[40] Here, the far-reaching consequences of colonialism become apparent, while "ancient colonial maps were drawn with little respect for natural conditions," once again sacrificing the poorest of the poorest.[41] Consequently, their already weakened internal and external autonomy deteriorates further.[42] One of the most impressive examples is, in fact, the "disappearance" of the low-lying island States in the South Pacific.[43]

---

[35] L. Elliot (note 169 in Chap. 3), 196; M. Bothe (note 125 in Chap. 2), 542.

[36] L. Elliot (note 169 in Chap. 3), 196.

[37] *Compare: Declaration on Environment and Development (note 12 in Chap. 2), Principle 18–19*; L. Elliot (note 169 in Chap. 3), 200.

[38] P. Wapner (note 39), 278.

[39] Ibid.

[40] Ibid., 279.

[41] *E. Benvenisti*, Management of Transboundary Resources: International Law and Optimal Resource Use, 23.

[42] L. Elliot (note 169 in Chap. 3), 196 et seq.

[43] Ibid., 196.

5.1.2.2 Autonomy Against External Interference

Not only is internal sovereignty threatened, but external sovereignty of States is also challenged, thereby challenging the principle of non-intervention. First, given the arguments above, we must realize that the more developed a country and its technology are, the less plausible the notion of unanticipated environmental harm becomes.[44] That cannot only be demonstrated by the effect of the environmental harm caused by the developed countries but also by the example of nuclear power, the use—or better the threat of use—of nuclear weapons.[45]

The use of armed force remains a key feature of State sovereignty, as it differentiates States from other organizations in national and international arenas and plays a crucial role in defending national interests and the sovereign domain.[46] As Barry stressed in 1989,

> *"Frontiers are established by power and maintained by the constant and known readiness to defend them by arms. It is absurd to think that professors of linguistics and collectors of folklore can do the work of statesmen and soldiers."*[47]

However, what seemed incontestable in 1989 appears doubtful now: the claim of State sovereignty to enforce interests of long-term security for the State territory stands in stark contrast "with the interaction of the use of military power and the properties of the biological and physical world".[48] Considering the damage nuclear weapons cause as well as their potential for permanent destruction of parts of life as we know it, they pose a threat to the vitality of not only the States but also the biosystem itself.[49] Furthermore, due to the continually developing technology, the scope of this risk in the near and far future—especially for the biosystem—seems incalculable. Consequently, bearing the immense ecological vulnerability in mind, the claim to the use of armed force to protect nations' sovereignty "will be undermined by the devastating impact of their use."[50] Therefore, the use of armed force to protect State sovereignty entails the destruction of this same State's sovereignty at the same time.[51] To summarize, "the loss of

---

[44] Ibid., 197.

[45] J. A. Camilleri (note 232 in Chap. 3), 179 et seq.

[46] Ibid., 179.

[47] B. M. Barry (note 40 in Chap. 3), 163.

[48] J. A. Camilleri (note 232 in Chap. 3), 180.

[49] Ibid.

[50] Ibid.

[51] Ibid.

protective power undermines State territorial integrity".[52] In Barry's words, it is time for "changes in the international regime that would reduce the importance of ownership of territory for military security and access to natural resources".[53]

The concept of the new world would involve a division into threatening and threatened communities, on the one hand, and, on the other, so-called States that celebrate their authority through military control.[54] Consequently, to confront this threat, security cannot rest at the State level in a "hard-shell territory". Still, it must become a global concern in the shape of "an alternative universalist system of global order".[55] We can say territoriality currently constitutes more of a "soft shell of deterrence" by "the dissuasive power of nuclear possession" than anything else.[56] Given these environmental threats, authority based on sovereignty appears relatively porous, almost irrelevant, and not the most suitable instrument.[57] Unlike the concept of "international" or "internationalization", which will always be based on claims to exclusive authority based on Statehood, "globalization, by contrast, admits to the fact that exclusivity is neither an actuality nor a historical possibility".[58]

5.1.2.3 Distribution of Jurisdiction

Besides using armed force, today's most important pillar of State sovereignty is found in "its supreme authority to claim to justice and truth" legitimately, which serves as the instrument for the State's implementation.[59] The structure of the modern industrial State relies on a panel of technical experts, technological departments, and elaborate scientific theories and processes. Its organs are highly dependent on their experts and technical consultants.[60] Bearing the primary sources of derived State authority in mind, the State frequently uses these technical means to solve problems. It demonstrates extraordinary success through its access to instrumental rationality.[61] However, the "single-minded approach"

[52] R. J. Harknett (note 43), 144.

[53] B. M. Barry (note 40 in Chap. 3), 176.

[54] J. A. Camilleri (note 232 in Chap. 3), 180.

[55] R. J. Harknett (note 43), 142.

[56] Ibid., 146.

[57] L. Elliot (note 169 in Chap. 3), 196; A. Linklater (note 35), 92.

[58] M. Williams (note 37), 117; A. Linklater (note 35), 104 et seq.

[59] J. A. Camilleri (note 232 in Chap. 3), 181.

[60] Ibid.

[61] Ibid.

can only be understood in the light of, and modeled by, the standard that technological thinking and invention have reached at that precise moment; this will always be a reductionist perspective, which will confront a highly complex system of the biosphere and environment at all times.[62] We can instead observe that

> *"Technological developments have robbed the territory requirement of much of its functional utility since the issues of security, resources, and jurisdiction can be seen as being more closely related to the globalized world than to a State's territory."*[63]

Even though the State is the "producer of technological thinking in contemporary society", the State itself, grounded in the theory of sovereignty, remains trapped in a reductionist perspective, unable to understand or confront the ongoing biophysical interactions.[64] Consequently, the effectiveness of sovereignty is—once again—called into question:

> *"The gap between the possession of sovereignty (formal sovereignty) and the capacity to exercise those rights (effective sovereignty) is so wide that it no longer makes sense to say that States possess supreme authority; the concept of sovereignty should be abandoned."*[65]

This becomes even more evident when one considers the primary purpose of international law, the "peaceful coexistence between sovereign States in the international arena via creating obstacles to excessive and unbalanced exercises of power", expressed and exercised by just one type of source of jurisdiction: the duties, which limit the unrestricted exercise of State authority.[66] International jurisdiction is based on principles that are exceptionally challenged in the context of climate change: territoriality and nationality.[67] Whereas territoriality defines the space within which States exercise power over persons, things, or events, in contrast to the extraterritorial application of legislation, nationality defines the

[62] Ibid., 181 et seq; C. Armstrong (note 46 in Chap. 2), 141 et seq.
[63] G. J. Abhimanyu (note 222 in Chap. 3), 51; C. Blanchard (note 151 in Chap. 3), 75.
[64] J. A. Camilleri (note 232 in Chap. 3), 182.
[65] M. Williams (note 37), 113.
[66] V. A. Ventura (note 206 in Chap. 3), 92.
[67] Ibid.

personal identity of the parties, giving them status and assignment within a specific jurisdictional system.[68] Both concepts appear to be at stake in the context of climate change and the associated problems, as explored in this research project.

This can be illustrated with the example of transboundary harm, which the Polluter State often attempts to justify by claiming it acted within its sovereign jurisdiction.[69] International corporations frequently relocate the most polluting production facilities to countries with less stringent environmental control standards, thereby taking advantage of those countries' sovereignty.[70] The preventative principle cannot effectively address these problems, given that all activities now produce effects beyond territorial boundaries.[71] The so-called "polluter pays" principle is often displaced by the "victim pays" principle, so that the State most affected by the pollution has to bear the costs.[72] The international system has failed to provide adequate compensation to victims for years.[73] Consequently, the effectiveness—not only of States as such but also of the whole international State system—is in question, as they are not guaranteed to head off and confront environmental harm in an adequate way, not even by means of the idea of distributional justice, as it is implemented nowadays.[74]

Moreover, the greater the State's strength and power is, the higher the risk of faster erosion of legitimacy, as it lacks the "ability to ameliorate the structure and pace of global development which lies at the root of the ecological crisis".[75] Furthermore, the democratic system, which "cut the State's attention span into short planning periods in line with the electoral timetable"—in the U.S., with the average time for the planning of 2,8 years –, is not particularly helpful in confronting and counteracting long-lasting environmental degradation and the deterioration of the biosphere.[76] This dilemma challenges every State trying to exercise its instrumental legitimacy properly, as it poses "a destructive ecological spiral".[77]

---

68 Ibid., 92–93, 182.

69 M. Bothe (note 125 in Chap. 2), 539; J. A. Camilleri (note 232 in Chap. 3), 185.

70 J. A. Camilleri (note 232 in Chap. 3), 186.

71 M. Bothe (note 125 in Chap. 2), 539 et seq.

72 J. A. Camilleri (note 232 in Chap. 3), 186 et seq.

73 Ibid., 187.

74 M. Bothe (note 125 in Chap. 2), 541; J. A. Camilleri (note 232 in Chap. 3), 187, 192–193.

75 J. A. Camilleri (note 232 in Chap. 3), 184.

76 Ibid.

77 Ibid., 184, 195.

5.1.2.4 Exercising Sovereign Rights Causing Environmental Degradation

One of the most significant dilemmas in this discussion is that exercising sovereignty primarily causes environmental degradation.[78] This can be most impressively illustrated by the example of States using the principle of permanent sovereignty over natural resources. Examining the situation regarding the Amazon, "the green lung of the world", the government of Brazil can justify its radical deforestation programs with its sovereign right to use timber resources within the territory of its State.[79] The same reasoning is employed to justify over-fishing within a State's territorial waters.[80] Consequently, exercising sovereign rights legitimately within the borders and enforcing purely selfish national interests and property rights can harm the environment, both within and outside the borders.[81] Moreover, the governments and political authorities aim to stay in power and invest their energy and focus their effort here, so that the exercise of "their fiduciary responsibilities" is sidelined, typically regarded as an afterthought, and "is more often than not made subject to their political survival".[82] Consequently, the question has to be raised if "the notions of State sovereignty and effective protection of the natural environment, including biodiversity, should be considered irredeemably contradictory".[83] Sovereigns are, as the ICJ once articulated in the Lotus case of 1927—nowadays better known as "Lotus principle" –

> *"free to dispose of the resources under their jurisdiction at their pleasure, unless a contrary international norm was proved."*[84]

This is considered an "optimistic belief in the international invisible hand".[85] With the increasing number of environmental disasters since the middle of the 20th century, the mismanagement of single sovereign powers has become obvious, but "there is very little room for redrawing political borders to conform to the

---

[78] L. Elliot (note 169 in Chap. 3), 197 et seq; *S. Kamieniecki/M. S. Granzeier*, in: K. T. Litfin, The greening of sovereignty in world politics, 1998, 260.

[79] L. Elliot (note 169 in Chap. 3), 198.

[80] Ibid.

[81] Ibid., 198.

[82] F. Venter (note 18 in Chap. 3), 66.

[83] Ibid.

[84] *Lotus Case,* ICJ No. 9, 07.09.1927, 20; *F. L. Bordin,* Reflections of Customary International Law: The Authority of Codification Conventions and ILC Draft Articles in International Law, International and Comparative Law Quarterly (2014), 564.

[85] E. Benvenisti (note 52), 22 et seq.

boundaries of natural resources."[86] This leads us remember the already mentioned tragedy of the commons:[87] every State is interested in gaining more profit from a resource with minimal costs of its own and at the expense of "the others". In the words of the World Commission on Environment and Development, this means: "The earth is one, but we are not."[88]

However, this approach fueled mistrust among developing countries. For these countries, as they argue, it would entail a "form of expropriating or extricating" for the greater good of declaring areas like the rainforest as public goods in the application of CHM.[89] To counterbalance the claims of developing States, the principle of common concern seems more appropriate, as it does not take territory away, but creates a kind of shared ownership.[90] It is considered a principle of greater versatility and lower practical commitments because it applies to matters both within and outside national jurisdiction, making it more suitable for addressing climate change-related issues.[91] However, this principle entails the risk of "unilateral extraterritorial environmental actions," which could constitute an attack on the sovereignty of developing countries.[92]

This, however, does not mean that the exercise of sovereignty and environmental protection are constantly at odds.[93] States can also act—individually or collectively—on behalf of the environment, entering into multilateral agreements, such as the Bamako Agreement between African countries.[94] This may become problematic when sovereign domestic environmental policy is "extra-territorialized" and attempts to enforce environmental protection by restricting other States. By way of example, the restriction on imports of tropical timber that does not comply with the EU's sustainable management rules necessarily infringes the sovereignty of the producing States.[95]

---

[86] Ibid., 23.

[87] *D. Steffens/F. Haberkuss*, Über Leben: Zukunftsfrage Artensterben: Wie wir die Ökorise überwinden, 2020, 138 et seq; *A. Serdy*, Commentary: Property rights in areas beyond national jurisdiction: not too late for proper debate?, The International Legal Regime of Areas beyond National Jurisdiction (2010), 147.

[88] L. Elliot (note 169 in Chap. 3), 198; E. Benvenisti (note 52), 31.

[89] A. Gonzalez Arreaza (note 14), 269.

[90] Ibid.

[91] M. Dervovic (note 202 in Chap. 2), 312 et seq.

[92] A. Gonzalez Arreaza (note 14), 270.

[93] L. Elliot (note 169 in Chap. 3), 199.

[94] Ibid.

[95] Ibid.

Consequently, environmental policy means there will always be "two competing sovereignty claims at stake":[96] the demand for autonomy and authority over internal sovereignty—the territory—and the mutual recognition and respect for other States within the international system.[97] A vivid example of this conflict is the recent WTO panel case against China concerning export duties and quotas on raw materials and rare earths.[98] In the case of *China—Raw Materials*, the Panel recognized that the principle of permanent sovereignty over natural resources, as a principle of general international law, equates to the principle of sustainable development.[99] However, it stressed that these two principles must be held in balance to "conserve and preserve the environment":[100]

> *"In the Panel's view, (...), our interpretation of Article XX(g) should "take into account" the principle of sovereignty over natural resources. The principle of sovereignty over natural resources allows Members to use their natural resources to promote their own development while regulating their use to ensure sustainable development. Conservation and economic development are not necessarily mutually exclusive policy goals; they can coexist. Can such policy goals also operate in harmony with WTO obligations, given that Members must exercise their sovereignty over natural resources consistent with their WTO obligations? In the Panel's view, Article XX(g) has been interpreted and applied in a manner that respects WTO Members' sovereign rights over their own natural resources."*[101]

In sum, if States want to benefit from their membership in the WTO, they must also accept the limits imposed on their sovereignty over natural resources. Therefore, in exercising sovereign rights to join international agreements, they also submit to the rights and duties under WTO law.[102] Consequently, for the first time, the transformation of the meaning of "S" in PSNR from "sovereign

---

[96] Ibid., 200.

[97] Ibid.

[98] A. Gonzalez Arreaza (note 14), 270 et seq.

[99] *China—Measures Related to the Exportation of Various Raw Materials,* WT/DS394/R, 05.07.2011, 7.380–7.381.

[100] A. Gonzalez Arreaza (note 14), 272.

[101] *China—Measures Related to the Exportation of Various Raw Materials,* WT/DS394/R, 05.07.2011, 7.381.

[102] A. Gonzalez Arreaza (note 14), 271.

authority" to "sovereignty responsibility" became palpable, allowing it to "operate in harmony with" sustainable development and the "preservation of the environment".[103]

It became even clearer in the case of *China—Rare Earths*, in which the Panel referred to the main goals of sustainable development pointed out in Principle 2 of the Rio Declaration in a broader way,[104] and stressed, once again, the importance of preservation and conservation of the environment in the context of intergenerational justice:

> *"In recognition of the permanent sovereignty that every Member exercises over its natural resources, WTO law recognizes the right of Members to adopt conservation measures should they wish to do so, in the light of their own objectives and policy goals, including economic and sustainable development. In other words, resource-endowed WTO Members are entitled to design conservation policies that meet their development needs, determine how much of a resource should be exploited today and how much should be preserved for the future, including for use by future generations, in a manner consistent with their sustainable development needs and their international obligations."*[105]

On the other hand, without the exercise of sovereign authority, implementing and enforcing international environmental law would not be possible.[106] This is because the assertiveness of enforcement norms lies with the State; it alone is obliged to choose the measures to implement environmental law.[107] Consequently, the argument of the "strong State" is renewed and strengthened, because the "menu of choices available to States" is extended.[108] However, this liberty for States can also be a burden, especially for economically weaker States.[109] The demands of the international community can therefore "undermine the territorial

[103] *China—Measures Related to the Exportation of Various Raw Materials,* WT/DS394/R, 05.07.2011, 7.372; A. Gonzalez Arreaza (note 14), 274 et seq; A. Jayagovind (note 63 in Chap. 2), 150; Y. Tyagi (note 15 in Chap. 2), 612.

[104] *China—Measures Related to the Exportation of Rare Earths, Tungsten, and Molybdenum,* WT/DS431/R, 25.03.2014, 7.263.

[105] *China—Measures Related to the Exportation of Rare Earths, Tungsten, and Molybdenum,* WT/DS431/R, 25.03.2014, 7.267.

[106] L. Elliot (note 169 in Chap. 3), 200.

[107] Ibid., 201.

[108] Ibid., 200 et seq.

[109] Ibid., 201.

integrity and right of self-determination of national communities" and intensify the less effective sovereignty (see above Chap. 3).[110]

Consequently, the existing form of sovereign Statehood seems old-fashioned and "morally parochial," "resting on the justice of their rule as on their de facto hold on power."[111] All the requirements and attributes of Statehood—territoriality, inviolability of borders, mutual recognition, and legitimate authority—maintain a *status quo,* which divides the world into an "inside", which protects itself from the "outside".[112] Through interaction and connection in international law, an interplay of rights and duties emerged, which extended and overwhelmed the State system, dividing it into "sameness and otherness".[113] Consequently, implementing a "global village sovereignty" in which every person is recognized as a global citizen would be the best model to face environmental degradation.[114] Going back to the roots of this principle, sovereignty facing environmental challenges should not be based on the "analogy with private ownership of territory and resources", but should be "re-envisioned as a public trust by which States exercise sovereignty to manage resources in the interests of the beneficiaries of the trust—the world's peoples".[115]

5.1.2.5 Pooled or Collective Sovereignty: The Better Way to Confront Environmental Degradation?

Yet, how can we address environmental degradation more effectively? Does it necessarily require and entail the dissolution of the model "sovereignty," or do we need a new form of sovereignty? In particular, when dealing with environmental challenges, bearing all the global and regional multilateral environmental agreements in mind, it is conspicuous that "the only way most States can realize and express their sovereignty is through participation in the various regimes that regulate and order the international system".[116] Considering the transboundary and global nature of environmental degradation, the State cannot manage

---

[110] *R. Eckersley*, The green state: Rethinking democracy and sovereignty, 2004, 249; L. Elliot (note 169 in Chap. 3), 201.

[111] L. Elliot (note 169 in Chap. 3), 206; A. Linklater (note 35), 90 et seq; *R. Bellamy/D. Castiglione*, in: D. Archibugi/D. Held/M. Köhler, Re-imagining political community: Studies in cosmopolitan democracy, 1998, 156.

[112] L. Elliot (note 169 in Chap. 3), 206; A. Linklater (note 35), 90 et seq.

[113] L. Elliot (note 169 in Chap. 3), 207; U. Beck (note 41), 62 et seq.

[114] L. Elliot (note 169 in Chap. 3), 207; D. Deudney (note 93 in Chap. 3); A. Linklater (note 35), 92.

[115] L. Elliot (note 169 in Chap. 3), 201.

[116] Ibid.

them on its own.[117] Instead, we can notice that the "post-modern sovereignty" will be exercised through "an intense cooperation between sovereign States", in the form of commissions, programs, funds, intergovernmental panels, or working groups.[118] Despite the complicated, rather bureaucratic system of "nested and polycentric governance," the fragmented, overlapping cooperation systems have repeatedly proved capable of delivering effective outcomes.[119] However, this represents a departure from the Westphalian tradition, in which individual States hold sovereignty.[120] It means a transfer of sovereign power to "interest groups and international bureaucrats" to such an extent that the individual State cannot exercise its sovereignty effectively on its own, but only "collectively" due to legitimization by the "world's peoples".[121]

There are already examples of such interest groups. For example, one of the fascinatingly well-working cooperations is the international water protection commission of Lake Constance (Internationale Gewässerschutzkommission für den Bodensee),[122] which is formed by Germany, Austria, and Switzerland and was founded in the middle of the 20th century due to the "steadily choked algae growth caused by the excessive drainage of wastewater".[123] Significant parts of the lake are thereby considered "condominiums", a legal figure in international law, considered temporary, which gives States the possibility to exercise their sovereignty over said territory together "as common property".[124] Here, the parallels between the convergence of "private" standard property regimes of pooled resources and "public" condominiums over shared territory are shockingly apparent.[125] Furthermore, this legal construct can be a "solution for existing boundary disputes" because it "allows States to collaborate and build a community of shared rights and responsibilities." Consequently, it represents an inversion of one of the main pillars of sovereignty: control over borders.[126]

---

[117] Ibid., 201 et seq.

[118] Ibid., 202; *G. Sorensen*, Sovereignty: Change and Continuity in a Fundamental Institution: Sovereignty: Change and Continuity in a Fundamental Institution, 602.

[119] C. Armstrong (note 46 in Chap. 2), 141.

[120] A. Linklater (note 35), 108.

[121] L. Elliot (note 169 in Chap. 3), 202; P. H. Sand (note 11), 537.

[122] *J. H. Samuels,* Condominium arrangements in international practice: Reviving an abandoned concept of boundary dispute resolution, Michigan Journal of International Law 29 (2008), 738 et seq.: *similar example: the Antarctica.*

[123] F. Venter (note 18 in Chap. 3), 72.

[124] J. H. Samuels (note 134), 768 et seq; F. Venter (note 18 in Chap. 3), 72 et seq.

[125] J. H. Samuels (note 134), 768 et seq; F. Venter (note 18 in Chap. 3), 73 et seq.

[126] J. H. Samuels (note 134), 774; F. Venter (note 18 in Chap. 3), 73.

The tripartite treaty between the Republic of Mozambique, the Republic of South Africa, and the Republic of Zimbabwe on the establishment of the Great Limpopo Transfrontier Park goes one step further, as Article 7 (4) of the Treaty of 2002 earmarked the establishment of a pluralist management board:[127]

> *"Where fences have been removed from previous international boundaries, each Party undertakes to respect the sovereign rights of a bordering Party and not to allow its officials to cross into a bordering Party's territory, unless previously agreed on through either arrangement with the JMB (Joint Management Board) or appropriate communication between mandated security or other designated agencies of the Parties."*

It is interesting to note that this treaty also declared in its preamble the parties' "responsibility to conserve and sustainably use natural resources for present and future generations."[128]

On the other hand, we must be aware that the traditional corpus concerning external sovereignty in international law remains unchanged. To negotiate and establish international treaties, such as multilateral environmental agreements, and subsequently create international organizations, working groups, or panels, the State must determine the framework for its external or foreign policy.[129] Notably, the 2015 Paris Agreement has also been ratified by supranational bodies—in this case, by the EU. However, additional ratification by each state is necessary to comply with the requirement, so a complete replacement of individual sovereignty has not yet been achieved.[130] States can still decide whether to become parties to environmental agreements (or not, as the United States has chosen regarding most international treaties).[131] However, the pressure for a more effective intergovernmental body to achieve adequate environmental protection is growing steadily.[132] Furthermore, multilateral environmental treaties can affect non-parties, *e.g.*, through trade restrictions.[133] Moreover, once the

---

[127] F. Venter (note 18 in Chap. 3), 74.

[128] Ibid., 75.

[129] L. Elliot (note 169 in Chap. 3), 202.

[130] Ibid; *J. Crawford*, in: J. Crawford/M. Koskenniemi, The Cambridge companion to international law, 2012, 132; Paris Agreement to the United Nations Framework Convention on Climate Change, 12.12.2015; UNFCCC.

[131] L. Elliot (note 169 in Chap. 3), 202 et seq.

[132] Ibid., 202.

[133] Ibid., 203.

State ratifies the environmental agreement, the "path dependency for policy-making" is unavoidable.[134] Hence, we can observe the growing independence of State authority within the regime of multilateral environmental agreements, such as the 1998 Rotterdam Convention[135] and the 2001 Stockholm Convention on Persistent Organic Pollutants.[136] Here, intergovernmental bodies can make recommendations and prepare decision-making guidelines documents for including new chemicals in the restricted lists, while the final decision about the "red list" is taken at the COP level.[137] Consequently, one of the "key features of globalization is interconnectedness", which refers not only to mutuality as in interdependence, but also stipulates the possibility of dependence.[138] In sum, there is a pool of independent "fragmented" authorities nowadays, not in the sense of shared and united sovereignty like the EU, but in more diffused ways:[139] "Power is shared and governance is increasingly diffused, located in both public and private spaces, characterized by the authority in multiple institutional arenas."[140] Across a broad range of institutions and actors, such as civil society movements, NGOs, business and corporate actors, and the scientific community, we can observe a "vertical global decision-making" process characterized by a "crisscrossing flow of transformed authority".[141] In particular, the growth of governmental organizations, quasi-governmental institutions, and non-governmental associations, like movements and activism of civil society and NGOs, is becoming louder and trying to fill the gap in the inactivity of States, together "check and balance on unbridled State sovereignty".[142] These tendencies reveal growing doubts about the functionality of today's social contract between the State and the people, thereby questioning the legitimacy of internal sovereignty of States and the "exclusionary nature of sovereignty and traditional ideas about community and citizenship."[143] In conclusion, civil society is considered an "alternative source of legitimacy as

[134] Ibid.

[135] Rotterdam Convention on the Prior informed Consent Procedure for Certain Hazardous Chemicals and Pesticides in International Trade, 10.09.1998.

[136] Stockholm Convention on Persistent Organic Pollutants, 22.05.2001.

[137] L. Elliot (note 169 in Chap. 3), 204.

[138] M. Williams (note 37), 116.

[139] *M. C. Love*, Global issues beyond sovereignty, 2020, 40.

[140] L. Elliot (note 169 in Chap. 3), 204; M. Williams (note 37), 113.

[141] L. Elliot (note 169 in Chap. 3), 204; *J. Rosenau*, in: D. Archibugi/D. Held/M. Köhler, Re-imagining political community: Studies in cosmopolitan democracy, 1998, 35.

[142] L. Elliot (note 169 in Chap. 3), 205; M. Williams (note 37), 113 et seq; B. C. Karkkainen (note 32), 208.

[143] L. Elliot (note 169 in Chap. 3), 205; A. Linklater (note 35), 109 et seq.

well as of authority," replacing the State's claim to sovereignty.[144] This "re-vision of sovereignty embedded in citizens or citizenship rather than in Statehood—ultimate authority within a territory is not the State but the people, returning the pendulum to the requirement that the State, acting as sovereign, is the product of demand for the right of self-determination and is sovereign only at the will of the people".[145]

5.1.3 The Strengthening of "People" in International Law

Focusing on State sovereignty and its struggle to find its role in the modern world, we will now examine the people. Here, the questions will focus on how they find their role in the contemporary world and how they make an impact. The most controversial and provoking question will be: "Does the prominence of NGOs at recent world conferences not evidence the fading legitimacy of the State system? Are human rights not steadily eroding domestic jurisdiction?"[146]

5.1.3.1 Climate Change Litigation: The Voice of People

However, how can the people's will—the "voice of the people"—be heard? A closer examination of the formal climate negotiation process reveals that the active participation of civil society is often lacking, in many cases nonexistent.[147] When it comes to the outcome of international treaty negotiations, civil society can observe, propose, pressure, prod, and even parody, but ultimately, it is controlled by governments.[148] However, an upcoming vehicle will help give people's voices greater value and "empower civil society": climate change litigation.[149] For instance, climate change was first brought to the agenda of the Inter-American Human Rights Commission by civil society, whereas governments and international institutions did not initially see the need for it.[150] Consequently, "climate

---

[144] L. Elliot (note 169 in Chap. 3), 206; M. Williams (note 37), 114.

[145] L. Elliot (note 169 in Chap. 3), 204 et seq.

[146] *B. Simma/A. L. Paulus,* The "International Community": Facing the Challenge of Globalization, European Journal of International Law 9 (1998), 272.

[147] *D. B. Hunter*, in: H. M. Osofsky/W. C. G. Burns, Adjudicating climate change: State, national, and international approaches, 2009, 370.

[148] Ibid.

[149] Ibid.

[150] Ibid.

litigation helps to democratize climate policy", both on the national level and on the international level.[151]

One notable example of this new development was the Inuit Petition, filed with the Inter-American Commission on Human Rights in December 2005, against the United States, to draw more attention to the problems faced by the Inuit due to climate change.[152] The intrigue of this case lies not only in its showing of the interaction between climate change and human rights for the first time. More importantly, it "serves as a bridge between Nation-States and civil society".[153] This petition is representative of "a multi-scalar regulatory dynamics" which breaks up the traditional Westphalian hierarchy, where international law only "rests on the contest of sovereign and equal Nation-States" and national authority remains untouched.[154] Even though the petition was filed on a supranational level, it "interacted with multiple types of actors operating at more than one level of governance" and thereby promoted a constructive process of "interrelation".[155] Moreover, the petition serves as an interconnection between different public levels and shows the "dynamics between governmental and private actors in the energy industry". Moreover, several NGOs together "represented a similar web of interconnection" as a counterbalance to industry interests.[156] In sum, the Inuit petition outlined "how creative lawyering may help to transform dialogue" for the first time.[157]

Even though the petition was not successful in the end, cases like this provoke a new "understanding and re-evaluation of key concepts in the legal system" in an inter- and multidisciplinary way, including human rights, nuisance, intergenerational equity, and justice.[158] Some scholars argue that unsuccessful litigation can be even more effective in the end, as it highlights the gap between governing law and moral understanding more clearly.[159] Consequently, climate change litigation is an essential component of the process of change, particularly in "supporting and reinforcing values and codes" and in strengthening the public's awareness of

---

[151] Ibid.

[152] H. M. Osofsky (note 211 in Chap. 4), 272 et seq.

[153] Ibid., 282; *J. Peel*, Climate Change Litigation, 2015, 241.

[154] H. M. Osofsky (note 211 in Chap. 4), 286.

[155] Ibid.

[156] Ibid., 287.

[157] Ibid., 291.

[158] *N. Rogers*, in: T. Bristow/Ford Thomas H., A Cultural History of Climate Change, 2016, 214.

[159] Ibid., 215.

the "awfulness and lawfulness" of this subject, symbolically and rhetorically.[160] We can therefore state that it is the fastest and most radical method, as it seeks to "challenge the establishment through the processes of the establishment" through "cultural performance".[161]

5.1.3.2 Groups of Populations as Claimants, NGOs, and Environmental Associations

Like all indigenous peoples, the Inuit—currently spread across three countries—Canada, the United States, and Greenland—are not entitled to the status of "nations" under international law.[162] However, their claims have gained significant influence through their powerful representative, the Inuit Circumpolar Council (ICC), an NGO.[163] In the international forum, this council is very present and active, making essential statements and recommendations in the PFII, which they joined with the Saami Council.[164]

NGOs are organizations, joined by people with specific interests and values, who want to "involve themselves in certain areas or issues with the permission of governments".[165] Consequently, environmental NGOs are probably the most active non-state actors in "ensuring compliance with environmental and climate change obligations" and "promoting environmental awareness among all people".[166] In contrast to States, the special nature of NGOs is that they are "sovereignty-free", which has the decisive advantage of enabling them to act transnationally and, therefore, independently of territory and population. Unlike companies, they do not intend to make a profit.[167] However, unlike individuals and moral legal persons—as we defined the "peoples"—they act to follow their own "egoistic interests immanent to them", often as the counterpart to the State and industry.[168]

---

[160] Ibid., 211, 214.

[161] J. Peel (note 166), 31; N. Rogers (note 171), 211.

[162] R. Tsosie (note 262 in Chap. 4), 92.

[163] Ibid; P. Wapner (note 39), 283.

[164] I. L. Stoyanova (note 211 in Chap. 4), 307.

[165] M. C. Love (note 151), 59; *R. Verheyen/S. Pabsch*, in: W. Kahl/M.-P. Weller, Climate change litigation: A handbook, 2021, 509.

[166] P. Wapner (note 39), 284; *I. Papanicolopulu/A. Rocha*, in: J. McDonald/J. McGee/R. Barnes, Research handbook on climate change, oceans and coasts, 2020, 203.

[167] R. Verheyen and S. Pabsch (note 178), 509.

[168] I. Papanicolopulu and A. Rocha (note 179), 196.

However, how can they exert influence if decision-making power and national authority are in the hands of States? The fact that the "Westphalian sovereignty system empowers States and restrains non-state actors" implies that NGOs are confined to a passive role as observers.[169] To put it in a nutshell, in the words of Wapner:

> *"States possess a monopoly over the legitimate use of violence within a given territory (...), [whereas] NGOs recognize this leading role and, in addition to their society-oriented types of practices, work to influence State action. In this context, these actions can be understood as attempts to enhance global responsibility among States."*[170]

Consequently, NGOs are interpersonal, "an odd category",[171] also called "the third sector",[172] as they are not governments, but receive resources from or even offer resources to governments, and, at the same time, promote ideas and point out possible responses to global problems.[173] They participate at different stages during the development of international law, like in (1) initiating law-making, (2) developing law, and (3) monitoring and calling for the enforcement of international law. [174] They also work as observers and advisors at international conferences. Nowadays, their "increasing role in all States or regime activities" allows them to support States in adaptively managing global challenges and complex interconnections, particularly in environmental questions, as well as in finding new responses to the "pressure of globalization" and to "diminish the self-regarding orientation of States".[175] In the case of environmental policy, this means:

> *"States and NGO efforts to create and sustain environmental regimes are attempts to qualify State sovereignty. They work to bring the dual needs of rights and responsibilities within the state system more into balance by restricting state sovereign authority. They represent the institutionalization of what policymakers called for in both the Stockholm and Rio Declarations."*[176]

---

[169] D. Deudney (note 93 in Chap. 3), 301.

[170] P. Wapner (note 39), 284 et seq.

[171] M. C. Love (note 151), 59.

[172] Ibid., 53; U. Beck (note 41), 38.

[173] M. C. Love (note 151), 53–80; P. Wapner (note 39), 283 et seq.

[174] *R. Wolfrum/N. Matz-Lück*, Conflicts in international environmental law, 2003, 204 et seq; I. Papanicolopulu and A. Rocha (note 179), 195.

[175] P. Wapner (note 39), 287; M. C. Love (note 151), 80; R. Wolfrum and N. Matz-Lück (note 188), 207; B. C. Karkkainen (note 32), 208 et seq.

[176] P. Wapner (note 39), 287.

Notably, in the past half-century, the number of NGOs has increased steadily, joined by members of the middle class, "who are frustrated with conventional party politics and the corrupted electoral system."[177] They strive to influence the system based on the understanding of a "global citizenship" detached from the straitjacket of democratic States, forming "the new constellation of a global sub-politics"—"the third force".[178] Sub politics means "direct politics"—the "shaping of the society of below"—without the detour via political institutions or the arduous journey across the hierarchical and bureaucratic hurdles created by States, to achieve "ad-hoc participation in political decisions".[179] By recognizing the growing weakness of States in coping with environmental matters, in particular, and the need for States to utilize tools such as laws, the "State-as-nation" is no longer the "primary theatre of political activity and participation".[180] We can refer to this polyarchic governance model for confronting complex ecological problems as "post-sovereign" governance.[181]

In Europe, this third force has already succeeded in the form of the environmental NGO ClientEarth. It has subsequently found its way into the EU's legal system through the adoption of the Aarhus Convention,[182] which entitles recognized environmental associations to bring third-party rights enforcement actions.[183] Here, once again, their altruistic role within the legal action comes to light, even though the legal concept behind this law is to be understood in the "sense of objective judicial review".[184] Although this legal concept is just one small step toward NGOs filing an action, in general, the entitlement requires a subjective right at its foundation, as codified in the German Constitution ("Grundgesetz") in Article 19(4) GG.[185] Consequently, NGOs typically have the power to file a lawsuit only in exceptional cases, such as the Peruvian

---

[177] A. Ong (note 279 in Chap. 3), 233; I. Papanicolopulu and A. Rocha (note 179), 197.

[178] U. Beck (note 41), 38.

[179] Ibid., 39.

[180] *C. van der Lugt*, Biermann, Global Environmental Change (s. Sovereignty), 230, 233.

[181] *B. C. Karkkainen*, Biermann, Global Environmental Change (s. Sovereignty), 210, 214.

[182] Convention on Access to Information, Public Participation in Decision-Making and Access to Justice in Environmental Matters, 31.10.2001; Aarhus Convention, Art. 15, implemented in German Law in the Environmental Appeals Act (UmwRG).

[183] R. Verheyen and S. Pabsch (note 178), 515, para. 24–25.

[184] *R. Verheyen/S. Pabsch*, in: W. Kahl/M.-P. Weller, Climate change litigation: A handbook, 2021, 515, para. 25.

[185] R. Verheyen and S. Pabsch (note 178), 514, para. 19–20.; *in German Code of Civil Procedure: § 51 ZPO.*

farmer Lliuya's case against the energy company RWE.[186] Even in the Netherlands, where the NGO Urgenda successfully challenged the Dutch government in one of the most significant climate change litigation cases,[187] several NGOs are now struggling to find "a remedy to a transformation towards climate neutrality" in a simple tort liability claim against Royal Dutch Shell.[188] However, in international law, NGOs have also used the remedies available to them as *amici curiae*, non-parties in court, who are "allowed to submit their comments or insights on the facts or law applicable for the proper administration of justice".[189] Even though to this day they are mostly not allowed to the traditional international courts—such as the ICJ and the International Tribunal for the Law of the Sea (ITLOS)—except in advisory opinions, they have managed to gain a certain level of legitimacy, transparency, and public participation by means of their efforts.[190]

However, the rising importance of the "third force" cannot be denied. Considering the questionable stability of the sovereignty of States, in particular, in the context of environmental concerns, a "new cluster of sovereign power—a cooperative State"—has to be considered carefully.[191] States do not have to see themselves as "the only key actors," but rather as the managers of matters.[192] On the one hand, they stand "in competition with a variety of organizations." Still, on the other hand, even if "sovereignty continues to limp along because of default," the complete replacement of State sovereignty by new forms of organization seems unrealistic.[193] However, even if non-state actors, such as NGOs or indigenous peoples with specific interests and knowledge about, *e.g.*, ecological processes, are excluded from the decision-making process, it results in an "incomplete picture of world politics".[194] Therefore, the UNGA, for instance, consistently incorporates this "third force" into its decision-making processes.[195] While approximately 1,400 NGOs were already involved in the Rio Conference,

[186] R. Verheyen and S. Pabsch (note 199), 511, para. 8.
[187] Ibid., 510–511, para. 7.
[188] Ibid., 513, para. 15.
[189] I. Papanicolopulu and A. Rocha (note 179), 199.
[190] *I. Papanicolopulu/A. Rocha*, in: J. McDonald/J. McGee/R. Barnes, Research handbook on climate change, oceans and coasts, 2020, 199 et seq.
[191] L. W. Pauly and E. Grande (note 124 in Chap. 3), 14.
[192] M. C. Love (note 151), 46.
[193] Ibid.
[194] S. Kamieniecki and M. S. Granzeier (note 89), 268.
[195] N. Matz-Lück and L. Christiansen (note 21 in Chap. 2), 526.

their participation continues to grow, and NGO involvement played a crucial role during the Rio + 20 Conference (WSSD) and the elaboration of the Paris Agreement.[196]

5.1.4 Conclusion

In reviewing all the considerations regarding the evanescent sovereignty challenged by climate change, on one hand, and the strengthening of the "voice" of people, represented by NGOs on the other, we must ask: What is sovereignty today? Is the absolute sovereignty of States still dominating the system of international law? Or is there already another form of sovereignty gradually replacing absolute State sovereignty and power?

Returning to the concept pool or collective sovereignty—as already developed above—the idea is not to "overcome, modify or capture" the concept of sovereignty, as it is only intended for a "state-centric sovereignty system", but rather to consider a system of "positive insight and guidance for building a sustainable society".[197] The false reasoning is that we are still thinking that all the environmentalist effort centers on "the privileged role of State claims to authority and autonomy" and "adding responsibilities to the rights of sovereign Statehood."[198] However, we have to be aware that sovereignty is not "synonymous with autonomy and supremacy of States", but it can also be exercised in another form, thereby reconsidering the "grass-roots dimensions of self-governing political associations".[199] As Deudney resumed:

> *"In short, a conception of political authority and community appropriate to the novel configuration of the global village must be terrapolitan rather than either Westphalian or cosmopolitan."*[200]

Focusing on this territorial approach, we must search for the source of sovereignty in this context, which we find in popular sovereignty.[201] Already, James Otis emphasized:

---

[196] N. Matz-Lück and L. Christiansen (note 20 in Chap. 2), 526.

[197] D. Deudney (note 93 in Chap. 3), 301 et seq.

[198] Ibid., 301.

[199] Ibid., 302 et seq.

[200] Ibid., 303.

[201] Ibid., 306.

"An original, supreme sovereign, absolute, and uncontrollable, earthly power must exist in precise over every society, from whose final decisions there can be no appeal but directly to Heaven. It is, therefore, originally and ultimately in the ***people*** *(...); and they never did in fact freely, nor can they rightfully, make an absolute unlimited renunciation of this divine right. It is ever like the thing given in trust and on a condition the performance of which no mortal can dispense with; namely, that the person or persons on whom the people confer the sovereignty, shall incessantly consult their good."*[202]

Popular sovereignty constitutes the cornerstone of every complex, legitimate authority, whether a federal, republican, democratic, or constitutional system.[203] In particular, reconsidering the republican political tradition, the idea behind this system is that "sovereignty is situated in the people" before hierarchical political authorities are established to construct a republic.[204] However, there is a strong opinion that even American Indian tribes possess sovereignty, in a temperate form, such as an "internal, culture-and community-based model of sovereignty" or simply "popular sovereignty".[205] For instance, "they have the sovereign right to develop their lands and resources, and they have the sovereign right to incorporate traditional environmental values into their own laws and policies."[206] In short, the power and authority are in the hands of the people, establishing their popular sovereignty in writing constitutions, which "can only be altered by supermajorities".[207]

In conclusion, sovereignty cannot be tied to the recognition of State sovereignty; even though "there is no evidence that the State has died," it merely seems to be the "most viable form of social organization."[208] However, the State nowadays takes on a more "competing role" alongside other actors, such as "individuals, international organizations, corporations, even the market

---

[202] *J. Otis*, The rights of the British colonies asserted and proved, 3rd ed., 1766, 12 et seq.
[203] D. Deudney (note 93 in Chap. 3), 306 et seq.
[204] Ibid., 307.
[205] E. Charles-Newton and E. A. Kronk (note 161 in Chap. 3), 77.
[206] R. Tsosie (note 262 in Chap. 4), 94.
[207] D. Deudney (note 93 in Chap. 3), 307.
[208] C. Blanchard (note 151 in Chap. 3), 74 et seq.

itself".[209] Consequently, we also have to think of sovereignty more unconventionally, because the absolute and unconstrained pursuit of freedom "for all human beings" is sovereignty.[210]

5.2 Reinterpretation of the Right of Self-Determination in the Context of Climate Change

One of the bases of this sovereignty—as we had already noted above—is the right of self-determination. However, this fundamental, inherent right of the people was subject to some change over the past half-century (see above Sect. 3.2). Traditionally, the self-determining people exercise their right "against another entity, a State or a colonial power".[211] Later, the omnipresence of the legal personality of States overshadowed every action of people, even though the State has never been and will not be the bearer of the right itself.[212] The state itself is not more than "the plenipotentiary or international dimension of peoples", a legal fiction, to ensure adequate enforcement of the rights of the people.[213]

Consequently, we must return to the origin of international law, to a law "less State-centered and more centered on people".[214] As we already ascertained above, the right of self-determination is "a right of the people, not of the governments", exercised and expressed based upon a collective interest or collective autonomy.[215] Drawing from the examples of history beginning with the "German nation" after World War II and ending up with the here relevant example of the disappearing island States, we must note, that the right of self-determination does not depend on any political relationship or political history. Still, the right must be amplified in an "abstract way" to "achieve equity".[216] In short, the right of

[209] C. Blanchard (note 17 in Chap. 3), 74 et seq.

[210] *N. Mansfield*, in: T. Bristow/Ford Thomas H., A Cultural History of Climate Change, 2016, 190.

[211] C. Blanchard (note 151 in Chap. 3), 114; *D. Thürer/T. Burri*, Self-Determination, Max Planck Encyclopedias of International Law (2008), para. 15–17.

[212] S. Willcox (note 7 in Chap. 1), 105.

[213] Ibid.

[214] S. J. Anaya (note 6 in Chap. 4), 156.

[215] S. Willcox (note 7 in Chap. 1), 112.

[216] C. Blanchard (note 151 in Chap. 3), 114.

self-determination has the task to "protect peoples' collective interest in autonomy and independence against grave (external or internal) threats over which they have little control." (compare Sect. 3.2).[217]

In this part of the Chapter, we will examine whether the right to self-determination is amenable to change in the context of climate change. Although the right of self-determination has likely not undergone a shift in meaning comparable to the sovereignty of States, we must find an alternative, broader scope of application for it. In particular, we need to determine whether the definition above applies to the case of the disappearing islands in the South Pacific, which are threatened by inundation caused by climate change.

5.2.1 Inundations Caused by Climate Change

Inundations of reef islands are described as "the diffusion of a high water level into or across an island, and flooding as the accumulation or flow of water from adjacent areas, as when rainwater ponds in island interiors during heavy precipitation such as may accompany tropical cyclones."[218] It provokes both "rapid and slow-onset processes" of multiplier consequences like, *i.a.*, the displacement of the inhabitants.[219] Consequently, climate change is not mono-causal; the displacement of people due to climate change results from an accumulation of many factors. Consequently, climate change cannot be described as a single act of menace, but as an "impact multiplier and accelerator."[220]

This accumulation of factors becomes particularly apparent in the cases of the States Kiribati, Tuvalu, and the Marshall Islands, which are "predicted to suffer the greatest impact, including the complete disappearance in a worst-case scenario".[221] As already recognized for the first time in Chapter 17 of Agenda 21

[217] A. Cassese (note 396 in Chap. 3), 319 et seq; P. Alston (note 353 in Chap. 3), 272, 292; S. Willcox (note 7 in Chap. 1), 104, 116.

[218] *C. D. Woodroffe,* Reef-island topography and the vulnerability of atolls to sea-level rise, Global and Planetary Change 62 (2008), 90.

[219] United Nations High Commissioner for Refugees (UNHCR), Summary of Deliberations on Climate Change and Displacement, 2011, 1.

[220] *E. Rasmusson/P. Presterud,* The Nansen Conference: Climate Change and Displacement in the 21st Century, 2011, 18; United Nations High Commissioner for Refugees (UNHCR), Summary of Deliberations on Climate Change and Displacement, 2011, 2; M. A. Brinker (note 133 in Chap. 3), 23.

[221] *C. Hamilton,* The Commonwealth and Sea-Level Rise, The Round Table (2003), 522.

> *"Small Island Developing States, and islands supporting small communities, are a special case for environment and development. They are ecologically fragile and vulnerable. Their small size, limited resources, geographic dispersion, and isolation from markets place them at a disadvantage economically and prevent economies of scale."*[222]

On these islands, the effects of climate change are evident in the accumulation of three main phenomena, resulting in one of the highest rates of vulnerability in the world. [223] First, the islands suffer from an extreme "likelihood of extreme weather events, *e.g.*, the increase of intense tropical cyclone activity", due to their highly exposed position in the Pacific, with large coastal regions.[224] Secondly, sea-level rise for this region is predicted to be 0.18 to 0.59 meters by 2100.[225] Tuvalu, for instance, is a State of only low-lying atolls, while Kiribati rises to 81 meters above the sea level at its highest elevation.[226] Meanwhile, the dwellings of the majority of the population and most of Kiribati's infrastructure lie just two meters above sea level, so that the estimated sea-level rise would, in this case, also lead to complete inundation.[227] Furthermore, this region is particularly vulnerable to a significant increase in surface temperatures, which in turn leads to increased ocean acidification. The side effects include coastal erosion, destruction of coral reefs, and the degradation of already scarce groundwater resources, among others.[228] In addition, the average rainfall is steadily decreasing. It will likely decline to 20% of current levels by 2050, which will be one of the main reasons for inhospitality in this area, as it will entail the disappearance of the freshwater lens.[229] In sum, while "droughts and storms have shortened lives and damaged or destroyed resources and assets as long as the atolls have

[222] Agenda 21: Sustainable Development, 14.06.1992a, Art. 17.123.

[223] *R. Ranasinghe/A. C. Ruane/R. Vautard*, IPCC—AR6 Synthesis Report—Climate Change 2021, 1836 ff; *R. Pachauri/L. Meyer*, IPCC—AR5 Synthesis Report—Climate Change 2014, 2015, 36.

[224] C. Hamilton (note 4 in Chap. 1), 527; G. J. Abhimanyu (note 222 in Chap. 3), 5; *R. Ranasinghe/A. C. Ruane/R. Vautard*, IPCC—AR6 Synthesis Report—Climate Change 2021, 1839; R. Pachauri and A. Reisinger (note 5 in Chap. 1), 15.

[225] C. Hamilton (note 237), 521; R. Pachauri and A. Reisinger (note 11 in Chap. 1), 45.

[226] *I. Kelman,* Islandness within climate change narratives of small island developing states (SIDS), Island Studies Journal (2018), 157.

[227] Republic of Kiribati (note 18 in Chap. 1), iii; I. Kelman (note 242), 157.

[228] R. Pachauri and A. Reisinger (note 11 in Chap. 1), 693, 697–698.

[229] R. Pachauri and A. Reisinger (note 5 in Chap. 1), 689.

been inhabited," there will most likely be a point in time at which they mean the end of said inhabitance.[230]

Additionally, the rate of vulnerability decreases with the level of development, meaning it is inversely related to the capacity to help oneself. As the IPCC noted, which was also recognized as "the best available science" for climate change and ocean acidification by ITLOS,[231]

> *"Climate change is projected to primarily affect human health adversely, particularly in lower-income populations of tropical and sub-tropical countries [through] direct effects (e.g. increased heat stress but reduced cold stress, loss of life in floods and storms) and indirect effects that operate through infectious disease vectors (e.g. mosquitoes), water-borne pathogens, water quality, air quality, food availability and quality (e.g. decreased protein content in some cereals), population displacement and economic disruption."*[232]

Consequently, developing States like Kiribati, Tuvalu, or the Marshall Islands are more threatened than States like the Netherlands, which likewise lie mainly below sea level.[233] In sum, the scholars see the root of the heightened vulnerability in the combination of "(1) internal community factors such as discrimination and prejudice, and (2) external factors such as governance, resource distribution, and exploitation by outsiders".[234] Even though these island States are perfectly adapted to the surrounding misanthropic environment, the "overpower" of climate change can seemingly overcome "this great resilience".[235] What can a state do when its entire population lives only up to two kilometers from the coast?[236] What happens when a unique and vulnerable ecosystem that has been functioning in absolute union with its inhabitants for centuries is at stake?[237]

---

[230] Republic of Kiribati (note 18 in Chap. 1), 19; R. Ranasinghe et al. (note 240), 1838.

[231] *Request For an Advisory Opinion submitted by the Commission of Small Island States on Climate Change and International Law,* No. 31, 21.05.2024, paras. 208, 374.

[232] R. Watson (note 24 in Chap. 1), 28; C. Hamilton (note 237), 519.

[233] E. Rasmusson and P. Presterud (note 236), 20.

[234] I. Kelman (note 242), 151.

[235] E. Rasmusson and P. Presterud (note 236), 20.

[236] C. Hamilton (note 237), 521.

[237] R. Pachauri and A. Reisinger (note 11 in Chap. 1), 19.

5.2.2 The Inhabitants of the Small Island Developing States (SIDS) Recognized as "People"

Consequently, in the multi-causal event of inundation evoked by climate change, the citizens of Kiribati, Tuvalu, and the Marshall Islands have to form a "firm ground on which the right to self-determination [can be] applied."[238] However, in accepting the challenge to "ground [the right out of the context of the] case of alien subjugation, domination or exploitation", the first task is to define "an identifiable people" to determine their collective "destiny".[239]

Taking a closer look at the inhabitants of the three small island States, the question arises whether they can be considered "people" in a new pluralist sense of self-determination. Hence, the development of the right to this collective "destiny" is not a single act, but a "continuous process",[240] that is, vested in the people."[241] Historically, Kiribati and Tuvalu were once united under British colonial rule as the Gilbert and Ellice Islands, before gaining independence from the British Empire in 1978. Even today, Tuvalu's head of State is still the King of England.[242] The Marshall Islands, in contrast, were dominated by various colonial powers: first by the Spanish Empire, then by Germany, and finally by Japan, before becoming part of the Trust Territory of the Pacific Islands under the military control of the United States.[243] In 1986, they achieved full sovereignty while remaining in a free association with the United States.[244] Consequently, these States have already outgrown the original scope of application of the right of self-determination—the process of decolonization. Consequently, the population and anyone standing under any form of non-self-government are entitled to the right of self-determination.[245] However, this assumption cannot be transferred automatically to the present times, because the right does not exist limitlessly or

---

[238] D. Thürer and T. Burri (note 227), para. 34.

[239] *D. Wong*, Sovereignty Sunk—The Position of Sinking States at International Law, Melbourne Journal of International Law (2013), 390.

[240] J. Crawford (note 304 in Chap. 3), 126.

[241] D. Thürer and T. Burri (note 227), para. 22.

[242] Encyclopedia Britannica.

[243] *C. Y. Mulalap*, in: R. Abate, Climate change and indigenous peoples: The search for legal remedies, 2013, 395.

[244] Ibid., 396 et seq.

[245] S. Willcox (note 7 in Chap. 1), 121; M. A. Brinker (note 133 in Chap. 3), 25 et seq.

endlessly. It is not a "once-and-for-all right" but a "constitutive" right that is constantly changing.[246]

However, taking a closer look at the hard law, Articles 1(1) of the ICCPR and 1 of the ICESCR, as well as Article VIII, Chap. 1, of the Helsinki Final Act, it is clear that "all peoples always have the right to self-determination." Beyond that, the ICJ has recognized this broad scope of application in several of the aforementioned decisions, so it is now recognized as *ius cogens*.[247]

In this context, we can conclude that the inhabitants of the islands continue to meet the criteria attributed to race, language, culture, religion, or attachment to their country.[248] Hence, the separation of Kiribati and Tuvalu was the first step toward achieving self-determination, as the two islands have distinct cultural backgrounds: one has a predominantly Polynesian population, while the other has a Micronesian population.[249] Moreover, the islanders are more strongly attached to their land than to the State per se, which stresses their identity and culture as critical essential values.[250] Consequently, returning to the question of attachment and interest in control over the resources of the territory (see above, Sect. 3.2), we can affirm this for the islanders.[251] As already stressed by the IPCC, the population has "a long developed and maintained unique lifestyle, adapted to their natural environment."[252] This goes so far that they "appear resigned to the fact that they might have to leave the island in the future, hoping to periodically return to have a connection to their heritage."[253] In conclusion, due to their long-standing culture, the firm desire of the population must be respected in these considerations.[254]

Moreover, the right of self-determination has to be interpreted as detached from state sovereignty as the "self itself" to express the "aspiration and efforts of a people to achieve self-determination" in the exercise and active claim of

[246] J. Crawford (note 14 in Chap. 3), 127.

[247] *Compare*: *South West Africa (Namibia)*, 21.06.1971, para. 52; *Western Sahara*, 16.10.1975, 54.

[248] M. A. Brinker (note 133 in Chap. 3), 26.

[249] Encyclopedia Britannica.

[250] C. Blanchard (note 151 in Chap. 3), 80; J. McAdam (note 10 in Chap. 1), 156.

[251] O. Angeli (note 237 in Chap. 4), 303.

[252] R. Pachauri and A. Reisinger (note 11 in Chap. 1), 59.

[253] *L. Yamamoto*, Atoll island states and international law, 2013, 176.

[254] D. Wong (note 255), 390; M. A. Brinker (note 133 in Chap. 3), 226.

this right.[255] The idea behind this is that "the integrity of a group intact can help preserve culture and national identities, [so that this] determination increase opportunities to formulate solutions that keep the integrity of a group intact."[256] The islanders are far from only casting blame and lamenting. Still, they are at the frontline suggesting "constructive ways for moving forward with action on achieving justice and on making prominent the voices that most need to be heard".[257] Tuvalu's inhabitants, for instance, are working on "an alternative, local green governmentality discourse based on indigenous knowledge, memory and eye-witness accounts" together with foreign environmentalists and journalists, by, *e.g.*, shooting a film about flooding with time-delay cameras, that were installed on the islands.[258] Moreover, the islanders are organized, for instance, in the Alliance of Small Island States (AOSIS), whose influence was and remains remarkable, for example, in negotiations for the United Nations Framework Convention on Climate Change (UNFCCC). This agreement was mainly the product of international cooperation between States and non-state actors.[259] Altogether, the islanders demonstrated strong resilience against climate-related extremes and adapted to slow-onset changes, which are also a consequence of their "dense social networks and their still-existing traditional knowledge".[260]

In conclusion, the nuclear right of self-determination is not based on political institutions or long-lasting continuing Statehood, but rather on cultural life and local identity.[261] The will and the skills to establish and maintain legitimate institutions and share the same "destiny", or in short, the will to fight for one's

---

[255] *W. G. Werner,* Self-Determination and Civil War, Journal of Conflict & Security Law (2001), 171; M. A. Brinker (note 133 in Chap. 3), 26; N. Berman (note 225 in Chap. 3), 90.

[256] *D. Hodgkinson/L. Young,* In the Face of Looming Catastrophe: A Convention for Climate-Change-Displaced Persons, Threatened Islands Nations (2013), 328.

[257] *I. Kelman,* Hearing local voices from Small Island Developing States for climate change, Local Environment (2010), 606.

[258] *F. R. Cameron,* Saving the "disappearing islands": Climate change governance, Pacific island states and cosmopolitan dispositions, Continuum: Journal of Media & Cultural Studies (2011), 877.

[259] *F. R. Cameron,* Saving the "disappearing islands": Climate change governance, Pacific island states and cosmopolitan dispositions, Continuum: Journal of Media & Cultural Studies (2011), 877.

[260] *J. Petzhold/A. K. Magnan,* Climate change: thinking small islands beyond Small Island Developing States (SIDS), Climate Change (2019), 146.

[261] S. Willcox (note 7 in Chap. 1), 125; J. McAdam (note 10 in Chap. 1), 156.

own "destiny", must be present.[262] Hence, "it is for the people to determine the destiny of the territory and not the territory the destiny of the people."[263]

5.2.3 Inundations Caused by Climate Change: A Threat to Self-Determination

To recognize a self-determining will, the "destiny of a people" has to be challenged by an external threat over which the people have little control.[264] This definition reflects the dual function of the right as both a human right and a traditional protective role.[265] Moreover, the threat's urgency must be of international relevance so that the international community may recognize it as an emergency.[266] Consequently, we must overcome the standard definition of threat—the traditional Nation-State as an oppressor of colonial inhabitants—to find a definition by which the "inundations caused by climate change as an external threat for the self-determination of the atoll island inhabitants" can be included.[267]

Focusing on this problem, we must ask whether such a "complex, multilateral, multi-causal web of past events and future harms" as climate change can be understood as an external threat to people's autonomy?[268] We are already aware that climate-related environmental phenomena have multi-level effects, not only on the environment as such but also on society, including infrastructure damage and disruptions to people's livelihoods.[269] Therefore, a phenomenon like this is often defined as a "disaster", which is "a serious disruption of the functioning of a community or a society at any scale due to hazardous events interacting with conditions of exposure, vulnerability, and capacity, leading to one or more of the following: human material, economic, and environmental losses, and impacts."[270] This definition aligns with the understanding of an external threat to self-determination. However, the opinions lean toward a broader approach to

---

[262] S. Willcox (note 7 in Chap. 1), 125; M. A. Brinker (note 133 in Chap. 3), 27.

[263] Opinion of Judge Dillard, *Western Sahara,* 16.10.1975, 114.

[264] P. Alston (note 353 in Chap. 3), 272; S. Willcox (note 7 in Chap. 1), 116.

[265] M. A. Brinker (note 133 in Chap. 3), 27.

[266] *C. R. Beitz,* The Idea of Human Rights, 2009, 189; M. A. Brinker (note 133 in Chap. 3), 27.

[267] M. A. Brinker (note 133 in Chap. 3), 27.

[268] S. Willcox (note 7 in Chap. 1), 126.

[269] I. Kelman (note 242), 151.

[270] I. Kelman (note 15 in Chap. 1), 151.

confront future problems of international law, to "give an accurate representation of the threats that exist to the enjoyment of the right to self-determination."[271]

As mentioned above, the ICJ has already emphasized the importance of the right in various decisions, yet has omitted more profound reflections on its scope of application. Hence, in underlining the *erga omnes* character of the right in the trailblazing decisions of *Barcelona Traction* and *East Timor,* the ICJ emphasized the importance of the right of self-determination.[272] Consequently, the status of *erga omnes* is acknowledged, "because of the protection of important rights, not because—or if—it is violated in a particularly serious way".[273] In the words of Crawford:

> *"Self-determination is primarily a process by which the peoples of the various States determine their future through constitutional processes without external interference."*[274]

Hence, based on the original idea of decolonization, it is now a right to "internal and external political status to promote the political, economic, social, and cultural development."[275] Consequently, to construct and preserve self-determination, justice needs to be established, so that "self-determination of a group is threatened because of the territorial dispositions of other groups" and, in consequence, "the group's lack of access to the territories of other States".[276]

In conclusion, the right of self-determination nowadays requires (1) a grave, foreseeable, external threat, (2) over which a people has little control, (3) to the destiny or autonomy of the people.[277] The inundations caused by climate change can be subsumed under this definition. Climate change-induced inundations are unpredictable events originating from outside and are ungovernable for the inhabitants of threatened island States. So, in the case of Kiribati, for instance, the forecasted sea level rise of probably two to three feet will devastate the atoll

---

[271] P. Alston (note 353 in Chap. 3), 272.

[272] *The Barcelona Traction, Belgium vs. Spain,* 24.07.1964; *East Timor Judgement,* 30.06.1995.

[273] *C. Tams,* Enforcing Obligations Erga Omnes in International Law, 2005, 137.

[274] D. Thürer and T. Burri (note 227), para. 17.

[275] Helsinki Final Act (note 350 in Chap. 3), Art. VIII, para. 2).

[276] J. Ödalen (note 373 in Chap. 3), 230.

[277] S. Willcox (note 7 in Chap. 1), 42 et seq.

island State.[278] In the long run, the autonomy of these people will suffer a serious threat due to the loss of their territory, which represents the basis of their existence.[279] In the words of an I-Kiribati, the inhabitants of Kiribati:

> *"Now, we hate the sea. Yes, the sea is good for us to get our food, but it is going to steal our land one day."*[280]

5.2.4 The Protection of the Self-Determination for the Islanders

However, the main question remains: Is there any possibility of finding means of protection against the acute threat to the islanders' right of self-determination? We must closely examine the already established scope of the right to self-determination in the context of developing States inhabiting small islands.[281]

First, the right is mainly recognized as *jus cogens* and an obligation erga omnes, as mentioned above (see Sect. 3.2).[282] The right represents a "basic right of the human person".[283] Recognizing fundamental legal principles, such as the right to self-determination, is one of the main pillars of the international community. Because of "the absence of a clear 'Grundnorm' in international law, norms and principles like this one, which is non-derogable, form the foundation of international law.[284]

Consequently, how can the international community react? Wyman emphasizes the moral importance of the international community and requests explicit action, particularly in light of vulnerabilities exacerbated by events such as climate change.[285] In the same vein, the General Assembly underlined the self-determination of people in Resolution 2625 (XXV), stressing "every State

---

[278] *N. Kristof,* New York Times, 01.12.1997.

[279] M. A. Brinker (note 133 in Chap. 3), 28.

[280] *K. Warne,* National Geographic, 11.2015.

[281] M. A. Brinker (note 133 in Chap. 3), 30.

[282] M. A. Brinker (note 129 in Chap. 3), 30.

[283] *The Barcelona Traction, Belgium vs. Spain,* 24.07.1964, para. 34.

[284] G. J. Abhimanyu (note 222 in Chap. 3), 39.

[285] *K. M. Wyman,* Are We Morally Obligated to Assist Climate Change Migrants?, Law & ethics of human rights (2013), 191; M. A. Brinker (note 133 in Chap. 3), 30.

has to promote, through joint and separate action".[286] Although the application of self-determination is highly controversial outside the colonial context,[287] the international community has recognized it as a *jus cogens* norm and an *erga omnes* obligation.[288] Abhimanyu pointed out that, even if the correlation between territorial integrity and the right of self-determination is not guaranteed, the right of self-determination as the relevant *jus cogens* norm serves as a "stapes holder" to realize connections like the permanent sovereignty over natural resources—the link between territorial integrity and sovereignty as a form of self-determination.[289]

Another approach focuses instead on cooperation within the international community and on States' mutual responsibility.[290] Described by Wyman as the "rescue principle", the principle of mutual aid asserts the moral obligation of everyone "to assist persons displaced by climate change because they are vulnerable".[291] Here, we can notice similarities with Article 1(2) of the International Covenants, which provides that "any obligations arise out of international economic co-operation, based upon the principle of mutual benefit and international law".[292] Consequently, the right of self-determination affects the intra-relationship between the State and the people, as well as the inter-relationship between States.[293] Therefore, the right exists in the "coordination between each other in responding to the threat posed by climate change inundation".[294]

In the context of vulnerability, we also have to discuss the criterion of capacity, here, in particular, in the negative sense of the responsibility of "high-income countries, which have been the leading contributors to cumulative emissions".[295] The intensely discussed topic of historical liability of the "rich democratic States"

---

[286] Resolution A/RES/2625(XXV): Declaration on Principles of International Law concerning Friendly Relations and Cooperation among States in accordance with the Charter of the United Nations. (note 353 in Chap. 3).

[287] I. Brownlie and J. Crawford (note 30 in Chap. 2), 131.

[288] D. Thürer and T. Burri (note 285 in Chap. 3), para. 9–11.

[289] G. J. Abhimanyu (note 222 in Chap. 3), 40.

[290] M. A. Brinker (note 133 in Chap. 3), 31.

[291] K. M. Wyman (note 301), 193.

[292] International Covenant on Civil and Political Rights (note 6 in Chap. 2), Art. 1(2), International Covenant on Economic, Social and Cultural Rights (note 6 in Chap. 2), Art. 1(2).

[293] M. A. Brinker (note 133 in Chap. 3), 31.

[294] S. Willcox (note 7 in Chap. 1), 141.

[295] K. M. Wyman (note 301), 193.

concerning the consequences of climate change comes to mind, leading to the logical result of an obligation to act for the sake of the islanders.[296] However, reality paints a different picture: the developing countries, with fewer opportunities and capacities to act, "are most likely to bear the brunt of the negative impacts of climate change."[297]

Following this approach, the extensions of the prevention principle—the so-called "causal connection principle" and "corrective justice"—express the concept that "the actor is responsible for the damaging consequences of his or her actions and has a special responsibility for the victims of those actions".[298] Although it seems challenging to link "the failure of the international community to curb greenhouse gas emissions to climate change and climate change to the rising sea levels and other physical changes, which is responsible for the loss of territory", it is not impossible.[299] The liability of governments and other global players is already under discussion in several national courts, as noted during the examination of NGOs and climate change litigation; therefore, recognition by international law is just a matter of time. However, the question remains, if all these efforts are sufficient to find a solution for the problem of losing territory, because this is the crux of the matter for the island States: "to ensure that it continues to be recognized—or, preferably, obtain acts of fresh recognition—by sovereign States."[300]

Another limiting factor in this controversy is the right of self-determination in other States. Every extension of the right of self-determination in favor of the islanders, whether it involves strengthening political autonomy or ceding territory to the detriment of another State, restricts the self-determination of others.[301] Consequently, the support of the threatened islands can provoke an "international problem of an economic, social, cultural and humanitarian character".[302]

Moreover, the previously mentioned liability issue arises, especially given the extremely unclear and hardly verifiable causal chain, as several courts have already affirmed.[303] Even though sporadic recognition of State responsibility or

---

[296] M. A. Brinker (note 133 in Chap. 3), 31.

[297] *K. M. Wyman,* Responses to climate migration, The Harvard environmental law review (2013b), 174.

[298] K. M. Wyman (note 301), 194.

[299] G. J. Abhimanyu (note 222 in Chap. 3), 43.

[300] D. Wong (note 255), 390.

[301] M. A. Brinker (note 133 in Chap. 3), 32.

[302] Charter (note 406 in Chap. 3), Art. 1(3).

[303] G. J. Abhimanyu (note 222 in Chap. 3), 43.

globally acting concerns in the context of climate change, like in the already mentioned case *Lliuya vs. RWE AG,* exists,[304] the search for “the causal link between the actions of one State and the threat that climate change poses to human rights in another State is already difficult.”[305]

5.2.5 Conclusion

In conclusion, climate change poses a significant threat to the atoll island States, given their highly vulnerable position in the South Pacific. Moreover, the populations of these States meet all the requirements to be the rightful holders of the right to self-determination. Their long-standing culture and deep ties to their territory enable the application of the right of self-determination in this context.[306]

Considering all the above-mentioned approaches, the right of self-determination as a pillar of statehood or other recognized legal personalities must be acknowledged. Otherwise, as Abhimanyu underlined,

> *“the inabilities of the international law, first of all, to prevent the physical loss of territory of island States by evolving to prevent or control climate change, secondly, to prevent the loss of Statehood (...) by adapting to recognize the extraordinary nature of these circumstances, nullifies the gain that individual States would ordinarily expect to derive from the social contract.”*[307]

As the former president of Kiribati, Anote Tong, already noted: “We have got to understand that climate change is not a national issue, it’s a global issue, and we need global thinking.”[308] The recognition of the right of self-determination for the people of the small island developing States would be the first step in the right direction.

[304] P. Minnerop (note 34 in Chap. 1), para. 44; R. Verheyen and S. Pabsch (note 178), 511, para. 8.

[305] S. Willcox (note 7 in Chap. 1), 132.

[306] M. A. Brinker (note 133 in Chap. 3), 33.

[307] G. J. Abhimanyu (note 222 in Chap. 3), 10 et seq.

[308] CBS News, As climate change threatens islands, Kiribati’s president plans development; https://www.cbsnews.com/news/climate-change-kiribati-president-taneti-maamau/ (last reviewed Oct. 9, 2025), 2017.

5.3 Reinterpretation of the Principle of Permanent Sovereignty over Natural Resources in the Case of the "Disappearing Islands"

Reconsidering the thoughts on the slowly changing process of sovereignty, in particular, regarding environmental degradation, and the reinterpretation of the right of self-determination in the context of climate change, the question arises whether the same considerations can also apply to the principle of permanent sovereignty over natural resources in the context of the disappearing island States.

5.3.1 Popular (Resource) Sovereignty

Reviewing the considerations above, we must admit that the traditional expression of sovereignty used for centuries is a "masculine defense against a hostile world of others".[309] This becomes particularly obvious in the context of the claim of permanent sovereignty over natural resources, specifically, sovereignty over the environment within the territory.[310] As noted in the last chapter, it became especially apparent in the context of climate change that the dual function of sovereignty—the protection against external threats and the control over resources and territory within—is incoherent. In the words of Wilmer:

> *"Claiming sovereignty over the environment precludes granting the environment any subject status of its own. This may not only be an unethical position from the perspective of environmentalists' claims but an inaccurate one in terms of understanding ecosystem processes in a way that enables us to live as humans within their constraints."*[311]

It is therefore not surprising that in the context of exploitation of natural resources, environmental concerns "have steadily made incursions into the scope of State sovereignty".[312] Hence, follow with the statement of Barrera-Hernández that "permanent sovereignty over natural resources is as much an issue of State duties as it is one of State rights."[313] So, for instance, China was recently made

[309] *F. Wilmer*, in: K. T. Litfin, The greening of sovereignty in world politics, 1998, 71.

[310] Ibid.

[311] Ibid.

[312] F. Venter (note 18 in Chap. 3), 77.

[313] *L. Barrera-Herández,* Sovereignty over Natural Resources under Examination: The Inter-American System for Human Rights and Natural Resource Allocation, Annual Survey of International & Comparative Law 12 (2006), 44.

painfully aware of this fact in the already discussed cases before the Appellate Body of the WTO, where the Panel limited China's permanent sovereignty over natural resources for the benefit of the international community by concluding that

> *"Natural resources products that will necessarily enter the market and are available for sale are subject to GATT disciplines in the same way as any other product."*[314]

This quote allows two conclusions: on the one hand, the "permanency" of the principle of absolute sovereignty over natural resources cannot be considered a "boundless discretion" for the State.[315] Hence, the States as members of the international community are instead entitled

> *"to pursue the optimal use of their natural resources in a manner consistent with their respective needs and concerns at different levels of economic development."*[316]

On the other hand, in an interdependent world, this type of sovereignty gives way to participation with the international community, specifically the international market.[317] Consequently, we can conclude in the words of Aqorau:

> *"Sovereignty has therefore never been absolute, although legally each sovereign State exercises unlimited territorial jurisdiction in respect of its own territory, subject only to such limitations as may be established by international customary law, treaties, and the general principles of law recognized by civilized nations."*[318]

Consequently, natural resources are subject to the international community, as the representative of "all people," when they come into contact with international law. However, there is also a dominant opinion among the scholars that entering the global market is a mandatory requirement for the "citizens [to] enjoy a real capacity to determine the conditions and benefits of the exploitation of

[314] *China—Measures Related to the Exportation of Rare Earths, Tungsten, and Molybdenum*, WT/DS431/R, 25.03.2014, para. 7.268; *J. Shi/X. Yang*, Reconciling Environmental Protection with Natural Resources Trade in International Law: A Perspective from China -Rare Earths, Frontiers of Law in China (2015), 562.

[315] *J. Shi/X. Yang*, Reconciling Environmental Protection with Natural Resources Trade in International Law: A Perspective from China -Rare Earths, Frontiers of Law in China (2015), 563.

[316] J. Shi and X. Yang (note 330), 564.

[317] Ibid., 563; *T. Aqorau*, in: M. Powles, Pacific futures, 2006, 218.

[318] *T. Aqorau*, in: M. Powles, Pacific futures, 2006, 218.

their resources", which only democratic States can meet.[319] Consequently, once again, we come back to our "popular [resource] sovereignty" and the simple conclusion that if the Nation-State owns its natural resources, "the only legitimate proprietors of the State are its people".[320] In conclusion, in the absence of the legal personality of a State, the people are the legitimate proprietors of the natural resources. Some cosmopolitans go a step further and conclude that "natural resources are the common heritage of all the people of the earth", whereby "moral claims being equal among all persons, a windfall resource's benefits should be universalized".[321] This idea is coherent with our conclusion in Chap. 3.

5.3.2 Self-determining Disappearing Islands

In the following, we have to ask whether the people of the disappearing island States are "self-determining" and hold sovereignty in a way that they "have the moral and political authority to establish justice within a geographic region."[322] This was already affirmed above, concerning the urgent threat of climate change. Hence, the people hold "at least a moral right to environmental self-determination that should entail the right to survive as a distinctive land-based people."[323] Thus, they should be able "to exercise sovereign control over what used to be their territorial waters," and in concrete terms, over their natural resources.[324]

Reviewing the traditional definition of sovereignty, the Pacific Island States have only held sovereignty since decolonization ended, when they reached the optimal stage of sovereignty of a Nation-State. Upon further review, can we continue to support this opinion? Does the classical definition of sovereignty, according to the "Island of Palmas Case," only include the sovereign State holding sovereignty?[325]

> ***"…sovereignty in the relations between States signifies independence. Independence in regard to a portion of the globe is the right to exercise therein, to the exclusion of any other State, the functions of a State. (…)Territorial sovereignty involves the***

---

[319] *C. Kutz,* Resources for the People—but Who Are the People?: Mistaken Nationalism in Resource Sovereignty, Ethics & International Affairs (2021), 120.

[320] Ibid., 121.

[321] Ibid., 122.

[322] J. Ödalen (note 373 in Chap. 3), 226.

[323] R. Tsosie (note 262 in Chap. 4), 92.

[324] J. Ödalen (note 373 in Chap. 3), 226.

[325] T. Aqorau (note 334), 216.

> *exclusive right to display the activities of a State. This right has as a corollary a duty: the obligation to protect, within the territory, the rights of other States, in particular their right to integrity and inviolability in peace and war, together with the rights each State may claim for its nationals in foreign territory. Without manifesting its territorial sovereignty in a manner corresponding to circumstances, the State cannot fulfil this duty."*[326]

Reading this definition carefully, we must admit that Pacific Island societies already held sovereignty before they were dominated and conquered by Western States. According to Aqorau, the islanders lived in societies "clustered by families and tribes, each of them within a geographic sphere of their influence, exercised power and authority" by excluding other families and tribes.[327] If we go along with this idea, "the Pacific Island societies have been exercising sovereign powers from time immemorial" within their "tribal and linguistic groupings".[328] For instance, even within the Nation–State of Tuvalu, as developed according to Western concepts, a comparison between Tuvaluans from the outer islands and those from Funafuti reveals completely different perceptions and understandings of government and allegiance. Hence, in the eyes of the islanders, there is no "sense of the State's role in their daily life" beyond the traditional community structures in which they live.[329] The same applies to the resources within the territory: 80 to 90 percent of the resources and land are under customary ownership, with no connection to any so-called State ownership or its jurisdictional power.[330] Consequently, we can stipulate that for the islanders of the Pacific Island States, the "government's influence" in the Western state-centric understanding is minimal to almost non-existent."[331]

Precisely for this reason, and mainly due to the understanding of sovereignty regarding their natural resources, the people of these States "could then continue to exercise sovereign control over what used to be their territorial waters".[332] Here, once again, one point becomes particularly clear:

---

[326] *Island of Palmas case (Netherland vs. United States),* 04.04.1928, 829 et seq., N. Schrijver (note 1 in Chap. 2), 236; T. Aqorau (note 221 in Chap. 2), 217.

[327] T. Aqorau (note 334), 217.

[328] T. Aqorau (note 333).

[329] J. McAdam (note 10 in Chap. 1), 156.

[330] Ibid.

[331] Ibid.

[332] J. Ödalen (note 373 in Chap. 3), 226.

> *"Sovereignty [– as we know it today –] is a social construction that has developed in relation to Western conceptions of power and political community."*[333]

However, if sovereignty is a social construct, we can reinterpret it as we see fit and as we need it to be. In the words of the former UNEP Executive Director Maurice Strong:

> *"People have learned to enlarge their circles of loyalty from the family via the tribe, the village, the town, and the city to the Nation-State, and that they now need to take the next step to the global level. Yet this did not mean an end to national governments. Taking the next step never meant automatically giving up the former circle of loyalty."*[334]

In conclusion, in the words of Tsosie:

> *"In an era of climate change, it is necessary to evaluate indigenous claims to "sovereignty" in relation to the right of self-determination, which belongs to all "peoples".*[335]

5.3.3 Recognition in the International Framework

However, can this idea of maintaining sovereignty over natural resources for the people of the disappearing island States be recognized within the international framework? Without a written legal declaration, sovereignty without territory remains an idea, slowly facing the threat of submersion of island States. However, this idea completely contradicts the fundamental principles of international law, as Abhimanyu clarified, there is

> *"a clear legal duty to not deprive a State of its territory, but there is no duty to protect a State from loss of territory."*[336]

International law offers two fora for the development of legal ideas that may become norms in international law, according to Article 38(1) of the ICJ Statute: the jurisdiction of the ICJ and the ITLOS, as well as the resolutions of the General

[333] F. Wilmer (note 325), 71.

[334] C. van der Lugt (note 194), 233.

[335] R. Tsosie (note 262 in Chap. 4), 91.

[336] G. J. Abhimanyu (note 222 in Chap. 3), 41 et seq.

Assembly. [337] The ICJ has already established the legal content, scope, and function of self-determination, which can, in part, be applied to permanent sovereignty over natural resources (see Chap. 3). The ITLOS has expressed its opinion on the continuity of the disappearing island States in the recently delivered judgment in the South China Sea Arbitration, which we will examine more closely in the next Chapter.[338] Consequently, although the court "has been induced to give priority to [the principle of] territorial integrity,"[339] self-determination—and also specifically the principle of permanent sovereignty over natural resources—"is applicable to all of [the new developments]."[340]

In addition, the General Assembly is recognized as an indicator of lawmaking and law elaboration.[341] For instance, it described and developed the relationship between human rights and climate change in the Human Rights Council Resolution 7/23.[342] Furthermore, Resolution 10/4 underlines that climate change has a range of "direct and indirect implications for the enjoyment of human rights," including the right to self-determination.[343] Moreover, in 2012, the Council initiated independent research to clarify the human rights obligations relating to environmental protection.[344] In the same year, Resolution 66/288 was adopted, affirming the particular vulnerability of Small Island Developing States and stressing the threats posed by sea-level rise, ocean acidification, coastal erosion, and the acute existential danger to coral reefs and mangroves.[345]

Moreover, the ICJ has recognized the General Assembly as a political institution or an "important stage in the development"[346] of international law.[347] Consequently, the ICJ emphasized in the Western Sahara case that there are

---

[337] *Compare:* Statute of the International Court of Justice, 26.05.1945, Art. 38(1); M. A. Brinker (note 133 in Chap. 3), 28.

[338] *The South China Sea Arbitration,* PCA Case No. 2013–19, 12.07.2016.

[339] *Western Sahara,* 16.10.1975, para. 50.

[340] *South West Africa (Namibia),* 21.06.1971, para. 52.

[341] J. Crawford (note 14 in Chap. 3), 114.

[342] Resolution 7/23: Human rights and climate change, 28.03.2008; Res. 7/23.

[343] Resolution 10/4: Human rights and climate change, 25.03.2009; Res. 10/4.

[344] *J. H. Knox,* Human Rights, environmental protection, and the sustainable development goals, Washington international law journal (2015), 518.

[345] Resolution 66/288. The future we want, 27.07.2012a; A/RES/66/288, para. 32–33, 164, 175–177.

[346] *South West Africa (Namibia),* 21.06.1971, para. 52.

[347] M. A. Brinker (note 133 in Chap. 3), 29.

"different ways in which the General Assembly resolutions dealt with the territory concerned".[348] That could lead to the conclusion that the Court has only a "secondary" or "administrative" role—rather than the role of "lead agency".[349] Consequently, to develop a legal basis for addressing the threat of disappearing islands and to acknowledge "possible security implications," we must leverage this recommendatory capacity to encourage States to act.[350]

Here, the opinions of scholars drift apart. Wyman, for instance, only appreciated that there is a "right gap, a lack of a right in existing law to remain permanently in another country due to environmental conditions in the home country".[351] Other scholars demand "a re-envisioning of [the entire discipline of law] to accommodate the unique circumstance of climate-induced human migration".[352] Moreover, they see the need for a "recognized and reconfigured international legal regime if the climate change predictions come true."[353] Consequently, we notice the growing call for a legal regime in this particular case of the natural resources of the disappearing islands related to the population of the threatened island.

In conclusion, we affirmed the reinterpretation of the principle of permanent sovereignty to a less unilateral orientation on States' sovereignty. Permanent sovereignty over natural resources is not only a privilege for States, which they may dispose of for unrestricted use and benefit, but also entails duties for States regarding their internal and external facets. Furthermore, the natural resources placed at the disposal of the population of the States—the people—are anchored in the right of self-determination. In the case discussed here, it means that the inhabitants of the disappearing island States have the right and claim to permanent sovereignty over the natural resources in the area of those States. The next logical step is to examine the possible solutions for the disappearing island States that international law offers.

---

[348] *Western Sahara,* 16.10.1975, para. 60.

[349] *J. Crawford*, in: V. Lowe/M. Fitzmaurice, Fifty years of the International Court of Justice, 1996, 592.

[350] Charter (note 406 in Chap. 3), Art. 14.

[351] *K. M. Wyman,* Responses to climate migration, The Harvard environmental law review (2013a), 169.

[352] M. Burkett (note 34), 347.

[353] *R. Rayfuse,* International Law and Disappearing States, Environmental Policy and Law (2011), 286.

Maintenance of the Right over the Maritime Zone According to the UNCLOS, Based upon the Reinterpreted Principle of Permanent Sovereignty over Natural Resources

6

The substrate of the State is not property, it is the people of the State seen as a collective. (J. Crawford (note 14 in Chap. 3), 717)

In A true union, nothing is lost, not even personality.

(*H. Grotius*, Hugonis Grotii De jure belli ac pacis libri tres, 1631, Bk II, Ch IX)

Many scholars have already endeavored to find solutions for threatened island States; as a result, various possibilities have been proposed. From the ceding of the territory of another State up to innovative ideas of the "de-territorialized island States", the opinions vary wildly. The older concepts of limited sovereignty—like public trusteeship or free association—were innovated. In the same way, the fusion of several States into the legal form of a federation or a union was celebrated during the heated debate over the disappearing island States. Consequently, it needs to be pondered whether State sovereignty—the for a long time so-called "grammar of politics", now being "reposed in abeyance"—can be replaced by another legal personality, giving "the opportunities for emergent forms of legal creativity".[1] It is time to take a closer look at these ideas and how they fit in the already developed concept of people as "principle-holder" of the principle of permanent sovereignty over natural resources.

[1] B. Knoll (note 88 in Chap. 3), 55.

M. A. Brinker, *The Principle of Permanent Sovereignty over Natural Resources as an Anchor in Times of Sealevel Rise*, https://doi.org/10.1007/978-3-658-50527-1_6

6.1 Statelessness and Sovereignty

Probably the most straightforward and unpolished solution is the cession of territory by another State. Approaching this idea, one matter must be discussed first: migration and climate change refugees. In this context, we need to be aware of one point: this is not the desired solution of the approach we are discussing here. As migration does not comply with the primary purpose of self-determination and sovereignty for the people, namely "the desire of these communities to stay together as a sovereign, self-determining community and continue as always within a new setting".[2] Even though the former President of Kiribati, Anote Tong, always spoke of "migration with dignity," he did not mean the migration of individual persons or the claim for refugee recognition.[3] He rather always called for collective resettlement or a "merit-based migration"[4] under the recognition and maintenance of sovereignty, which included "adaptation for Kiribati beyond our borders"[5] and "relocation is by far the only option; this is where migration with dignity comes in."[6]

Although the discussion was conducted at the academic level, a decision has not yet been reached in the international forum. This vacuum the international community leaves behind, when it comes to acknowledging the status of climate refugees within the Refugee Convention, is already called a "right gap".[7] Even though in January 2020 the UN Human Rights Committee announced that the

---

[2] *T. Skillington,* Reconfiguring the Contours of Statehood and the Rights of Peoples of Disappearing States in the Age of Global Climate Change, Social sciences (2016), 2.

[3] ABC News, Pacific Islanders reject 'climate refugee' status, want to 'migrate with dignity', SIDS conference hears; https://www.abc.net.au/news/2014-09-05/pacific-islanders-reject-calls-for-27climate-refugee27-status/5723078 (last reviewed Oct. 9, 2025), 2014.

[4] *J. McAdam,* Swimming against the Tide: Why a Climate Change Displacement Treaty is Not the Answer, International Journal of Refugee Law (2011), 20; M. Burkett (note 34 in Chap. 5), 361.

[5] Climate Change Secretariat UNFCCC, climate change, small island developing States, 2005, 13; J. McAdam (note 10 in Chap. 1), 144.: similar statement by the Tuvaluan Prime Minister 2000 COP 6: "*the potential impacts of climate change on the country were so serious for our people, that the Cabinet has been exploiring the possibility of buying land in a near-by country, in case we become refugees to the impacts of climate change.*"

[6] *M. E. Vaha,* Hosting the Small Island Developing States: two scenarios, International Journal of Climate Change Strategies and Management (2018), 234.

[7] M. Burkett (note 34 in Chap. 5), 350; G. J. Abhimanyu (note 222 in Chap. 3), 12; *S. McAnaney,* Sinking Islands—Formulating a Realistic Solution to Climate Change Displacement, New York University Law Review (2012), 1183; C. Hamilton (note 4 in Chap. 1), 527 et seq.

deportation of the asylum seeker and I-Kiribati Ioane Teitiota by New Zealand in 2015 was a violation of international standards of human rights, while international newspapers already headlined the recognition of the first "Climate Change Refugee", this was, in fact, irrelevant for international law.[8] First, because the decision of the UN Human Right Committee is not binding in international law—where the expression of environmentally displaced persons" is preferred—and, secondly, it does not further the actual objective of the threatened island States.[9]. As the former president of Kiribati, Anote Tong, expressed it, "I don't like our people to be categorized as a refugee. Having lost a home, the last thing I would push to see them lose is their dignity".[10]

Considering the inadequacy of a status as refugees, it is a legitimate question, "whether communities facing such threats have a legal, as well as moral right to resettle on the land of another State."[11] The ceding of territory from one state to another seems to be the most appropriate solution and is easily carried out. However, the ceding of the territory is a highly political affair, in particular, because of the self-limitation of the other State in giving up land.[12]

The idea of ceding territory is discussed, *e.g.*, in the context of Kiribati's nationhood. It is not the first instance of involuntary land cession in this region. In 1945, the population of Banaba Island, one of the present-day Kiribati territories, had to make way for mining operations by a British enterprise and was collectively relocated to Rabi Island in Fiji.[13] At first, Kiribati shows no interest in acquiring land on Viti Levu, an island of the Republic of Fiji.[14] Hence, in the current situation, scholars like Michael Gerrard have already suggested,

[8] *E. Wasuka*, Landmark decision from UN Human Rights Committee paves way for climate refugees, https://www.abc.net.au/news/2020-01-21/un-human-rights-ruling-worlds-first-climate-refugee-kiribati/11887070 (last reviewed Oct. 9, 2025), 2020; *F. Biermann/I. Boas*, in: F. Biermann/R. Brohm/K. Dingwerth, "Global environmental change and the nation state", 2002, 255 et seq.

[9] *F. Biermann/I. Boas*, in: F. Biermann/P. Pattberg/F. Zelli, Global climate governance beyond 2012, 2010, 256.

[10] *J. Quinones/K. Cherry/A. Lajka*, Climate Refugees: Kiribati, https://www.cbsnews.com/news/climate-refugees-kiribati-cbsn-on-assignment/ (last reviewed Oct. 9, 2025), 2017.

[11] T. Skillington (note 19), 1 et seq.

[12] Ibid., 2.

[13] *J. McAdam*, Caught between homelands, https://insidestory.org.au/caught-between-homelands/ (last reviewed Oct. 9, 2025), 2013.

[14] *L. Yamamoto/M. Esteban*, Atoll Island States and international law: Climate change displacement and sovereignty, 2014, 191; *S. Reardon*, Pacific island to buy piece of Fiji as climate plan, https://www.newscientist.com/article/dn21581-pacific-island-to-buy-piece-of-fiji-as-climate-plan/ (last reviewed Oct. 9, 2025), 2012.

"if Fiji were to cede the land and give it up and say it's no longer within their jurisdiction, then it would become the new Kiribati".[15]

Regarding international law, the cession of territory refers to the transfer of territorial sovereignty from one State to another, typically through a bilateral treaty signed by governmental authorities within the framework of civil law, or by means such as sale, donation, or mutual exchange.[16] Here, again, we notice the similarity between the civil law construct of ownership and the public law construct of territory. Taking a closer look at this idea, the problematic legal constructions that "a sovereign State exists on the leased territory" are striking.[17] Moreover, it is obvious that "it would be quite difficult to find a land which incorporates the whole population of a country."[18] Furthermore, it is difficult to find "uninhabited, uninhabitable [land], that is not subject to any property, personal, cultural or other claims and devoid of all resources and any value."[19] Even though the right of self-determination provides "the right of a community which has a distinct character to have this character reflected in the institutions of government under which it lives" for the people, this does not reach as far as to claim the land of an existing State, and violate "the territorial integrity and State sovereignty".[20] Nevertheless, some scholars consider this the "most straightforward and appealing solution from the legal perspective,"[21] because in this scenario, the people would not lose the pre-existing maritime zone, even if the new territory is far from it.[22]

However, this legal construct entails yet more problems, including, for instance, the practicability of "full governmental powers" over a portion of the earth's surface,[23] because "a semi-autonomous region within another sovereign

---

[15] *M. Ward*, Planning to sink: What happens if Kiribati drowns?, https://www.pbs.org/newshour/world/planning-sink-happens-kiribati-drowns (last reviewed Oct. 9, 2025), 2014.

[16] I. Brownlie and J. Crawford (note 30 in Chap. 2), 214 et seq; R. Jennings et al. (note 126 in Chap. 3), 680 et seq; J. McAdam (note 10 in Chap. 1), 148.

[17] G. J. Abhimanyu (note 222 in Chap. 3), 48.

[18] L. Yamamoto and M. Esteban (note 31), 188.

[19] R. Rayfuse (note 15), 284.

[20] J. McAdam (note 10 in Chap. 1), 147.

[21] R. Rayfuse (note 15), 284.

[22] Ibid; J. McAdam (note 10 in Chap. 1), 144 et seq.: similar statement of Tuvaluan Prime Minister in 2008: *„Tuvalu would be based in Australia but continue to function as a sovereign nation, in the hope of one day returning to its island home. The Tuvalu Government would continue to exercise its economic exclusion zone of about one million square kilometres and maintain its seat and vote at the United Nations."*

[23] D. Wong (note 255 in Chap. 5), 369.

State would not still be [Kiribati]."[24] Consequently, the status of a fully autonomous State could be at stake, in particular, considering that the "totality of international rights and duties recognized by international law" is an attribute of States, not a precondition.[25] However, if full recognition as a State is not secured, the possibility of being downgraded to refugee status or losing statehood remains.

Concerning the maritime zone remaining where the island States had historically been located, the already discussed attachment problem can be consulted, which always depends on the people more than the territory as such,[26] because it "is not the territorial nature of self-determination or Statehood, but the claim that self-determining people are necessarily tied to one territory in particular."[27] Regarding the loss of attachment to their homeland, the example of the citizens of Banaba can be used again, as they were displaced to Rabi Island not only due to mining but also due to the devastation caused by the war in the 1940s.[28] The promised sovereignty for the Banabans over their homeland was not only questioned by various police actions and litigation, but also proved unrealistic to realize and, in practice, pointless—almost impossible.[29] As years and generations went by, a growing lack of awareness among younger Banabans—"a poignancy (…) fades with time"—was noted regarding the relocation story to Rabi.[30] Nowadays, the connection between the Banabans and the island of Banabas is often called the "mud-blood" connection.[31] Consequently, the importance of land and cultural identity should not be underestimated, particularly in the Pacific Island region, where the ties to the homeland are powerful.[32] Moreover, as McAdam noticed:

> *"The effects of dislocation from home can last for generations, and can have significant ramifications for the maintenance and enjoyment of cultural and social rights by resettled communities."*[33]

---

[24] *R. Rayfuse/E. Crawford,* Climate Change, Sovereignty and Statehood, Sydney Law School (2011), 7.

[25] J. Crawford (note 14 in Chap. 3), 32, 46.

[26] S. Willcox (note 7 in Chap. 1), 154.

[27] Ibid., 155.

[28] *V. Sutton,* in: R. Abate, Climate change and indigenous peoples: The search for legal remedies, 2013, 374.

[29] Ibid., 374 et seq.

[30] J. McAdam (note 30).

[31] V. Sutton (note 45), 374.

[32] J. McAdam (note 10 in Chap. 1), 153.

[33] Ibid.

With the same tendency, but a more juridical argumentation, the Arbitral Tribunal constituted under Article 10 of Annex VII to UNCLOS ("Arbitral Tribunal") registered by Permanent Court of Arbitration (PCA) delimited the term of an island in comparison to a rock according to Article 121 (1) and 121 (3) UNCLOS in the South China Sea Arbitration Award of July 12, 2016.[34] It is considered the "human habitation" with a "non-transient character" as mandatory for the classification as an island, primarily as the capacity "to generate EEZ rights, dependent on the presence of a population to benefit from the resources within that zone".[35] In this context, it stressed that the "stable community of people" of an island and its economic activity must be "oriented around the feature itself, and not focused solely on the waters or seabed of the surrounding territorial sea".[36] Therefore, it sees it as a necessary and fundamental requirement of the characterization as an island for the piece of land itself to be of use and importance to the community, as it may not be "entirely dependent on external resources or devoted to using a feature as an object for extractive activities without the involvement of a local population".[37] Despite the principle of "case-by-case-assessment", this very narrow and strict interpretation of the Tribunal lets us doubt whether the Atoll Island States will comply with this "high bar to generate EEZ and continental shelf rights" shortly.[38] However, we must always bear in mind the principle of consistency of legal personality, in this case, the existing State. Consequently, for Atoll Island States, the Arbitral Tribunal, regarding the size of "human habitation", specifically stipulated that "in remote atolls, a few individuals or family groups could well suffice".[39]

Consequently, the cession of territory is only "an attempt to protect, rather than subvert the principle of territorial integrity and State sovereignty" to conserve

[34] *The South China Sea Arbitration,* PCA Case No. 2013–19, 12.07.2016, para. 478–551; *C. Schofield/D. Freestone,* Islands Awash Amidst Rising Seas: Sea Level Rise and Insular Status under the Law of the Sea, The International Journal of Marine an Coastal Law 34 (2019), 409.

[35] *The South China Sea Arbitration,* PCA Case No. 2013–19, 12.07.2016, para. 489, 542; C. Schofield and D. Freestone (note 51), 409 et seq.

[36] *The South China Sea Arbitration,* PCA Case No. 2013–19, 12.07.2016, para. 512, 542–543; C. Schofield and D. Freestone (note 51), 410.

[37] *The South China Sea Arbitration,* PCA Case No. 2013–19, 12.07.2016, para. 512, 542–543; C. Schofield and D. Freestone (note 51), 410.

[38] C. Schofield and D. Freestone (note 51), 410.

[39] *The South China Sea Arbitration,* PCA Case No. 2013–19, 12.07.2016, para. 542; C. Schofield and D. Freestone (note 51), 411.

international peace and security.[40] Still, it does not align with the interests of the people. What the inhabitants of Kiribati and the other island States are afraid of is "primarily one of loss: loss of control over territory and resources, over land, rights, sovereignty and power—the power to shape one's destiny", or in a few words, "at its heart, it is the loss of self-determination."[41] Therefore, in 2011, the former president of Kiribati, Anote Tong, considered moving his 100,000-person population to "man-made floating islands" to "maintain a connection to the place and continue to have sovereignty over it".[42] The former Tuvaluan Prime Minister leaned in a similar direction with his statement during the COP14 in 2008:

> *"We are not contemplating migration. We are a proud nation of people with a unique culture that cannot be relocated. We want to survive as a people and as a nation."*[43]

6.2 "De-territorialized" Nation-States

Considering the disadvantages of ceding territory and the consequences of this idea, such as the recognition of climate refugees and Statehood as such, we will move on to examine other solutions that international law offers. One of them is the innovative idea of a "de-territorialized" Nation-State.

6.2.1 A New Form of an International Entity

This highly debated approach of the "deterritorialized" Nation-State addresses the formalized principle of territoriality in Article 1 of the Montevideo Convention, which states that Statehood is "based on the principle of effectiveness among territorial units."[44] Statehood and other legal entities are based on the conclusion that international law (possibly solely) entitles an entity to be a State, provided it exercises full governmental power over a defined territory.[45]

---

[40] S. Willcox (note 7 in Chap. 1), 162; J. McAdam (note 10 in Chap. 1), 149.

[41] J. McAdam (note 30).

[42] V. Sutton (note 45), 375; *P. Mercer*, Fiji, Climate Change Concerns Dominate Pacific Bloc Summit, https://www.voanews.com/a/fiji-climate-change-concerns-dominate-pacific-bloc-summit-129368308/144896.html (last reviewed Oct. 9, 2025), 2011.

[43] J. McAdam (note 10 in Chap. 1), 145.

[44] J. Crawford (note 14 in Chap. 3), 46.

[45] Ibid.

The classical understanding of a State—as already developed above—demands "territory in which the people are settled."[46] However, how do we define the relationship between a territory and the people who settled it? Can it be described as the relationship between property and owner, or more as a "vehicle for maintaining exclusive jurisdiction and exploitation of resources?"[47] Independent of the description of attachment, one point we can conclude with absolute certainty:[48] there must be at least a territorial base where the government can be installed. In the words of Wong, "the leg [of territory] may be bent, but it must exist."[49]

However, is this leg essential to maintaining the status of Statehood or that of any other legal entity? Which functions crucially require the State to have a territory? As already developed in Chap. 5, we can derive four functional sources of Statehood from the territory: it serves as a source of security, as well as economic, historical, and cultural resources, and it facilitates the effective exercise of jurisdiction.[50]

However, as we have already seen, these essential functions of Statehood are partly already assumed by the international community. In particular, in the case of climate change, State sovereignty is on shaky ground, as we saw impressively above (see Chap. 5). Even though the threat of attacks on territorial integrity remains in the 21st century, such attacks are now more effectively repelled through international cooperation than through the efforts of a single territorial government.[51] Referring to the second function of territoriality, globalization has a particularly significant impact on the economy, which is enmeshed in an international web of cooperation and transboundary trade.[52] Consequently, a State is more dependent on global market correlations than on domestic production.[53] Furthermore, even the inherent source of territorial competence,[54] jurisdiction, is gradually being transferred to international institutions, as seen in the case of the EU. Regarding the last function of territoriality, historical and cultural resources are not necessarily related to the territory, as we have already seen in the case

46 R. Jennings et al. (note 126 in Chap. 3), 120.

47 G. J. Abhimanyu (note 222 in Chap. 3), 20.

48 M. A. Brinker (note 133 in Chap. 3), 62.

49 D. Wong (note 255 in Chap. 5), 354.

50 G. J. Abhimanyu (note 222 in Chap. 3), 23.

51 Ibid., 25.

52 M. A. Brinker (note 133 in Chap. 3), 63.

53 M. Burkett (note 34 in Chap. 5), 358 ff.

54 *J. Anaya,* The Capacity of International Law to Advance Ethnic or Nationality Rights Claims, Human Rights Quarterly 13 (1991), 410.

of the Pacific Island States. In this case, as in many others, the culture refers to a specific region of the world, such as the Pacific Ocean, but is not bound to a particular landmass.[55] For instance, Kiribati and the Marshall Islands are part of Micronesia, which extends beyond their borders. At the same time, Tuvalu is mainly inhabited by a Polynesian population.[56]

In conclusion, nowadays, the international community or other global players easily replace the main functions of territory, so that "in a globalized world regulated by de-territorialized international or transnational law, the State loses its centrality."[57] Consequently, even the decentralization of a State without territory is possible.

On the other hand, the recognition of de-territorialized entities may create an unpredictable uncertainty in the international community. For instance, the number of States could rise significantly, leading to a growing, uncontrollable complexity in international relations.[58] The equality of these legal entities with other States and the endowment of the same sovereign rights would entitle them to competencies, such as the capacity to claim territorial rights.[59] This could lead to paralysis of the already established States in their territorial sovereignty.[60] Moreover, the physical movement of people into another State's territory would constitute an invasion, introducing new customs, values, and rules into the host State's existing social, legal, and political institutions.[61]

However, by accepting the legal personality of a deterritorialized Nation-State only in the exceptional case of disappearing island States, the existing doubts about the evanescent significance of territoriality persist.[62] In the present-day world, where territory is often limited to mere functional utility, it is time to make room for the establishment and recognition of other legal entities.

---

[55] G. J. Abhimanyu (note 222 in Chap. 3), 26.

[56] *E. Stratford/C. Farbotko/H. Lazrus,* Tuvalu, Sovereignty and Climate Change: Considering Fenua, the Archipelago and Emigration, Island Studies Journal 8 (2013), 71.; Encyclopedia Britannica, Kiribati Land.

[57] *V. Bilková,* in: M. Kuijer/W. Werner, Netherlands Yearbook of International Law: The Changing Nature of Territoriality in International Law, 2016, 25.

[58] G. J. Abhimanyu (note 222 in Chap. 3), 26.

[59] M. A. Brinker (note 133 in Chap. 3), 63.

[60] G. J. Abhimanyu (note 222 in Chap. 3), 26.

[61] E. Stratford et al. (note 73), 75; M. A. Brinker (note 133 in Chap. 3), 64.

[62] M. A. Brinker (note 133 in Chap. 3), 64.

6.2.2 The People's Will in this New International Entity

However, recognizing the legal status of a State without territory must allow its people to exercise their right of self-determination effectively—the second pillar of the PSNR.[63] "Can the population of an Atoll Island State continue to exist as a self-determining people without a territory of its own?"[64] Regardless of the international community's external recognition of the legal entity "de-territorialized States," the full range of rights, including sovereignty, is at stake.[65] For instance, a de-territorialized entity might be able to control goods and people transport, as well as people's movement. However, other inherent attributes and capacities originally intertwined with sovereign States, such as currency, a military, a police force, or an independent judicial system, stand and fall with "a given portion of the earth."[66] In particular, inherent features, such as the enforcement of legislation and the collection of taxes, depend on a fixed landmass and can be effectively exercised only by the State.[67] Consequently, the continuity of sovereignty without territory is limited, "with the sovereign power in respect of its own people and citizens, wherever they are."[68]

However, in practice, the "people will start to migrate, legally or with an irregular situation, and overall the society will slowly disintegrate."[69] The model would prevent the people "from establishing their own justice within a geographic area; thus, this model would fail to meet the criterion for Statehood of preserving the people's self-determination".[70] After a specific period, the government would become fictional, as it would be ineffective.[71] Consequently, at some point, an adequate exercise of the right of self-determination may be questioned.[72] According to Ödalen, it might be possible that "people [are] self-determining to a degree", but that this concept would be too weak to reach the

---

[63] M. A. Brinker (note 129 in Chap. 3), 64.

[64] S. Willcox (note 7 in Chap. 1), 194.

[65] M. A. Brinker (note 133 in Chap. 3), 64.

[66] S. Willcox (note 7 in Chap. 1), 195.

[67] M. A. Brinker (note 133 in Chap. 3), 64.

[68] R. Jennings et al. (note 126 in Chap. 3), 384 et seq.

[69] M. Burkett (note 34 in Chap. 5), 368.

[70] *K. R. Lal,* Legal Measures to Address the Impacts of Climate Change-Induced Sea Level Rise on Pacific Statehood, Sovereignty and Exclusive Economic Zones, Auckland University Law Review (2017), 260.

[71] Ibid.

[72] M. A. Brinker (note 133 in Chap. 3), 64.

top of the scale of what might be defined as full sovereignty, in the gradual concept of self-determination.[73] According to this line of argument, the groups' right to self-determination can only reach its full potential through the creation of a State. At the same time, other legal personalities only have limited forms of self-determination at their disposal.[74] In line with this thought, Ödalen refers to the two different facets of the right of self-determination—the internal and external self-determination—and stresses that the group, irrespective of their capability to exercise political self-determination by their government-in-exile, will "no longer possess a domain of political control independent of other political units".[75] Consequently, they would lack external self-determination.

Ultimately, it will always come down to acceptance by the international community, such as recognition of the new legal status.[76] There is always hope for a continued community with some form of sovereignty, as seen in the case of the Sovereign Order of Malta, where the nucleus of peoplehood can be preserved by conserving its history, spirituality, and service.[77] At the beginning, it is only the formal membership based on plain identity, which will be passed down to the generations and form a multigenerational bond, tied by the formerly abstract citizenship. Ultimately, the legal definition of citizenship is intertwined with the psychosocial interest in preserving the endangered State's culture and traditional way of life. Change is transformed into a concrete legal construct that people would fight for.[78] Moreover, at least in the case of the legal entity of a State, there is "a strong presumption within international law that favors the continuity and disfavors the extinction of an established State" or other legal entity.[79] The EU, as a recognized entity, also represents a case of functional sovereignty in international law.[80] Moreover, the term "other entity" is used in numerous treaties, for example, in the UN Fish Stock Agreement.[81]

[73] A. E. Buchanan (note 373 in Chap. 3), 47; J. Ödalen (note 373 in Chap. 3), 234.

[74] J. Ödalen (note 373 in Chap. 3), 230.

[75] J. Ödalen (note 371 in Chap. 3), 232.

[76] J. Ödalen ((note 373 in Chap. 3), 234.

[77] K. R. Lal (note 87), 260.

[78] M. Burkett (note 34 in Chap. 5), 369.

[79] K. R. Lal (note 87), 245; D. Wong (note 255 in Chap. 5), 361 et seq; M. Burkett (note 34 in Chap. 5), 362.

[80] R. Rayfuse (note 15), 286; K. R. Lal (note 87), 260.

[81] *Compare*: Fish Stocks Agreement, 04.12.1995; UNFSA, Art. 1(2)(b), 40, 41, 43.

However, all these examples lead to the conclusion that, on the one hand, statehood does not seem to be the consummate form of full sovereignty attainable for the disappearing islands. Still, on the other hand, self-determination will not be lost regardless. The right of self-determination is not cast in stone or an all-or-nothing concept.[82] However, self-determination can continue to exist in a different political status. Hence, it lies in the hands of the population of the Atoll Island States to maintain their right of self-determination, *e.g.*, by signing an appropriate agreement with another State that gives refuge to the islanders.[83] Moreover, they can strengthen their self-determination by "circumscribing the peoplehood in law" or by constituting their "territorial" sovereignty over the territory in the sea.[84] In sum, there are possible solutions to maintain the right of self-determination, perhaps not in the legal form of a de-territorialized State, but more likely in another legal form.

In conclusion, the significant disadvantage of this new model of Statehood is undeniably the limited independence of this State form, in particular, when the host State exerts substantial control over a de-territorialized State, overruling its decisions "on a wide range of matters and doing so systematically and on a continuing basis."[85] Nevertheless, "in such settings, international law can no longer continue with the fiction of a uniform model of the State, founded historically upon the territorial rights of a "unified" and self-determining people."[86]

6.3 Public Trusteeship as a New Idea in Modern Environmental Law

Bearing in mind the weaknesses of the legal entity of the so-called "de-territorialized Nation-State"—in particular, the recognition by the international community and the continuance of self-determination—we have to turn to already established legal personalities well known to the international community, namely the legal entity of trusteeship.

With the heated debate regarding the erosion of operational sovereignty in mind, we must consider another aspect of the law of natural resources: the strong attachment of people (see above, Chap. 4). Furthermore, we can understand the

[82] M. A. Brinker (note 133 in Chap. 3), 65.

[83] M. Burkett (note 34 in Chap. 5), 366.

[84] S. Willcox (note 7 in Chap. 1), 197; L. Yamamoto and M. Esteban (note 31), 201.

[85] I. Brownlie and J. Crawford (note 30 in Chap. 2), 130 et seq.

[86] T. Skillington (note 19), 3.

rise of sovereignty in the context of the need for "an organizing element for the post-Stockholm 1972 and post-Rio 1992 global ecological order".[87] Consequently, we can notice an "expansion of national jurisdiction" and, consequently, of sovereignty, *e.g.,* to the new area of the EEZ in UNCLOS and to the even larger range of plant and animal genetic resources considered "common concern of humankind" in the CBD or the International Treaty on Plant Genetic Resources for Food and Agriculture 2001.[88] Hence, the legal concept of the "common concern of humankind" regarding areas or natural resources situated within the territorial boundaries of States, but with limited sovereign rights, might be considered a kind of trusteeship, with the State acting as trustee.[89] However, this does not go as far as the idea of the UNESCO World Heritage Convention recognizing cultural and natural heritage as "property, to whatever people they might belong".[90] In sum, the extension of sovereign rights, especially in the context of UNCLOS, goes along with "specific obligations owed to other States and the international community" about conserving living marine resources threatened by climate change impacts (*e.g.,* Articles 61 to 70 UNCLOS). [91] Therefore, Roscoe Pound described the "limited" role of States in managing common natural resources as "a sort of guardianship for social purposes".[92]

However, as with the equation of ownership and sovereignty, the legal construct of the "common concern of humankind" does not reach as far as property; it is somewhat comparable to the concept of public trusteeship.[93] In this case, the State does not assume the role of a proprietary proprietor of natural resources, but rather that of a fiduciary.[94] This idea can, to some extent, already be found in Principle 2 of the 1972 Stockholm Declaration:[95]

---

[87] P. H. Sand (note 11 in Chap. 5), 520.

[88] P. H. Sand (note 202 in Chap. 2), 194; P. H. Sand (note 11 in Chap. 5), 519 et seq; *P. H. Sand*, in: L. J. Kotzé, Transboundary Governance of Biodiversity: Transboundary Governance of Biodiversity, 2014, 49.

[89] P. H. Sand (note 202 in Chap. 2), 195.

[90] P. H. Sand (note 11 in Chap. 5), 521.

[91] Ibid; Convention on Biological Diversity (note 252 in Chap. 4), Art. 1(2), 5–14; International Treaty on Plant Genetic Resources for Food and Agriculture, 11.2001; ITPGRFA, 10(2); *Request For an Advisory Opinion submitted by the Commission of Small Island States on Climate Change and International Law,* No. 31, 21.05.2024, para. 418.

[92] P. H. Sand (note 11 in Chap. 5), 531.

[93] P. H. Sand (note 202 in Chap. 2), 195.

[94] Ibid; P. H. Sand (note 11 in Chap. 5), 519.

[95] P. H. Sand (note 105), 49.

> *"The natural resources of the Earth, including the air, water, land, flora and fauna, and especially representative samples of natural ecosystems must be safeguarded for the benefit of present and future generations through careful planning or management, as appropriate."*

The question remains if this construction is also suitable for the people as "fiduciary" and, further, for the future of disappearing island States.

6.3.1 The Triumphal Development of Trusteeship

Reviewing, once again, the beginning of the philosophy of law, John Locke already described the government as a "fiduciary trust" on behalf of their people,[96] and Marx considered the societies of the world not as proprietors but as "*boni patres familias*" of the earth:[97]

> *"Selbst eine ganze Gesellschaft, eine Nation, ja, alle gleichzeitigen Gesellschaften zusammengenommen sind nicht Eigentümer der Erde. Sie sind nur ihre Besitzer, ihre Nutznießer, und haben sie als boni patres familias den nachfolgenden Generationen verbessert zu hinterlassen."*[98]

Having originated from Roman law, this idea is nowadays not found in European civil law, like in the German contractual relation between the *trustor* and the *trustee* for the benefit of the *beneficiary*, but also in other legal systems like the Anglo-American trust law,[99] the *waqf* of Islamic law, or the *moramati* of African customary land law.[100] Contrary to the widespread assumption, the model is not based on a bilateral contractual relationship between a trustor and a trustee, as in a civil contract, nor on the trustee's duties to the beneficiary. [101] It instead represents a trilateral structure.[102]

---

[96] P. H. Sand (note 202 in Chap. 2), 198; P. H. Sand (note 105), 37.

[97] P. H. Sand (note 202 in Chap. 2), 198.

[98] Translated in English: "*Even a whole society, a nation, indeed all simultaneous societies taken together are not owners of the earth. They are only its owners, its beneficiaries, and have to leave it improved as boni patres familias to the following generations.*"

[99] P. H. Sand (note 105), 38; *D. D. Caron,* Time and the Public Trust Doctrine: Law Knowledge of Climate Change, University of Hawai'i Law Review 35 (2013), 443.

[100] P. H. Sand (note 202 in Chap. 2); P. H. Sand (note 105), 42 et seq.

[101] P. H. Sand (note 202 in Chap. 2), 198.

[102] Ibid.

In the context of public trusteeship over environmental resources, the trustee is the State, the trustor is the community, and the beneficiary is the people.[103] Nevertheless, this construction could also be extended or limited to members of specific international regimes, *e.g.*, contracting parties to a multilateral convention, as trustors; intergovernmental institutions, such as the ISA, as trustees; and future generations, individuals, or groups, as beneficiaries.[104] Similarly, the main idea behind the principles of common concern in the CBD and CHM in UNCLOS is that States act as "trustees" for the oceans and marine environmental protection within and beyond their territorial boundaries.[105] Consequently, as the trustee, the State exercises the sovereign rights over natural resources, much like a proprietor over the corpus in civil law, in this model, but with the interests of the beneficiary in mind and in accordance with the terms of the arranged trust.[106] The main task and duty of the trustee is to safeguard the rights of beneficiaries. In the context of international environmental law, this concept is understood as "resource stewardship", as "man's obligations as Earth's custodian," or as "man's stewardship or trustee responsibilities for Earth's natural resources and life systems".[107] In conclusion, even the "international community" has a responsibility towards the beneficiaries "to ensure that they can enforce the terms of the trust against trustee-states, through appropriate remedies and institutions", *e.g.*, by designating representative civil bodies to overcome the "democratic deficit" of global governance.[108]

However, according to these considerations, the general assumption of an "erosion of sovereignty" seems disproved, seeing as the public trust concept empowers the "legitimacy of environmental governance by Nation-States". [109] The fundamental power remains in the hands of the State, as it controls the beneficiary and acts on behalf of the community.[110] Concluding, we can hypothesize that the legal fiction of the "heritage of humankind" is abandoned more and more, so that the State assumes additional tasks, as seen recently in Article 10 (1) of the FAO Plant Gene Treaty 2001:[111]

---

[103] Ibid.

[104] Ibid., 199.

[105] V. A. Ventura (note 206 in Chap. 3), 142; P. H. Sand (note 11 in Chap. 5), 521.

[106] P. H. Sand (note 202 in Chap. 2), 199.

[107] Ibid., 198 et seq; P. H. Sand (note 105), 53.

[108] P. H. Sand (note 202 in Chap. 2), 200.

[109] Ibid.

[110] *R. Wilde*, International territorial administration, 1st ed., 2008, 317.

[111] P. H. Sand (note 11 in Chap. 5), 520.

"In the relationship with other States, the Contracting Parties recognize the sovereign rights of States over their own plant genetic resources for food and agriculture, including that the authority to determine access to those resources rests with national governments and is subject to national legislation."

However, this additional power of States is double-edged because, like in Article 10 of the FAO Plant Gene Treaty, the legitimization of the State goes along with a "substantial measure of external accountability".[112] In other words, as Robert Keohane noted:

"Global governance can impose limits on powerful States and other powerful organizations, but it also helps the powerful, because they shape the terms of governance."[113]

Nevertheless, having been judged as a successful idea, the concept of public trusteeship, in particular, in the context of environmental resources, has found its way into the national and international rules, like in the already cited paragraph 27 of the Pennsylvania Constitution (compare Chap. 4):

"Pennsylvania's natural resources are the common property of all the people, including generations yet to come. As trustee of these resources, the Commonwealth shall conserve and maintain them for the benefit of the people."[114]

In particular, in the context of intergenerational justice, the idea of trusteeship seems widespread, like in Article 2 of the Philippine Environmental Policy Decree of 1977:

"The responsibilities of each generation as trustee and guardian of the environment for succeeding generations,"[115]

or in Eritrea's Environment Proclamation of 1996, which designated the State as

"custodian for the harmonized and integrated management and protection of the national environment and the sustainable use of natural resources".[116]

---

[112] Ibid., 537.

[113] Ibid.

[114] P. H. Sand (note 202 in Chap. 2), 195.

[115] Ibid.

[116] Ibid; P. H. Sand (note 105), 40.; *compare*: *South African National Environmental Management Act 1998, South African Biodiversity Act 2004.*

Nowadays, the idea of shared environment or shared natural resources appears in many forms, such as the "common heritage" doctrine, the doctrine of bon voisinage regarding "shared natural resources", or the "World Heritage Convention". [117] Similarly, a "stewardship" status for continental shelf areas 60 to 120 miles beyond the EEZ or marine resources exists in specific regional seas, such as the Mediterranean and the South Pacific.[118] The definition of biological resources is highly diversified nowadays, ranging from the governance of particular living resources to the protection of abstract intellectual property rights in genetic resources, ultimately encompassing the "intrinsic value" of biological diversity and its components.[119] The most prominent illustration of a kind of public trusteeship in "area-based" or "habitat-based" conservation is the World Heritage Convention (WHC), initially referred to as the "World Heritage *Trust* Convention".[120] So, for instance, one of the first "species-based" examples is the preamble of the 1946 Whaling Convention,

> *"Recognizing the interest of the nations of the world [as trustee] in safeguarding for future generations [as beneficiaries] the great natural resources represented by the whale stocks [as a corpus of the trust]."*

However, we have to consider these last examples with caution. Even if the trusteeship is recognized, the States retain unrestricted sovereignty over the area where the World Heritage is located and identified. Moreover, the 1946 Whaling Convention served mainly the interests of the whaling industry.[121]

6.3.2 A Trusteeship for the Disappearing Island States?

Trusteeship is also not new in the context of disappearing islands. In particular, regarding the discussion of a new category of de-territorialized States, "the political trusteeship system provides a helpful model in "how to govern a nation without a habitable territory".[122] In this model, the government of a "Nation

---

[117] P. H. Sand (note 202 in Chap. 2), 196 et seq.

[118] Ibid., 197.

[119] P. H. Sand (note 105), 57.

[120] Ibid., 58.

[121] *Compare*: last sentence of the preamble: „*Having decided to conclude a convention to provide for the proper conservation of whale stocks and thus make possible the orderly development of the whaling industry.*"

[122] M. Burkett (note 34 in Chap. 5), 363.

Ex-Situ" would manage "the State without territory", which would include the "maritime zone to the benefit of the displaced population"in the case of the disappearing islands".[123]

Established in a similar context as the principle of permanent sovereignty over natural resources in the aftermath of World War II, the purpose of the UN Trusteeship System was the development of self-government, "while respecting the right of the peoples of the territory to permanent sovereignty over indigenous natural wealth and resources".[124] Following the traditional arrangement, the trustor for this new system would be another State, a group of States, or the United Nations itself, while "elected citizens of the Nation Ex-Situ themselves would serve as trustees."[125] According to the supporters of the idea, this new trusteeship system was necessary for the endangered States to recognize in their sovereign equality and "to persist as international personalities".[126] In this context, it is essential to emphasize that the trustor plays a supportive role in the transition and in establishing "respect for the continued sovereign equality".[127] The trustee would first serve as an interim body to manage and simplify the "process of transition for the peoples and governance mechanisms", such as developing effective working mechanisms for representing the interests of the diaspora in international affairs, *e.g.*, for their diplomatic protection.[128] After the process of territorial dislocation was completed, the interim body would merge with the dislocated governing body "to form a single locus of power" to act in the function of the interim body, "coordinating all social, economic, and commercial matters related to its former territory for the benefit of its dispersed citizens".[129] This so-recognized State, or however this legal fiction would be called, is created in perpetuity.[130] Essential for maintaining this perpetuity is the recognition by the international community because "without international legitimacy, the trustee will likely lack necessary resources, and may face State-sponsored resistance".[131]

According to supporters of this model, one advantage would be resolving the growing problem of uncontrolled migration and providing a way to admit

---

[123] Ibid.

[124] Ibid., 364.

[125] Ibid., 363 et seq.

[126] Ibid., 364.

[127] Ibid.

[128] Ibid., 365.

[129] Ibid., 366.

[130] Ibid.

[131] Ibid., 367.

refugees, as the status of these people would be recognized as that of citizens of a Nation Ex-Situ.[132] However, we must be aware of the inevitable result: this Nation Ex-Situ would only exist for a specific, limited time. As Rachel Morris expressed:

> *"For a certain time, there will be a government, but it will be a fiction. It will be a slow process of whole nations dying in the social sense in addition to the geographical sense."*[133]

Moreover, the structure of the Nation Ex-Situ would allow the exercise of jurisdiction over its citizens, which would, on the one hand, be a relief for other States that cannot exercise jurisdiction over a stateless individual and, on the other hand, protect citizens from mistreatment.[134] Hence, the benefits of citizenship are diverse, ranging from the perpetuation of culture and traditional ways of life to the hope of continued community, in the sense of a bonded community or shared purpose, as seen in the case of the Sovereign Order of Malta.[135]

6.3.3 Trusteeship as an Outdated Model

However, the problem with this legal construct is that people, once again, remain in a passive role as beneficiaries without any possibility to act. Even though the role of the trustee would be granted to an intergovernmental organization due to the loss of State, the people will not have any influence on the contract between trustor and trustee because the trustee always takes the controlling part—"the ayant-droit"[136]—over the beneficiary, in acting on behalf of the legal personality of the trust.[137] Examples of peremptory passive beneficiaries, such as the environment, future generations, or natural resources, illustrate this concept. However, in the case discussed here, where people, as active representatives of a still-existing State, are willing and able to fill this position and claim these rights, this legal figure seems inadequate and outdated.

---

[132] Ibid., 367 et seq.

[133] *R. Morris*, What Happens When Your Country Drowns?, https://www.motherjones.com/environment/2009/11/tuvalu-climate-refugees/ (last reviewed Oct. 9, 2025), 2009.

[134] M. Burkett (note 34 in Chap. 5), 368.

[135] Ibid., 369.

[136] B. Knoll (note 88 in Chap. 3), 61.

[137] R. Wilde (note 127), 318.

Considering that most of the concerned States have already been under UN trusteeship, as per Chapters XII and XIII of the UN Charter, and were able to liberate themselves through a lengthy process, the return to the concept of trusteeship in the described model would be interpreted as a step backward.[138] For instance, the Marshall Islands were under United States trusteeship as the Trust Territory of the Pacific Islands (TTPI), along with Palau, Yap, Chuuk, Pohnpei, and the Northern Mariana Islands, before they gained independence.[139] The process of gaining independence stretched over 15 years after World War II, "exposing several gaps between the US's stated goals of fostering the TTPI's socio-economic development and the realities on the ground", leading to the creation of the Congress of Micronesia in 1965.[140] A similar, even more challenging road was in store for the population of Nauru, a small island developing State in the South Pacific, adjacent to Kiribati and the Marshall Islands. After being colonized and exploited by the Germans in the 19th century, Nauru was placed under a British mandate following World War I on behalf of the League of Nations, comprising Australia, the United Kingdom, and New Zealand. During this time, extensive areas of Nauru were utilized for phosphate mining.[141] As a result, the Nauruans had to be resettled in Australia in the 1960s, due to the immense environmental destruction, without any prospect of "seeking full sovereign independence" on the territory of Australia.[142] Consequently, the government could not

> *"see its way clear to transferring the sovereignty of territory which is at present part of Australia".*[143]

Consequently, this dispute was brought before the ICJ in 1989 and decided in 1992, again highlighting the problematic concept of transferring territory to another State.[144]

In retrospect, the trusteeship system—developed from the mandatory system based on the idea of a colony – was considered "a synthesis between two initially

---

[138] B. Knoll (note 88 in Chap. 3), 53 et seq; K. R. Lal (note 87), 260.

[139] C. Blanchard (note 151 in Chap. 3), 101; C. Y. Mulalap (note 259 in Chap. 5), 394.

[140] C. Y. Mulalap (note 259 in Chap. 5), 394; B. Knoll (note 88 in Chap. 3), 66.

[141] J. McAdam (note 10 in Chap. 1), 150.

[142] Ibid.

[143] Ibid., 151.

[144] *Compare*: *Phosphate Lands in Nauru (Nauru vs. Australia),* 26.06.1992.

opposed concepts."[145] On the one hand, the aim was "to liberate the peoples from the strenuous conditions of the modern world" with the purpose of the realization of self-determination, on the other hand, the aim of "restoration of sovereignty [to] the empowered peoples repatriated from legal exile", consequently to impose the Western system of Nation-State sovereignty.[146] The idea of the trusteeship system as an interim solution to "transfer governmental power to the new sovereign" never reflected the reality.[147] Some scholars go as far as to say that this concept was already based on the assumption that "societies of certain peoples in the world were either completely lacking or at least of an inferior character compared to that of 'civilized' peoples, so that they had to be introduced carefully to the concept of a 'sovereign State'.[148] Consequently, the trusteeship system—"the mandate"- can be described as "a cobweb of obligations to keep pending sovereignty questions at bay", maintaining "latent sovereignty" over the mandated territory "in abeyance".[149] The result was that the population of the trusteeship often stood under "double dependence under two competing authorities": one exercising control within a territory and the other exercising external control.[150] This mechanism of separated powers can also be described as an attempt to fuse two entities—the sub-state (the peoples) and the supra-state (an international organization)—without an intermediate level of State sovereignty.[151]

Therefore, it is not surprising that many scholars express concerns that the trusteeship would revive the perception of "benevolent colonialism" in the eyes of the island States, considering the origins of the concept of a "standard of civilization".[152] Referring to the concrete situation, Yamamoto and Esteban considered:

> *"Trusteeship could therefore be seen as undermining sovereignty and be interpreted as a lack of capacity of SIDS to deal with the impacts of sea-level rise by themselves."*[153]

---

145 B. Knoll (note 88 in Chap. 3), 80.
146 Ibid.
147 Ibid.
148 R. Wilde (note 127), 317.
149 B. Knoll (note 88 in Chap. 3), 66, 73,
150 Ibid., 103.
151 R. Wilde (note 127), 318.
152 Ibid., 295, 317–320.
153 C. Blanchard (note 151 in Chap. 3), 101; L. Yamamoto (note 269 in Chap. 5), 207 et seq.

The only possible solution in this context is for people—not the State—to assume the role of active trustee. Here, we return to the necessity of "the development in international law, the sovereigns-as-trustees model must admit that States are not the only sovereign actors cognizable to international law."[154] Burkett developed the idea, which she considered a "Nation Ex-Situ" without the United Nations or any other foreign state "holding the territory under its supervision in trust".[155] She stressed that the UN and its member States would only play a supportive role, if any—"a political trustee"- in the transition to and the establishment of the "deterritorialized entity".[156] On the other hand, the interim body of the "Nation Ex-Situ" would make every decision, *e.g.*, determining appropriate modifications to relevant political and economic institutions or representing the people in international affairs, such as diplomatic protection.[157] In sum, Burkett considered this theory only for an interim period, for the time of "territorial dislocation", so that, once completed, the interim body could merge with the dislocated governing body "to form a single locus of power".[158] However, Burkett also foresaw specific political factors—"State-sponsored resistance" and "a critical mass of the international community"—on whose consent the international legitimacy of this model depended.[159] Burkett assumed that the international community would mainly welcome the model of "ongoing Statehood" because this status would support and ensure the main objectives of sovereignty: self-determination, governmental effectiveness, economic stability, and protection of rights.[160]

However, it is questionable whether revitalizing a model with such a burdensome history and dubious reputation seems suitable, particularly in the case of the Pacific Island States, which experienced this past in a very unpleasant way. Here, we can agree with Jane McAdam, who said:

> *"The traditional ways in which law and policy have been divided into 'fields' of inquiry and operation, such as 'human rights', 'trade', 'development', and so on, do not reflect the messy, complex interconnectedness of the issue."*[161]

---

[154] *E. Fox-Decent/I. Dahlman,* Sovereignty as Trusteeship and Indigenous Peoples, Theoretical Inqueries in Law (2015), 530.

[155] M. Burkett (note 34 in Chap. 5), 365.

[156] Ibid., 364 et seq.

[157] Ibid.

[158] Ibid., 366.

[159] Ibid., 367.

[160] Ibid.

[161] Ibid., 372.

In summary, the model of trusteeship may be experiencing a revival, with a renewed focus on protecting the environment and natural resources. Regarding the disappearing island States, however, it does not offer an adequate solution because it would represent a step back in the level of sovereignty and reopen old wounds. Unlike the environment and natural resources, which are considered passive and unchangeable actors in international law, the people's representation must be adequately secured. Consequently, in this case, historical models should be left behind to find a solution for the islanders' future.

6.4 Foundation of an Association, Union, or Cooperation

After rejecting the model of trusteeship, particularly a UN Trusteeship, as a possible legal figure for the disappearing island States, we have to review other models of "limited self-determination" offered by international law that could suit the island States in their current predicament.[162]

6.4.1 Free Association

Another legal form of self-government—particularly in the context of exemption from non-self-governing status—must be considered: association with another State, as outlined in Chapter XI of the UN Charter.[163] Unlike the trusteeship model in Chapters XII and XIII, this legal figure is designed for a permanent solution to self-government; consequently, it guarantees the "continuum of self-determination" in a progressive manner, as provided for in Principle VII of the aforementioned Resolution 1541 (XV).[164] By complying with the specific obligations outlined in Articles 73, 73a, and 73c of the UN Charter, the integrated State continues to exist under the influence of the associated State.[165] Reviewing the rigorous, hardly executable conditions of Article 73, 73a, and 73c UN-Charter, the same conclusion as in the case of UN trusteeship could be extrapolated, namely, that the "prerequisite of self-government is a certain standard of material, social

[162] J. Ödalen (note 373 in Chap. 3), 230 et seq.

[163] J. Crawford (note 14 in Chap. 3), 621.

[164] S. Willcox (note 7 in Chap. 1), 214.

[165] J. Crawford (note 14 in Chap. 3), 622.

and educational process", so that this legal personality does not reach the legal status of sovereignty.[166]

However, does this mean that people, when choosing free association or any other form of integration, are "participating in their own disappearance"?[167] Even though the association with the other State entails a specific restriction for the associated people concerning their rights over the existing territory and maritime claims,[168] it does not mean the "dissolution of the political entity (...) itself".[169] In this case, the associated people would remain a sovereign entity together with the "host State", unlike other legal forms, such as the cession of territory, where Statehood would be lost.[170] Therefore, the "pre-existing maritime zone would remain effective, but the zones would belong to the host State".[171] This model could even be a "win-win situation" for the associated people and the host State, as the host State would purchase new land, particularly the valuable and extensive EEZ of the disappearing territory, and the associated people could be resettled to a new territory as a whole.[172] Consequently, the permanent sovereignty over natural resources would be preserved for the islanders and the host State's population.

Depending on the specific content of the negotiated agreement, the free association will enable the islanders to maintain a better international legal status, including the capacity to continue diplomatic relations and participate in international organizations.[173] For instance, the Cook Islands are members of international bodies such as the Food and Agriculture Organization (FAO), the World Health Organization (WHO), and the Asian Development Bank through a free association with New Zealand.[174] As determined in Principle VII (b) of Resolution 1541 (XV), the associated people enjoy full executive and legislative power by establishing democratic governing institutions and a judicial system, so that they can "determine their internal constitution without interference".[175] In the Niue Assembly, the people were granted the power to "make laws for the

---

[166] Ibid., 621.

[167] S. Willcox (note 7 in Chap. 1), 213.

[168] L. Yamamoto (note 269 in Chap. 5), 200; S. Willcox (note 7 in Chap. 1), 213.

[169] J. McAdam (note 10 in Chap. 1), 154.

[170] L. Yamamoto (note 269 in Chap. 5), 200.

[171] Ibid.

[172] *L. Yamamoto*, Atoll island states and international law, 2013, 200.

[173] S. Willcox (note 7 in Chap. 1), 213.

[174] Ibid., 214.

[175] Ibid; J. McAdam (note 10 in Chap. 1), 154 et seq.

peace, order and good government of Niue," which provides for the authority to amend any law in force in Niue, including the Constitution itself.[176]

Consequently, as Crawford described, this model is "one of the more significant possibilities of self-government communities—especially island communities—that are too small to be economically and politically viable standing alone".[177] Hence, it is not surprising that the majority of the islanders—represented, *i.a.*, by the president of Kiribati—support this idea.[178] According to McAdam, who evaluated interviews with governmental officials and community members in Kiribati and Tuvalu:

> *"The issues of key importance to many Tuvaluans and I-Kiribati [are]the retention of home – land, community, and identity – rather than preserving the political entity of the State itself."*[179]

As already affirmed above, "self-determination does not necessarily involve a claim to Statehood and secession," as this legal figure is instead considered a remnant of the colonial period, "to secure and promote European interests, rather than local culture and identity."[180] In the harsh words of Aqorau:

> *"The idea of sovereign Statehood or the State as an instrument through which they align themselves is anathema to their notions of sovereignty. Sovereignty to them is limited to their own religious, tribal, landholding, and language groups."*[181]

Consequently, the fact that the submergence of territory results in "facts no longer supporting the State's existence" seems an insignificant side effect for the islanders.[182]

That is all the more true because the Pacific Islands have had positive experiences with this model, *e.g.*, with the already-mentioned free association of the Cook Islands and Niue with New Zealand, or Palau and the Marshall Islands

---

176 Niue Constitution Act, 1974, Art. 28, 35, 37.

177 J. Crawford (note 14 in Chap. 3), 626.

178 J. McAdam (note 10 in Chap. 1), 154.

179 Ibid., 154, 156.

180 Ibid.

181 T. Aqorau (note 334 in Chap. 5), 219.

182 M. Burkett (note 34 in Chap. 5), 367.

with the United States.[183] The States entered into free association, maintaining their full executive and legislative powers, while their citizens acquired citizenship of the associated State.[184] It seems doubtful, however, whether this model is suitable for the disappearing island States of Kiribati and Tuvalu, as these island States lack a strong historical relationship with the eligible States—New Zealand or Australia –, which do not seem willing to accept the Islanders as citizens.[185] Moreover, the conditions and legal consequences of this association might be unclear, controversial, or unresolvable, as there is always the risk of asymmetric legal competencies and overreach by one party. Consequently, an association would be one option for the islanders, but we must also consider other, better alternatives.

6.4.2 Federation or Union

"Merging" with another State could also be achieved by forming a federation or union with this State, creating a new State, or joining the other State.[186] Hence, by integrating into another State, the associated people will lose their status as a State, while maintaining "equal rights and opportunities for representation and effective participation at all levels in the executive, legislative and judicial organs of government"[187].[188] In contrast to free association, the federal State acts as "a sole person in the eyes of international law", which means "all the external sovereignty [of the member States] is absorbed by the federal State". [189] In the words of Willcox:

---

[183] J. McAdam (note 10 in Chap. 1), 154 et seq; D. Wong (note 255 in Chap. 5), 374; *H. Lazrus*, Sea Change: Island Communities and Climate Change: Sea Change: Island Communities and Climate Change, 2012, 287.

[184] J. McAdam (note 10 in Chap. 1), 155.

[185] Ibid., 156; L. Yamamoto (note 269 in Chap. 5), 200.

[186] L. Yamamoto (note 269 in Chap. 5), 200.

[187] Resolution A/RES/1541 (XV): Principles which should guide Members in determining whether or not an obligation exists to transmit the information called for under Article 73 e of the Charter (note 300 in Chap. 3), Principle VIII.

[188] L. Yamamoto (note 269 in Chap. 5), 200.

[189] J. McAdam (note 10 in Chap. 1), 156; R. Jennings et al. (note 126 in Chap. 3), 252; S. Willcox (note 7 in Chap. 1), 215–217.

> *"Where free association sits at the maximal end of both axes of autonomy and international legal status, federation offers substantial opportunities for the former but less scope for the latter."*[190]

Even though the individual federal States do not play an active role on the international floor, they are "recognized as subjects of international law". [191] They leave room for their capacity to unfold "distinctiveness internationally" and establish a "form of multi-ethnic pluralism", like in the cases of Belgium, Germany, or Switzerland.[192]

Consequently, federalism is an "association of different, overlapping and interacting communities", in which the members exercise their power, both in "self-rule" and in "shared rule".[193] Hence, the federation or union can be described as a vivid example of reciprocity and interdependence, with and within a permanent process of negotiating and balancing the rights and obligations of each member.[194] Hence, "sovereignty is divided between the federal State and the Member State" means that the member States can exercise unlimited sovereignty and independence "as far as their competence reaches".[195]

Brownlie regards federalism as

> *"probably better able than any other system to provide a regime of stable autonomy which provides group freedoms within a wider political cosmos and keeps the principle of nationality in line with ideas of mutuality and genuine coexistence of peoples."*[196]

In this discussion, we must know that the border between a union and a federation is always fluid. For instance, it was not surprising that the 2004 agreement for "deeper and closer cooperation" between the Pacific Island States included the association of a Union, based on the most famous example, the EU.[197] In this case, the competencies and tasks previously held by the national authority

---

[190] S. Willcox (note 7 in Chap. 1), 216.

[191] *G. I. Hernández*, in: D. French, Statehood and self-determination, 2013, 508, 501–507; S. Willcox (note 7 in Chap. 1), 217.

[192] *G. I. Hernández*, in: D. French, Statehood and self-determination, 2013, 508, 501–507; S. Willcox (note 7 in Chap. 1), 217.

[193] S. Willcox (note 7 in Chap. 1), 215.

[194] Ibid., 215 et seq.

[195] R. Jennings et al. (note 126 in Chap. 3), 249.

[196] I. Brownlie (note 58 in Chap. 4), 6.

[197] T. Aqorau (note 334 in Chap. 5), 216.

were transferred to the supranational authority, the Union.[198] In this way, the EU acquired further competencies and authority, becoming a supranational entity and, ultimately, recognized as a legal personality in 2009.[199] Thus, the EU is exemplary for the steadily growing tendency in the last fifty years to strengthen the position of subnational entities.[200] Nowadays, the EU "stands as the poster child for an attempt to parallelize social-economic and political spaces in functional integration".[201] This tendency aligns with the previously discussed concept of sovereignty, which is steadily shifting towards "popular sovereignty".[202] Venter expressed:

> *"In contrast to the Nation-State of the 19th Century, the democratic State of the 19th and 20th century, and the welfare State of the 20th century, the notion of a sixth form of modern statehood, [is labelled] the "transnational cooperation State" or the "networked State".*[203]

For instance, the legal personality of a federation can also enforce "enhancing global warming policy," bringing together various actors and opening the floor for additional forums and agents in global warming legislation and litigation.[204] Hence, whether we label the new legal personality resulting from the fusion of the host State and the island State "union" or "federation", the island State will be capable of maintaining its autonomy and enforcing rights, such as permanent sovereignty over its natural resources. In the United States, for example, as early as 1953, the Supreme Court recognized the Union's rights to the subsoil of territorial waters.[205] Similar legislation has been enacted in the federal States of Canada and Australia.[206] In sum, this fusion will also only be "a mirror of our time", combining power, by "transferring national authority in three directions", and:

---

[198] K. Kern and T. Löffelsend (note 180 in Chap. 5), 117.

[199] *compare*: Treaty on European Union, 29.07.1992; TEU, Art. 47.

[200] K. Kern and T. Löffelsend (note 180 in Chap. 5), 117.

[201] *M. Klöpfer/R. D. Neugärtner*, in: W. Kahl/M.-P. Weller, Climate change litigation: A handbook, 2021, para. 55.

[202] F. Venter (note 18 in Chap. 3), 78.

[203] Ibid., 79.

[204] *M. Klöpfer/R. D. Neugärtner*, in: W. Kahl/M.-P. Weller, Climate change litigation: A handbook, 2021, para. 54.

[205] R. Jennings et al. (note 126 in Chap. 3), 252.

[206] Ibid., 252 et seq.

> *"upwards, to the level of international and supranational institutions: sideways, to civil society actors; and downwards, to sub-national actors."*[207]

6.4.3 Cooperation and Other Legal Cooperative Personalities

Hence, to close this discussion: which legal personality should the disappearing island States choose for the future? At the forefront of the dispute, two main stances can be identified. Mainly, older politicians still advocate for an absolute sovereign nation for all the Pacific Islands.[208] For instance, they reject a currency's peg to the Australian dollar, considering it "an affront to its sovereignty and integrity".[209] However, confronting climate change, the single institutional response of one State actor is often (too) slow, particularly if someone has to pick up on "the multiple voices and views of the Pacific countries and their populations".[210]

Therefore, on the other hand, we can notice a strong tendency among the younger generation to lean away from the "fear of loss of the national voice" and toward "stronger and closer collective action" among the Pacific Islands, recognizing the "diversity of responses" in, *e.g.*, regional programs.[211] It goes so far that some Pacific Island States are questioning the concept of Statehood itself, doubting "the utility and efficacy of the constitution they were given at independence" after their liberation from colonial rule.[212] According to McAdam,

> *"The idea that there is some supranational authority exercising power and responsibilities in a spatial jurisdictional zone is not widely accepted."*[213]

Moreover, they recall their old strength, regional cooperation, which has a long-standing history among the Pacific Island States.[214] The islanders have a very far-reaching history not only regarding their tribal and linguistic ties, which can

---

[207] K. Kern and T. Löffelsend (note 180 in Chap. 5), 116.

[208] T. Aqorau (note 334 in Chap. 5), 216.

[209] T. Aqorau (note 333 in Chap. 5), 216.

[210] J. Bryant-Tokalau (note 5 in Chap. 1), 19.

[211] T. Aqorau (note 334 in Chap. 5), 217; J. Bryant-Tokalau (note 5 in Chap. 1), 19.

[212] T. Aqorau (note 334 in Chap. 5), 220.

[213] J. McAdam (note 10 in Chap. 1), 156.

[214] T. Aqorau (note 334 in Chap. 5), 221.

already be considered a form of sovereignty (see above Chap. 4), but also in their manner of living together in a "non-interventionist and non-provocative way."[215]

For instance, one of the first significant steps toward regional cooperation was the founding of AOSIS in 1990 at the Second World Climate Conference, which made them very active at the Rio meeting in 1992.[216] The "nexus that links the relationship" between Pacific Island States is their immense vulnerability to environmental disasters, climate change, and sea-level rise, collectively intensifying their impact on environmental change.[217] This cooperation did not remain the only one. It was followed by further agreements like the Pacific Islands Countries Trade Agreement (PICTA), the Pacific Agreement on Closer Economic Relations (PACER), the Treaty on Fisheries between the Governments of certain Pacific Island States and the Government of the United States, and the Pacific Island Air Services Agreement (PIASA).[218]

However, the Pacific Island States did not only come together in the AOSIS but also made use of the concept of "community-based management" (CBM), which is known as "people-centered, community-oriented, and resource-based", whether people have the innate capacity to understand and act on their own problems".[219] Encouraging and strengthening collective responsibility and "stewardship", this legal figure is found, in particular, in the context of ocean and fisheries management, where several agreements have been established under the "general umbrella of co-management or CBM".[220] For instance, the Pacific Island States have collaborated through the Nauru Agreement (PNA), which is joined by eight Pacific States, to coordinate and develop fisheries management in this region.[221] Moreover, there is cooperation with private actors in deep-sea mining, including Nauru Ocean Resources (NORI) and Tonga Offshore Mining Ltd. (TOML).[222] In this way, also the "Pacific consensus" was found, to establish fixed baselines based on geographic coordinates rather than baselines "without

---

[215] T. Aqorau (note 333 in Chap. 5), 221.

[216] J. Bryant-Tokalau (note 5 in Chap. 1), 21 et seq; H. Lazrus (note 202), 287.

[217] H. Lazrus (note 202), 289; J. Bryant-Tokalau (note 5 in Chap. 1), 21.

[218] T. Aqorau (note 334 in Chap. 5), 223.

[219] *M. Binkley/A. Gill/P. Saunders/G. Wescott*, in: D. L. VanderZwaag, Towards Principled Oceans Governance, 2006, 250.

[220] Ibid., 254.

[221] *K. N. Scott*, in: D. R. Rothwell/D. Letts, Law of the Sea in South East Asia: Environmental, Navigational and Security Challenges, 2020, 113.

[222] M. W. Lodge (note 134), 138.

taking into account sea level rise", adopted in the 2014 Palau Declaration,[223] the 2015 "Taputapuatea Declaration on Climate Change", and the 2016 Declaration of Baselines and Outer Zone Limits of the Marshall Islands.[224] The 50th Pacific Island Leaders meeting in 2019 even stressed in its statement that:

> *"Leaders committed to a collective effort, including to develop international law, with the aim of ensuring that once a Forum Member's maritime zones are delineated in accordance with the 1982 UN Convention on the Law of the Sea, that the Members' maritime zones could not be challenged or reduced as a result of sea-level rise and climate change."*

The "community-based management" led to the idea of "non-territorial functional space", which could compensate or replace the sovereign State in the near future.[225] In particular, regarding ecosystem management, we notice an "evolution to nonexclusive territoriality" because ecological entities "cross existing State boundaries".[226] Therefore, in the context of common property management, such as land, water, and other natural resources, connectivity and cooperation appear to be among the most critical instruments.[227] Here, greater effectiveness and decentralization can be achieved by involving not only State actors but also other stakeholders, such as indigenous peoples and relevant local communities, "to ensure the connectivity between management strategies and the socio-cultural peculiarities of the pertinent resource".[228] So, for instance, in the case of biological diversity and natural and associated cultural resources, the example of a "transboundary protected area" already exists, which is "an area of land or sea that straddles one or more boundaries between States, sub-national units such as

---

[223] Article 10: "*We call for strengthened regional efforts to fix baselines and maritime boundaries to ensure that the impact of climate change and sea level rise does not result in reduced jurisdiction.*"

[224] *K. N. Scott*, in: D. R. Rothwell/D. Letts, Law of the Sea in South East Asia: Environmental, Navigational and Security Challenges, 2020, 114; R. Strating and J. Wallis (note 26 in Chap. 4), 4 et seq; *D. Freestone/C. Schofield*, Republic of the Marshall Islands. 2016 Maritime Zones Declaration Act: Drawing "Lines in the Sea", The International Journal of Marine an Coastal Law 31 (2016), 740 et seq; *D. Freestone/C. Schofield*, Pacific Islands Countries Declare Permanent Maritime Baselines, Limits and Boundaries, The International Journal of Marine and Coastal Law 36 (2021), 687.

[225] V. Ward (note 27 in Chap. 5), 82.

[226] Ibid.

[227] Ibid., 83; *T. Marauhn/A.-M. Böhringer*, in: L. J. Kotzé, Transboundary Governance of Biodiversity: Transboundary Governance of Biodiversity, 2014, 98.

[228] T. Marauhn and A.-M. Böhringer (note 8 in Chap. 7), 98.

provinces and regions, autonomous areas and areas beyond the limits of national sovereignty or jurisdiction (...)."[229]

Moreover, it is not unrealistic for people—irrespective of the legal concept of state or other derived legal personality—to manage a portion of land on their own, as the example of the Saami shows. The Saami are indigenous people in Norway, Finland, and Sweden, whose communities extend far beyond borders. Their territory is therefore regarded separately from the boundaries of the Nation-States.[230] They are represented by local and national governing bodies. They are granted special legislative and executive powers, including the authority to collect taxes and manage political institutions, which are crucial for preserving their language, education, religion, and culture.[231] Consequently, this living example can also serve as the poster child for the disappearing island States to form cooperative arrangements or acquire any other legal personality to preserve their rights over the natural resources within the areas of their present territories. This is particularly possible since "the Pacific is already a community sharing values and a common heritage linked by the vast Pacific Ocean", irrespective of their legal personality.[232]

6.5 Conclusion

In this chapter, we considered models for "solution finding" and alternatives for Statehood, because "notions of consistency and finality, like the State-territory link, are increasingly moribund".[233] Consequently, we had to answer whether a system "still so heavily rooted in notions of territoriality, sovereignty, jurisdiction, regulation, and accountability" is ready to challenge the '*2.0 reality*', a world of "erosion of State-driven framing."[234]

Further, we took a closer look at the legal personalities the disappearing island States have access to, at least to preserve sovereignty over their natural resources. We considered the idea of Statelessness and the integration of the people into another State by means of cession of Statehood, which seems the most realistic solution, but does not in any way reflect the adequate realization of the right

[229] Ibid., 100.

[230] S. Willcox (note 7 in Chap. 1), 218.

[231] Ibid.

[232] T. Aqorau (note 334 in Chap. 5), 222.

[233] M. Burkett (note 34 in Chap. 5), 373.

[234] C. Blanchard (note 151 in Chap. 3), 104.

of self-determination for the people. In the next part, we examined the innovative concept of the "de-territorialized" Nation-State, which has recently been the subject of a heated debate in the international community. The concept of recognizing a State without territory seems revolutionary but unachievable in this still territory-dependent world. There are particular fears regarding the dilution of the concept of Statehood and its permanence without territory if the population has to leave the land.

Consequently, we had to step back and reconsider the legal forms of limited sovereignty that international law offers us. The concept of public trusteeship, introduced in international law by the UN Trusteeship system outlined in the UN Charter, has found its way into various national and international rules and has experienced a revival, particularly in environmental law. However, even if the concept of trusteeship for the natural resources of the disappearing islands is an appropriate idea, it would still fail to adequately represent the will of self-determining people, because it does not allow for full sovereignty of peoplehood. Particularly due to the negative experiences of the Pacific Island States during their long-standing UN trusteeship in the aftermath of colonization, the concept would be viewed more as a step back than a step forward.

Hence, we had to consider other forms of self-government, as they are developed in international law and are based more on the concept of cooperation and fusion. The free association, a legal personality similar to trusteeship, but designed for continuance, seems to be the most adequate solution for the islands because it retains full external sovereignty, so that it can appear as a whole sovereign legal personality on the international floor, but can be supported in internal affairs by the associated State. In particular, for the islanders with a small understanding of the legal concept of the State, it seems an adequate solution. However, for Tuvalu and Kiribati, the Pacific Island States have a strained relationship with the possible associated States, Australia and New Zealand, and the implementation could be challenging.

Moreover, we considered a federation or union similar to the EU. A federation offers islanders a range of options for internal affairs, whereas on the external level, the federation would act as a single legal entity. Consequently, the islanders could maintain their sovereignty, *e.g.,* over their natural resources, but would have no room to maneuver in the international forum. Consequently, in this context, we asked whether international law is ready to "accept a [completely new] alternative of the territorial State itself"[235]. As we have noted, the Pacific Island States are already tied together through several cooperative agreements, so they are

[235] C. Blanchard (note 17 in Chap. 3), 104.

moving toward the creation of a new legal personality. In ecosystem management, community-based management seems to be a resounding success, so the question must be seriously posed: Will the disappearing islands usher in the era of "new forms of ecological self-governmentality"? [236] Can they be considered the shining paradigm, *e.g.*, the SIDS as a social organization that will allow the international community to move towards the recognition of the "complete dissociation of a State as a social community?" [237] While we will not be able to find a final answer, we can note a so far thoroughly positive tendency.

[236] C. Blanchard (note 151 in Chap. 3), 104; F. R. Cameron (note 275 in Chap. 5), 874.

[237] C. Blanchard (note 151 in Chap. 3), 104; F. R. Cameron (note 275 in Chap. 5), 874.

Compatibility and Compliance with UNCLOS

7

By the law of nature, these things are common to mankind – the air, running water, the sea, and consequently the shores of the sea. (Institutiones Iustiniani, 535 A.D., 2.1.1.)

After considering the legal personality of the disappearing islands, we will now examine the compatibility of these legal concepts with the most crucial international treaty on this topic: UNCLOS.

This treaty "may be a promising instrument" according to several scholars, *e.g.*, "due to its expansive definition of pollution, the clear obligations on States parties to preserve the health of the environment" and its "advancing climate change litigation".[1] First, however, we must determine whether UNCLOS, upon its adoption, triggers a territorial expansion of sovereignty, or whether the principle of the CHM does not contradict this theory. If not, what does the legal construct of the CHM represent so that we can render it feasible for the issues raised? Then, we will focus on one of the main principles of UNCLOS: protecting and preserving the marine environment, and how this supports our approach to climate change. In the last part, we will challenge the State as the dominant and sole actor in UNCLOS and raise the question of whether this concept is compatible with our idea of a new legal personality for the disappearing islands.

[1] C. Blanchard (note 151 in Chap. 3), 91; *M. Burkett*, A justice paradox: Climate change, small island developing states, and the absence of international legal remedy, 2015, 652 et seq.

M. A. Brinker, *The Principle of Permanent Sovereignty over Natural Resources as an Anchor in Times of Sealevel Rise*, https://doi.org/10.1007/978-3-658-50527-1_7

7.1 "Territorial Temptation" Versus "Common Heritage of Humankind"

As we concluded in Chap. 3, UNCLOS is primarily based on the principle of State sovereignty. However, the CHM was introduced in UNCLOS for the Area and its resources simultaneously. Did it serve as a counterpart to keep the expansion of State sovereignty at bay, or has this idea failed?

7.1.1 Sovereignty Expansion Under UNCLOS

Taking a closer look at the 1982 UN Convention on the Law of the Sea, we have to realize that the treaty, in the form it was reached in 1982 and came into force in 1994 after 60 States had ratified it, does not have much in common with the already mentioned original concept of the "mare liberum" by Grotius. The idea that up to half a century ago, the ocean existed without boundaries—"free and open to all"—a blind spot on the map, or in Judge Jesus' words, "no-man's land", seems unrealistic and ironic these days.[2] Today, we have to search—at least in the Northern hemisphere—for the few "stateless spaces"—or in the case of the Arctic, so-called "donut-holes"—in the sea, not claimed as sovereign territory by a State.[3] Currently, the reality is that "with the advent of the 200-mile resource zones [is that,] every coastal and island State would have at least one maritime boundary to negotiate with at least one neighbor".[4]

The signature of UNCLOS initiated what is probably the most excellent peaceful undertaking: the "territorial expansion of coastal States sovereignty, sovereign rights and jurisdiction seaward".[5] In particular, because of the "insufficient precision and deliberate vagueness of UNCLOS", the "territorial temptation" of the States was open to—probably unwarranted—enhancement of their jurisdiction

---

[2] *J. L. Jesus*, in: J. Frowein/K. Scharioth/I. Winkelmann/R. Wolfrum, Verhandeln für den Frieden—Negotiating for Peace, 2003, 594.

[3] H. Türk (note 204 in Chap. 3), 38; *C. Schofield/T. Potts*, Current Legal Developments: The Arctic, International Journal of Marine and Coastal Law (2008), 164; *E. Roszko*, Maritime territorialisation as performance of sovereignty and nationhood in the South China Sea: Maritime territorialisation: Maritime territorialisation as performance of sovereignty and nationhood in the South China Sea: Maritime territorialisation, Nations and Nationalism (2015), 233.

[4] J. L. Jesus (note 21), 594; H. Türk (note 204 in Chap. 3), 26–27, 38.

[5] V. A. Ventura (note 206 in Chap. 3), 156; H. Türk (note 204 in Chap. 3), 26 et seq; J. L. Jesus (note 21), 579 et seq.

seaward, so that UNCLOS was used as a "springboard for coastal States to expand the prerogatives given to them over parts of the sea".[6] Going back to Grotius, in the words of Ventura:

> *"In this sense, Selden's mare clausum would continue to haunt the law of the sea."*[7]

Also, for the small island States, the adoption of UNCLOS led to the most significant change in their previously insignificant international status, "transforming some of the world's smallest States into massive territories", even with different levels of sovereign rights respectively in the EEZ.[8] So, for instance, Kiribati, with a land area of around 820 km^2, was granted an EEZ of approximately 3.5 million km^2,[9] and Tuvalu, with a land area of only 26 km^2, was given an EEZ of roughly 900,000 km^2, which made it several times larger than the EEZ of the whole EU.[10] Consequently, this change opened a proverbial sea of new opportunities for the "sea-rich, but land-poor small island States", who had a limited range of options to secure their food supply, livelihoods, and revenue, except for their maritime natural resources—the fish stocks.[11] In the following, Kiribati increased its income through the award of fishing licenses, earning 42 to 44 percent of its total government revenue from access fees for foreign fleet fisheries within the EEZ in 2010, while Tuvalu had corresponding earnings totaling 11 percent of its total government revenue.[12] This data reflects the socio-economic and cultural significance of—we can also call it dependence on—maritime resources for the SIDS. Still, it also shows the unlocked potential of growing industries like blue-sea fishing and deep-sea mining.[13] Therefore, the loss of these maritime and

---

[6] V. A. Ventura (note 206 in Chap. 3), 157.

[7] Ibid.

[8] *R. Davis/Q. Hanich,* Small Island States and the LOS Convention 30 Years On: Have the Benefits Been Realized?, Ocean Yearbook 26 (2012), 63.

[9] Ibid.

[10] *A. J. Tilling/E. Fihaki,* Tuvalu National Biodiversity Strategy and Action Plan: Fourth National Report To the Convention on Biological Diversity, 2009, 6 et seq; C. Blanchard (note 151 in Chap. 3), 81.

[11] R. Davis and Q. Hanich (note 27), 63.

[12] Ibid., 63 et seq; C. Blanchard (note 151 in Chap. 3), 81; *A. Powers/C. Stucko,* Introducing the Law of the Sea and the Legal Implications of Rising Sea Levels, Threatened Islands Nations (2013), 132., Kiribati, 2011, Annual Report to the Commission, Part 1.

[13] C. Blanchard (note 151 in Chap. 3), 82; *J. Petzhold/A. K. Magnan,* Climate change: thinking small islands beyond Small Island Developing States (SIDS), Climate Change (2019), 146.

resource-related rights would be fatal to the recognition of SIDS as States and to their economies.[14]

Hence, we must note that introducing this new legal concept laid the groundwork for greater sovereignty for the States, thereby increasing the exploration and exploitation of marine resources.[15] With the introduction of the principle of permanent sovereignty over natural resources, which is also defined in UNCLOS as the "sovereign right to exploit their natural resources"[16], the exploration and exploitation of marine mineral resources were legitimized. So, some degree of disposability of the jurisdiction of coastal States was reached, albeit in the limited scope of sovereign rights over the EEZ and the continental shelf.[17]

The same point is made for introducing the CHM for the submerged space beyond the jurisdiction of coastal States or "the Area", as the Articles 136 and 137 UNCLOS call it.[18] However, must we necessarily conclude that adopting a new legal concept concerning the *'white spots'* of the oceans automatically results in the "undesirable consequence" of the "tragedy of the commons"?[19] Is this principle the abandonment of the freedom of the seas found in Article 87 UNCLOS, or rather a principle of conscious regulation in the common interest of the international community, as mainly the developing countries argue?[20] However, does this innovative new concept, which emerged from the belief in free access and exclusive exploitation in the common interest of the international community and was propagated accordingly, represent only a preliminary step toward the unilateral exploitation of natural resources?[21]

[14] C. Blanchard (note 151 in Chap. 3), 80.

[15] *F. L. Bastos*, in: M. C. Ribeiro, 30 Years After the Signature of the United Nations Convention on the Law of the Sea: The Protection of the Environment and the Future of the Law of the Sea: Proceedings of the International Conference—15–17 November 2012, 2014, 126, 132, 134.

[16] *Compare*: Article 2, 56, 77, 82, 193 UNCLOS.

[17] F. L. Bastos (note 34), 132 et seq.

[18] Ibid., 134.

[19] *Y. Huang/C. Hu,* The Principle of the Common Heritage of Mankind Can be Applied to Marine Genetic Resources, Global Commons and the Law of the Sea 5 (2018), 53.

[20] *E. M.* de *Santo/E. Mendenhall/E. Nyman/R. Tiller,* Stuck in the middle with you (and not much time left): The third intergovernmental conference on biodiversity beyond national jurisdiction, Marine Policy (2020), 4.

[21] Y. Huang and C. Hu (note 38), 53, 55.

7.1.2 The Innovative Principle of the Common Heritage of Humankind

The opposite is the case. The idea of the CHM was primarily advanced by Arvid Pardo, Malta's ambassador to the UN, in his well-known speech before the First Committee on November 1, 1967.[22] He replicated the idea of an "indivisible common patrimony", first conceptualized by Andrés Bello, a Chilean international jurist, who pleaded for "areas of the planet set apart in common for the use of all people and not capable of being subject to claims of State sovereignty or ownership, but to certain defined rights of common use".[23] Consequently, Pardo considered the exploration of natural resources—originally including all of the oceans' resources, living or not-living—"primarily in the interests of mankind and with particular regard to the interests and needs of poor countries:"[24]

> *"(...) a vision shaped by the history of an ancient island community, one that had come to understand that only in order and the rule of law can there be real protection for the weak and small."*[25]

Bearing in mind the well-known "tragedy of the commons," Pardo worried about the legal status of natural resources in the deep seabed beyond the limits of national jurisdiction, considering both existing principles of sovereignty and freedom as gateways to unregulated exploitation by wealthy and technologically advanced States.[26] Consequently, he campaigned in this speech that:

> *"The seabed and the ocean floor are the common heritage of mankind and should be used and exploited for peaceful purposes and the exclusive benefit of mankind as a whole."*[27]

---

[22] Ibid., 58; V. A. Ventura (note 206 in Chap. 3), 101; *K. Baslar*, The concept of the common heritage of mankind in international law, 1998, 235 et seq.

[23] H. Türk (note 204 in Chap. 3), 32.

[24] Y. Huang and C. Hu (note 38), 58.

[25] R. Davis and Q. Hanich (note 27), 60.

[26] *Compare:* Convention on the Law of the Sea 1982 (note 194 in Chap. 2), Art. 143(1); Y. Huang and C. Hu (note 38), 62; *C. Wang/Y.-C. Chang,* A new interpretation of the common heritage of mankind in the context of the international law of the sea, Ocean and Coastal Management (2020), 4.

[27] Y. Huang and C. Hu (note 38), 63, 67; H. Türk (note 204 in Chap. 3), 33.

In sum, the idea behind this concept was to prevent the "move of coastal States towards the exercise of unilateral jurisdiction over the waters immediately adjacent to their shore" to outpace "colonial-like spoliation of marine natural resources therein" once and for all.[28] Considering this so-called "creeping jurisdictionalism" a real threat causing political tension, economic injustice, and pollution risks, he brought the idea of this "benefit of humankind as a whole" into being, relying on the concept that financial and economic cooperation and distribution among the States derive from activities within.[29] Consequently, he combined two concepts: on the one hand, the "solidarity between all participating States, in particular, about the weaker members" and, on the other hand, the effective implementation of the marine environment against pollution.[30] The SIDS still rely on this idea.[31]

However, what does the "internationalization of the submerged space beyond national jurisdiction" and, in the following, the "communitarisation of natural resources" mean in a legal sense?[32] The fact is that the CHM occupies a hybrid status; it represents

> *"the counterpoint to the concept of the freedom of the high seas and the subjection of marine spaces to national jurisdiction."*[33]

The expression of "common interest" in this context was chosen deliberately in contrast to the already known and defined principle of "*res communis*" and its counterpart "*res nullius*".[34] While "*res nullius*" establishes a space that belongs to nobody, even though everyone can appropriate it, "res communis" is defined as a common area that no one can appropriate, but is used by everyone.[35] During the negotiation process, developing countries favored the idea of a common property, similar to the concept of "res communis".[36] However, industrialized countries

---

[28] V. A. Ventura (note 206 in Chap. 3), 102.

[29] Y. Huang and C. Hu (note 38), 62; V. A. Ventura (note 206 in Chap. 3), 102; H. Türk (note 204 in Chap. 3), 3.

[30] *N. Matz-Lück*, in: A. G. O. Elferink/E. J. Molenaar, The International Legal Regime of Areas Beyond National Jurisdiction, 2010, 65; P. Ferrara (note 103 in Chap. 3), 211; K. Baslar (note 41), 235 et seq.

[31] R. Davis and Q. Hanich (note 27), 59 et seq.

[32] F. L. Bastos (note 34), 141.

[33] Ibid., 134.

[34] Y. Huang and C. Hu (note 38), 70.

[35] Ibid., 71.

[36] 3th United Nations Conference on the Law of the Sea 1978.

rejected this idea, instead campaigning for the "principle of non-appropriation."[37] As Dolman noticed astutely:

> *"International resources management cannot be based on the classical Roman-law concept of private ownership and the classical static concept of national sovereignty. Both the concept of ownership and sovereignty are being (and should be) transferred by the new, revolutionary concept of the common heritage of mankind."*[38]

The problem with the concept of common property—also known as "open-access space"—is the absence of rights and duties, which, in consequence, leads to a lack of responsibility, and, further, to "overexploitation and degradation".[39] There is no right for spatial exclusion or power of transmissibility or transfer of resources; the only guaranteed right of the "authorized users" is to use the property and generate income for all.[40] So, for instance, in the case of fishery resources, the concept of "property rights" does not set the right priorities for the relevant conservation and management of fishing, among other things, because, as we already noticed, "property rights" are not equated to sovereign rights of States.[41] Like sovereign rights within the EEZs, this legal figure creates the "temptation" of overfishing, giving the impression of "owning" quotas for fish stocks, which were at their highest level of degradation in the early 1990 s.[42] The new principle should instead be based on equity, "limited to a certain improvement in the distribution of the benefits".[43] Consequently, this principle is closely connected with the term "community interest", which involves the exploitation of natural resources 'under

---

[37] H. Türk (note 204 in Chap. 3), 36 et seq; *E. Egede/E. Charles,* Common Heritage of Mankind and the Deep Seabed Area Beyond National Jurisdiction: Past, Current and Future Prospects, Marine Technology Society Journal (2021), 43.

[38] *A. J. Dolman,* Resources, regimes, world order, 1981, 247 et seq; K. Baslar (note 41), 372.

[39] V. Ward (note 27 in Chap. 5), 90.

[40] Ibid.

[41] *L. A. La Fayette,* Entitlement To Marine Living Resources In Areas Beyond National Jurisdiction: Commentary On Richard Barnes, The International Legal Regime of Areas beyond National Jurisdiction (2010), 159 et seq; *A. Serdy,* Commentary: Property rights in areas beyond national jurisdiction: not too late for pa proper debate?, The International Legal Regime of Areas beyond National Jurisdiction (2010), 143.

[42] L. A. La Fayette (note 60), 160 et seq; *R. Rayfuse/D. Freestone,* Precaution and the Protection of Marine Biodiversity in Areas beyond National Jurisdiction: Precaution and the Protection of Marine Biodiversity in Areas beyond National Jurisdiction, International Journal of Marine and Coastal Law (2012), 774.

[43] H. Türk (note 204 in Chap. 3), 36.

an international management regime applied in favor of all people of present and future generations'.[44]

Consequently, the CHM, born in the context of the law of the sea, was later carbon-copied into the law of outer space and, to a lesser extent, into international environmental law.[45] So, for instance, Pardo already hoped to make the principle suitable for the conservation and protection against environmental pollution, "to close the oceans to all human use as a result of nuclear waste and other pollution", even if it is, to date, a peripheral issue in the panorama of CHM.[46] The concept was also considered for application to the continental shelf beyond the 200-mile limit. However, Article 82(4) UNCLOS does not grant the ISA adequate scope of maneuver but limits it to the distribution of levies based on equitable sharing criteria, so this idea could be considered a previous provision of CHM within the 200-miles zone.[47] However, the discussion regarding the extension of this principle to uninhabited land—"no man's land"—came up soon after Pardo's statement, recognizing that the language used in, *e.g.*, the 1959 Antarctic Treaty reminded one of the "*res communis*" idea, the predecessor of the CHM.[48] Later, this principle was frequently invoked when regulatory questions arose concerning the exploitation of resources in the relevant areas and the prevention of environmental disasters, for example, in the failed case of the Regulation of Antarctic Mineral Resources Activities (CRAMRA).[49] To date, the principle is considered the only possible way for developing States to "put forth their arguments of *res communis*".[50]

However, the CHM is still considered the legal instrument to usher in the "transformation of the Westphalian World Order" towards a time of "supranational law" or "global law".[51]

---

[44] Y. Huang and C. Hu (note 38), 70.

[45] K. Baslar (note 41), 159 et seqq., 243 et seqq., 277 et seqq.

[46] Ibid., 235 et seq; *E. van Doorn*, Legal Implications of the "Common Heritage" Principle for Atlantic Bluefine Tuna, 2021, 144.

[47] K. Baslar (note 41), 239.

[48] Ibid., 243 et seq.

[49] *K. Baslar*, The concept of the common heritage of mankind in international law, 1998, 248 et seq.

[50] Ibid., 263.

[51] Ibid., 372 et seq.

7.1.3 The Common Heritage of Humankind: a Legal Personality for People?

Furthering this idea, the CHM was difficult to define, combining "bundles of rules, principles and theories, such as the stewardship doctrine and theory of inter- and intra-generational justice and the principle of sustainable development".[52] Because of its non-exhaustive nature, its rather "nebulous nature" which invites a broad range of interpretations, some scholars even consider it a new international legal personality, an improved version of the legal personality of a State—"the primary unit".[53] In those days, it was considered the starting point of a new era "from State-centered international law to anthropocentric international law, or from law of nations to the law of humankind, or even from individualism to egalitarianism."[54] After centuries—probably from Grotius' era until the second half of the 20th century—of considering the State as the "sole subject of international relations having rights and duties", it is time to bring the anthropocentric character of the concept of the CHM to the fore.[55] The idea was that the State was no longer the "mere juxtaposition of individual units constitute the international community", but forms together "an overarching system embodying a common interest of all States and humankind".[56] "Humankind" cannot only be "the steward of the earth charged with the protection of the earth and living organisms therein as a *custodi in terram*", but it could also be considered a new legal personality in international law.[57] Pursuing this idea, the representative of humankind would, without a doubt, be the international community as a figure *sui generis*, reflecting its growing importance within the international legal system, "distinct from these constituting nuclei—the States".[58] So, for instance, Baslar referred to the term "humankind" as

> *"all human beings as a collective body of peoples wherever they may be found, and thus it includes both men and women."*

[52] E. Egede and E. Charles (note 56), 42.

[53] Ibid., 43; B. Simma and A. L. Paulus (note 159 in Chap. 5), 269 et seq.

[54] P. Ferrara (note 103 in Chap. 3), 210; K. Baslar (note 41), 71; E. Egede and E. Charles (note 56), 43.

[55] P. Ferrara (note 103 in Chap. 3), 210.

[56] B. Simma and A. L. Paulus (note 159 in Chap. 5), 271.

[57] P. Ferrara (note 103 in Chap. 3), 210 et seq.

[58] Ibid., 211; K. Baslar (note 41), 75.

To develop and strengthen this legal personality, scholars call for an organization for the protection and supervision of "the common heritage of humankind", based on the concept of the UN Trusteeship Council, "a body acting for humanity, (…) for our great surrounding environments, (…) on behalf of all nations and future generations in the governance of the global commons".[59] Part of these tasks of a "special agent" acting as a "trustee" are already being undertaken by the ISA, particularly by granting new exploration licenses for seabed mining, *e.g.*, to Kiribati in 2012.[60] However, as Article 137 (2) UNCLOS stresses, "all rights to the resources of the Area are vested in mankind as a whole", and the ISA only acts on behalf of humankind, while all States parties, meanwhile, are "*ipso facto*" members of the ISA according to Article 156 UNCLOS.[61] Consequently, the primary purpose of the principle becomes clear: "avoid exploitative opportunities, ensure substantive fairness and give priority to the interests and needs of developing States".[62] However, it is apparent in the discussion that the "common heritage of humankind" is and remains a "passive legal personality", only capable of acting by means of humankind's trustees, namely, once again, the States.[63] As we noted above, the legal figure of trusteeship or even stewardship is not the preferred legal concept for the continued existence of the island States.

Unfortunately, in UNCLOS, humankind is understood in a relatively narrow and misleading sense: "all States".[64] Even though UNCLOS is "based on the fundamental premise that all the problems of the oceans are closely interrelated and need to be considered a whole" for and with the help of the entire international community, UNCLOS itself equates this community with the community of States as seen, *e.g.*, in Article 139 (3), 153 (4) and Annex III, Article 4 (4).[65] In conclusion, even if UNCLOS offers an innovative legal concept—the CHM, which paves the way to a "supranational world" and overcomes the "Westphalian World Order"—this treaty is still based on the nearly insurmountable supremacy of States.

---

[59] K. Baslar (note 41), 375 et seq.

[60] E. Egede and E. Charles (note 56), 42; *D. Freestone,* The Law of the Sea Convention at 30: Successes, challenges and new agendas, International Journal of Marine and Coastal Law (2012), 678.

[61] C. Wang and Y.-C. Chang (note 45), 3.

[62] *C. Wang/Y.-C. Chang,* A new interpretation of the common heritage of mankind in the context of the international law of the sea, Ocean and Coastal Management (2020), 4.

[63] K. Baslar (note 41), 78.

[64] Ibid., 72; P. Ferrara (note 103 in Chap. 3), 214.

[65] P. Ferrara (note 103 in Chap. 3), 214; H. Türk (note 204 in Chap. 3), 2.

7.1.4 The Common Heritage of Humankind Nowadays

This already addresses the main problem of the CHM: it remains a principle under the sponsorship of States, whereas the ISA, as custodian for the CHM, only realizes the common interests of all States.[66] For instance, the ISA takes steps to protect the environment in the case of deep-sea mining; however, due to States' influence, it appears more like a redistribution of resources than conservation.[67] Even if the original idea of CHM allows "a variety of stakeholders," such as civil society, industry, academic societies, the scientific community, and coastal communities, the ISA, as an intergovernmental organization, rarely involves these groups in its decision-making processes, at best, in an observer status.[68] It is even worse when we consider that CHM is all about shared assets, so the exploitation of resources to derive monetary benefits. In contrast, other principles included in the CHM, like the inter-generational justice, sink into oblivion.[69] In particular, regarding resources, the shared asset system is considered with caution, given that it applies only to mineral resources and inevitably affects environmental resources.[70] In more drastic words, the rights granted to the States by UNCLOS, referring to deep-ocean mining, are "rights vested in mankind as a whole were transferred to the States, their companies, etc."[71]

Consequently, the question arises of how to comply with the main characteristics and goals of the CHM, including its peaceful purpose and the benefits of sharing resources in the area, as set out in Articles 137, 141, and 143 of UNCLOS.[72] Nowadays, benefit sharing seems mainly equated with economic benefits from deep-seabed mining and the exploitation of mineral resources, as it was feared and debated during the negotiation of UNCLOS. Hence, the CHM seems to have degenerated into a sole concept of exploitation.[73] The crux of the matter

---

[66] E. Egede and E. Charles (note 56), 44.

[67] *E. Egede/E. Charles,* Common Heritage of Mankind and the Deep Seabed Area Beyond National Jurisdiction: Past, Current and Future Prospects, Marine Technology Society Journal (2021).

[68] E. Egede and E. Charles (note 56), 45.

[69] E. Egede and E. Charles (note 86), 47.

[70] Ibid., 46.

[71] *E. van Doorn,* Legal Implications of the "Common Heritage" Principle for Atlantic Bluefine Tuna, 2021, 114.

[72] E. Egede and E. Charles (note 56), 45.

[73] *E. M.* de *Santo/E. Mendenhall/E. Nyman/R. Tiller,* Stuck in the middle with you (and not much time left): The third intergovernmental conference on biodiversity beyond national

is that, because developing countries essentially advocate this principle, it provokes resistance from developed countries to equitable benefit sharing, regardless of their actual participation in exploration and exploitation.[74] The consequence led to the non-ratification of UNCLOS by some developed countries due to their disagreement with the deep-sea mining regime.[75] Even if a compromise was found in the establishment of the ISA, the question of its influence and margin of discretion is repeatedly questioned, as recently shown in the request of Nauru on behalf of the foreign-owned NORI challenging the 2-year-rule under Chap. 1 (15) (b) and (c) of the 1994 Agreement.[76] Consequently, it remains questionable whether the CHM and its regulation by the ISA are a boon or a bane for the original purpose of protecting the maritime resources of the seabed. Does more regulation by an international organization result in better and controlled protection, or in only more exploitation? However, the follow-up question that comes up automatically is whether the unregulated status of the "freedom of the seas" is the better choice.

Additionally, during negotiations of the recently signed Biodiversity Beyond National Jurisdiction Agreement (BBNJ), the CHM and benefit sharing were discussed and supported by developing countries, particularly the 134 State members of the G77/China.[77] According to the EU and Tuvalu, as representatives of the Pacific SIDS, it should be "an effective, practicable and future-proofed implementing agreement for the conservation and sustainable use of marine biodiversity in areas beyond national jurisdiction".[78] This idea took up the original purpose of Pardo, who considered the principle "part of sustainable management of humankind's heritage".[79] Moreover, it extends beyond the scope of UNCLOS, including the marine genetic resources that were still unknown at the time UNCLOS was negotiated.[80] So, for instance, Palestine insisted on the inclusion of the CHM during the 3rd intergovernmental conference on biodiversity beyond

jurisdiction, Marine Policy (2020), 3; K. Baslar (note 41), 264; E. van Doorn (note 90), 114 et seq.

[74] M. Dervovic (note 202 in Chap. 2), 311.

[75] E. van Doorn (note 90), 116.

[76] *P. A. Singh,* The Invocation of the "Two-Year Rule" at the International Seabed Authority: Legal Consequences and Implications, The International Journal of Marine and Coastal Law 37 (2022); E. Egede and E. Charles (note 56), 48 et seq.

[77] E. M. de Santo et al. (note 92), 3.

[78] E. M. de Santo et al. (note 39).

[79] K. Baslar (note 41), 236.

[80] *J. A. Roach,* The BBNJ Process: Gaps and Prospects for Success, Ocean Yearbook 35 (2021), 69.

national jurisdiction and pleaded against the significant resistance of developed countries, mainly supporters of the "freedom of the sea" idea:[81]

> *"The principle of Common Heritage of Mankind, the polluter pays, the principle of Common Heritage of mankind, the precautionary principle/ approach, the principle of Common Heritage of Mankind, equity; did I mention the principle of Common Heritage of Mankind? The ecosystem approach, best available scientific information and traditional knowledge of indigenous peoples and local communities, and of course the principle of Common Heritage of Mankind."*[82]

Hence, according to the G77/China-States, the "overall goal of conservation and sustainable use of marine biodiversity in ABNJ can only be achieved when guided by the bedrock principle of CHM".[83] The African Group, represented by Algeria, also considered the principle of such importance, so its lack of inclusion would be "like putting a ship in the water without a navigational instrument".[84] Consequently, the final version of the BBNJ includes the CHM as a general principle in Article 7, taking into account crucial topics such as benefit sharing, but remains uncoupled from the legal status of the resources as such.[85] In conclusion, even if the original purpose of the CHM seems to be upstaged steadily, there are always someone—in particular the developing States -, who remember us of it, of the idea of *res communis*, the benefit sharing in the intra- as well as intergenerational context, and the complete protection of environmental resources, in particular, as Pardo pictured it as:[86]

> *"a sort of bridge to the future and unite the world community in its quest to preserve the planet for generations to come."*[87]

---

[81] E. M. de Santo et al. (note 92), 3 et seq; *J. A. Roach,* The BBNJ Process: Gaps and Prospects for Success, Ocean Yearbook 35 (2021), 69.

[82] State of Palestine, Statement on Behalf of the Group of 77 and China, Working Group on Cross-Cutting issues: The 3rd Session of the Intergovernmental Conference on an International Legally Binding Instrument under the United Nations Convention on the Law of the Sea on the Conservation and Sustainable Use of the Marine Biological Diversity of Areas Beyond National Jurisdiction, 2019.

[83] E. M. de Santo et al. (note 92), 3.

[84] E. M. de Santo et al. (note 39).

[85] E. Egede and E. Charles (note 56), 51; Agreement under the United Nations Convention on the law of the Sea on the conservation and sustainable use of marine biological diversity of areas beyond national jurisdiction, 19.06.2023.

[86] E. M. de Santo et al. (note 92), 3 et seq; E. Egede and E. Charles (note 56), 47 et seq.

[87] K. Baslar (note 41), 236.

Consequently, even if the BBNJ Agreement does not change the UNCLOS content, it can be considered an amendment to the Convention and, consequently, also a progress in the development of the CHM, written down and established as a general principle of the protection of biological diversity and natural resources.

7.2 Protection and Preservation of the Marine Environment

Consequently, in its original status, the CHM can be considered one pillar of innovative tendencies, and it may remain so in the future. This pillar can therefore pave the way for a reinterpretation of UNCLOS, consistent with the new legal concept for disappearing islands. Thus, let us take a closer look at one of the equally essential pillars of UNCLOS, which is groundbreaking in the context of climate change: the protection and preservation of the marine environment.

7.2.1 Preventive Principle and Due Diligence in UNCLOS

Regardless of the concrete legal nature of the CHM—either a principle, concept, notion, doctrine, regime, ideal, theory, right, or legal term of art—since its creation, it has pursued one purpose: the peaceful benefit-sharing of resources and the protection of the maritime environment[88].[89] You could say that protecting the marine environment and conserving marine resources go hand in hand with UNCLOS, trying to achieve its goal mainly through "compliance with the 'due diligence' obligation among the States".[90] This is found in many different Articles in UNCLOS, *e.g.,* in Article 78 (1) and (2) UNCLOS, where obligations with due regard to the rights and freedoms of other States are established, in the "attempt to harmonize contrary values" like the interests of Nation-States as well as the interests of the international community.[91] Therefore, for instance, these

[88] *Compare*: Convention on the Law of the Sea 1982 (note 194 in Chap. 2), Art. 192, 194.

[89] *N. Matz-Lück*, in: A. G. O. Elferink/E. J. Molenaar, The International Legal Regime of Areas Beyond National Jurisdiction, 2010b, 62; M. Dervovic (note 202 in Chap. 2), 310.

[90] *L. N. Nguyen,* Expanding the Environmental Regulatory Scope of UNCLOS Through the Rule of Reference: Potentials and Limits, Ocean Development & International Law (2021), 438.

[91] V. A. Ventura (note 206 in Chap. 3), 141 et seq.

articles are built on the premise that coastal States are "trustees" of common concerns of humankind, such as the oceans and marine protection.[92]

Hence, even though climate change and sea level rise were neither on the agenda during UNCLOS negotiations nor known to the negotiating parties at the time, the treaty appears remarkably amenable to an environmentally friendly interpretation.[93] Although the preventive principle had only been formulated a few years before UNCLOS was adopted, it already found its way into Article 194(2) of UNCLOS. They expressed the principles of "due diligence" and "harm prevention".[94] However, the obligation imposed by the Convention for the States "to prevent the spread of pollution" is much "more stringent" than the principle laid down in the Stockholm or the Rio Declaration, referring to damages, moreover, in comparison to Art. In 194 (1) UNCLOS, the ITLOS stated in its Advisory Opinion that Article 194 (2) UNCLOS concerns a particular obligation for States regarding transboundary pollution.[95] This also includes an obligation of "due diligence" like Art. 194 (1) UNCLOS, but to a "lesser degree of effort to achieve the intended result", so mainly at the discretion of a State.[96]

Even if it is not expressly mentioned in the paragraph itself, this interpretation has been developed by ITLOS jurisdictions, *i.a.*, in the *South China Sea* Arbitration, obligating flag States to investigate the situation and take action if necessary.[97] Wolfrum even goes a step further and claimed that with the beginning of the negotiation of UNCLOS III, the protection and conservation of the marine environment as set out in Article 192 UNCLOS, in particular referring to the high seas—even if not explicitly declared as CHM—"are the shared responsibility of all States".[98] Otherwise, "Article 192 UNCLOS would render void and

---

[92] Ibid., 142.

[93] N. Matz-Lück (note 108), 62; *A. Boyle,* Law of the sea perspectives on climate change, International Journal of Marine and Coastal Law (2012), 831.

[94] *J. Kateka,* in: R. Wolfrum, Coexistence, cooperation and solidarity, (2012), 925; A. Proelß (note 198 in Chap. 3), Sec. 194, para. 20, 22; *Request For an Advisory Opinion submitted by the Commission of Small Island States on Climate Change and International Law,* No. 31, 21.05.2024, para. 246.

[95] *Request For an Advisory Opinion submitted by the Commission of Small Island States on Climate Change and International Law,* No. 31, 21.05.2024, para. 253.

[96] *Request For an Advisory Opinion submitted by the Commission of Small Island States on Climate Change and International Law,* No. 31, 21.05.2024, paras. 254–257.

[97] *The South China Sea Arbitration,* PCA Case No. 2013–19, 12.07.2016, para. 743 et seqq; A. Proelß (note 198 in Chap. 3), Sec. 194, para. 20.

[98] K. Baslar (note 41), 237; *R. Wolfrum,* Purposes and Principles of International Environmental Law, German Yearbook of International Law 33 (1990).

would arguably violate the principle of good faith as enshrined in Article 300 UNCLOS."[99] ITLOS also affirmed in of 2024, that Article 192 UNCLOS "imposes upon States a legal obligation (…) and a legal order for the protection and preservation of the marine environment."[100] However, this was never mentioned explicitly in the convention, so it is even an indirect interpretation.

However, at first glance, the norms of UNCLOS seem well-suited to the challenges of climate change and the possibility of the disappearance of States. First of all, the Convention defines marine pollution in Article 1, paragraph 1, subparagraph 4, as follows:

> *"Pollution of the marine environment means the introduction by man, directly or indirectly, of substances or energy into the marine environment, including estuaries, which results or is likely to result in such deleterious effects as harm to living resources and marine life, hazards to human health, hindrance to marine activities, including fishing and other legitimate uses of the sea, impairment of quality for use of sea water and reduction of amenities."*

Moreover, ITLOS specified the three main criteria of this definition in "(1) there must be a substance or energy; (2) this substance or energy must be introduced by humans, directly or indirectly, into the marine environment; and (3) such introduction must result or be likely to result in deleterious effects."[101] Here, we can notice the similarity to the definition of the climate change threat for the disappearing island States, the threat is always coming from the anthropogenic sources, "produced by man", as the Tribunal also recognized.[102]

Moreover, upon closer examination of the protection of the marine environment, the treaty identifies six distinct sources of marine pollution: land-based sources, seabed activities subject to national jurisdiction, activities in the Area,

[99] *B. E. Klerk,* Protecting the Marine Environment from the Impacts of Climate Change: A Regime Interaction Study, Review of European, Comparative and International Environmental Law 32 (2022), 44, 50; *Request for Advisory Opinion submitted by the Commission of Small Island States on Climate Change and International Law,* Case No. 31, 16.06.2023, 125 et seq.

[100] *Request For an Advisory Opinion submitted by the Commission of Small Island States on Climate Change and International Law,* No. 31, 21.05.2024, para. 184.

[101] *Request For an Advisory Opinion submitted by the Commission of Small Island States on Climate Change and International Law,* No. 31, 21.05.2024, para. 161.

[102] *Request For an Advisory Opinion submitted by the Commission of Small Island States on Climate Change and International Law,* No. 31, 21.05.2024, para. 165.

dumping, vessels, and the atmosphere.[103] Consequently, the system regarding marine pollution appears to be principally designed on the basis of self-regulation and the principle of reciprocity to secure each State's national interests.[104] The complex, intertwined mechanism of climate change, producing sea level rise, poses a dramatic threat to the Island States and, in turn, raises the possibility of their complete disappearance, which does not seem to align with the simple concept of the treaty. ITLOS also noted difficulties in categorizing anthropogenic GHG emissions, including pollution from land-based sources, from vessels, and through the atmosphere.[105] However, working in a complementary manner, this system of rights and obligations can provide us with the foundation we need to address the present-day challenges. In particular, Article 207(4) of UNCLOS requires States to take into account "internationally agreed rules, standards and recommended practices and procedures", such as "climate change treaties such as the UNFCCC and the Paris Agreement", as the Tribunal affirmed.[106] Moreover, the Tribunal states that the enforcement rules of Articles 213 to 222 of UNCLOS impose an obligation on States to "adopt laws and regulations and to take measures necessary to implement rules and standards set out in climate change treaties and other relevant instruments".[107]

So, for instance, Article 192 UNCLOS obliges States "to protect and preserve the marine environment", which first and foremost comprises the ocean as a whole, "all maritime areas", without distinguishing between marine spaces under or beyond national jurisdiction.[108] ITLOS affirmed this in its Advisory Opinion, determining this Article as a "cover of all contemporary threats to the marine environment, including those that have emerged following the adoption of the

[103] *Y. Tanaka*, The international law of the sea, 2019, 325; *Request For an Advisory Opinion submitted by the Commission of Small Island States on Climate Change and International Law*, No. 31, 21.05.2024, paras. 259 et seqq.

[104] Y. Tanaka (note 123), 324.

[105] *Request For an Advisory Opinion submitted by the Commission of Small Island States on Climate Change and International Law*, No. 31, 21.05.2024, para. 262.

[106] *Request For an Advisory Opinion submitted by the Commission of Small Island States on Climate Change and International Law*, No. 31, 21.05.2024, para. 270.

[107] *Request For an Advisory Opinion submitted by the Commission of Small Island States on Climate Change and International Law*, No. 31, 21.05.2024, para. 286.

[108] Y. Tanaka (note 123), 332 et seq; *The South China Sea Arbitration*, PCA Case No. 2013–19, 12.07.2016, para. 940; *Request For Advisory Opinion submitted by the Commission of Small Island States on Climate Change and International Law*, Case No. 31, 15.06.2023, p. 16, para. 55.

Convention".[109] This idea contradicts the holistic approach to climate change.[110] However, this article not only referred to existing damage but also, in accordance with the preventive principle, to future damage. Consequently, it now includes the obligation to preserve, which means maintaining or improving the current condition.[111] This obligation, in turn, involves, on the one hand, the "positive obligation to take active measures to protect and preserve the marine environment as a whole, and, on the other hand, the negative obligation not to degrade the marine environment at the same time".[112]

Moreover, ITLOS affirmed the principle of due diligence for States in its 2011 Advisory Opinion, which was reiterated in 2024, not only in Article 194 but also in Article 192 of UNCLOS.[113] There, it not only demanded to "take necessary measures to prevent, reduce and control marine pollution", but also appealed to the States to "put in place a national system, including legislation, administrative procedures and an enforcement mechanism necessary to regulate the activities in question, and to exercise adequate vigilance to make such a system function efficiently."[114] That is of particular importance "in a situation in which private persons or entities mostly carry out the activities in question."[115] Moreover, the Tribunal stated that "the standard of due diligence has to be more severe for the riskier activities, but depending on the States' capabilities and available resources."[116] Moreover, the precautionary approach is considered an "integral part of the general obligation of due diligence".

Moreover, Article 194 (1) UNCLOS clarifies that these rules refer to *any* possible source of marine pollution, and thereby amplifies the scope of its application—in contrast to the earlier Geneva Convention—to the utmost, by

---

[109] *Request For an Advisory Opinion submitted by the Commission of Small Island States on Climate Change and International Law,* No. 31, 21.05.2024, paras. 384, 400.

[110] *Request For Advisory Opinion submitted by the Commission of Small Island States on Climate Change and International Law,* Case No. 31, 15.06.2023, p. 16, para. 55.

[111] Y. Tanaka (note 123), 333.

[112] Ibid; *The Iron Rhine Railway Arbitration,* 24.05.2005a.

[113] *Request For an Advisory Opinion submitted by the Commission of Small Island States on Climate Change and International Law,* No. 31, 21.05.2024, para. 234.

[114] *Request For an Advisory Opinion submitted by the Commission of Small Island States on Climate Change and International Law,* No. 31, 21.05.2024, paras. 234–235.

[115] *Request For an Advisory Opinion submitted by the Commission of Small Island States on Climate Change and International Law,* No. 31, 21.05.2024, 236.

[116] *Request For an Advisory Opinion submitted by the Commission of Small Island States on Climate Change and International Law,* No. 31, 21.05.2024, paras. 239–240.

utilizing vocabulary like "*inter alia*" or "*designed to minimize to the fullest possible extent*".[117] However, as ITLOS clarified in this Advisory Opinion, it does not mean the "immediate cessation of marine pollution", but rather the reduction and control of existing marine pollution "within the "scientific, technical, economic and financial capacities" of the States, as well as the "harmonization of their policies".[118] We can already note that this is not only designed to depict former, groundbreaking jurisdiction, like the *Trail Smelter* case[119] and the *Nuclear Weapons* case,[120] but it was meant to be open to continuation and re-interpretation, as can be seen in the latest modifications and elaborations in the *Iron Rhine* case[121] or the already discussed *South China Sea* case.[122]

In particular, the *South China Sea* case is not only known because of the innovative interpretation of the term of an island in contrast to Article 121 (3) UNCLOS (see above Chap. 6) but also because the concept of protection and preservation of the marine environment—in Part XII of UNCLOS—was amplified and re-interpreted with the condition and duty to cooperate.[123] Thereby, the Arbitral Tribunal not only declared a breach of the obligation to protect and preserve the marine environment, referring to Article 192 UNCLOS, but also appealed to China to take all measures to protect and preserve rare or fragile ecosystems and the habitat of depleted, threatened, or endangered species and other forms of marine life under Article 194 (5) UNCLOS.[124] However, ITLOS specifies in its Advisory Opinion that the necessary measures are understood broadly and "in accordance with its ordinary meaning", so that "rarity" and "fragility" must be

---

[117] Y. Tanaka (note 123), 333.

[118] *Request For an Advisory Opinion submitted by the Commission of Small Island States on Climate Change and International Law,* No. 31, 21.05.2024, para. 199, 225, 230.

[119] *Trail Smelter case (United States vs. Canada),* 16.04.1938, 11.03.1941.

[120] *Legality of the Threat or Use of Nuclear Weapons,* 08.07.1996.

[121] *The Iron Rhine Railway Arbitration,* 24.05.2005a, para. 59; *C. Kojima,* South China Sea arbitration and the protection of the marine environment: Evolution of UNCLOS part XII through interpretation and the duty to cooperate, Asian Yearbook of International Law 21 (2015a), 171.

[122] *The South China Sea Arbitration,* PCA Case No. 2013–19, 12.07.2016.

[123] *C. Kojima,* South China Sea arbitration and the protection of the marine environment: Evolution of UNCLOS part XII through interpretation and the duty to cooperate, Asian Yearbook of International Law 21 (2015), 166.

[124] C. Kojima (note 141), 168; *The South China Sea Arbitration,* PCA Case No. 2013–19, 12.07.2016, para. 1203, B(12).

defined on a case-by-case review.[125] Even though the due diligence principle is not found explicitly in UNCLOS, the Arbitral Tribunal referred to it on several occasions, by underlining the importance of the preventive principle in Article 194 (1), (2) UNCLOS, as well as in Article 192 UNCLOS.[126] It is stressed that Article 192 UNCLOS could also be violated by the omission of taking active measures to protect and preserve the marine environment:[127]

> *"Article 192 thus entails the positive obligation to take active measures to protect and preserve the marine environment, and by logical implication, entails the negative obligation not to degrade the marine environment. The corpus of international law relating to the environment, which informs the content of the general obligation in Article 192, requires that States ensure that activities within their jurisdiction and control respect the environment of other States or of areas beyond national control."*

Thereby, it referred to the previously mentioned famous jurisdictions, such as the Trail Smelter case and the Nuclear Weapons case, as well as to customary international law.[128] Moreover, in recent jurisdictions, such as the Iron Rhine case, it has reiterated the "positive" duty to prevent and mitigate significant environmental harm, as well as the "negative" duty not to degrade the environment.[129] This award not only demonstrates the living application of UNCLOS in protecting and preserving the marine environment but also provides insight into a remarkable development in the interpretation of a so-called outdated treaty. Furthermore, the court explicitly emphasized its commitment to complying with the obligations of other international agreements under Article 237 UNCLOS, which envisages the harmonization of international treaties under Article 30 of the Vienna Convention on the Law of Treaties (VCLT).[130] Consequently, in no other treaty is the interaction with and the inclusion of other treaties as vivid and flexible as in

---

[125] *Request For an Advisory Opinion submitted by the Commission of Small Island States on Climate Change and International Law,* No. 31, 21.05.2024, paras. 402–403.

[126] *The South China Sea Arbitration,* PCA Case No. 2013–19, 12.07.2016, 743 et seqq; C. Kojima (note 143), 171; *Request For Advisory Opinion submitted by the Commission of Small Island States on Climate Change and International Law,* Case No. 31, 15.06.2023b, 15, para. 51–55; *Request For an Advisory Opinion submitted by the Commission of Small Island States on Climate Change and International Law,* No. 31, 21.05.2024, para. 234.

[127] *The South China Sea Arbitration,* PCA Case No. 2013–19, 12.07.2016, para. 941; C. Kojima (note 143), 171.

[128] *The South China Sea Arbitration,* PCA Case No. 2013–19, 12.07.2016, para. 941.

[129] *The Iron Rhine Railway Arbitration,* 24.05.2005b, para. 59; C. Kojima (note 143), 171.

[130] *The South China Sea Arbitration,* PCA Case No. 2013–19, 12.07.2016, 942; C. Kojima (note 143), 172.

UNCLOS—the Constitution of the Ocean.[131] Like in the *South China Sea* case, and now in the Advisory Opinion of ITLOS in 2024, where the CBD and the Convention on International Trade in Endangered Species of Wild Fauna and Flora (CITES) were taken into account and "systematically integrated" for the interpretation and definition of terms, like "ecosystem", of Articles 192 and 194 (5) UNCLOS, the court has once again shown the character of the treaty as "a living instrument".[132] Consequently, the systematic integration of and the numerous cross-references to other international treaties found in this treaty are nothing but the realization of the meaning of Article 31 (3) (c) VCLT, which expresses the flexible interpretation of international treaties.[133] In conclusion, UNCLOS not only includes several customary rules but also provides an "umbrella or framework provisions capable of being implemented at a later date".[134]

7.2.2 Cooperation in UNCLOS

As discussed in the previous Chapter, cooperation is one of the key features of the international law instruments SIDS use to address climate change and sea level rise. This principle is also found in the system of protection and preservation of the marine environment in UNCLOS, in particular, as the cooperation between States and international organizations, specified in Article 123 and Article 197 UNCLOS:[135]

> *"States shall cooperate on a global basis and, as appropriate, on a regional basis, directly or through competent international organizations, in formulating and elaborating international rules, standards, and recommended practices and procedures consistent with this Convention, for the protection and preservation of the marine environment, taking into account characteristic regional features."*

---

[131] C. Kojima (note 143), 170.

[132] *The South China Sea Arbitration,* PCA Case No. 2013–19, 12.07.2016, Dispositif, para. 1203, B(12); C. Kojima (note 143), 170, 180; *Request For an Advisory Opinion submitted by the Commission of Small Island States on Climate Change and International Law,* No. 31, 21.05.2024, paras. 169, 401.

[133] C. Kojima (note 143), 170; *L. N. Nguyen,* Expanding the Environmental Regulatory Scope of UNCLOS Through the Rule of Reference: Potentials and Limits, Ocean Development & International Law (2021), 424.

[134] C. Kojima (note 143), 170; L. N. Nguyen (note 155), 421.

[135] Y. Tanaka (note 123), 335.

Originally developed and mentioned in Principle 7 of the Rio Declaration, this Article, already at this early stage of international interrelationship, at which UNCLOS was negotiated, shows the significance of cooperation to confront problems and challenges regarding the marine environment, one of the core principles in international agreements, *e.g.,* also included in the now-negotiated BBNJ Agreement (Article 8).[136] It is also interesting to note that States are mentioned on the same level as international organizations, so that they are not only considered interchangeable but also a better way to find solutions on the global stage. Also in the Advisory Opinion in 2024, ITLOS defined the two actors as interchangeable, so that "States Parties refer to States and international organizations".[137] Furthermore, the Tribunal recognized that this duty of cooperation "was central to the examination of the Request".[138] However, it affirmed that the duty to cooperate according to Article 197 UNCLOS goes not further than it requires States to act with "due diligence"—as set in Article 194 (1), (2) UNCLOS—and to fulfil this obligation in good faith.[139]

Moreover, the treaty acknowledges that regional particularities must be considered and that global cooperation does not necessarily yield a better solution; however, this is also possible on a regional level.[140] These considerations were confirmed and strengthened in various cases, for instance, in the *MOX Plant* case in 2001, where cooperation was acknowledged as a "fundamental principle".[141] However, in the South China Sea case, this idea was also a substantial component of the overall decision.[142] For instance, the court emphasized that China

[136] C. Kojima (note 143), 178; E. M. de Santo et al. (note 92), 3; Agreement under the United Nations Convention on the law of the Sea on the conservation and sustainable use of marine biological diversity of areas beyond national jurisdiction (note 104).

[137] *Request For an Advisory Opinion submitted by the Commission of Small Island States on Climate Change and International Law,* No. 31, 21.05.2024, para. 155.

[138] *Request For an Advisory Opinion submitted by the Commission of Small Island States on Climate Change and International Law,* No. 31, 21.05.2024, para. 295.

[139] *Request For an Advisory Opinion submitted by the Commission of Small Island States on Climate Change and International Law,* No. 31, 21.05.2024, paras. 309, 321.

[140] Y. Tanaka (note 123), 335.

[141] *The MOX Plant Case (Ireland vs. United Kingdom),* 03.12.2001, para. 82; *Request For an Advisory Opinion submitted by the Commission of Small Island States on Climate Change and International Law,* No. 31, 21.05.2024, para. 296.

[142] *The South China Sea Arbitration,* PCA Case No. 2013–19, 12.07.2016, 946, 984–986; C. Kojima (note 143), 177; Y. Tanaka (note 123), 335.

had failed in this specific duty "to cooperate and coordinate with other States bordering the South China Sea".[143] Remarkably, the court underlined the stronger wording of Article 197 UNCLOS "shall cooperate", in contrast to the weaker formulation of the general norm of Article 123 (b) UNCLOS: "should endeavor to coordinate the implementation of their rights and duties concerning the protection and preservation of the marine environment".[144]

Here, once again, the importance of cooperation for provisional measures is appreciated by the international courts, in particular, for the prevention of future environmental harm, because "as marine pollution may easily spread beyond man-made delimitation lines, the protection of the marine environment [...] can hardly be achieved by a single State.[145] Moreover, the question arises whether this award opened the door to a broad enough application of Article 192 UNCLOS to make it "a weapon against every threat to the marine environment," and whether it extends the duty to cooperate into a binding norm.[146] Assuming it did both, is it not the ideal "weapon" for the disappearing islands to confront the industrial countries as the main polluters and emitters, as vividly seen in the advisory opinions before the two most important international courts, the ICJ and ITLOS?[147] As long as the island States are recognized as States, they should use this legal instrument to enforce their rights, taking advantage of the possibilities and power the international stage offers them.

7.2.3 Climate Change in UNCLOS?

However, it remains unclear whether this broadened concept can also be applied to disappearing islands. Specifically, can disappearing islands acquire legal personality under UNCLOS, even when they lose the character of a State? In the same breath, the question arises whether States can be held responsible for a

---

[143] *The South China Sea Arbitration,* PCA Case No. 2013–19, 12.07.2016, 986.

[144] *The South China Sea Arbitration,* PCA Case No. 2013–19, 12.07.2016, 984, 986; C. Kojima (note 143), 178.

[145] C. Kojima (note 143), 179; Y. Tanaka (note 123), 335; *Request For an Advisory Opinion submitted by the Commission of Small Island States on Climate Change and International Law,* No. 31, 21.05.2024, para. 191.

[146] C. Kojima (note 143), 180.

[147] *Request for an Advisory Opinion submitted by the Commission of Small Island States on Climate Change and International Law (Request for Advisory Opinion submitted to the Tribunal),* Case No. 31, exp. Spring 2024; *Request for Advisory Opinion: Obligations of States in respect of Climate Change,* Case No. 187, 23 July 2025.

multi-causal, intertwined event like climate change and its serious consequences, such as sea level rise, which go far beyond the scope of the here presented protection and preservation from marine pollution. This question was often a point of discussion in the last years, particularly because the disappearing islands do not tire of announcing their upcoming claim against the leading global polluter—mainly Australia—to the international courts—mainly the ICJ—concerning the responsibility to avoid emissions causing climate change damage.[148] Neither Tuvalu in 2002 nor Palau in 2011 realized their ambitions to file a suit, but instead concentrated on the international climate negotiations leading up to the Paris Agreement.[149] However, at least Palau sought a legally non-binding advisory opinion of the ICJ, "hoping to close the rhetorical gap between State action and international legal responsibilities".[150] Some scholars even went a step further and considered that such an advisory opinion on climate change would "have the power to reshape positively the international approach to greenhouse gas emissions."[151] Until now, it might be too early to see any further reaching impact of the Advisory Opinion rendered by ITLOS in 2024 for the SIDS, but the scholars read it with raising interest, in particular, about the intertwined interpretation of UNFCCC and the Paris Agreement.[152] However, as ITLOS acknowledged, the UNFCCC and the Paris Agreement were incorporated into the Convention as interpretative instruments.[153]

Simply put, climate change and global warming result from pollution emitted by States' conduct, affecting other States' existence; thus, we can resume "legal rights and interests protected under UNCLOS are affected", as ITLOS

[148] C. Hamilton (note 237 in Chap. 5), 529; *K. Boom*, See you in court: the rising tide of international climate litigation; https://theconversation.com/see-you-in-court-the-rising-tide-of-international-climate-litigation-3542 (last reviewed Oct. 9, 2025), 2011.

[149] K. Boom (note 170); M. Burkett (note 20), 656; *Request For an Advisory Opinion submitted by the Commission of Small Island States on Climate Change and International Law,* No. 31, 21.05.2024, para. 325.

[150] M. Burkett (note 20), 658.

[151] *M. Burkett*, A justice paradox: Climate change, small island developing states, and the absence of international legal remedy, 2015, 658.

[152] *Request for Advisory Opinion: Obligations of States in respect of Climate Change,* Case No. 187, 23 July 2025; *Request for an Advisory Opinion submitted by the Commission of Small Island States on Climate Change and International Law (Request for Advisory Opinion submitted to the Tribunal),* Case No. 31, exp. Spring 2024.

[153] C. Kojima (note 143), 179; Y. Tanaka (note 123), 335; *Request For an Advisory Opinion submitted by the Commission of Small Island States on Climate Change and International Law,* No. 31, 21.05.2024, para. 191.

concluded.[154] However, there are some difficulties concerning the exact value of marine environmental damage.[155] Questions like the precise volume of emissions emitted by a specific State over a given period, their precise impact on climate change, and the consequences of induced sea level rise, such as the destruction of coral reefs and atoll islands, seem unresolvable. [156] As we have seen in the *Lliuya vs. RWE* case, general principles of civil and penal law, such as questions of proof and causation, are not easily applicable in general terms.[157] Consequently, even if the disappearing island States finally brought an action before the international courts, the question arises whether these efforts would be better invested in regional cooperation and negotiations on international rules and standards, given the seemingly insurmountable burden of proof.[158] The ITLOS advisory opinion does not address this problem; instead, it cites the IPCC as the best scientific standard. Moreover, the Tribunal clarified the relationship between UNCLOS and other international instruments by holding that "UNFCCC and the Paris Agreement are *lex specialis* in respect of the obligations of States Parties under the more general provisions of the Convention," but "nonetheless should be applied in such a way as not to frustrate the very goal of the Convention".[159] Following the advisory opinions, we will see how this problem is resolved in the forthcoming procedures.

Despite this, the Pacific Island States have already demonstrated that they have taken advantage of the opportunities provided by UNCLOS on several occasions, such as the legal concept of cooperation. Consequently, in terms of protecting and preserving the marine environment, UNCLOS served as a guiding hand for the disappearing island States to develop new survival strategies. In sum, UNCLOS also provides legal concepts that can make the latest and innovative solution for the disappearing islands manageable.

---

[154] *M. Jaén,* Protecting the Oceans from Climate Change: An Analysis of the Role of Selected International Instruments on Resources and Environmental Portection in the Context of UNCLOS, Ocean Yearbook 21 (2007), 126 C. Kojima (note 143), 179; Y. Tanaka (note 123), 335; *Request For an Advisory Opinion submitted by the Commission of Small Island States on Climate Change and International Law,* No. 31, 21.05.2024, para. 191.

[155] M. Jaén (note 176), 126.

[156] Ibid.

[157] R. Verheyen and S. Pabsch (note 178 in Chap. 5), 511, para. 8; P. Minnerop (note 34 in Chap. 1), para. 44; S. Willcox (note 7 in Chap. 1), 132.

[158] M. Jaén (note 176), 127.

[159] *Request For an Advisory Opinion submitted by the Commission of Small Island States on Climate Change and International Law,* No. 31, 21.05.2024, paras. 220, 224.

7.3 New Treaty?

Regarding all the considerations above regarding the United Nations Convention on the Law of the Sea, in light of recent developments, we must consider whether a new treaty on the law of the sea is necessary to address the problems of the day. This will be the content of the next part of this chapter.

7.3.1 The State as a Single and Absolute Actor in UNCLOS?

The question remains whether a new treaty is necessary to develop a solution for the disappearing island States. Does UNCLOS offer solutions beyond the concept of States, and is it open to an interpretation "outside of the box", outside the narrow scope of an international regime of States?[160] This matter is controversial and not as easily ticked off as some scholars believe.[161] The "Nation-State" as a "territorial State" is the leading actor under the Westphalian system, as reflected in the United Nations Convention on the Law of the Sea and in most international law.[162]

Consequently, we have to take a closer look at two reasons: firstly, States, next to the numerous rights granted to them by UNCLOS, are also submitted to a broad range of obligations, and secondly, that UNCLOS offers the same range of rights to "juridical persons" as it does to the States. An example found quite often in UNCLOS is the so-called "rule of reference," which follows the principle of the primacy of international law over national law by obligating the active actor in UNCLOS —the State.[163] Consequently, a rule of reference always contains (1) the obligation to the State party and (2) the rule that is referred to.[164] There are different kinds of rules of reference, and each has a different level of obligation for the State to comply.[165] For instance, Articles 60, 207, 212, and 262 UNCLOS only require "taking into account the external rules and

---

[160] C. Blanchard (note 151 in Chap. 3), 117.

[161] K. R. Lal (note 87 in Chap. 6), 266.

[162] C. Blanchard (note 151 in Chap. 3), 73.

[163] L. N. Nguyen (note 155), 421.

[164] L. N. Nguyen (note 109), 421.

[165] L. N. Nguyen (note 155), 421 et seq.

standards", which represents a low standard.[166] Articles 208, 210, 211 UNCLOS, meanwhile, oblige the State to adopt rules that "have the same effect" or be "not less effective" than international rules, whereas provisions like Article 211 (5) UNCLOS request national rules "conforming" or "giving effect to" international standards.[167] These different wordings cover the two opposite poles of the standard of conduct, the minimum and the maximum.[168] There are a handful of other phrasings found in UNCLOS, like "must take account of", "action the basis of", "be in conformity with", "without prejudice to" or territorial sea sovereignty "should be exercised", which make us aware of one decisive factor, namely, that absolute sovereignty of States is not absolute, but somewhat limited in UNCLOS.[169] According to Ward,

> *"Absolute sovereignty, in the sense of total control, authority, and autonomy of action, is not granted, for States are authorized to act subject to limits."*[170]

This conclusion shows us even more what we already assumed: absolute sovereignty was never completely granted, not even in the peak phase of belief in absolute sovereignty, in the 1970 s and 1980 s,[171] when UNCLOS was negotiated:

> *"Sovereignty has therefore never been absolute. (…) [The fact that] States are interdependent on each other for trade and economic development demonstrates that no one State can be totally independent."*[172]

Consequently, this is a reason for hope that the power of States is limited, providing us with scope for a broader interpretation of "other actors" in UNCLOS. However, the yield is still sobering when seeking other actors aside from the States in UNCLOS, such as persons, who are also attributed rights and duties.[173] The leading actor and addressee of the responsibilities and claims is the State; even private parties are not addressed directly in the Convention.[174] Other actors

[166] L. N. Nguyen (note 109), 421.

[167] Ibid., 422.

[168] Ibid.

[169] V. Ward (note 27 in Chap. 5), 92.

[170] Ibid.

[171] F. Nawrot (note 118 in Chap. 2), 100.

[172] T. Aqorau (note 334 in Chap. 5), 218.

[173] *I. Papanicolopulu,* The Law of the Sea Convention: No place for persons?, International Journal of Marine and Coastal Law (2012), 871.

[174] A. Boyle (note 112), 833.

are rarely found in UNCLOS, except in the already mentioned Article 137 UNCLOS, which allows active claims of "juridical and natural persons" against the ISA, but only in the specific constellation of seabed mining.[175] However, apart from this, these other actors can only derive rights—in particular, participatory rights—in a limited scope, based on previous sponsorship and the will of a State, as specified in Part XI[176] of UNCLOS.[177] Therefore, other actors under UNCLOS may act only through State sponsorship and, consequently, only under the control of a State party.[178]

However, the treaty allows some room for interpretation, for example, by taking fundamental human rights into account. So, for instance, Articles 293 and 311 UNCLOS give us the possibility to include "the needs and concerns of persons and aims", in allowing or even mandating "the direct attribution of rights, the uniform regulation of States' duties vis-à-vis persons and the consistent interpretation of rights and duties under the Convention, taking into account "considerations of humanity".[179] Even though this development of "a consistent and effective regime applicable to persons at sea is still in the initial phase", a change in the field of human rights is often the first step in a grassroots movement to a global change, as we have already noticed in various examples in this research project. [180] Thus, whether in the history of indigenous peoples or in the examples of climate change litigation, this development offers us hope for a more positive perspective on the participation of people and various actors in UNCLOS.

7.3.2 Change by Interpretation: Following the Main Purposes of UNCLOS

Reviewing the possibilities for change that international law offers, we can examine its primary sources, such as the Vienna Convention on the Law of Treaties. So, for instance, according to Article 31 of the Vienna Convention on the Law of Treaties, every treaty "shall be interpreted in good faith" and "in the context

[175] I. Papanicolopulu (note 195), 869.

[176] Convention on the Law of the Sea 1982 (note 194 in Chap. 2), Art. 153, para. 2(b), Annex III: Art. 4, Art. 139 and Seabed Disputes Chamber.

[177] I. Papanicolopulu (note 195), 869; I. Papanicolopulu and A. Rocha (note 179 in Chap. 5), 194.

[178] I. Papanicolopulu (note 195), 869.

[179] I. Papanicolopulu (note 17 in Chap. 4), 874.

[180] I. Papanicolopulu (note 195), 874.

and the light of its object and purpose", so that UNCLOS has to be seen in this "light of change" as well.[181] According to some scholars, no treaty offers flexibility in addressing changing circumstances or "encompasses new activities".[182] Nevertheless, the treaty is the "product of its time in which it was negotiated" and is therefore not a "climate change convention".[183] Hence, we look in vain for terms like "global warming" or "climate change" in the 1970 s and 1980 s, nothing but indeterminate concepts of a science-fictional, apocalyptic, and distant future.[184] However, this treaty—negotiated in the aftermath of the Stockholm Declaration—had already incorporated concepts such as the CHM and the protection and preservation of the marine environment, as seen above. These concepts express the original idea of the United Nations Conference on the Law of the Sea (UNCLOS III), the "assurance of peace, security, cooperation and friendly relations among all nations".[185]

Let us take a closer look at the new developments regarding the disappearing islands. An example of dynamic development is the regime of baselines, which encouraged an interpretation in favor of the islands by allowing them to freeze the baselines or the outer limits of their maritime zones when facing the submergence of landmass.[186] While the Polynesian Leaders Group—*i.a.*, the Marshall Islands, Kiribati, and Tuvalu—initially showed preference for the concept of freezing the baselines by coordinates, having already provided the appropriate legislation, *e.g.*, in the 2014 Palau Declaration,[187] the dominant opinion considers it preferable to freeze the outer limits, keeping the EEZ and continental shelf intact independently from the submerged area.[188] This new concept appears to prevent the creeping erosion of sovereignty over the territorial sea and the EEZ, stemming from the misleading notion that baselines remain ambulatory.[189] This means they are constantly measured against the steadily changing low-tide

[181] *S. V. Busch*, in: E. Johansen/S. V. Busch/I. U. Jakobsen, The law of the sea and climate change: Solutions and constraints, 2021, 326; R. Strating and J. Wallis (note 26 in Chap. 4), 4.

[182] *I. U. Jakobsen/E. Johansen/P. P. Nickels*, in: I. U. Jakobsen/E. Johansen/S. V. Busch, The law of the sea and climate change: solutions and constraints, 2021, 377.

[183] N. Matz-Lück (note 108), 63; I. U. Jakobsen et al. (note 204), 376.

[184] I. U. Jakobsen et al. (note 204), 376; R. Rayfuse and D. Freestone (note 61), 774.

[185] S. V. Busch (note 203), 309; J. L. Jesus (note 21), 593.

[186] S. V. Busch (note 203), 312 et seq.

[187] R. Strating and J. Wallis (note 26 in Chap. 4), 4 et seq.

[188] S. V. Busch (note 203), 317; K. N. Scott (note 5), 114.

[189] *M. Hayashi*, in: D. Vidas/P. J. Schei, The World Ocean in Globalisation: Climate Change, Sustainable Fisheries, Biodiversity, Shipping, Regional Issues, 2011, 188 et seq.

elevation—in a more figurative sense, "the drying rocks" –, which has led to continually evolving uncertainty about the size of the State's territory and the EEZ.[190] Consequently, this legal instability can lead to disputes with neighboring States, particularly where countries share a maritime space of fewer than 400 miles, which is the case in most instances.[191] In this context, *e.g.,* the European Commission already pointed out "there might be a need to revisit existing rules of international law, particularly the Law of the Sea, as regards the resolution of territorial and border disputes".[192] Consequently, in October 2020 the majority of the Pacific Islands—the Cook Islands, Fiji, Federated States of Micronesia, Papua New Guinea, Solomon Islands, Palau, Tonga, Tuvalu, Tokelau, and Kiribati—together with Australia, New Zealand, and France filed a submission under Article 76 (9) UNCLOS before the UN Commission on the Limits of the Continental Shelf to "describe permanently the outer limits of its continental shelf".[193] In August 2021, the Declaration on Preserving Maritime Zones in the Face of Climate Change-Related Sea-Level Rise was issued at the 51st virtual Annual Meeting of the South Pacific Forum by the eighteen member States.[194] This shows us—once again—the tireless, cooperative action of the Pacific Islands to rescue their territory, no matter what.

Thus, regardless of the legal solution found for the Pacific Islands, the delimitation of maritime zones can be considered an endorsement of the primary purpose of UNCLOS: "the strengthening of peace, security, cooperation and friendly relations among all nations".[195] However, the question of the quality of a "State without territory" remains in the case of complete submergence because even if fixation of baselines seems an adequate solution for partially submerged territory, it is far from clear "at present whether this solution is acceptable for a completely submerged island State."[196]

Going back to the beginning, the starting point of the interpretation concerning baselines is found in the well-known *Anglo-Norwegian Fisheries* case, one of the first cases before the ICJ, which involved the law of the sea (see above,

---

[190] Ibid., 188; *D. D. Caron*, in: H. N. Schreiber/J.-H. Paik, Regions, Institutions, and Law of the Sea, 2013, 533 et seq.

[191] M. Hayashi (note 211), 188 et seq; D. D. Caron (note 212), 533 et seq.

[192] M. Hayashi (note 211), 201.

[193] R. Strating and J. Wallis (note 26 in Chap. 4), 5.

[194] Pacific Island Forum, Declaration on Preserving Maritime Zones in the Face of Climate Change-Related Sea-Level Rise, 2021; D. Freestone and C. Schofield (note 5), 686.

[195] S. V. Busch (note 203), 318; J. L. Jesus (note 21), 593 et seq.

[196] C. Blanchard (note 151 in Chap. 3), 83.

Chap. 3).[197] Later, international jurisdictions issued numerous judgments, regularly influencing and changing complex rules, such as the recent *South China Sea* Arbitration.[198] This case illustrates, for example, that the strict differentiation between rocks and islands, once conceptualized to guarantee "stability and continuity of maritime borders," now seems outdated, at least in the case of the disappearing Island States.[199] Moreover, it no longer serves its former purpose of fostering peace, security, cooperation, and friendly relations.

In sum, this short paragraph has already shown us two things: on the one hand, that there is always a way to innovate in interpreting treaty law, either through additional cooperative agreements or litigation. Moreover, both remedies—a new agreement and litigation—are always a very important "adjusting screw" in the process of changing the interpretation of hard law, which the Pacific Island States have already taken advantage of.

7.3.3 Change by Fragmentation

Moreover, these new tendencies not only show us the possibility of changing the law dynamically through contemporary interpretation but also highlight how to bridge the gap in hard law, *e.g.*, the UNCLOS.[200] Even though UNCLOS, as the "Constitution of the Ocean", pursues the aim "to govern all aspects of the resources and uses of the oceans" and it is considered "the pillar of rules-based order governing international interactions",[201] we have to be aware that it is "impossible for UNCLOS to regulate every legal issue with depth or specificity".[202] However, fragmentation of international law, in the words of Anne Peters, does not need to be seen in a "negative or pejorative connotation", but instead offers scope for diversity, specialization, and pluralism[203]:

---

[197] *Compare: Anglo-Norwegian Fisheries Case,* 18.12.1951.

[198] *Compare*: *The South China Sea Arbitration,* PCA Case No. 2013–19, 12.07.2016.

[199] J. L. Jesus (note 21), 593.

[200] K. N. Scott (note 5), 101.

[201] R. Strating and J. Wallis (note 26 in Chap. 4), 1.

[202] L. N. Nguyen (note 155), 419.

[203] V. A. Ventura (note 206 in Chap. 3), 164.

> *"Finally, [fragmentation] is a term which describes not only a legal process in the real world of law but has also been a label for the accompanying discourse (mostly among academics, less among judges, and even less among political law-making actors)."*[204]

Hence, soft law, *e.g.*, the UN Resolution 66/288 in 2012, can fill a gap and bring about the desired process.[205] Nowadays, this Resolution, for instance, is considered one of the most critical non-legally binding documents to have arisen from the WSSD.[206] Unsurprisingly, one of the most essential documents on climate change is a non-legally binding instrument, reflecting States' reluctance to enter into a binding international agreement.[207] Consequently, it is even less surprising that other global players set foot on the stage to act. For the first time during this elaboration process, the UNGA allowed collaborative initiatives, private actors, and NGOs to realize "multiple projects associated with resilience, adaptation, and sea level rise."[208] At the same time, the voice of AOSIS—the previously mentioned cooperation between the Pacific Island States—grew louder, leading to one of the greatest successes for these States in 2015: the adoption of the Paris Agreement under the United Nations Framework Convention on Climate Change (Paris Agreement).[209]

The relationship between UNCLOS and the Paris Agreement is hardly clear-cut.[210] Although the overlap of regimes appears problematic, it can also be viewed as an advantage, as it imposes a mandatory claim to an interrelationship between the two regimes, as demonstrated recently in the 2024 advisory opinion of the ITLOS.[211] Moreover, Article 237 of UNCLOS provides for the possibility of "apply in harmony with environmental rights and obligations" rather than

[204] Ibid., Peters, Anne, MPIL Research Paper Series, 2016–2019: 1–29.

[205] *Compare*: Resolution 66/288. The future we want (note 6 in Chap. 6); K. N. Scott (note 5), 101.

[206] N. Matz-Lück and L. Christiansen (note 21 in Chap. 2), 525.

[207] N. Matz-Lück and L. Christiansen (note 20 in Chap. 2), 525.

[208] K. N. Scott (note 5), 102; N. Matz-Lück and L. Christiansen (note 21 in Chap. 2), 525.

[209] F. R. Cameron (note 275 in Chap. 5), 877.

[210] *A. Boyle*, in: M. C. Ribeiro, 30 Years After the Signature of the United Nations Convention on the Law of the Sea: The Protection of the Environment and the Future of the Law of the Sea: Proceedings of the International Conference—15–17 November 2012, 2014, 380.

[211] Ibid.

supersede or undermine them.[212] Here, once again, we can see that fragmentation in international law does not necessarily mean a disadvantage; instead, it helps to approach a complex problem like climate change from different angles, exploiting the full potential of interrelationships and cooperation between various international regimes and institutions.[213] Once again, we must admit that "climate change engages many different areas of international law"—not least UNCLOS.[214]

Furthermore, the "disappearing islands" have not only found a way through the "jungle of fragmented international law", but they are also an expression of considerable "fragmentive dynamics" by committing "meta discourses" either on the global and local neoliberal level, on the global and local green governmental level, or in the international and local environmentally engaged civil society.[215] The event of their disappearance served as a catalyst for a worldwide movement of connectivity and ecological responsibility, promoting the concept of environmental citizenship.[216] Hence, we can identify "new forms of ecological self-governmentality"—as seen above—in which the here-discussed reinterpretation of the principle of permanent sovereignty over natural resources fits perfectly.[217] In summary, the islands serve as a living example of the appeal made by the Permanent Court of Arbitration in the South China Sea case, which calls for increased collaboration, as already noted above (Chap. 7.2).[218]

7.3.4 Re-thinking old Concepts: "A Sea of Islands"

Following the recognition of new forms of self-governmentality, we also have to find a way to integrate this new concept into the UNCLOS regime, which is based on the idea that "land dominates the sea".[219] In this context, the gap in UNCLOS is so evident that it provokes enormous "tension between different perspectives

[212] *Request for an Advisory Opinion submitted by the Commission of Small Island States on Climate Change and International Law,* Case No. 31, 20.09.2023, 8; *M. H. Nordquist (ed),* United Nations Convention on the Law of the Sea, 1982: A commentary, 2002, Art. 237.1.

[213] A. Boyle (note 232), 381.

[214] I. U. Jakobsen et al. (note 204), 382.

[215] F. R. Cameron (note 275 in Chap. 5), 874.

[216] F. R. Cameron (note 274 in Chap. 5), 882.

[217] F. R. Cameron (note 275 in Chap. 5), 874.

[218] C. Kojima (note 143), 179.

[219] R. Strating and J. Wallis (note 26 in Chap. 4), 2.

of the relationship between land and sea".[220] In this context, the South China Sea Arbitration serves as an example to analyze the different perspectives on the phenomenon of "maritime territorialization" and to clarify the tension between the varying opinions of States.[221] Maritime territorialization is used, on the one hand, to "clarify, change, or replace UNCLOS-led maritime rules-based order" and, on the other hand, to express and intensify "maritime sovereignty, symbolically linking the sea to their sovereign identity and nationhood".[222] In response, the Pacific Island States introduced a new, innovative perspective, stressing that their lifestyle and identities cannot be described by land-sea boundaries but by an "incorporating maritime space".[223] Hence, the Pacific Islands have to be considered a "sea of islands rather than islands in a vast sea", following the former predominant approach among the Pacific people that

> *"the ocean [is seen] as early continentals [and] the land as a provider of the necessities of life."*[224]

This approach opposes the concept that "maritime entitlements run with the land"—our doctrine of "land dominates the sea"—and, in continuing on this road, contradicts the Westphalian—"west-centric system"—of the domination of State sovereignty completely.[225] Unfortunately, this principle dominates the treaty and persists in climate change litigation, where "sea-based rights and obligations are almost non-existent" and the State remains the dominant and active actor.[226]

However, we have noticed a growing shift in thinking in societies. So, for instance, at the 2017 Pacific Island Forum (PIF), the islanders established the concept of the "Blue Pacific Continent" as a new basis for their maritime sovereignty, introduced and discussed as the "2050 Strategy of the Blue Pacific Continent".[227] The choice of the wording "continent" is not without reason: the continent is typically understood as consisting of land, consequently, this concept favors "a territorialization of the sea, based on an understanding of Pacific Island States

---

220 R. Strating and J. Wallis (note 193 in Chap. 2), 1.

221 R. Strating and J. Wallis (note 26 in Chap. 4), 1.

222 R. Strating and J. Wallis (note 193 in Chap. 2), 1.

223 Ibid., 6.

224 Ibid; *G. Fry*, Framing the Islands: Power and Diplomatic Agency in Pacific Regionalism, 2019, 300.

225 R. Strating and J. Wallis (note 26 in Chap. 4), 6.

226 I. U. Jakobsen et al. (note 204), 381.

227 R. Strating and J. Wallis (note 26 in Chap. 4), 6.

as the largest oceanic continent in the world with the ocean connecting cultures, identities, resources and development aspirations."[228] In conclusion, the so-called "world's seventh continent" pursues the purpose to

> *"free the land of these bonds, to restore the essential regional viewpoint and unity, to overlook the dividing waters, to see the land and its people as united."*[229]

Nowadays, this concept does not only mean a regional administration community, but was founded to "ensure a strong and collective voice [and] regional position and action".[230] This idea includes many approaches, which we have already discussed in this research project, from "promotion of regional solidarity" to "Oceanic identity" and "Pacific island ownership", by stressing the unique connection between people and their environment.[231] These "large ocean States" shall determine and ensure indigenous control in this architecture of regional diplomacy and climate policy, so that the "Pacific voice" is heard in the global forums. This seems successful because the world cannot be imagined without the PIF and the extreme opinions of the PSIDS.[232] It even goes so far as to say that Australia and New Zealand's views are certainly valued, but their objectives are no longer tolerated.[233] Only this can promote the idea of "direct inclusion of the Pacific peoples", combining the new strengthening of self-determination with new Pacific diplomacy.[234]

7.4 Conclusion

In conclusion, we can say with certainty that we do not need a new treaty in the law of the sea to implement the concept of a new legal personality for the disappearing island States, within UNCLOS. Regardless of the practical reason that time is running out due to the imminent threat of sea-level rise, UNCLOS can be considered a treaty open to interpretation.

[228] R. Strating and J. Wallis (note 193 in Chap. 2), 6.

[229] R. Strating and J. Wallis (note 26 in Chap. 4), 6.

[230] G. Fry (note 8 in Chap. 8), 301.

[231] Ibid., 302; *Request for an Advisory Opinion submitted by the Commission of Small Island States on Climate Change and International Law,* Case No. 31, 20.09.2023, p. 8, para.

[232] G. Fry (note 8 in Chap. 8).

[233] Ibid., 302.

[234] *G. Fry*, Framing the Islands: Power and Diplomatic Agency in Pacific Regionalism, 2019, 303.

Firstly, the treaty established an entirely new legal personality for the CHM. This innovative principle was not only open to interpretation and reinterpretation but also ensured a legal concept of a standard legal figure, thereby banishing any territorial temptations kindled by the States. Based on the simple trusteeship system, the CHM included the idea of a common space preserved for humankind, supervised by an international organization—the ISA —thereby representing an advancement over the already-discussed weaknesses of the UN trusteeship, despite the adverse developments of the last years. Consequently, in developing this legal personality alone, the treaty already ushered in a new era of "anthropocentric international law," which will replace "State-centered law."

However, the central concept of protecting and preserving the marine environment in UNCLOS does not reflect absolute sovereignty or state dominance, as it may seem at first glance. Even though notions like climate change and sea-level rise were unknown at the time of its negotiation, so that "it is tailored to the geographical circumstances of its own time, not the ones yet to come", the treaty provides the foundation for a re-interpretation in favor of the disappearing island States.[235] For instance, UNCLOS advocates for greater cooperation, which aligns with the legal principles that island States already follow. Hence, the treaty is often considered "tailor-made" for the Pacific Islands.[236] This is not only because of their already mentioned immense expansion of territorial sovereignty by the legal figure of the EEZ, but also because it has allowed the Pacific Island States "to formalize a system for the use and management of the region's most important resource base fisheries".[237] This tendency is recorded in several agreements, which, as a side effect, further promoted cooperation between the Pacific Island States.

Finally, we can conclude that UNCLOS provides a basis for reinterpreting the law in favor of a new legal personality for the disappearing island States. Even though the State still dominates the treaty as the sole active legal actor, the process of interpretation through legislation and jurisdiction is steadily filling the numerous legal gaps in the treaty. For instance, even the concept of the Blue Pacific Continent appears to fit within the State-dominated international treaty framework, as outlined in the United Nations Convention on the Law of the Sea.

---

[235] K. R. Lal (note 87 in Chap. 6), 261.

[236] Ibid.

[237] Ibid.

Closing Considerations

8

> *We have got to understand that climate change is not a national issue, it's a global issue, and we need global thinking.* (CBS News (note 324 in Chap. 5). Anote Tong, former president of Kiribati)

Reviewing this research project, what can we conclude? In the first chapter, we developed the international principle at stake, the principle of permanent sovereignty over natural resources. We took a closer look at the history and development of the principle, from its initial appearance in the aftermath of World War II to its subsequent strengthening and growing importance during decolonization. Grown as soft law through resolutions of the General Assembly, it was recognized within half a century in several treaties, *i.a.*, the United Nations Convention on the Law of the Sea. Due to its appearance in several international judgments, it is primarily recognized as international customary law.

The second chapter focused on the two main pillars of this principle, the sovereignty of States and the right of self-determination. We took a closer look at the sovereignty of States from a philosophical perspective, building on a weaker model of property rights—occupancy rights. In the following, it was identified that the predominant model of State sovereignty in the present world is based upon the Western Westphalian concept of the Nation-State, which is also the definition of Statehood in the Montevideo Convention. However, reviewing the trends of the last few years, the concept of State sovereignty has become unstable, particularly in addressing environmental problems and climate change on the one hand, and in the face of growing globalization on the other. The second pillar, of the permanent sovereignty over natural resources, is built upon the right of self-determination, reflecting the people's voice. Nowadays, it can be divided into

M. A. Brinker, *The Principle of Permanent Sovereignty over Natural Resources as an Anchor in Times of Sealevel Rise*, https://doi.org/10.1007/978-3-658-50527-1_8

internal and external aspects of self-determination, which mirror the two facets of State sovereignty: authority and independence. In the context of permanent sovereignty over natural resources, economic self-determination is critical.

In the third chapter, we dealt with the right-holder—or, better, principle-holder—of permanent sovereignty over natural resources, which the State primarily assumes. However, since the principle was developed, people have already played a not-insignificant role as principle-holders, particularly in the context of decolonization. Later, the "main active players" in international law—the States—displaced them. This development climaxed in the 1970s and 1980s, when the State was not even questioned as the only and true actor in international law.[1] With the realization of the phenomenon of climate change and the resulting imminent threat, this phenomenon shook up the concept of the single Nation-State as an actor, so that the question of another principle-holder arose. Consequently, we took a closer look at the different shapes of people—principal holders, the whole population of a state, and minorities within states or indigenous peoples—who have gained importance in recent years. Referring to the second pillar of the principle of permanent sovereignty over natural resources, we must note that people are morally firmly attached to their territory and its natural resources, as underscored in several jurisdictions regarding indigenous peoples. In conclusion, we have to assume that the people are morally the better principle-holders for permanent sovereignty over natural resources.

The fourth chapter addressed the emerging trends in international law in the context of climate change. On the one hand, we focused on the main pillars upon which absolute sovereignty over natural resources is based and discovered that, in particular, in environmental degradation and climate change, State sovereignty is unstable and contributes to environmental degradation. Consequently, the tendency leans toward more pooled and collective sovereignty in international cooperation. On the other hand, we have noticed the growing influence of the public in international law, whether through NGO participation or in climate change litigation. The final part addressed climate change-induced inundations in the South Pacific and the application of self-determination to the people in this specific example. We reaffirmed that the right of self-determination is threatened in this case and is, therefore, applicable to the phenomenon of sea-level rise. In conclusion, the principle of permanent sovereignty over natural resources should be applied in this context in favor of collective or popular sovereignty—in concrete terms, in favor of the people.

[1] F. Nawrot (note 118 in Chap. 2), 100.

In the fifth chapter, we focused on the legal framework for this reinterpretation of permanent sovereignty over natural resources. We established that Statelessness due to the loss of territory is not an adequate solution for the islanders. The idea of the recognition of a "de-territorialized" State would also not be able to reflect the self-determining will of the people adequately, in particular, because the recognition of a State without territory seems doubtful. In the following, we took a closer look at the different models of self-government that international law offers. We concluded that all models already established in international law do not provide an adequate solution for the islanders to maintain their permanent sovereignty over natural resources. This led us to assume that the best solution lies along the path that the Pacific Island States have already begun to walk, recognizing a new legal personality in cooperation.

The last chapter raised the question of whether this new legal personality in international law would be compatible with the most important international treaty in the law of the sea, UNCLOS. This is questionable because the treaty is based on the principle of State sovereignty and the States as the primary actors. However, within UNCLOS, we found many links to make the idea of a new legal personality feasible. For instance, the CHM possesses legal personality and internalizes the notion of collective sovereignty. Moreover, one of the main principles of UNCLOS—protecting and preserving the marine environment—can be applied to climate change and cooperation, as the South China Sea Arbitration has impressively demonstrated. In conclusion, we must admit that, even though the treaty is tailored to the State as forerunner for all actions, rights, and duties, it creates the necessary scope for interpretation, particularly in light of fragmentation, as we can observe in the judgments and agreements already discussed.

Considering all the opinions, judgments, and agreements examined in the context of the disappearing islands, the question may arise whether these complex considerations even make sense. We have not yet found a solution in the combination of the principle of preservation of baselines or outer limits so that the legal status of an island, according to Article 121 (1) UNCLOS, can be maintained.[2] Can we not simply close the discussion on the principle "once an island, always an island"?[3] It is also appropriate that, with this method, the sovereign rights over the natural resources in the maritime zone be preserved for the Pacific Island

---

[2] *N. Oral,* International Law as an Adaptation Measure to Sea-level Rise and Its Impacts on Islands and Offshore Features, The International Journal of Marine an Coastal Law 34 (2019), 429.

[3] Ibid.

States.[4] At the same time, the opposing voices persistently refer to the natural State doctrine according to which "extended maritime zones can never prevail, if the former population of the island is dispersed, and no stable community lives in or uses the surrounding ocean area".[5] However, this application of the natural state doctrine leads us to a "perfidious situation": that "climate change, assessed as a non-artificial intervention," would reveal that the "natural state" of islands is only maintained by artificial human intervention—*e.g.,* coastal protection and sea defenses.[6] Consequently, we must admit, "most of the world has been subject to significant human modification over millennia through transformations," either by physical or intellectual improvements.[7]

Consequently, we have to be aware of one thought: State sovereignty—a legal fiction—is not eternal and endless and cannot serve as a "once and for all" right, in the same way that there is not a sole perfect solution for all of our problems. Matters must be addressed through consensus and cooperation, hopefully leading to the best solution.[8]

What remains at the end? We are living in a century of change, a century in which old traditional concepts are losing their value and sense, and "human interactions with ocean-space are even more intense and complex".[9] "Climate change poses significant challenges to international law", it provokes the mandatory "issues at stake [to] transcend purely inter-state interests" and requires the "participation of non-state actors".[10] Consequently, not only the small Pacific Island States are at immense risk but also "the impact of climate change on people is immediately an impact on the Nation-State, and (…) climate change puts national sovereignty (…) at risk precisely because of the way it may impact on human welfare and human rights".[11] The Pacific Island States—in this way—only serve as an very figurative example because of "their very nature, highly dependent on oceans and seas for the livelihoods of their people, while also remaining extremely vulnerable to sea-level rise and the adverse effects of climate change,

[4] Ibid., 429 et seq.

[5] *I. Saunders*, in: D. R. Rothwell/D. Letts, Law of the Sea in South East Asia: Environmental, Navigational and Security Challenges, 2020, 129.

[6] Ibid.

[7] Ibid., 122.

[8] J. Crawford (note 14 in Chap. 3), 127.

[9] *A. Østhagen*, Coast Guards and Ocean Politics in the Arctic, 2020, 13.

[10] I. Papanicolopulu and A. Rocha (note 179 in Chap. 5), 194.

[11] *J. Barnett/W. N. Adger*, Climate Dangers and Atoll Countries, Climate Change (2003), 327.

pollution and other stresses on oceans and marine resources."[12] Therefore, if we do not act, we will likely face the catastrophe of a "legal feedback mechanism", in which "the economic viability of the small island States might be threatened" because of "the shrinking or eventual disappearance of their maritime zones."[13] However, as Palau concluded in its written statement to ITLOS: "in no case may a people be deprived of its own means of subsistence".[14]

Consequently, why should we not broaden our horizons and try to think outside the box? Why do we not grant the disappearing Island States what they depend upon and desire most: "full participation in the benefits and opportunities linked with the oceans and seas"?[15] They already live in "a network of related maritime features where the populations might sustain themselves", as we have seen above.[16] The United Nations Convention on the Law of the Sea once "provided small island States with a degree of stability and security, allowing them to deal on a more even footing with larger and more prosperous nations and to more easily access the benefits of marine resources".[17] Why can this concept not be applied again by re-interpreting UNCLOS, *e.g.*, by recognizing the Blue Pacific Continent?

---

[12] R. Davis and Q. Hanich (note 27 in Chap.7), 49.

[13] Ibid., 83.

[14] *Request For Advisory Opinion submitted by the Commission of Small Island States on Climate Change and International Law,* Case No. 31, 15.06.2023, 20, para. 65.

[15] R. Davis and Q. Hanich (note 27 in Chap. 7), 60.

[16] C. Schofield and D. Freestone (note 51 in Chap. 6), 411.

[17] R. Davis and Q. Hanich (note 27 in Chap. 7), 49.

Literature

Abhimanyu, George Jain (2014): The 21st century Atlantis. The International Law of Statehood and Climate Change-Induced Loss of Territory. In: Stanford Journal of International Law 50, Artikel 1, pp. 1–52.

Abi-Saab, Georges (1991): Permanent Sovereignty over Natural Resources and Economic Activities. In: Mohamed Bedjaoui (ed.): International law. Achievements and prospects. Dordrecht, Boston, Norwell, MA, U.S., Paris: Nijhoff; Sold and distributed in the U.S.A. and Canada by Kluwer Academic Publishers; UNESCO.

Adler-Nissen, Rebecca; **Gammeltoft-Hansen**, Thomas (2008): An Introduction to Sovereignty Games. In: Rebecca Adler-Nissen und Thomas Gammeltoft-Hansen (eds.): Sovereignty games. 1. publ. New York: Palgrave Macmillan (Palgrave studies in governance, security, and development), pp. 1–17.

Agnew, John (2018): Globalization and Sovereignty. Beyond the Territorial Trap.

Ahmed, Masood; **Sirohi**, Nishant (2015); Permanent Sovereignty over Natural Resources and the Indigenous People: Revisited; In: Civil, and Military Law Journal (51), Article 1, pp. 110–120.

Alston, Philip (ed.) (2001): Peoples' rights. Oxford: Oxford Univ. Press (The collected courses of the Academy of European Law, 9,2).

Anaya, James (1991): The Capacity of International Law to Advance Ethnic or Nationality Rights Claims. In: Human Rights Quarterly 13 (3), pp. 403–411.

Anaya, James (2009): International Human Rights and Indigenous Peoples.

Anaya, S. James (2004): Indigenous peoples in international law. 2. ed. Oxford [i.a.]: Oxford Univ. Press.

Angeli, Oliviero (2017): Self-Determination and Sovereignty over Natural Resources. In: Ratio Juris (30), Article 3, pp. 290–304.

Aqorau, Transform (2006): Rethinking Sovereignty in the Pacific. In: Michael Powles (ed.): Pacific futures. Canberra: Pandanus Books, Research School of Pacific and Asian Studies, Australian National University, pp. 216–224.

Aquilina, Kevin (2014): Territorial Sea and the Contiguous Zone. In: David Joseph Attard, Malgosia Fitzmaurice und Norman A. Martínez Gutiérrez (eds.): The IMLI Manual on International Maritime Law. Volume I: The Law of the Sea.

Armstrong, Chris (2015): Against "Permanent Sovereignty" over Natural Resources. In: Politics, Philosophy and Economics (14 (2)), pp. 129–151.

M. A. Brinker, *The Principle of Permanent Sovereignty over Natural Resources as an Anchor in Times of Sealevel Rise*, https://doi.org/10.1007/978-3-658-50527-1

Armstrong, Chris (2017): Justice and natural resources. An egalitarian theory. First edition. Oxford, New York: Oxford University Press.

Atapattu, Sumudu (2009): Climate change, human rights and forced migration. Implications for International Law. In: Wisconsin International Law Journal (27), Article 3, pp. 607–636.

Banai, Ayelet (2013): Political Self-Determination and Global Egalitarianism: Towards an Intermediate Position. In: Social Theory and Practice 39 (1), pp. 45–69.

Banai, Ayelet (2014): The territorial rights of legitimate states: a pluralist interpretation. In: International Theory (6), Article 1, pp. 140–157.

Banai, Ayelet; **Moore,** Margaret; **Miller,** David; **Nine**, Cara; **Dietrich,** Frank (2014): Symposium 'Theories of Territory beyond Westphalia'. In: Int Theory 6 (1), pp. 98–104. https://doi.org/10.1017/S1752971914000013.

Barnett, Jon; **Adger**, W. Neil (2003): Climate Dangers and Atoll Countries, In: Climate Change, pp. 321–337.

Barrera-Herández, Lila (2006): Sovereignty over Natural Resources under Examination. The Inter-American System for Human Rights and Natural Resource Allocation. In: Annual Survey of International & Comparative Law 12 (1), Article 4, pp. 43–58.

Barry, Brian M. (1989): Democracy, power and justice. Essays in political theory. Oxford: Clarendon Pr. online available on http://www.loc.gov/catdir/enhancements/fy0636/89002937-d.html.

Bartelson, Jens (2008): Sovereignty Before and After the Linguistic Turn. In: Rebecca Adler-Nissen und Thomas Gammeltoft-Hansen (eds.): Sovereignty games. 1. publ. New York: Palgrave Macmillan (Palgrave studies in governance, security, and development).

Barth, William Kurt (2008): On Cultural Rights: The Equality of Nations and the Minority Legal Tradition. Chapter 3: Minority Protection in the Era of Human Rights, pp. 69–98.

Baslar, Kemal (1998): The concept of the common heritage of mankind in international law. The Hague [i.a.]: Nijhoff (Developments in international law).

Bastos, Fernando Loureiro (2014): Setting the field for future "mineral rushes": some reflections on the international regime for the exploration and exploitation of marine minerals. In: Marta Chantal Ribeiro (ed.): 30 Years After the Signature of the United Nations Convention on the Law of the Sea: The Protection of the Environment and the Future of the Law of the Sea. Proceedings of the International Conference—15–17 November 2012, pp. 119–146.

Baxi, Upendra (2019): Sovereign rights, state obligations and natural resources. In: Shawkat Alam, Jahid Hossain Bhuiyan und Jona Razzaque (ed): International Natural Resources Law, Investment and Sustainability.

Beck, Ulrich (1999): World risk society. Cambridge [i.a.]: Polity Press.

Bedjaoui, Mohammed (1979): Towards a new international economic order. Paris: Unesco (New challenges to international law).

Beitz, Charles R. (1999): Political theory and international relations. Princeton, NJ [i.a.]: Princeton Univ. Press (Princeton paperbacks).

Beitz, Charles R. (2009): The Idea of Human Rights. Oxford: Oxford University Press USA – OSO. Online available on https://ebookcentral.proquest.com/lib/gbv/detail.action?docID=472202.

Bellamy, Richard; **Castiglione**, Dario (1998): Between Cosmopolis and Community: Three Models of Rights and Democracy within the European Union. In: Daniele Archibugi,

David Held und Martin Köhler (ed.): Re-imagining political community. Studies in cosmopolitan democracy. Oxford: Polity Press, pp. 152–178.

Benvenisti, Eyal (2002): Management of Transboundary Resources. International Law and Optimal Resource Use.

Berman, Howard; **Lyons**, Oren; **Falk**, Richard (1993): Indigenous Peoples and the Right to Self-Determination. In: American Society of International Law, pp. 190–204.

Berman, Nathaniel (1988): Sovereignty in Abeyance. Self-Determination and International Law.

Biermann, Frank (2002): Global Environmental Change and the Nation State: The Scope of the Challenge. In: Frank Biermann, Rainer Brohm und Klaus Dingwerth (eds.): "Global environmental change and the nation state". Potsdam: PIK (PIK report), pp. 1–9.

Biermann, Frank; **Boas**, Ingrid (2002): Global adaptation governance: the case of protecting climate refugees. In: Frank Biermann, Rainer Brohm und Klaus Dingwerth (eds.): "Global environmental change and the nation state". Potsdam: PIK (PIK report), pp. 255–269.

Biermann, Frank; **Boas,** Ingrid (2010): Global adaptation governance: the case of protecting climate refugees. In: Frank Biermann, Philipp Pattberg und Fariborz Zelli (eds.): Global climate governance beyond 2012. 1. publ. Cambridge [i.a.]: Cambridge Univ. Press, pp. 255–269.

Biersteker, Thomas; **Weber**, Cynthia (1996): Reconstructing the analysis of sovereignty: concluding reflections and directions for future research. In: Thomas Biersteker (ed.): State sovereignty as social construct. Cambridge: Cambridge University Press (Cambridge studies in international relations), pp. 278–286.

Bilková, Veronika (2016): A State Without Territory? In: Martin Kuijer und Wouter Werner (ed.): Netherlands Yearbook of International Law. The Changing Nature of Territoriality in International Law.

Binkley, Marian; **Gill**, Alison; **Saunders,** Phillip; **Wescott**, Geoff (2006): Community involvement in marine and coastal management in Australia and Canada. In: David L. VanderZwaag (ed.): Towards Principled Oceans Governance: Taylor and Francis, pp. 249–280.

Bjorklund, Andrea K. (2008): National Treatment. In: August Reinisch (ed.): Standards of investment protection. 1. publ. Oxford [i.a.]: Oxford Univ. Press, pp. 29–58.

Blanchard, Catherine (2015): Evolution or revolution? Evaluating the Territorial State-Based Regime of International Law in the Context of the Physical Disappearance of Territory Due to Climate Change and Sea-Level Rise. In: Canadian Yearbook of International Law 53, pp. 66–118.

Boom, Keely: See you in court: the rising tide of international climate litigation. In: The Conversation 28.09.2011. online available on https://theconversation.com/see-you-in-court-the-rising-tide-of-international-climate-litigation-3542.

Bordin, Fernando Lusa (2014): Reflections of Customary International Law: The Authority of Codification Conventions and ILC Draft Articles in International Law, In: International and Comparative Law Quarterly (63), pp. 535–567.

Bothe, Michael (2006): Whose environment? Concepts of commonality in international environmental law. In: Gerd Winter (ed.): Multilevel governance of global environmental change. 1. publ. Cambridge [i.a.]: Cambridge Univ. Press, pp. 539–558.

Boyle, Alan (2012a): Climate Change and Ocean Governance. In: Marta Chantal Ribeiro (ed.): 30 Years after the Signature of the United Nations Convention on the Law of the Sea: The Protection of the Environment and the Future of the Law of the Sea. Proceedings of the International Conference, pp. 357–382.

Boyle, Alan (2012b): Law of the sea perspectives on climate change. In: International Journal of Marine and Coastal Law, pp. 831–838.

Boyle, Alan (2014): Climate Change and Ocean Governance. In: Marta Chantal Ribeiro (ed.): 30 Years After the Signature of the United Nations Convention on the Law of the Sea: The Protection of the Environment and the Future of the Law of the Sea. Proceedings of the International Conference—15–17 November 2012, pp. 357–382.

Boyle, Alan (2019): Climate Change, Sustainable Development and Human Rights. In: Markus Kaltenborn, Markus Krajewski und Heike Kuhn (ed.): Sustainable Development Goals and Human Rights.

Brinker, Mara Alin (2020): The Right of Self-Determination in the Context of Climate Change. How to deal with the disappearing islands in the exemplary case of the Atoll State Kiribati under the International Law: GRIN.

Brownlie, Ian (1988): The Rights of Peoples in Modern International Law. In: James Crawford (ed.): The rights of peoples. Oxford: Clarendon.

Brownlie, Ian (1997): Rebirth of Statehood. In: Malcolm D. Evans (ed.): Aspects of statehood and institutionalism in contemporary Europe. Aldershot [i.a.]: Dartmouth (EC, international law forum), pp. 5–8.

Brownlie, Ian; **Crawford**, James (2019): Brownlie's principles of public international law. Ninth edition. Oxford: Oxford University Press.

Bryant-Tokalau, Jenny (2018): Indigenous Pacific Approaches to Climate Change. Pacific Island Countries. Cham: Palgrave Pivot (Springer eBook Collection Social Sciences).

Buchanan, Allen E. (1991): The Right of Self-Determination. Analytical and Moral Foundations. In: Arizona Journal of International and Comparative Law (8), Article 2, pp. 41–50.

Buchanan, Allen E. (2003): The Making and Unmaking of Boundaries: What Liberalism Has to Say. In: Allen E. Buchanan und Margaret Moore (ed.): States, nations, and borders. The Ethics of Making Boundaries. 1. publ. Cambridge [i.a.]: Cambridge Univ. Press (The Ethikon series in comparative ethics), pp. 231–261.

Bungenberg, Marc (2015): Evolution of Investment Law. In: Marc Bungenberg und Stephan Hobe (ed.): Permanent Sovereignty over Natural Resources: Springer.

Bungenberg, Marc; Hobe, Stephan (ed.) (2015): Permanent Sovereignty over Natural Resources: Springer.

Burkett, Maxine (2011): The Nation Ex-Situ: On Climate Change, Deterritorialized Nationhood and the Post-Climate Era. In: Climate Law (2), pp. 345–374.

Burkett, Maxine (2015): A justice paradox. Climate change, small island developing states, and the absence of international legal remedy.

Burns, William C.G. (2003): The Impact of Climate Change on Pacific Island Developing Countries in the 21st Century. In: Alexander Gillespie und William C.G. Burns (ed.): Climate Change in the South Pacific: Impacts and Responses in Australia, New Zealand, and Small Island States, pp. 233–250.

Busch, Signe Veierud (2021): Law of the Sea Responses to Sea-Level Rise and Threatened Maritime Entitlements. Applying an Exception Rule to Manage an Exceptional Situation. In: Elise Johansen, Signe Veierud Busch und Ingvild Ulrikke Jakobsen (ed.): The law of the sea and climate change. Solutions and constraints. Cambridge, UK, New York, NY, Port Melbourne, New Delhi, Singapore: Cambridge University Press, pp. 309–335.

Cambou, Dorothée; **Smis**, Stefaan (2013): Permanent Sovereignty over Natural Resources from a Human Rights Perspective: Natural Resources Exploitation and Indigenous Peoples' Rights in the Arctic. In: Michigan State International Law Review (22), pp. 347–376.

Cameron, F. R. (2011): Saving the "disappearing islands": Climate change governance, Pacific island states and cosmopolitan dispositions. In: Continuum: Journal of Media & Cultural Studies (25), Article 6, pp. 873–886.

Camilleri, Joseph A. (1992): The end of sovereignty? Aldershot: Elgar.

Campins-Eritjia, Mar; **Gupta**, Joyeeta (2004): The Role of "Sustainability Labelling" in the International Law of Sustainable Development. In: Nicolaas Schrijver und Friedl Weiss (ed.): International law and sustainable development. Leiden [i.a.]: Nijhoff (Developments in international law).

Caron, David D. (2013a): Climate Change and Oceans. In: Harry N. Schreiber und Jin-Hyun Paik (Hg.): Regions, Institutions, and Law of the Sea. Leiden, Boston: Martinus Nijhoff Publisher, pp. 515–537.

Caron, David D. (2013b): Time and the Public Trust Doctrine. Law Knowledge of Climate Change. In: University of Hawai'i Law Review 35 (35), Article 2, pp. 441–458.

Carty, Antony (1992): The Third World claim to economic self-determination: economic rights of peoples: theoretical aspects. In: Subrata Roy Chowdhury, Erik M.G. Denters und Paul de Waart (ed.): The right to development in international law. Dordrecht i.a.: Nijhoff.

Cassese, Antonio (1979): The Helsinki Declaration and Self-Determination. In: Thomas Buergenthal (ed.): Human rights, international law and the Helsinki accord. Montclair: Allanheld Osmun/Universe Books (Landmark studies).

Cassese, Antonio (1986): International law in a divided world. Oxford i.a: Clarendon.

Cassese, Antonio (1995): Self-determination of peoples. A legal reappraisal. 1. publ. Cambridge: Cambridge Univ. Press (Hersch Lauterpacht memorial lecture series, 12).

Cassese, Antonio (1996): The International Court of Justice and the Right of Peoples to Self-Determination. In: Vaughan Lowe und Malgosia Fitzmaurice (ed.): Fifty years of the International Court of Justice. 1. publ. Cambridge [i.a.]: Cambridge Univ. Press (Grotius publications).

Castellino, Joshua (2005a): International Law and Indigenous Peoples. Part I—Human Rights Instruments and Indigenous Peoples.

Castellino, Joshua (2005b): The right to land, International Law and indigenous peoples. In: Joshua Castellino und Niamh Walsh (ed.): International Law and Indigenous Peoples.

Castellino, Joshua; **Walsh**, Niamh (ed.) (2005): International Law and Indigenous Peoples.

Charles-Newton, Eugenia; **Kronk**, Elizabeth Ann (2013): Introduction to indigenous sovereignty under international and domestic law. In: Randall Abate (ed.): Climate change and indigenous peoples. The search for legal remedies. Cheltenham, UK: Edward Elgar, pp. 63–78.

Charlesworth, Hilary (2000): The boundaries of international law. 1. publ. Manchester: Manchester Univ. Pr. [i.a.] (Melland Schill studies in international law).

Charney, Jonathan I. (2018): The Marine Environment and the 1982 United Nations Convention on the Law of the Sea. In: John Norton Moore (ed.): Common Resources—Law of the Sea, Outer Space, and Antarctica, pp. 258–284.

Chekera, Yolanda T.; **Nmehielle,** Vincent O. (2013): The International Law Principle of Permanent Sovereignty over Natural Resources as an Instrument for Development: The Case of Zimbabwean Diamonds. In: African Journal of Legal Studies 6, Article 1, pp. 69–102.

Chowdhuri, Ramendra Nath (1955): International mandates and trusteeship systems. s'Gravenhage: Nijhoff.

Connolly, William E. (1995): The ethos of pluralization. Minneapolis: University of Minnesota Press (Borderlines, v. 1).

Craven, Matthew; **Parfitt**, Rose (2018): Statehood, Self-determination and recognition. In: Malcolm Evans (ed.): International law. Fifth edition. Oxford: Oxford University Press.

Crawford, James (1979): The creation of states in international law. Oxford: Clarendon Press.

Crawford, James (ed.) (1988): The rights of peoples. Oxford: Clarendon. Online available on http://www.loc.gov/catdir/enhancements/fy0635/88005298-d.html.

Crawford, James (1996): The General Assembly, the International Court and self-determination. In: Vaughan Lowe und Malgosia Fitzmaurice (ed.): Fifty years of the International Court of Justice. 1. publ. Cambridge [i.a.]: Cambridge Univ. Press (Grotius publications).

Crawford, James (1998): State practice and international law in relation to succession.

Crawford, James (2001): The Right of Self-Determination in International Law: Its Development and Future. In: Philip Alston (ed.): Peoples' rights. Oxford: Oxford Univ. Press (The collected courses of the Academy of European Law, 9,2).

Crawford, James (2006): The creation of states in international law. 2. ed. Oxford: Clarendon Press. Online available on http://www.loc.gov/catdir/enhancements/fy0725/200600 0256-b.html.

Crawford, James (2012): Sovereignty as legal value. In: James Crawford und Martti Koskenniemi (eds.): The Cambridge companion to international law. With the collaboration of Surabhi Ranganathan. 1. publ. Cambridge: Cambridge Univ. Press (Cambridge companions to law), pp. 117–133.

Cristescu, Aureliu (1981): The right to self-determination. Historical and current development on the basis of United Nations instruments. New York: United Nations.

Daes, Erica-Irene (2005): Globalization, Intellectual Property and indigenous peoples. In: Svein Jentoft, Henry Minde und Ragnar Nilsen (eds.): Indigenous peoples. Resource management and global rights. 2. ed. Delft: Eburon, pp. 67–73.

Daes, Erica-Irene A. (2021): Working Paper by the Chairperson-Rapporteur, Mrs. Erica-Irene A. Daes, on the concept of "indigenous people". Ed. de Equipo Nizkor. 10.06.1996. Online available on http://www.derechos.org/nizkor/bolivia/doc/daes.html, last checked on 01.02.2021.

Davis, Ruth; **Hanich**, Quentin (2012): Small Island States and the LOS Convention 30 Years On: Have the Benefits Been Realized? In: Ocean Yearbook 26, pp. 49–85.

Denters, Erik M.G. (2004): Free Riders, Claims and Countermeasures in Combating Climate Change. In: Nicolaas Schrijver und Friedl Weiss (ed.): International law and sustainable development. Leiden [i.a.]: Nijhoff (Developments in international law).

Dervovic, Medy (2021): Sharing Arctic Science: Applying the Common Heritage and Common Concern of Humankind in the Arctic. In: The Yearbook of Polar Law 13, pp. 301–320.

Deudney, Daniel (1998): Global Village Sovereignty. Intergenerational Sovereign Publics, Federal-Republican Earth Constitutions, and Planetary Identities. In: Karen T. Litfin (ed.): The greening of sovereignty in world politics. Cambridge [i.a.]: MIT Press (Global environmental accord), pp. 299–325.

Diethe, Carol; **Nietzsche**, Friedrich (n.d.). Introduction: On Nietzsche's critique of morality. Friedrich Nietzsche: On the Genealogy of Morality, xiii–xxix.

Doehring, Karl (2012): Article 1: Self-Determination. In: Bruno Simma (ed.): The Charter of the United Nations—A Commentary. 3rd ed. Oxford: Oxford Univ. Press [i.a.].

Dolman, Antony J. (1981): Resources, regimes, world order. New York, i.a.: Pergamon Pr (Pergamon policy studies on international development).

Doty, Roxanne Lynn (1996): Sovereignty and the nation: constructing the boundaries of national identity. In: Thomas Biersteker (ed.): State sovereignty as social construct. Cambridge: Cambridge University Press (Cambridge studies in international relations), pp. 121–147.

Duruigbo, Emeka (2006): Permanent Sovereignty and Peoples' Ownership of Natural Resources in International Law. In: The George Washington International Law Review 38, pp. 33–100.

Eckersley, Robyn (2004): The green state. Rethinking democracy and sovereignty. Cambridge, Mass.: MIT Press.

Egede, Edwin; **Charles**, Eden (2021): Common Heritage of Mankind and the Deep Seabed Area Beyond National Jurisdiction: Past, Current and Future Prospects. In: Marine Technology Society Journal (55), Article 6, pp. 40–52.

Elian, George (1979): The principle of sovereignty over natural resources.

Elian, George; **Bantas**, Andrei (1979): The principle of sovereignty over natural resources. Alphen aan den Rijn: Sijthoff & Noordhoff.

Elliot, Lorraine (2008): Sovereignty and the Global Politics of the Environment: Beyond Westphalia? In: Trudy Jacobsen, Charles J. G. Sampford und Ramesh Thakur (ed.): Re-envisioning sovereignty. The end of Westphalia? Aldershot: Ashgate (Law, ethics and governance series), pp. 193–209.

Escobar, Arturo (1998): Whose Knowledge, Whose Nature? Biodiversity, Conservation, and the Political Ecology of Social Movements. In: Journal of Political Ecology (5), pp. 53–82.

Falk, Richard (1997): 'The Right of Self-Determination under International Law: The Coherence of Doctrine Versus the Incoherence of Experience'. In: Wolfgang Danspeckgruber (ed.): Self-determination and self-administration. Boulder, Colo. [i.a.]: Rienner.

Falk, Richard (2008): On the Quasi-Legislative Competence of the General Assembly. In: Nicholas Greenwood Onuf (ed.): International legal theory. 1. publ. London [i.a.]: Routledge-Cavendish.

Falk, Richard A. (1981): Human rights and state sovereignty. New York i.a.: Holmes & Meier.

Farmer, Alice (2006): Towards a Meaningful Rebirth of Economic Self-Determination: Human Rights Realization in Resource-Rich Countries. In: International Law and Policies 39, pp. 417–473.

Ferrara, Pablo (2018): Multinational Corporations and International Environmental Liability: International Subjectivity and Universal Jurisdiction (Backs and Forths after Kiobel). In: Markus Kotzur, Nele Matz-Lück, Alexander Proelß, Roda Verheyen und Joachim

Sanden (ed.): Sustainable ocean resource governance. Deep-sea mining, marine energy, and submarine cables. Leiden, Boston: Brill Nijhoff (ProQuest Ebook Central), pp. 204–233.

Fitzmaurice, Malgosia (2008): Intergenerational Equity Revisited. In: Isabelle Buffard, James Crawford, Alain Pellet und Stephan Wittich (ed.): International Law Between Universalism and Fragmentation.

Fox-Decent, Evan; **Dahlman**, Ian (2015): Sovereignty as Trusteeship and Indigenous Peoples. In: Theoretical Inquiries in Law (16), pp. 507–533.

Franck, Thomas M. (1992): The emerging right to democratic governance. In: The American Journal of International Law (86), Article 1, pp. 46–91.

Freestone, David (2012): The Law of the Sea Convention at 30. Successes, challenges, and new agendas. In: International Journal of Marine and Coastal Law (27), Article 4, pp. 675–682.

Freestone, David; **Schofield**, Clive (2016): Republic of the Marshall Islands. 2016 Maritime Zones Declaration Act: Drawing "Lines in the Sea". In: The International Journal of Marine and Coastal Law 31, pp. 732–758.

Freestone, David; **Schofield**, Clive (2021): Pacific Islands Countries Declare Permanent Maritime Baselines, Limits and Boundaries. In: The International Journal of Marine and Coastal Law 36, pp. 685–695.

Fry, Greg (2019): Framing the Islands. Power and Diplomatic Agency in Pacific Regionalism. Canberra: ANU Press (ANU Press Pacific Series). Online available on https://search.ebscohost.com/login.aspx?direct=true&scope=site&db=nlebk&db=nlabk&AN=3093622.

Fuentes, Ximena (2004): International Law-Making in the Field of Sustainable Development. The Unequal Competition between Development and the Environment. In: Nicolaas Schrijver und Friedl Weiss (ed.): International law and sustainable development. Leiden [i.a.]: Nijhoff (Developments in international law).

Gilbert, Jérémie (2007): Indigenous Rights in the Making: The United Nations Declaration on the Rights of Indigenous Peoples. In: Int J Minor Group Rights 14 (2–3), pp. 207–230. https://doi.org/10.1163/138548707X208818.

Gilbert, Jérémie (2013a): Land Rights as Human Rights: The case for a specific Right to Land. In: International Journal on Human Rights (18), pp. 114–135.

Gilbert, Jérémie (2013b): The Right to Freely Dispose of Natural Resources. In: Netherlands Quarterly of Human Rights 31 (3), pp. 314–341. https://doi.org/10.1177/016934411303100305.

Gillespie, Alexander; **Burns**, William C.G. (ed.) (2003): Climate Change in the South Pacific: Impacts and Responses in Australia, New Zealand, and Small Island States.

Giorgetta, Sueli (2004): The Right to a Healthy Environment. In: Nicolaas Schrijver und Friedl Weiss (ed.): International law and sustainable development. Leiden [i.a.]: Nijhoff (Developments in international law).

Goethe, Johann Wolfgang von, Faust I, 1808.

Gonzalez Arreaza, Alejandro (2017): Natural resource sovereignty and economic development in the WTO in light of the recent case law involving raw materials and rare earths. In: Review of European, Comparative & International Environmental Law (26), pp. 266–275.

Grewe, Wilhelm G. (2012): History. In: Bruno Simma (ed.): The Charter of the United Nations—A Commentary. 3rd ed. Oxford: Oxford Univ. Press [i.a.].

Grote Stoutenburg, Jenny (2013a): When Do States Disappear? In: Michael B. Gerrard (ed.): Threatened Island Nations. New York: Cambridge University Press, pp. 57–87.

Grote Stoutenburg, Jenny (2013b): When Do States Disappear?: Thresholds of Effective Statehood and the Continued Recognition of "Deterritorialized" Island States. In: Michael B. Gerrard und Gregory E. Wannier (ed.): Threatened Island Nations. Legal Implications of Rising Seas and a Changing Climate. Cambridge: Cambridge University Press, pp. 57–88.

Grotius, Hugo (1604): De jure praedae commentarius. Oxford: Clarendon Press (Publications of the Carnegie Endowment for International Peace).

Grotius, Hugo (1631): Hugonis Grotii De jure belli ac pacis libri tres. Editio secunda emendatior & multis locis auctior. Amsterdam: Apud Guilielmum Blaeuw.

Grotius, Hugo 1583–1645 (1916): The Freedom of the seas or the right which belongs to the Dutch to take part in the Indian trade. NY: Oxford Univ. Press (Carnegie Endowment for International Peace. Div. of International Law).

Gullberg, Tom (2000): State, territory and identity. The principle of national self-determination and the question of territorial sovereignty in Carinthia and other post-Habsburg territories after the First World War. Zugl.: Åbo, Akad. Akad. avh., 2000. Åbo: Åbo Akad. Förl.

Gümplová, Petra (2014): Restraining permanent sovereignty over natural resources. In: Quarderns de Filosofia 53, pp. 93–114.

Gümplová, Petra (2019): Sovereignty over natural resources—A normative reinterpretation. In: Global Constitutionalism, pp. 1–31.

Hamilton, Clive (2003): The Commonwealth and Sea-Level Rise. In: The Round Table, pp. 517–531.

Hannum, Hurst (1993): Rethinking Self-Determination. In: Virginia Journal of International Law 34 (1), pp. 1–70.

Harknett, Richard J. (2003): Territoriality in the Nuclear Era. In: Eleonore Kofman (ed.): Globalization. Theory and practice. 2. ed. London: Continuum, pp. 138–149.

Harris, David John (2010): Cases and materials on international law. 7. ed. London: Sweet & Maxwell.

Hayashi, Moritaka (2011): Sea-Level Rise and the Law of the Sea: Future Options. In: Davor Vidas und Peter Johan Schei (eds.): The World Ocean in Globalisation. Climate Change, Sustainable Fisheries, Biodiversity, Shipping, and Regional Issues. Leiden, Boston: Martinus Nijhoff Publisher, pp. 187–206.

Henriksen, John B. (2001): Implementation of the Right of Self-Determination of Indigenous Peoples. In: Indigenous Affairs (3), pp. 6–21.

Hernández, Gleider I. (2013): Federated entities in international law: disaggregating the federal State? In: Duncan French (ed.): Statehood and self-determination. 1. publ. Cambridge [i.a.]: Cambridge Univ. Press, pp. 491–512.

Higgins, Rosalyn (1994): Problems and process. International law and how we use it. Oxford: Clarendon. Online available on http://www.loc.gov/catdir/enhancements/fy0637/93035770-d.html.

Hinsley, Francis H. (1986): Sovereignty. 2. ed. Cambridge: Cambridge Univ. Press.

Hobbes, Thomas (2000): Leviathan. South Bent: Information.

Hobbes, Thomas. (1651): Leviathan. Oxford: Oxford University Press.

Hobe, Stephan (2015): Evolution of the Principle on Permanent Sovereignty over Natural Resources. In: Marc Bungenberg und Stephan Hobe (ed.): Permanent Sovereignty over Natural Resources: Springer.

Hodgkinson, David; **Young**, Lucy (2013): In the Face of Looming Catastrophe. A Convention for Climate-Change-Displaced Persons. In: Threatened Islands Nations, pp. 299–335.

Hofbauer, Jane A. (2009): The Principle of Permanent Sovereignty over Natural Resources and Its Modern Implications.

Hossain, Kamal (2004): Preface. In: Nicolaas Schrijver und Friedl Weiss (eds.): International law and sustainable development. Leiden [i.a.]: Nijhoff (Developments in international law).

Huang, Yao; **Hu**, Changshun (2018): The Principle of the Common Heritage of Mankind Can be Applied to Marine Genetic Resources. In: Global Commons and the Law of the Sea 5, Article 3, pp. 50–75.

Hunter, David B. (2009): The Implication of Climate Change Litigation: Litigation for International Environmental Law-Making. In: Hari M. Osofsky und William C. G. Burns (ed.): Adjudicating climate change. State, national, and international approaches. Cambridge, New York: Cambridge University Press, pp. 357–374.

Icduygu, Ahmet (2003): Immigration and the Nation-State. In: Eleonore Kofman (ed.): Globalization. Theory and practice, pp. 150–162. 2. ed. London: Continuum.

Iglesias Sánchez, Sara (2017): Arctic indigenous peoples at European courts. Issues concerning their effective judicial protection at the CJEU and the ECtHR. In: Elena Conde Pérez und Sara Iglesias Sánchez (ed.): Global challenges in the Arctic region. London, New York: Routledge, pp. 217–235.

Inoguchi, Takashi; **Bacon,** Paul: Sovereignties: Westphalian, liberal and anti-utopian. Sovereignties; In: International Relations of the Asia-Pacific (1), 2001, pp. 285–304.

Iorns Magallanes, Catherine J. (2017): Indigenous peoples and self-determination, Challenging State Sovereignty. In: Victoria University of Wellington Legal Research Papers (7), Article 5.

Jaén, Monica (2007): Protecting the Oceans from Climate Change: An Analysis of the Role of Selected International Instruments on Resources and Environmental Protection in the Context of UNCLOS. In: Ocean Yearbook 21, pp. 91–128.

Jakobsen, Ingvild Ulrikke; **Johansen**, Elise; **Nickels**, Philipp Peter (2021): The law of the sea as part of the climate-change regime complex. In: Ingvild Ulrikke Jakobsen, Elise Johansen und Signe Veierud Busch (ed.): The law of the sea and climate change: solutions and constraints, pp. 374–385.

Jayagovind, A. (2012): Impact of Permanent Sovereignty over Natural Resources on WTO: A Critique of WTO Ruling in China: Exportation of Raw Material Case 52, pp. 141–151.

Jennings, Ivor (1958): The approach to self-government. Reprint. Cambridge: Univ. Press.

Jennings, Robert (1963, 2017): The Acquisition of Territory in International Law.

Jennings, Robert; **Watts**, Arthur; **Oppenheim**, Lassa Francis Lawrence (ed.) (1992): Oppenheim's international law. 9. ed. Harlow: Longman.

Jesus, José Luís (2003): Rocks, New-Born Islands, Sea Level Rise and Maritime Space. In: Jochen Frowein, Klaus Scharioth, Ingo Winkelmann und Rüdiger Wolfrum (eds.): Verhandeln für den Frieden – Negotiating for Peace. Springer.

Kamieniecki, Sheldon; **Granzeier**, Margaret Scully (1998): Eco-Cultural Security and Indigenous Self-Determination: Moving Toward a New Conception of Sovereignty. In: Karen T. Litfin (ed.): The greening of sovereignty in world politics. Cambridge [i.a.]: MIT Press (Global environmental accord), pp. 257–274.

Kant, Immanuel (1795): Zum ewigen Frieden.

Karkkainen, Bradley C.: Post-Sovereign Environmental Governance: The Collaborative Problem-Solving Model. In: Biermann, Global Environmental Change (s. Sovereignty), Bd. 2002, pp. 206–225.

Karkkainen, Bradley C. (2002): Post-Sovereign Environmental Governance: The Collaborative Problem-Solving Mode. In: Frank Biermann, Rainer Brohm und Klaus Dingwerth (eds.): "Global environmental change and the nation state". Potsdam: PIK (PIK report), pp. 206–216.

Kateka, James (2012): Protection and Preservation of the Marine Environment in the Area under UNCLOS. In: Rüdiger Wolfrum (ed.): Coexistence, cooperation and solidarity. Leiden [i.a.]: Nijhoff, pp. 919–931.

Keal, Paul (2003): European Conquest and the Rights of Indigenous Peoples: The moral backwardness of international society.

Kelman, Ilan (2010): Hearing local voices from Small Island Developing States for climate change. In: Local Environment (15), Article 7, pp. 605–619.

Kelman, Ilan (2018): Islandness within climate change narratives of small island developing states (SIDS). In: Island Studies Journal (13), Article 1, pp. 149–166.

Kern, Kristine; Löffelsend, Tina (2008): Governance beyond the Nation State: Transnationalization and Europeanization of the Baltic Sea Region. In: Marko Joas, Detlef Jahn und Kristine Kern (ed.): Governing a common sea. Environmental policies in the Baltic Sea region. London: Earthscan, pp. 115–141.

Kingsbury, Benedict (1998): "Indigenous peoples" in international law. A constructivist approach to the Asian controversy (92 (1998)).

Kingsbury, Benedict (2001a): Reconciling Five Competing Conceptual Structures of Indigenous Peoples' Claims in International and Comparative Law. In: New York University Journal of International Law and Politics (34), Article 1, pp. 189–250.

Kingsbury, Benedict (2001b): Reconciling Five Competing Conceptual Structures of Indigenous Peoples' Claims in International and Comparative Law. In: Philip Alston (ed.): Peoples' rights. Oxford: Oxford Univ. Press (The collected courses of the Academy of European Law, 9,2), pp. 69–110.

Kiwanuka, Richard (1988): The Meaning of "People" in the African Charter on Human and Peoples' Rights, pp. 80–101.

Klerk, Bastiaan E. (2022): Protecting the Marine Environment from the Impacts of Climate Change. A Regime Interaction Study. In: Review of European, Comparative and International Environmental Law 32, pp. 44–56.

Klöpfer, Michael; **Neugärtner**, Rico David (2021): Liability for climate damages, sustainability and environmental justice. In: Wolfgang Kahl und Marc-Philippe Weller (ed.): Climate change litigation. A handbook. München, Oxford, United Kingdom, New York, NY, U.S., Baden-Baden: Beck; Hart; Nomos, pp. 21–43.

Knoll, Bernhard (2008): The legal status of territories subject to administration by international organisations. Cambridge: Cambridge Univ. Press.

Knop, Karen (2002): Diversity and self-determination in international law. 1. publ. Cambridge: Cambridge Univ. Press (Cambridge studies in international and comparative law, N.S., 20).

Knop, Karen (2012): Statehood: Territory, people, government. In: James Crawford und Martti Koskenniemi (ed.): The Cambridge companion to international law. Under the collaboration of Surabhi Ranganathan. 1. publ. Cambridge: Cambridge Univ. Press (Cambridge companions to law), pp. 95–116.

Knox, John H. (2015): Human Rights, environmental protection, and the sustainable development goals. In: Washington international law journal (24), Article 3, pp. 517–536.

Kofele-Kale, Ndiva (2006): The international law of responsibility for economic crimes. Holding state officials individually liable for acts of fraudulent enrichment. [2nd ed.]. Aldershot: Ashgate.

Kojima, Chie (2015): South China Sea arbitration and the protection of the marine environment. Evolution of UNCLOS Part XII through interpretation and the duty to cooperate. In: Asian Yearbook of International Law 21, pp. 166–180.

Koskenniemi, Martti (1994): National self-determination today. Problems of legal theory and practice.

Kristof, Nicholas, *Island Nations Fear Sea Could Swamp Them*, New York Times, 01.12.1997.

Kuehls, Thom (1998): Between Sovereignty and Environment: An Exploration of the Discourse of Government. In: Karen T. Litfin (ed.): The greening of sovereignty in world politics. Cambridge [i.a.]: MIT Press (Global environmental accord), pp. 31–53.

Kuper, Adam (2003): The Return of the Native. In: Current Anthropology 44 (3), pp. 389–402. https://doi.org/10.1086/368120.

Kuper, Adam (2009): Discussion on the Concept of Indigeneity. In: Amelia Cook und Jeremy Sarkin (ed.): Who is indigenous? Indigenous rights globally, in Africa, and among the san in Botswana (18).

Kutz, Christopher (2021): Resources for the People—but Who Are the People? Mistaken Nationalism in Resource Sovereignty. In: Ethics & International Affairs (35), Article 1, pp. 119–144.

Kymlicka, Will, The Internationalization of minority rights, In: International Journal of Constitutional Law (6), Article 1, 2008, pp. 1–32.

La Fayette, Louise A. (2010): Entitlement To Marine Living Resources In Areas Beyond National Jurisdiction. Commentary On Richard Barnes. In: The International Legal Regime of Areas beyond National Jurisdiction (26), pp. 159–162.

Lal, Kya Raina (2017): Legal Measures to Address the Impacts of Climate Change-Induced Sea Level Rise on Pacific Statehood, Sovereignty and Exclusive Economic Zones. In: Auckland University Law Review (23), pp. 235–268.

Lansing, Robert (1921): The peace negotiations. A personal narrative. London.

Lapidoth, Ruth; Owada, Hisashi (1997): Commentary to Falk, The Right of Self-Determination Under International Law. In: Wolfgang Danspeckgruber (eds.): Self-determination and self-administration. Boulder, Colo. [i.a.]: Rienner.

Lazrus, Heather (2012): Sea Change: Island Communities and Climate Change. Sea Change: Island Communities and Climate Change. Palo Alto, CA: Annual Reviews.

Lewis, Bridget (2018): Environmental Human Rights and Climate Change. Current Status and Future Prospects.

Linklater, Andrew ((1949) 2007): Critical theory and world politics. 1. publ. London [i.a.]: Routledge.

Lodge, Michael W. (2013): Implementation of the Common Heritage of Mankind. In: Harry N. Schreiber und Jin-Hyun Paik (ed.): Regions, Institutions, and Law of the Sea. Leiden, Boston: Martinus Nijhoff Publisher, pp. 129–144.

Loibl, Gerhard (2004): The Evolving Regime on Climate Change and Sustainable Development. In: Nicolaas Schrijver und Friedl Weiss (ed.): International law and sustainable development. Leiden [i.a.]: Nijhoff (Developments in international law).

Loukacheva, Natalia (2009): Arctic indigenous peoples' internationalism: in search of a legal justification. In: Polar Record 45 (1), pp. 51–58. https://doi.org/10.1017/S0032247408007742.

Love, Maryann Cusimano (2020): Global issues beyond sovereignty. Fifth edition. Lanham: Rowman & Littlefield.

MacLean, Robert (1994): Public International Law Textbook. 16. ed.

Mansfield, Nick (2016): Climate Change. Politics, excess, sovereignty. In: Tom Bristow und Ford Thomas H. (ed.): A Cultural History of Climate Change, pp. 177–191.

Marauhn, Thilo; **Böhringer**, Ayse-Martina (2014): An Ecosystem Approach to the Transboundary Protection of Biodiversity. In: Louis J. Kotzé (ed.): Transboundary Governance of Biodiversity. Transboundary Governance of Biodiversity. Under the collaboration of Thilo Marauhn. 1st ed. Leiden: BRILL (Legal Aspects of Sustainable Development Ser, v.19), pp. 90–104.

Matsui, Yoshiro (2004): The Principle of "Common but Differentiated Responsibilities". In: Nicolaas Schrijver und Friedl Weiss (ed.): International law and sustainable development. Leiden [i.a.]: Nijhoff (Developments in international law).

Matz-Lück, Nele (2010): The Concept of the Common Heritage of Mankind: Its Viability as a Management Tool for Deep-Sea Genetic Resources. In: Alex G. Oude. Elferink und Erik J. Molenaar (ed.): The International Legal Regime of Areas Beyond National Jurisdiction. 1st ed. Leiden: BRILL (Nova et Vetera Iuris Gentium Ser), pp. 61–75.

Matz-Lück, Nele; Christiansen, Liv (2020): UNGA as the Anchor: Global Environmental Conferencing. In: Environmental Policy and Law (50), pp. 519–530.

McAdam, Jane (2011): Swimming against the Tide. Why a Climate Change Displacement Treaty is Not the Answer. In: International Journal of Refugee Law (23), Article 1, pp. 2–27.

McAdam, Jane (2013a): Climate change, forced migration, and international law. 1. publ. In paperback. Oxford: Oxford Univ. Press.

McAdam, Jane (2013b): Caught between homelands. In: Inside Story, 15.03.2013.

McAnaney, Sheila (2012): Sinking Islands—Formulating a Realistic Solution to Climate Change Displacement. In: New York University Law Review (87), Article 4, pp. 1172–1209.

McCorquodale, Robert (2018): The Individual and the International Legal System. In: Malcolm Evans (ed.): International law. Fifth edition. Oxford: Oxford University Press.

Meine, Anna (2021): Beyond Westphalia. Democratic Conceptions of Sovereignty and Constellations of Plural Territories. In: Andre Santos Campos und Susana Cadliha (ed.): Sovereignty as value. Lanham, Boulder, New York, London: Rowman & Littlefield (Values and identities: Crossing philosophical borders), pp. 127–145.

Melandri, Manuela (2016): Self-determination and state-building in international law: a right in abeyance? Self-determination and state-building in international law: a right in abeyance?: UCL (University College London).

Mensah, Thomas A. (2008): Using Judicial Bodies for the Implementation and Enforcement of International Environmental Law. In: Isabelle Buffard, James Crawford, Alain Pellet und Stephan Wittich (ed.): International Law Between Universalism and Fragmentation.

Mercer, Phil (2011): Fiji, Climate Change Concerns Dominate Pacific Bloc Summit. In: Voa News, 06.09.2011.

Miller, David (1995): On nationality. Reprinted. Oxford [i.a.]: Clarendon Press (Oxford political theory).

Miller, David (2000): Citizenship and national identity. 1. publ. Cambridge [i.a.]: Polity Press.

Miller, David (2007): National responsibility and global justice. 1. publ. Oxford [i.a.]: Oxford Univ. Press (Oxford political theory).

Miller, David (2012): Territorial Rights: Concept and Justification. In: Political Studies (60), pp. 252–268.

Miller, Marian A. L. (1998): Sovereignty Reconfigured: Environmental Regimes and Third World States. In: Karen T. Litfin (ed.): The greening of sovereignty in world politics. Cambridge [i.a.]: MIT Press (Global environmental accord), pp. 173–192.

Minnerop, Petra (2018): Climate Protection Agreements. In: Max Planck Encyclopedias of International Law.

Moore, Margaret (2001): The Ethics of Nationalism. Oxford: Oxford University Press U.S. – OSO.

Moore, Margaret (2012): Natural Resources, Territorial Right, and Global Distributive Justice. In: Political Theory (40), pp. 84–107.

Moore, Margaret (2013): Place-related attachments and global distributive justice. In: Journal of Global Ethics 9 (2), pp. 215–226. https://doi.org/10.1080/17449626.2013.818465.

Moore, Margaret (2015): A Political Theory of Territory: Oxford University Press.

Moore, Margaret (2021): Can we Forfeit Our Territorial Rights? In: Andre Santos Campos und Susana Cadliha (ed.): Sovereignty as value. Lanham, Boulder, New York, London: Rowman & Littlefield (Values and identities: Crossing philosophical borders), pp. 147–166.

Morgan, Edmund S. (1988): Inventing the people. The rise of popular sovereignty in England and America. New York: Norton.

Morgenthau, Hans J. (1940): Positivism, functionalism, and international law. In: American Journal of International Law, pp. 260–284.

Morris, Rachel (2009): What Happens When Your Country Drowns? In: Mother Jones 2009, 30.11.2009 (Nov./Dec 2009).

Mühlebach, Andrea (2001): "Making Place" at the United Nations: Indigenous Cultural Politics at the U.N. Working Group on Indigenous Populations, pp. 415–448.

Mulalap, Clement Yow (2013): Islands in the stream: addressing climate change from a small island developing state perspective. In: Randall Abate (ed.): Climate change and indigenous peoples. The search for legal remedies. Cheltenham, UK: Edward Elgar, pp. 377–408.

Murphy, Alexander B. (1996): The sovereign state system as political-territorial ideal: historical and contemporary considerations. In: Thomas Biersteker (ed.): State sovereignty as social construct. Cambridge: Cambridge University Press (Cambridge studies in international relations), pp. 81–120.

Nawrot, Filip (2020): Principle of permanent sovereignty over natural resources in rulings of international courts. In: Prawne Problemy Gronictwa i Ochrony Srodowiska (2), Article 1. pp. 97–109.

Ng'ambi, Sangwani Patrick (2015): Permanent Sovereignty Over Natural Resources and the Sanctity of Contracts, From the Angle of Lucrum Cessans, In: Loyola University Chicago International Law Review (2), Article 3, pp. 153–172

Nguyen, Lan Ngoc (2021): Expanding the Environmental Regulatory Scope of UNCLOS Through the Rule of Reference: Potentials and Limits. In: Ocean Development & International Law (52), Article 4, pp. 419–444.

Nicholson, Rowan (2019): Statehood and the State-Like in International Law.

Nine, Cara (2012): Global justice and territory. 1. publ. Oxford [i.a.]: Oxford Univ. Press.

Nine, Cara (2016): Water Crisis Adaptation: Defending a Strong Right Against Displacement from the Home. In: Res Publica 22 (1), p. 37–52. https://doi.org/10.1007/s11158-015-9310-1.

Nordquist, Myron H. (2003): United Nations Convention on the Law of the Sea, 1982. Dordrecht: Nijhoff.

Northcott, Heather A. (2012): Realisation of the right of indigenous peoples to natural resources under international law through the emerging right to autonomy. In: The International Journal of Human Rights 16 (1), pp. 73–99. https://doi.org/10.1080/13642987.2011.611335.

Oda, Shigeru (2003): Fifty Years of The Law of the Sea. With a Special Section on the International Court of Justice.

Ödalen, Jörgen (2014): Underwater Self-determination: Sea-level Rise and Deterritorialized Small Island States. Underwater Self-determination: Sea-level Rise and Deterritorialized Small Island States. In: Ethics, Policy & Environment (17), Article 2, pp. 225–237.

Oeter, Stefan (2012): The protection of indigenous peoples in international law revisited. From non-discrimination to self-determination. In: Holger P. Hestermeyer (ed.): Coexistence, cooperation and solidarity. Liber amicorum Rüdiger Wolfrum. Under the collaboration of Rüdiger Wolfrum. Leiden: Nijhoff, pp. 477–502.

Oguamanam, Chidi (2013): Rio+20: Indigenous Knowledge and Intellectual Property in Coastal and Ocean Law. In: Ocean Yearbook 27, pp. 121–146.

Oklopcic, Zoran (2009): Populus Interruptus: Self-Determination, the Independence of Kosovo, and the Vocabulary of Peoplehood. In: Leiden Journal of International Law 22 (4), pp. 677–702. https://doi.org/10.1017/S0922156509990161.

Olson, Mancur (1971): The logic of collective action. 2. print. Cambridge, Mass. [i.a.]: Harvard Univ. Press (Harvard economic studies).

Ong, Ai-hwa (1999): Flexible citizenship. Durham [i.a.]: Duke Univ. Press.

Orakhelashvili, Alexander (2006): Peremptory norms in international law. Teilw. zugl.: Cambridge, Univ.., Diss., 2004. 1. publ. Oxford: Oxford Univ. Press (Oxford monographs in international law).

Oral, Nilüfer (2019): International Law as an Adaptation Measure to Sea-level Rise and Its Impacts on Islands and Offshore Features. In: The International Journal of Marine and Coastal Law 34, pp. 415–439.

Osofsky, Hari M. (2009): The Inuit Petition as a Bridge? Beyond Dialectics of Climate Change and Indigenous Peoples' Rights. In: Hari M. Osofsky und William C. G. Burns (ed.): Adjudicating climate change. State, national, and international approaches. Cambridge, New York: Cambridge University Press, pp. 272–291.

Østhagen, Andreas (2020): Coast Guards and Ocean Politics in the Arctic. Singapore.

Otis, Ghislain; **Laurent**, Aurélie (2013): Indigenous land claims in Europe. In: Arctic Review on Law and Politics 4, pp. 156–180.

Otis, James (1766): The rights of the British colonies asserted and proved. 3rd ed., corr. S.l.: Boston, New-England printed, London reprinted for J. Williams.

Oxman, Bernard H. (2018): The Territorial Temptation: A Siren Song at Sea. In: John Norton Moore (ed.): Common Resources—Law of the Sea, Outer Space, and Antarctica.

Özmen, Elif (2019): Das Recht(e) in Das Recht der Völker. In: Henning Hahn und Reza Mosayebi (ed.): John Rawls: Das Recht der Völker, pp. 13–28.

Papanicolopulu, Irini (2012): The Law of the Sea Convention. No place for persons? In: International Journal of Marine and Coastal Law (27), Article 4, pp. 867–874.

Papanicolopulu, Irini; **Rocha**, Armando (2020): Oceans, climate change and non-state actors. In: Jan McDonald, Jeffrey McGee und Richard Barnes (ed.): Research handbook on climate change, oceans and coasts, pp. 193–208.

Parrish, Austen L. (2019): The interplay between extraterritoriality, sovereignty, and the foundations of international law. In: Daniel S. Margolies (ed.): The Extraterritoriality of Law. History, Theory, Politics. Under the collaboration of Umut Özsu, Maia Pal, and Ntina Tzouvala. Milton: Routledge (Politics of Transnational Law Ser), pp. 169–182.

Pauly, Louis W.; **Grande**, Edgar (2005): Reconstituting Political Authority: Sovereignty, Effectiveness, and Legitimacy in a Transnational Order. In: Edgar Grande und Louis W. Pauly (eds.): Complex Sovereignty. Reconstituting Political Authority in the Twenty-First Century. Toronto: University of Toronto Press, pp. 3–21.

Paxman, John T. (1989): Minority indigenous populations and their claims for self-determination.

Peel, Jacqueline (2015): Climate Change Litigation. Cambridge: Cambridge University Press (Cambridge studies in international and comparative law).

Pentassuglia, Gaetano (2009): Evolving Protection of Minority Groups: Global Challenges and the Role of International Jurisprudence. In: Int Community Law Rev 11 (2), pp. 185–218. https://doi.org/10.1163/187197309X430918.

Pentassuglia, Gaetano (2017): Self-Determination, Human Rights, and the Nation-State. In: ICLR 19 (4–5), pp. 443–484. https://doi.org/10.1163/18719732-12340007.

Pereira, Ricardo (2012): Exploration and Exploitation of Energy Resources. In: Karen. Makuch (ed.): Environmental and Energy Law. 1st ed. Hoboken: John Wiley & Sons, Incorporated.

Pereira, Ricardo; **Gough**, Orla (2013): Permanent Sovereignty over Natural Resources in the 21st Century: Natural Resource Governance and the Right of Self-Determination of Indigenous Peoples under International Law. In: Melbourne Journal of International Law 14, pp. 451–495.

Perrez, Franz Xaver (1996): The Relationship Between "Permanent Sovereignty" and the Obligation not to cause transboundary environmental damage. In: Environmental Law (26).

Perrez, Franz Xaver (2000): Cooperative sovereignty. The Hague [i.a.]: Kluwer Law International.

Petzhold, Jan; **Magnan**, Alexandre K. (2019): Climate change: thinking small islands beyond Small Island Developing States (SIDS). In: Climate Change (152), pp. 145–166.

Pfeiffer, Thomas; **Nowak**, Martin A. (2006): All in the game. In: Nature, Article 441, pp. 583–584.

Pitty, Roderic (2001): Indigenous Peoples, Self-determination and International Law. In: The International Journal of Human Rights 5 (4), pp. 44–71. https://doi.org/10.1080/714003733.

Plato, Timaeus, 360 BC.

Powers, Ann; **Stucko**, Christophe (2013): Introducing the Law of the Sea and the Legal Implications of Rising Sea Levels. In: Threatened Islands Nations, pp. 123–140.

Prip, Christian (2021): Integrating Climate Change in the Governance of Areas. In: Elise Johansen, Signe Veierud Busch und Jakobsen Ingvild Ulrikke (ed.): The Law of the Sea and Climate Change.

Proelß, Alexander (2017): United Nations Convention on the Law of the Sea. A Commentary. 1st ed. Baden-Baden: Nomos Verlagsgesellschaft (Kooperationswerke Beck – Hart – Nomos). Online available on https://ebookcentral.proquest.com/lib/gbv/detail.action?docID=5519090.

Quinones, Julian; **Cherry**, Kacey; **Lajka**, Arijeta (2017): Climate Refugees: Kiribati. In: CBS News, 21.08.2017. Online available on https://www.cbsnews.com/news/climate-refugees-kiribati-cbsn-on-assignment/.

Raič, David (2002): Statehood and the law of self-determination. Available: Leiden, Univ. fra, Diss., 2002. The Hague: Kluwer Law International (Developments in international law, 43).

Rasmusson, Elisabeth; **Presterud**, Pal (2011): The Nansen Conference. Climate Change and Displacement in the 21st Century. Oslo, Norway.

Rawls, John (2002): Das Recht der Völker. Berlin [i.a.]: De Gruyter (Ideen & Argumente).

Rayfuse, Rosemary (2011): International Law and Disappearing States. In: Environmental Policy and Law (41), Article 6, pp. 281–287.

Rayfuse, Rosemary; **Crawford**, Emily (2011): Climate Change, Sovereignty and Statehood. In: Sydney Law School.

Rayfuse, Rosemary; **Freestone**, David (2012): Precaution and the Protection of Marine Biodiversity in Areas beyond National Jurisdiction. Precaution and the Protection of Marine Biodiversity in Areas beyond National Jurisdiction. In: International Journal of Marine and Coastal Law (27), pp. 773–781.

Reardon, Sara (2012): Pacific island to buy a piece of Fiji as climate plan. In: New Scientist, 13.03.2012.

Reisman, William Michael (1975): Puerto Rico and the international process. New roles in association: a report for the Conference on "Puerto Rico and the Foreign Policy Process". Washington, DC: West Publ (Studies in transnational legal policy, 6).

Rich, Roland (1988): The right to development. A right of peoples?

Risse, Mathias (2012): On global justice. Princeton [i.a.]: Princeton Univ. Press.

Roach, J. Ashley (2021): The BBNJ Process: Gaps and Prospects for Success. In: Ocean Yearbook 35, pp. 52–84.

Rogers, Nicole (2016): Litigation, activism, and the paradox of lawfulness in an age of climate change. In: Tom Bristow und Ford Thomas H. (ed.): A Cultural History of Climate Change, pp. 211–228.

Rosenau, James (1998): Governance and Democracy in a Globalizing World. In: Daniele Archibugi, David Held und Martin Köhler (ed.): Re-imagining political community. Studies in cosmopolitan democracy. Oxford: Polity Press, pp. 28–57.

Roszko, Edyta (2015): Maritime territorialisation as performance of sovereignty and nationhood in the South China Sea: Maritime territorialisation. In: Nations and Nationalism (21), Article 2, pp. 230–249.

Rousseau, Jean-Jacques 1712–1778 (1791): An inquiry into the nature of the social contract. London: printed for G. G. J. and J. Robinson.

Ruhl, J. B. (2010): Climate Change Adaptation and the Structural Transformation of Environmental Law. Climate Change Adaptation and the Structural Transformation of Environmental Law, pp. 363–435.

Ruppel, Oliver; **Ruppel-Schlichting**, Katharina (2011): Environmental Law and Policy in Namibia.

Sack, Robert David (1986): Human territoriality. 1. publ. Cambridge i.a.: Cambridge Univ. Pr (Cambridge studies in historical geography).

Samuels, Joel H. (2008): Condominium arrangements in international practice. Reviving an abandoned concept of boundary dispute resolution. In: Michigan Journal of International Law 29 (4), pp. 727–776.

Sand, Peter H. (2002): Global Environmental Change and the Nation State: Perspectives of International Law. In: Frank Biermann, Rainer Brohm und Klaus Dingwerth (eds.): "Global environmental change and the nation state". Potsdam: PIK (PIK report), pp. 194–206.

Sand, Peter H. (2006): Global environmental change and the nation state: sovereignty bounded? In: Gerd Winter (ed.): Multilevel governance of global environmental change. 1. publ. Cambridge [i.a.]: Cambridge Univ. Press, pp. 519–538.

Sand, Peter H. (2014): The Concept of Public Trusteeship in the Transboundary Governance of Biodiversity. In: Louis J. Kotzé (ed.): Transboundary Governance of Biodiversity. Transboundary Governance of Biodiversity. Under the collaboration of Thilo Marauhn. 1st ed. Leiden: BRILL (Legal Aspects of Sustainable Development Ser, v.19), pp. 34–64.

Sands, Philippe (2018): Principles of international environmental law. Fourth edition. Cambridge: Cambridge University Press.

Santo, Elizabeth M. de; **Mendenhall**, Elizabeth; **Nyman**, Elizabeth; **Tiller**, Rachel (2020): Stuck in the middle with you (and not much time left): The third intergovernmental conference on biodiversity beyond national jurisdiction. In: Marine Policy, Article 103957, pp. 1–9.

Saunders, Imogen (2020): The limits of the natural state doctrine. Rocks, islands, and artificial intervention in a changing world. In: Donald R. Rothwell und David Letts (ed.): Law of the Sea in South East Asia. Environmental, Navigational, and Security Challenges. London, New York: Routledge, pp. 118–135.

Schofield, Clive; **Freestone**, David (2019): Islands Awash Amidst Rising Seas: Sea Level Rise and Insular Status under the Law of the Sea. In: The International Journal of Marine and Coastal Law 34, pp. 391–414.

Schofield, Clive; **Potts**, Tavis (2008): Current Legal Developments: The Arctic. In: International Journal of Marine and Coastal Law (23), pp. 151–176.
Schrijver, Nico (1997): Sovereignty over Natural Resources. Balancing Rights and Duties.
Schrijver, Nico (2008a): Evolution of Sustainable Development in International Law.
Schrijver, Nico (2008b): Unravelling State Sovereignty? The Controversy on the Right of Indigenous Peoples to Permanent Sovereignty over their Natural Wealth and Resources. In: Ineke Boerefijn und Cees Flinterman (ed.): Changing perceptions of sovereignty and human rights. Essays in honour of Cees Flinterman. Antwerp, i.a.: Intersentia.
Schrijver, Nico (2009): Development without Destruction. The UN and Global Resource Management.
Schrijver, Nico (2015): 50 years of Permanent Sovereignty over Natural Resources. In: Marc Bungenberg und Stephan Hobe (ed.): Permanent Sovereignty over Natural Resources: Springer.
Schrijver, Nicolaas (2013): Self-determination of peoples and sovereignty over natural wealth and resources.
Schrijver, Nicolaas; Weiss, Friedl (ed.) (2004): International law and sustainable development. Leiden [i.a.]: Nijhoff (Developments in international law).
Schwarzenberger, Georg (1970): Economic world order? A basic problem of international economic law. Manchester: Manchester Univ. Press (The Melland Schill lectures).
Scott, Karen N. (2020): Climate change and the law of the sea in the Asia Pacific. In: Donald R. Rothwell und David Letts (ed.): Law of the Sea in South East Asia. Environmental, Navigational, and Security Challenges. London, New York: Routledge, pp. 94–117.
Serdy, Andrew (2010): Commentary. Property rights in areas beyond national jurisdiction: not too late for proper debate? In: The International Legal Regime of Areas beyond National Jurisdiction (26), pp. 143–158.
Shaw, Malcolm N. (2008): International law. 6. ed. Cambridge [i.a.]: Cambridge Univ. Press.
Shaw, Malcolm N. (2014): International law. 7. [updated] ed. Cambridge [i.a.]: Cambridge Univ. Press.
Shi, Jingxia; **Yang**, Xingxing (2015): Reconciling Environmental Protection with Natural Resources Trade in International Law. A Perspective from China -Rare Earths. In: Frontiers of Law in China (10), Article 3, pp. 537–566.
Shrinkhal, Rashwet (2014): Problems in Defining Indigenous Peoples under International Law. In: Chotanagpur Law Journal, pp. 187–195.
Sidgwick, Henry (1897): The elements of politics. 2nd ed., rev. Throughout. London, New York: Macmillan.
Simma, Bruno; **Paulus**, Andreas L. (1998): The "International Community": Facing the Challenge of Globalization. In: European Journal of International Law 9, pp. 266–277.
Simmons, John A. (2001): On the Territorial Rights of States. In: Philosophical Issues, pp. 300–326.
Simmons, John A. (2016): Boundaries of authority. New York, NY: Oxford University Press.
Singh, Pardeep A. (2022): The Invocation of the "Two-Year Rule" at the International Seabed Authority: Legal Consequences and Implications. In: The International Journal of Marine and Coastal Law 37, pp. 375–412.
Skillington, Tracey (2016): Reconfiguring the Contours of Statehood and the Rights of Peoples of Disappearing States in the Age of Global Climate Change. In: Social sciences (5).

Skordas, Achilles (2007): Self-determination of peoples and transnational regimes: a foundational principle of global governance. Cambridge University Press.

Smith, Jeffrey (2013): Fishing for Self-Determination: European Fisheries and Western Sahara—The Case of Ocean Resources in Africa's Last Colony. In: Ocean Yearbook 27, pp. 267–290.

Sodan, Helge; **Ziekow**, Jan (2023): Grundkurs Öffentliches Recht. Staats- und Verwaltungsrecht. 10. ed.: C.H. Beck Verlag.

Sorensen, Georg: Sovereignty: Change and Continuity in a Fundamental Institution. Sovereignty: Change and Continuity in a Fundamental Institution. Oxford, UK and Boston, U.S.: Blackwell Publishers Ltd.

Soroos, Marvin S. (1986): Beyond sovereignty. Cap. 8: Ocean Resources—Negotiating a New Law of the Sea. Columbia, SC: Univ. of South Carolina Press (Studies in international relations).

Stavenhagen, Rodolfo (2011): How Strong Are the Rights of Indigenous Peoples? In: Journal of Human Rights 10 (3), pp. 414–421. https://doi.org/10.1080/14754835.2011.596079.

Steffens, Dirk; **Haberkuss**, Fritz (2020): Über Leben. Zukunftsfrage Artensterben: Wie wir die Ökokrise überwinden: Pinguin-Verlag.

Stilz, Anna (2011): Nations, States, and Territory. In: Ethics 121 (3), pp. 572–601. https://doi.org/10.1086/658937.

Stilz, Anna (2019): Territorial sovereignty. First edition. Oxford: Oxford University Press (Oxford Scholarship Online).

Stoyanova, Irina L. (2013): The Saami facing the impacts of global climate change. In: Randall Abate (ed.): Climate change and indigenous peoples. The search for legal remedies. Cheltenham, UK: Edward Elgar, pp. 287–312.

Stratford, Elaine; **Farbotko**, Carol; **Lazrus**, Heather (2013): Tuvalu, Sovereignty and Climate Change: Considering Fenua, the Archipelago and Emigration. In: Island Studies Journal 8 (1), pp. 67–83.

Strating, Rebecca; **Wallis**, Joanne (2022): Maritime sovereignty and territorialisation. Comparing the Pacific Islands and South China Sea. In: Marine Policy, Article 141, pp. 1–8.

Summers, James (2014): Peoples and international law. Second revised edition. Leiden, Boston: Brill Nijhoff (The Erik Castren Institute monographs on international law and human rights, volume 17).

Sutton, Victoria (2013): Fiji: climate change, tradition and Vanua. In: Randall Abate (ed.): Climate change and indigenous peoples. The search for legal remedies. Cheltenham, UK: Edward Elgar, pp. 363–376.

Tams, Christian (2005): Enforcing Obligations Erga Omnes in International Law.

Tanaka, Yoshifumi (2012): The International Law of the Sea.

Tanaka, Yoshifumi (2019): The international law of the sea. Third edition. Cambridge, New York, NY, Port Melbourne, VIC, New Delhi, Singapore: Cambridge University Press.

Thornberry, Patrick (1991): International law and the rights of minorities. Oxford: Clarendon Press. Online available on http://www.loc.gov/catdir/enhancements/fy0639/90039511-d.html.

Thornberry, Patrick (1993): The Democratic or Internal Aspect of Self-Determination with Some Remarks on Federalism. In: Christian Tomuschat (ed.): Modern law of self-determination. Dordrecht: Nijhoff (Developments in international law, 16).

Thornberry, Patrick (1998): Images of Autonomy and Individual and Collective Rights in International Instruments on the Rights of Minorities. In: Markku Suksi (ed.): Autonomy. Applications and implications. The Hague: Kluwer Law International.

Thornberry, Patrick (2002): Indigenous peoples and human rights. New York: Juris Pub.; Manchester, UK; Manchester University Press (Melland Schill studies in international law).

Thürer, Daniel; **Burri**, Thomas (2008): Self-Determination. In: Max Planck Encyclopedias of International Law.

Tilling, A. J.; **Fihaki**, E. (2009): Tuvalu National Biodiversity Strategy and Action Plan. Fourth National Report to the Convention on Biological Diversity. 4th ed. UNDP.

Tsosie, Rebecca (2013): Climate Change and Indigenous Peoples: Comparative Models of Sovereignty. In: Randall Abate (ed.): Climate change and indigenous peoples. The search for legal remedies. Cheltenham, UK: Edward Elgar, pp. 79–95.

Türk, Helmut (2012): Reflections on the contemporary law of the sea. Leiden: Nijhoff (Publications on ocean development, 71).

Tyagi, Yogesh (2015): Permanent Sovereignty over Natural Resources. In: Cambridge Journal of International and Comparative Law (4), Article 3, pp. 588–615.

Vaha, Milla Emilia (2017): "We as Peoples Have the Right to Exist". Threatened Nations and Climate Justice. In: Climate Justice and Human Rights (90), Article 4, pp. 767–776.

Vaha, Milla Emilia (2018): Hosting the Small Island Developing States: two scenarios. In: International Journal of Climate Change Strategies and Management (10), Article 2, pp. 229–224.

Van der Lugt, Cornis (2002): Thirty Years After Stockholm: What Role for State Sovereignty? In: Frank Biermann, Rainer Brohm und Klaus Dingwerth (eds.): "Global environmental change and the nation state". Potsdam: PIK (PIK report), pp. 226–236.

Van Doorn, Erik (2021): Legal Implications of the "Common Heritage" Principle for Atlantic Bluefin Tuna. Berlin: Duncker & Humblot.

Van Wyk, Sanita (2017): The Impact of Climate Change Law on the Principle of State Sovereignty over Natural Resources (Law and Constitution in Africa, 35).

Venter, Francois (2014): Transfrontier Protection of the Natural Environment, Globalization and State Sovereignty. In: Louis J. Kotzé (ed.): Transboundary Governance of Biodiversity. Transboundary Governance of Biodiversity. Under the collaboration of Thilo Marauhn. 1st ed. Leiden: BRILL (Legal Aspects of Sustainable Development Ser, v.19), pp. 65–89.

Ventura, Victor AMF (2020): Environmental Jurisdiction in the Law of the Sea. The Brazilian Blue Amazon. Cham, Switzerland: Springer.

Verheyen, Roda; **Pabsch**, Severin (2021): The role of non-governmental organizations for climate change litigation. In: Wolfgang Kahl und Marc-Philippe Weller (eds.): Climate change litigation. A handbook. München, Oxford, United Kingdom, New York, NY, U.S., Baden-Baden: Beck; Hart; Nomos, pp. 507–531.

Vukas, Budislav (2012): Self-Determination of Peoples. In: Holger P. Hestermeyer (ed.): Coexistence, cooperation and solidarity. Liber amicorum Rüdiger Wolfrum. With the collaboration of Rüdiger Wolfrum. Leiden: Nijhoff.

Waart, Paul J.I.M. de (2004): Sustainable Development through a Socially Responsible Regime. In: Nicolaas Schrijver und Friedl Weiss (ed.): International law and sustainable development. Leiden [i.a.]: Nijhoff (Developments in international law).

Wälde, Thomas W. (2004): Natural Resources and Sustainable Development: From "Good Intentions" to "Good Consequences". In: Nicolaas Schrijver und Friedl Weiss (ed.): International law and sustainable development. Leiden [i.a.]: Nijhoff (Developments in international law).

Wang, Chuanliang; **Chang**, Yen-Chiang (2020): A new interpretation of the common heritage of mankind in the context of the international law of the sea. In: Ocean and Coastal Management, Article 191, pp. 1–7.

Wapner, Paul (1998): Reorienting State Sovereignty. Rights and Responsibilities in the Environmental Age. In: Karen T. Litfin (ed.): The greening of sovereignty in world politics. Cambridge [i.a.]: MIT Press (Global environmental accord), pp. 275–297.

Ward, Molly (2014): Planning to sink: What happens if Kiribati drowns? In: PBS News Hour Weekend, 27.07.2014.

Ward, Veronica (1998): Sovereignty and Ecosystem Management: Clash of Concepts and Boundaries? In: Karen T. Litfin (ed.): The greening of sovereignty in world politics. Cambridge [i.a.]: MIT Press (Global environmental accord), pp. 80–108.

Warne, Kennedy, *Rising Seas Threaten These Pacific Islands but Not Their Culture*, National Geographic, 11.2015.

Wasuka, Evan (2020): Landmark decision from UN Human Rights Committee paves way for climate refugees. In: ABC News, 21.01.2020. Online available on https://www.abc.net.au/news/2020-01-21/un-human-rights-ruling-worlds-first-climate-refugee-kiribati/11887070.

Weisburd, Mark (2009): The International Court of Justice and the Concept of State Practice.

Weiss, Friedl; **Scherzer**, Bernhard (2015): Existence of Common or Universal Principles for Resource Management (?). In: Marc Bungenberg und Stephan Hobe (ed.): Permanent Sovereignty over Natural Resources: Springer.

Werner, Wouter G. (2001): Self-Determination and Civil War. In: Journal of Conflict & Security Law (6), Article 2, pp. 171–190.

Wilde, Ralph (2008): International territorial administration. 1. publ. Oxford [i.a.]: Oxford Univ. Press (Oxford monographs in international law).

Willcox, Susannah (2015): Climate Change Inundation and Atoll Island States: Implications for Human Rights, Self-Determination and Statehood.

Williams, Marc (2003): Rethinking Sovereignty. In: Eleonore Kofman (ed.): Globalization. Theory and practice, pp. 109–123. 2. ed. London: Continuum.

Wilmer, Frank (1998): Taking Indigenous Critiques Seriously: the Enemy "R" Us. In: Karen T. Litfin (ed.): The greening of sovereignty in world politics. Cambridge [i.a.]: MIT Press (Global environmental accord), pp. 55–78.

Wilmer, Franke (1993): The indigenous voice in world politics. Newbury Park, i.a.: Sage Publ (Violence, cooperation, peace).

Winter, Gerd (2006): The legal nature of environmental principles in international, EU, and exemplary national law. In: Gerd Winter (ed.): Multilevel governance of global environmental change. 1. publ. Cambridge [i.a.]: Cambridge Univ. Press, pp. 587–604.

Wolfrum, Rüdiger (1990): Purposes and Principles of International Environmental Law. In: German Yearbook of International Law 33, pp. 308–330.

Wolfrum, Rüdiger; **Matz-Lück**, Nele (2003): Conflicts in international environmental law. Berlin, Heidelberg: Springer (Beiträge zum ausländischen öffentlichen Recht und Völkerrecht, 164). Online available on http://www.loc.gov/catdir/enhancements/fy0818/2003376828-d.html.

Wong, Derek (2013): Sovereignty Sunk—The Position of Sinking States at International Law. In: Melbourne Journal of International Law (14), Article 2, pp. 349–391.

Woodroffe, Colin D. (2008): Reef-island topography and the vulnerability of atolls to sea-level rise. In: Global and Planetary Change 62, pp. 70–96.

Wyman, Katrina Miriam (2013a): Are We Morally Obligated to Assist Climate Change Migrants? In: Law & ethics of human rights (7), Article 2, pp. 185–212.

Wyman, Katrina Miriam (2013b): Responses to climate migration. In: The Harvard environmental law review (37), Article 1, pp. 167–216.

Yamamoto, Lilian (2013): Atoll island states and international law. Heidelberg [i.a.]: Springer.

Yamamoto, Lilian; **Esteban**, Miguel (2014): Atoll Island States and international law. Climate change, displacement, and sovereignty. Berlin, Heidelberg: Springer.

Young, Stephen (2019): Re-historicising dissolved identities: Deskaheh, the League of Nations, and international legal discourse on Indigenous peoples. In: London Review of International Law 7 (3), pp. 377–408. https://doi.org/10.1093/lril/lraa004.

Ypi, Lea (2014): A permissive theory of territorial rights. In: European Journal of Philosophy (22), Article 2, pp. 288–312.

Jurisdiction

Ad Hoc Arbitration, *BP Exploration Company (Libya) Limited v. Libya,* Award on the Merits of 10.10.1973.

Ad Hoc Arbitration, *LIAMCO v. Libya (Libyan American Oil Company v. The Government of the Libyan Arab Republic),* Award of 12.04.1977.

Ad Hoc Arbitration, *The American Independent Oil Company v. The Government of the State of Kuwait (Aminoil v. Kuwait),* Final Award of 24.03.1982.

Administrative Court of Cologne (Verwaltungsgericht Köln), *Case "Sealand"*, Judgment of 03.05.1978, Reference number 9 K 2565/77. In: Deutsches Verwaltungsblatt, pp. 510–512.

An Arbitrational Tribunal Constituted under Annex VII to the 1982 United Nations Convention on the Law of the Sea, Award of 12.07.2016, Reference number PCA Case No. 2013–19.

European Commission of Human Rights, *Könkämä and 38 other Saami villages v. Sweden,* No. 27033/95, 25.11.1996.

Inter-American Commission on Human Rights, Report No. 40/04; Case 12.053 of 11.10.2004, Reference number OEA/Ser.L/V/II.122, doc. 5 rev. 1 (2004).

Inter-American Court of Human Rights, *Case of Saramaka People v. Suriname,* No. 172, Judgment of 28.11.2007.

Inter-American Court of Human Rights, *The Mayagna (Sumo) Awas Tingni Community v. Nicaragua,* No. 79, Judgment of 31.08.2001.

Inter-American Commission on Human Rights, *Maya indigenous communities of the Toledo District v. Belize*, Report No. 40/04; Case 12.053, OEA/Ser.L/V/II.122, doc. 5 rev. 1, 11.-29.10.2004.

International Arbitral Award, *Texaco Overseas Petroleum Co. v. Libya,* Award on the Merits of 19.01.1977.

Permanent Court of International Justice, *Lotus Case*, Judgment of 07.09.1927, No. 9.

International Court of Justice, *The Corfu Channel Case,* Judgment of 25.03.1948.

International Court of Justice, *Anglo-Norwegian Fisheries Case,* Judgment of 18.12.1951, pp. 116–144.

International Court of Justice, *South West Africa Cases,* Judgment of 21.12.1962, pp. 319–348.

International Court of Justice, *The Barcelona Traction, Belgium v. Spain,* Judgment of 24.07.1964.

International Court of Justice. *North Sea Continental Shelf Cases (Federal Republic of Germany/ Denmark; Federal Republic of Germany/ Netherlands)*, in: Reports 1969.

International Court of Justice, *South West Africa (Namibia),* Judgment of 21.06.1971.

International Court of Justice, *Western Sahara,* Advisory Opinion of 16.10.1975.

International Court of Justice, *Case Concerning Military and Paramilitary Activities in and against Nicaragua—Nicaragua v. U.S.,* Judgment of 26.11.1984.bor

International Court of Justice, *Case Concerning the Frontier Dispute—Burkina Faso v. Republic of Mali,* Judgment of 22.12.1986.

International Court of Justice, *Phosphate Lands in Nauru (Nauru v. Australia),* Judgment of 26.06.1992.

International Court of Justice, *East Timor Judgement,* Judgment of 30.06.1995.

International Court of Justice, *Legality of the Threat or Use of Nuclear Weapons,* Advisory Opinion of 08.07.1996.

International Court of Justice, *Case Concerning The Cabcikovo-Nagymaros Project (Hungary v. Slovakia),* Judgment of 25.09.1997.

International Court of Justice, *Israeli Wall,* Advisory Opinion of 09.07.2004.

International Court of Justice, *Case Concerning Armed Activities on The Territory of the Congo (Congo v. Uganda),* Judgment of 19.12.2005.

International Court of Justice, *Construction of a road in Costa Rica along the San Juan River*, Judgment of 16.12.2015 (No. 1088).

International Court of Justice, *Request for Advisory Opinion: Obligations of States in respect of Climate Change,* Case, Advisory Opinion, 23.07.2025, Reference number Case No. 187.

International Tribunal for the Law of the Sea, *The MOX Plant Case (Ireland v. United Kingdom),* Advisory opinions and orders of 03.12.2001.

International Tribunal for the Law of the Sea, Request for *an Advisory Opinion submitted by the Commission of Small Island States on Climate Change and International Law,* Written Statement of the Republic of Nauru of 15.06.2023, Reference number Case No. 31.

International Tribunal for the Law of the Sea, Request for *an Advisory Opinion submitted by the Commission of Small Island States on Climate Change and International Law,* Written Statement of the Commission of Small Island States on Climate Change and International Law of 16.06.2023, Reference number Case No. 31.

International Tribunal for the Law of the Sea, Request for *an Advisory Opinion submitted by the Commission of Small Island States on Climate Change and International Law,* Public sitting of 20.09.2023, Reference number Case No. 31.

International Tribunal for the Law of the Sea, *Request for an Advisory Opinion submitted by the Commission of Small Island States on Climate Change and International Law,* Advisory Opinion, 21.05.2024, Reference number Case No. 31.

Permanent Court of Arbitration (PCA), *The Iron Rhine Railway Arbitration,* Award of 24.05.2005.

Permanent Court of Arbitration (PCA), *The South China Sea Arbitration,* Case No. 2013–19, 12.07.2016

Sapporo District Court, *The Nibutani Dam Decision, Kayano et. al. v. Hokkaido Expropriation Committee,* Judgment of 27.03.1997. In: International Legal Materials (38).

United Nations International Arbitral Award, *Island of Palmas case (Netherlands v. United States),* 04.04.1928.

United Nations International Arbitral Award, *Trail Smelter case (United States v. Canada,* Award of 16.04.1938, 11.03.1941.

Reports

Brundtland, Gro Harlem (1987): Report of the World Commission on Environment and Development: Our Common Future.

CBS News (2017): As climate change threatens islands, Kiribati's president plans development, https://www.cbsnews.com/news/climate-change-kiribati-president-taneti-maamau/; 20.11.2017.

Chen, Deliang; **Rojas,** Maisa; **Samset,** Bjørn (2021): IPCC—AR6 Synthesis Report—Climate Change 2021. The Intergovernmental Panel on Climate Change.

Climate Change Secretariat, UNFCCC (2005): Climate Change and Small Island Developing States. Ed. of Climate Change Secretariat UNFCCC. Bonn, Germany.

Government of Tuvalu, UNFCCC (2007): Tuvalu's National Adaptation Programme of Action. Ministry of Natural Resources, Environment, Agriculture, and Lands. Tuvalu.

Indigenous Peoples Council on Biocolonialism (20.08.2002): International Indigenous Peoples Summit on Sustainable Development, Khoi-San Territory, Kimberly, South Africa. The Kimberly Declaration.

Pachauri, Rajendra; **Meyer,** Leo (2015): IPCC—AR5 Synthesis Report—Climate Change 2014. The Intergovernmental Panel on Climate Change.

Pachauri, Rajendra; **Reisinger,** Andy (2007): IPCC—AR4 Synthesis Report—Climate Change 2007. The Intergovernmental Panel on Climate Change.

Pacific Island Forum (2021): Declaration on Preserving Maritime Zones in the Face of Climate Change-Related Sea-Level Rise. Online available on https://www.forumsec.org/2021/08/11/communique/.

Pacific Islanders reject 'climate refugee' status, want to 'migrate with dignity', SIDS conference hears (2014). In: ABC News, 06.09.2014.

Ranasinghe, Roshanka; **Ruane**, Alex C.; **Vautard**, Robert (2021): Climate Change Information for Regional Impact and for Risk Assessment. Chapter 12. In: IPCC—AR6 Synthesis Report—Climate Change 2021. The Intergovernmental Panel on Climate Change, p. 1767–1925.

Republic of Kiribati (2007): National Adaptation Program of Action (NAPA). Ministry of Environment, Land, and Agricultural Development, Government of Kiribati.

The Human Rights Committee, Communication 26.03.1990, reference number Communication No. 167/1984. In: U.N. Doc. Supp. No. 40 (A/45/40).

The World Bank (2021): Adapting to rising sea levels in the Marshall Islands. Understanding the Pacific atoll nation's adaptation pathways to build resilience to sea level rise and climate change.

Watson, Robert (2001): IPCC—AR3 Synthesis Report—Climate Change 2001. The Intergovernmental Panel on Climate Change.

WTO Panel, Reports of the Panel 05.07.2011, *China—Measures Related to the Exportation of Various Raw Materials,* reference number WT/DS394/R.

WTO Panel, Reports of the Panel 25.03.2014, *China—Measures Related to the Exportation of Rare Earths, Tungsten, and Molybdenum,* reference number WT/DS431/R.

Resolutions, Declarations, and Conventions

African Union, African Charter on Human and Peoples' Rights, Banjul Charter, 27.06.1981.

Governments of Finland, Norway, and Sweden, Nordic Saami Convention, 16.11.2005.

International Labour Organization (ILO), Organization for Security and Co-operation in Europe, Helsinki Final Act, 01.08.2975.

Organization of African Unity (OAU), Rapporteur's Report, CM/1149 (XXXVII), 1981.

United Nations, 26.12.1933, Montevideo Convention on Rights and Duties of States.

United Nations, 14.08.1941, The Atlantic Charter.

United Nations, 26.05.1945, UN Charter.

United Nations, 26.11.1951, Doc. L81.

United Nations, 20.12.1951, Doc. A/C2/L120.

United Nations, 16.04.1952, Doc. E/CN4/L24.

United Nations, 06.05.1952, Doc E/CN4/SR260.

United Nations, 11.12.1952, Doc. A/C2/SR237.

United Nations, 21.12.1952, Doc. A/PV.411 (VII).

United Nations, 27.10.1955, Doc. A/C3/SR 646.

United Nations, 29.11.1955, Doc. A/C3/SR676.

United Nations, 29.04.1958, Convention on the Continental Shelf.

United Nations, 18.05.1959, Doc. A/AC97/SR.1.

United Nations, 01.03.1960, Doc. A/AC.97/SR.10.

United Nations, 05.11.1962, Doc. A/C2/L.165.

United Nations, 23.05.1969, Vienna Convention on the Law of Treaties.

United Nations, 14.06.1971, Doc. A/CONF 48/PC.12 Annex II.

United Nations, 13.04.-21.05.1972, Proceedings of the United Nations Conference on Trade and Development; Third Session; Santiago de Chile, Volume I – Report and Annexes.

United Nations, 16.06.1972, Declaration of the United Nations Conference on the Human Environment (Stockholm Declaration).

United Nations, 23.08.1978, Vienna Convention on Succession of States in respect of Treaties.

United Nations, Convention on the Law of the Sea, 1982 (UNCLOS).

United Nations, 08.04.1983, Vienna Convention on Succession of States in respect of State Property, Archives and Debts.

United Nations, 22.05.1992, Convention on Biological Diversity (CBD).

United Nations, 14.06.1992, Agenda 21: Sustainable Development.

United Nations, 12.08.1992, Declaration on Environment and Development (Rio Declaration).

United Nations, 25.06.1993, Vienna Declaration and Programme of Action.

United Nations, 17.12.1994, The Energy Charter Treaty.

United Nations, 04.12.1995, Fish Stocks Agreement.

United Nations, 13.09.2007, reference number A/RES/61/295, Declaration on the Rights of Indigenous Peoples (UNDRIP).

United Nations, 12.12.2015, Paris Agreement to the United Nations Framework Convention on Climate Change.

United Nations Economic and Social Council (ECOSOC), 19.07.2000, reference number: E/CN.4/Sub.2/2000/10, Prevention of Discrimination Against and the Protection of Minorities

United Nations Economic Commission for Europe, 31.10.2001, Convention on Access to Information, Public Participation in Decision-Making and Access to Justice in Environmental Matters (UNECE).

United Nations Educational, Scientific, and Cultural Organization (UNESCO), International Meeting of Experts on Further Study on the Concept of the Rights of Peoples; Final Report and Recommendations, 27.-30.11.1989, SHS-89/CONF.602/7.

United Nations Environment Programme, 10.09.1998, Rotterdam Convention on the Prior Informed Consent Procedure for Certain Hazardous Chemicals and Pesticides in International Trade. e

United Nations Food and Agriculture Organization, 11.2001, International Treaty on Plant Genetic Resources for Food and Agriculture (ITPGRFA).

UNHCR (2011): Summary of Deliberations on Climate Change and Displacement. United Nations High Commissioner for Refugees.

United Nations Educational, Scientific, and Cultural Organization (UNESCO), 27.11.1989, reference number SHS-89/CONF.602/7.

United Nations General Assembly, Official Reports of the General Assembly; Sixth Session, Third Committee, 397th meeting.

United Nations General Assembly, Resolution of 10.12.1948, reference number A/RES/3/217 A, 217 A (III): Universal Declaration of Human Rights.

United Nations General Assembly, Resolution of 12.01.1952, reference number A/RES/523 (VI): Integrated economic development and commercial agreements.

United Nations General Assembly, Resolution of 12.01.1952, reference number A/RES/545 (VI): Inclusion in the International Covenant or Covenants on Human Rights.

United Nations General Assembly, Resolution of 21.12.1952, reference number A/RES/626 (VII): Right to Exploit Freely Natural Wealth and Resources.

United Nations General Assembly, Resolution of 1955, reference number A/2929: Annotations on the text of the draft International Covenants on Human Rights.

United Nations General Assembly, Resolution of 12.12.1958, reference number A/RES/1314: Recommendations Concerning International Respect for the Rights of Peoples and Nations to Self-Determination.

United Nations General Assembly, Resolution of 14.12.1960, reference number A/RES/15/1514: Declaration on the Granting of Independence to Colonial Countries and Peoples.

United Nations General Assembly, Resolution of 15.12.1960, reference number A/RES/1541 (XV): Principles which should guide Members in determining whether or not an obligation exists to transmit the information called for under Article 73 e of the Charter.

United Nations General Assembly, Resolution of 14.12.1962, reference number A/RES/1803 (XVII): Permanent sovereignty over natural resources.

United Nations General Assembly, Resolution of 30.11.1966, reference number: A/RES/2160 (XXI): Strict observance of the prohibition of the threat or use of force in international relations, and of the right of peoples to self-determination.

United Nations General Assembly, International Covenant on Civil and Political Rights (ICCPR), Resolution of 16.12.1966.

United Nations General Assembly, International Covenant on Economic, Social and Cultural Rights (ICESCR), Resolution of 16.12.1966.

United Nations General Assembly, Resolution of 24.10.1970, reference number: A/RES/2625(XXV): Declaration on Principles of International Law concerning Friendly Relations and Cooperation among States in accordance with the Charter of the United Nations.

United Nations General Assembly, Resolution of 29.12.1971, reference number: A/RES/2869(XXVI): Question of American Samoa, Bahamas, Bermuda, British Virgin Islands, Brunei, Cayman Islands, Cocos (Keeling) Islands, Gilbert and Ellice Islands, Guam, Montserrat, New Hebrides, Pitcairn, St. Helena, Seychelles, Solomon Islands, Turks and Caicos Islands, and the United States Virgin Islands.

United Nations General Assembly, Resolution of 27.11.1972, reference number: A/RES/2925 (XXVII): Strengthening of the role of the United Nations with regard to the maintenance and consolidation of international peace and security, the development of co-operation among all nations and the promotion of the rules of international law in relations between States.

United Nations General Assembly, Resolution of 29.11.1972, reference number: A/RES/2936 (XXVII): Non-use of force in international relations and permanent prohibition of the use of nuclear weapons.

United Nations General Assembly, Resolution of 18.12.1972, reference number: A/RES/3016(XXVII): Permanent sovereignty over natural resources of developing countries.

United Nations General Assembly, Resolution of 13.12.1973, reference number: A/RES/3129(XXVIII): Co-operation in the field of the environment concerning natural resources shared by two or more States.

United Nations General Assembly, Resolution of 01.05.1974, reference number: Resolution A/RES/3201(S-VI): Declaration on the Establishment of a New International Economic Order.

United Nations General Assembly, Resolution of 12.12.1974, reference number A/RES/3281(XXIX), Charter of Economic Rights and Duties of States.

United Nations General Assembly, Resolution of 16.12.1974, reference number: A/RES/3326 (XXIX): Report of the Governing Council of the United Nations Environment Program.

United Nations General Assembly, Resolution of 17.12.1974, reference number: A/RES/3336 (XXIX): Permanent sovereignty over national resources in the occupied Arab territories.

United Nations General Assembly, Resolution of 19.12.1983, reference number: A/Res/38/161: Process of preparation of the Environmental Perspective to the Year 2000 and Beyond.

United Nations General Assembly, Resolution of 04.12.1986, reference number: A/RES/41/128: Declaration on the Right to Development.

United Nations General Assembly, Resolution of 04.08.1987, reference number: A/42/427. Report of the World Commission on Environment and Development: Our Common Future: Annex 1.

United Nations General Assembly, Resolution of 18.09.2000, reference number: A/RES/55/2: United Nations Millennium Declaration.

United Nations General Assembly, Resolution of 22.05.2001, Stockholm Convention on Persistent Organic Pollutants.

United Nations General Assembly, Resolution of 15.03.2002, reference number: E/CN.4/2002/98, Report of Working Group for Draft United Nations Declaration on the Rights of Indigenous Peoples.

United Nations General Assembly, Resolution of 02.12.2004, reference number A/59/565, Report of the High-Level Panel on Threats, Challenges and Change on a More Secure World: Our Shared Responsibility.

United Nations General Assembly, Resolution of 2005, reference number A/RES/60/1, 2005 World Summit Outcome.

United Nations General Assembly, Resolution of 11.09.2009, reference number: A/RES/63/281: Climate change and its possible security implications.

United Nations General Assembly, Resolution of 27.07.2012, reference number: A/Res/66/288. The future we want.

United Nations General Assembly (19.06.2023): Agreement under the United Nations Convention on the Law of the Sea on the conservation and sustainable use of marine biological diversity of areas beyond national jurisdiction. Online available on https://documents-dds-ny.un.org/doc/UNDOC/LTD/N23/177/28/PDF/N2317728.pdf?OpenElement.

United Nations High Commissioner for Refugees (UNHCR), 2011, Summary of Deliberations on Climate Change and Displacement.

United Nations Human Rights Committee (HRC), 02.12.1985, Ivan Kitok v. Sweden, Communication No. 197/1985, CCPR/C/33/D/197/1985.

United Nations Human Rights Committee (HRC), 26.03.1990, Communication No. 167/1984, U.N. Doc. Supp. No. 40 (A/45/40), Lubicon Lake Band v. Canada.

United Nations Human Rights Committee (HRC), 25.04.2000, Concluding Observations: Guyana.

United Nations Human Rights Committee (HRC), 24.04.2002, Concluding Observation: Sweden.

United Nations Human Rights Committee (HRC), 04.05.2004, Concluding observations: Suriname.

United Nations Human Rights Council, 28.03.2008, Resolution 7/23: Human rights and climate change.

United Nations Human Rights Council, 25.03.2009, Resolution 10/4: Human rights and climate change.

World Council of Indigenous Peoples, Declaration from the First General Assembly, Port Albemi, BC, Canada, 10.1975.

MIX
Papier aus verantwortungsvollen Quellen
Paper from responsible sources
FSC® C105338

If you have any concerns about our products,
you can contact us on
ProductSafety@springernature.com

In case Publisher is established outside the EU,
the EU authorized representative is:
Springer Nature Customer Service Center GmbH
Europaplatz 3, 69115 Heidelberg, Germany

Printed by Libri Plureos GmbH
in Hamburg, Germany